1970

The Notebooks for The Possessed

The Notebooks for

The Possessed

Fyodor Dostoevsky

Edited and with an Introduction by Edward Wasiolek

Translated by Victor Terras

The University of Chicago Press
CHICAGO & LONDON

Library of Congress Catalog Card Number: 68-26723

The translation is based upon the Russian edition of Dostoevsky's notebooks: *Zapisnye tetradi F. M. Dostoevskogo,* edited by E. N. Konshina (Moscow, 1935).

The University of Chicago Press, Chicago 60637
The University of Chicago Press, Ltd., London W.C.1

Published 1968. Printed in the United States of America

Contents

Illustrations

The illustrations included in this edition of Dostoevsky's *Notebooks for "The Possessed"* are facsimiles of original pages of the notebooks.

Introduction

I

The first impression one gets of *The Possessed* is of incongruity, disharmony, and disfigurement. Everything is what it should not be. Intellectuals are not intellectuals, governors do not govern, and family relationships have unraveled: sons scoff at fathers, a niece finds the affection of an uncle an insult, and the respect a husband has for his wife increases when she takes a lover. Murder is considered fidelity; ugliness, beauty; blasphemy, religion; error, truth; and a million heads on the chopping block is the vision of the social millenium.

Some kind of measure has been lost; some proportion unperceived; and personal dignity and identity forgotten. Everyone and everything is in some way mutilated, and even holiness, in Maria Timofeevna, hobbles and truth speaks in madness. The earth has opened up in a small provincial town and monsters—little, grotesque, comic, serious, and awesome—have scurried to take possession of the surface. *The Possessed* is about men who have forgotten who and why they are. It is both fact and prophecy.

The body politic is sick, and the sickness has palsied the people's actions, corroded their social relations, twisted their bodies, clouded their thoughts, and confused their feelings. There is no communion of ideas, feelings, or souls; and language itself—fed by poisoned spiritual sources—has begun to disintegrate. There are no dialogues, only silence and noise, hysterical outbursts, and people talking to themselves. Stepan Trofimovich Verkhovensky does not communicate when he orates to his circle to the thumpings of Liamshin's piano; Barbara Stavrogin commands but does not converse; Shatov communes only with himself; Kirilov speaks, from misuse and misapplication, a mutilated Russian; Peter talks and talks but says nothing; and Stavrogin does not talk.

Men are set against each other and against themselves. Their intentions do not match their actions: will is set against act, head against fact, and belief against words. Virginsky thinks he is a liberal husband who respects his wife for taking a lover; he is actually a jealous husband. Liputin thinks he is a socialist dedicated to the advancement of Fourier's ideas; he is actually a miser, family tyrant, and roué. Shatov bases his view of the world and of history on God, but he cannot believe in God. Kirilov proves the freedom of man by killing himself. And Shigalyov proposes to establish the freedom of men by reducing nine-tenths of them to the condition of beasts.

Words have detached themselves from things, ideas from substance, and men from the earth. If one listens closely to the noise and commotion, and to the rhetoric and confusion, one hears finally only the silence of a spectral world. Stepan Trofimovich's rhetoric is without substance, and Peter's torrent of words sounds into silence, as his riot of action passes into nothingness. Peter raises the phantoms of programs, plans, and procedures; he populates the country with "committees of five" that do not exist; and at the end he himself disappears as if he had never existed. At the center of this world, like Dante's devil, is Stavrogin, fixed in silence and glacial calm. The silence flows from him and to him, and the twisted beliefs men cling to have been discarded by him. He has searched and rejected, believed and unbelieved, until there is nothing left but the silence and emptiness of his soul; for even the courage, will, and fierce honesty of Stavrogin issue into emptiness and annihilation. Stavrogin alone is real; and he is unreal.

The Possessed is a difficult and a magnificent novel, a novel prophetic of the Russian revolution and the twentieth century. It is a novel that engaged Camus in a lifelong fascination with Kirilov and a lifelong struggle against the compelling logic of Dostoevsky's world. It is also a novel that engaged Dostoevsky in a three-year struggle between his heart and his political passion, and between what he wanted to say and what he had to say. The novel tells us how well he succeeded, and the notebooks for *The Possessed*, how hard he tried.

II

The years in Europe, during which Dostoevsky wrote the bulk of *The Possessed*, were sheer misery. The money was short: in letters and notes

Dostoevsky whines, pleads, begs, explains, and there is always only a kopek left and none expected. The period of separation from Russia is long and the ache to return sharp. His health is as desperate as his finances: fits, shortness of breath, hemorrhoids, poor digestion. His wife is in poor health, and his daughter Liuba is teething; the French have been routed at Sedan; the weather is ugly; his mind is clouded by recent fits; he cannot work, and everything is in disarray. Paris is under siege by the Prussians, and Dostoevsky is under siege by penury, delays, nonunderstanding editors, and lost letters. In remarkable autobiographical notes that have been included in these published notebooks, we get not only the facts of Dostoevsky's misery, but his feelings about them, and the near hallucinatory associations that come as he expresses them. I am referring to the first section of these notes, where several dreams, a letter, and the record of fits he experienced between August, 1869, and October, 1870, are grouped. The following, from the middle of June, 1870, is typical:

The weather keeps changing; it is rainy and relatively cold. The money has not arrived, and I don't know if I'll get any at all. I've completed the fifth chapter of the novel.

~~In the evenings~~ at night (two ~~evenings~~ nights in a row) I can hardly work: the blood rushes to my head, I feel torpid, sleepy, I'm afraid of the bad consequences of working at night (a stroke, or something of that kind?).

Most of his fits come at three-week intervals, but at the time of writing they have increased in frequency. They come mostly at night, but not always without harm to himself from falls; the effects—headaches, heaviness of thought, and shattered nerves—last as many as five or six days. He cannot work, and the fits—either in Dostoevsky's imagination or in reality—are connected with other events. His misery is both personal and general: "I have great worries. The hot months lie ahead, terribly strenuous work—the novel for *The Russian Messenger* (I put no trust in it). I have thought up a letter to N. Let it rest until Sept. 1. Something's got to give! We shall be very short of money right until fall."

Almost mystically he notes the time of the fits and the coincidences with the phase of the moon, or the hour of Tropman's[1] execution:

The fit occurred during an almost full moon. <January>7/19. A fit at 6 o'clock in the morning (the day and almost the hour of Tropman's execution). I did not feel it, awoke after 8 o'clock, with a feeling that I had had a fit. I had a headache and my body was aching all over. N.B. (Altogether, the aftereffects of my fits, i.e., nervousness, shortness of memory, and intensified and foggy, quasi-contemplative state, persist longer now than in previous years. They used to pass after three days, while now it may take six. Especially at night, by candle-light, an indefinite hypochondriac melancholy, and as if a red, bloody shade (not color) upon everything. Almost impossible to work during those days.

The weather, the war, his situation, health, work, are all by some personal and near hallucinatory association meaningfully connected:

My head won't clear up even in a whole week. The weather is hot; there was a full moon on the 13th; rare light, warm rainshowers. I am struggling with the 1st part of my novel, and I'm desperate. War has been declared.[2] Ania is quite exhausted. Liuba is nervous and restless. N.B. Kashpirev[3] sent the money two months later than promised. Our situation has hardly improved, even though the money has been sent. All my hope rests with the novel and my trip to K<issinge>n.[4] I wonder about the war.

Added to all this Dostoevsky did not want to write *The Possessed.* He wanted to write his great work, "Atheism," or "The Life of a

---

[1] See the introductory comments to Section I for an account of the Tropman case.

[2] War between Prussia and France was officially declared on July 19, 1870.

[3] Vassily V. Kashpirev, editor of the journal, *Dawn,* in which Dostoevsky published his short novel *The Eternal Husband* (January and February, 1870).

[4] Dostoevsky visited Kissingen for gambling.

Great Sinner," a work that had ripened in his soul and would crown his creative career. The political pamphlet he speaks of in early 1870 was to be an interruption, and, he hoped, a short one. He hopes to have it done in the summer of 1870, and then in the fall, then in December, and then in the spring of 1871. It was not finished until the end of 1872. He writes to Maikov in the middle of October, 1870: "never has any work cost me so much work"; and in December, 1870, to Strakhov, that the novel "has cost him a year of suffering"; and to S. A. Ivanova: "The work on this novel has exhausted me physically and morally." He tore up two hundred and forty pages in July, 1870; in December he complained to Strakhov that he had revised the novel at least ten times, and in January, 1871, to his niece, that he had revised it at least twenty times.

Nor is he sure what he is writing: at first it is a pamphlet, something he has to get out of his system and out of his schedule so that he can sit down to what he has been aching to write, "The Life of a Great Sinner"; then it is in part indistinguishable from what he had been aching to write. Nor is he sure whom he is writing about. Nechaev, who provoked him to have his say, is not the hero; nor is Stepan Trofimovich Verkhovensky, who starts and finishes the novel; nor is Kirilov, who appears only in the very latest period of creation. The hero is perhaps Stavrogin, who forced his way into the novel and into Dostoevsky's tormented heart. But if Stavrogin is the hero, Dostoevsky was no longer writing the pamphlet he had wanted to write.

What kind of work came out of all this? One of the world's great novels, as any novel with Kirilov, Stavrogin, Stepan Verkhovensky, and Peter Verkhovensky would have to be. But it is also a novel with a biased political point of view, an unfair assessment of the political and social movements of the sixties and seventies, and a cruel caricature of Turgenev. It has its share of ignorance, spite, and cruelty. And Dostoevsky meant it to be that way. He knew what he was doing and did it not from ignorance, but from malice. It is idle to remind him and us —as Soviet commentators often do and as American commentators sometimes do—that Nechaev's cynical politics were not the only politics of the sixties and early seventies. Dostoevsky was not a political *ingénu*. He combed the newspapers and watched the political pulse of Russia and Europe with feverish attention and expectancy. But one man's distinction is another's triviality. He knew that Chernyshevsky, Pisarev,[5] and Dobroliubov[6] were not Nechaev, and he knew that neither the radical critics nor Nechaev were the Chaikovtsys and the budding populists. But he didn't care. From his point of view they were all the same. They all believed that man could be shaped by the arbitrary abstractions that arose in their brains. He did not. He believed that these conceptions—no matter how beautiful in theory—were vicious and destructive. Nechaev confirmed what Belinsky, Chernyshevsky, and Pisarev were, and destroyed what they thought they were.

Dostoevsky first learned of Nechaev in December of 1869, probably in the reading room of the Dresden library, hunched over one of those Russian newspapers which he pursued and read all over Europe. Nechaev, the conspiracy, the murder of Ivanov, and the trial of the Nechaevists—all these had an enormous impact on Dostoevsky, dredging up all his fears for the future of Russia, reinforcing his conviction that the godless liberalism that had betrayed him in the forties led to destruction and chaos, and justifying his irrational and ungenerous disgust with Belinsky. The Nechaev case moved Dostoevsky toward what was contemporary, historical, and journalistic, and the change—his interest in contemporary events notwithstanding—went against the grain of his deepest urgings. He wanted at this time to immerse himself in "The Life of a Great Sinner," its five books, and its Miltonic imaginings of battles between faith and unfaith, fall and regeneration.

In the deepest sense, Dostoevsky is not by nature a political writer and a commentator of the social scene. What Pisarev has to say about *Fathers and Sons* and what Dobroliubov has to say about *Oblomov*

---

[5] Dmitri Ivanovich Pisarev (1840–68), one of the three most important radical critics, along with Dobroliubov and Chernyshevsky. His extreme utilitarian view of literature was formulated in "The Destruction of Aesthetics" and other essays.

[6] Nikolay Aleksandrovich Dobroliubov (1836–61), is an important radical critic of the sixties. He held literature in more respect than did Pisarev and Chernyshevsky, but like them, he insisted on its contemporary social relevance. His most famous essay is "What is Oblomovism?"

is always relevant, if not always true. But what Dobroliubov has to say about *The Double* and what Pisarev has to say about *Crime and Punishment* are beside the point, if not actually stupid. Raskolnikov, Myshkin, Ivan Karamazov, Stavrogin, and Kirilov are not of their age as are Bazarov, Rudin, and Oblomov. *The Possessed* is, of course, more political than the other great novels: Nechaev, the murder of Ivanov, the committees of five, Granovsky,[7] Uspensky,[8] and Miliukov[9] are all history; and even the actual names fill the notes. But behind them and through them Dostoevsky's imagination could not help picturing his universal, mythic battles of will and faith, fall and redemption. He was not interested in the historical Nechaev, as he himself stated, but only in what Nechaev represented. He was interested in the type and not the individual, in the logic of history and not the empirical event: "I do not know Nechaev, or Ivanov, or the circumstances of this murder," he wrote. "Even if I knew, I would not use them. I take only the completed act. My imagination can in the highest degree differ from what actually happened, and my Peter Verkhovensky can in no way resemble Nechaev; still, I believe that my imagination has created that person, that type, which corresponds to the crime." Unlike Zola, Dostoevsky does not have to know the buttons on Nechaev's shirt, or the occupation of Nechaev's father, or the habits of his mother. He knows only the "accomplished fact," and the logic of human nature that corresponds to that accomplished fact. In a century in which Balzac catalogued the mores of Parisians, Zola of provincials, Dickens of aspiring gentlemen, and Norris of robber barons, it is startling to hear what sounds like a tenet from French classical criticism: not the individual, but the type. But the type for Dostoevsky is not what usage and the

---

[7] Timofei Nikolaevich Granovsky (1813–55), a professor of history at Moscow University, and a Western liberal in political and social outlook. He was a friend of Hertsen, Stankevich, and Belinsky, and he is the prototype of Stepan Trofimovich Verkhovensky in *The Possessed*.

[8] Pyotr G. Uspensky (1847–81), one of Nechaev's accomplices in the murder of the student Ivanov, and prototype in large part of Virginsky.

[9] Aleksandr P. Miliukov (1817–97), writer and teacher, personally known to Dostoevsky. At the time he was writing *The Possessed,* Dostoevsky became disenchanted with him and criticized him in his letters. Miliukov is in part the prototype for Liputin, but also of Virginsky.

age have decreed—rather what the imagination had conceived. Journalism confirmed, but it did not determine.

Dostoevsky had his version of that "purposive history" which afflicted virtually every Russian thinker of the nineteenth century. Whether Belinsky,[10] Chernyshevsky,[11] Dobroliubov, Grigoriev,[12] or later Mikhailovsky[13] and Plekhanov,[14] they all believed in the "logic" of history. The logics were different, of course; Dostoevsky's brand was most nearly formulated and exposited philosophically by his close friend Grigoriev. Not for Belinsky or Chernyshevsky, or for Dostoevsky—and Dostoevsky would hate the company—was history the undifferentiated flow of empirical data. For all of them, history was reality and reality was the idea of history; what we call events were empirical data, which might or might not express the idea-reality of true history. For Dostoevsky, Nechaev did express this. In him, reality and idea were one. The fantastic, as Dostoevsky reminds us often, was real; and as Grigoriev exposited and Dostoevsky practiced, the imagination of the great writer was the spark that ignited and illumined reality.

---

[10] Vissarion G. Belinsky (1811–48), the most important Russian critic in the nineteenth century. He was largely responsible for the reputations of Dostoevsky, Gogol, Lermontov, the later Pushkin, Turgenev, and others. He was an immense presence in Russian criticism and literature, and his influence may be compared to that of Dr. Johnson in English literature and Sainte-Beuve in French literature.

[11] Nikolay G. Chernyshevsky (1828–89), the most important of the radical critics, and a follower of Belinsky. Imprisoned from 1862 to 1883, he wrote his most famous novel, *What Is To Be Done?* in prison. The novel provided inspiration for generations of revolutionaries.

[12] Apollon A. Grigoriev (1822–64), the most important non-utilitarian critic writing in the 1850's and 1860's. He is the exponent of "organic criticism," that is, a view of literature in which the writer is necessarily tied to his country, time, and even region, while expressing the absolute which is constant in every man's soul. His views are close to those of Dostoevsky, who was his friend. Grigoriev's best-known work is *My Literary and Moral Wanderings.*

[13] Nikolay K. Mikhailovsky (1842–1904), leader of the "Populist" movement *(narodnichestvo)* and an important social critic. Like so many of the nineteenth-century critics, he insisted on the social relevance of literature, but unlike the radical critics, he placed great emphasis on the psychological and moral characteristics of the writer.

[14] Georgi V. Plekhanov (1856–1918), the most important pre-revolutionary Marxist thinker and literary critic in Russia. In literary criticism, examples of his Marxist approach to literature may be seen in *Letters Without Address* and in *Art and Social Reality.*

Dostoevsky had very little to add to the real-life Nechaev. He was as fantastic as anything the imagination could invent, or discover. At the age of sixteen he was illiterate; by nineteen he was a teacher of religion; by twenty-one he was one of a group of protesting St. Petersburg students; and by twenty-one and a half he was Bakunin's intimate. Five months after he arrived in Europe in early 1869 he had convinced much of the *émigré* revolutionary establishment that Russia was ripe for revolution and a new order, and had enlisted their aid to effect that revolution by giving him unqualified support. In the early fall of 1869 he reappeared in Moscow as Bakunin's official representative and the head of a fictitious international revolutionary committee.

As the organizer of a "network" of committees of five, Nechaev was always arrogant and unbending; he insisted on total obedience in the name of the "cause." Ivanov, a student at the Petrovsk Agricultural Academy, had at meetings of the central committee of five consistently opposed him, refused to obey an order of Nechaev's, and threatened to start a rival group. Nechaev managed to convince the other members of the committee that Ivanov was going to inform on them. Ivanov was lured to a distant part of the Academy park on the pretext of unearthing a printing press. There he was set upon by Nechaev and the others, brutally beaten, strangled, and finally—because of the furious struggle—shot in the back of the neck by Nechaev. His body was weighed down with bricks and dropped into a pond.

The police quickly traced the murder to Nechaev, but only in a way that sent a chill through their hearts and mystery and terror into their consciousness. The Third Section had been investigating the appearance of mysterious proclamations and an upsurge of student disturbances; in a raid on a bookstore they found, along with the proclamations, a notebook of addresses, a copy of "The Cathechism of a Revolutionary" in cipher, data calling for a revolution on February 19, 1870, and plans for the assassination of the highest dignitaries. Among the addresses, they found the name of Ivanov. Although arrest after arrest was made, the police were unable to penetrate further than the surface. No one seemed to know where the committee was, how large it was, what its organization was. The committee seemed omnipresent and yet invisible; the plans for revolution seemed detailed and imminent, yet undiscoverable. But all names led to Nechaev.

Like Peter Verkhovensky, Nechaev had managed to raise the fantasies and vagaries of his mind to substantial fact in the minds of his followers and the minds of the police, and had managed to provoke in those followers, by fear and bullying, grudging dedication to a cause no one quite understood. But one fact was real—the murder of Ivanov—and the witnesses who confessed to Nechaev's part in the murder were real. The tsarist government was determined to bring Nechaev to trial for the murder, but he had quickly slipped out of the country after the murder was discovered, leaving his comrades to shift for themselves. And there, undismayed by the murder, his perfidy, exile, and even the fact that the tsarist government had alerted its embassies and enjoined the help of friendly powers in the search for him, Nechaev set to work with indefatigable energy to disseminate the "cause" and himself.

Most European countries did not permit the extradition of political refugees but did permit the extradition of common criminals, and it was as common criminal that the tsarist government persuaded the European powers to help in the search for Nechaev. He was finally arrested near Zurich, Switzerland, in the fall of 1872, extradited to Russia (after some liberal protests), quickly tried, and quickly sentenced to twenty years of hard labor in Siberia. He never reached Siberia, however, because the government had no intention of sending him where he could influence other political prisoners. He was sent instead to the Alexei-Ravelin in St. Petersburg. There he continued to invoke fantasmal worlds, convincing his guards and his keepers that invisible threads tied him to every tremor that touched the empire. Shortly before his unrepentant death in 1882, he had extensive and intimate contacts with members of "The People's Will" and their successful attempt on the Tsar's life in 1881.

Scorned by every liberal group in the nineteenth century for his unabashed cynicism, he nevertheless continued to live in reputation long after his death. The Soviets early in their post-revolutionary theorizing seemed ready to accept him as a true predecessor, before the terror of what they were about to admit sent them rushing for qualification, evasion, and silence. Nechaev and the spirit of Nechaevism were more powerful and enduring than his contemporaries knew. Only Nechaev, and Dostoevsky, believed in that power.

III

The notes for *The Possessed* consist of some autobiographical materials: the accounts of several dreams and a record of fits for more than a year; notes for several related but unpublished works, notably those for "The Life of a Great Sinner"; and, in great bulk, variants, outlines of plots, sketches of scenes, and analyses of characters for *The Possessed* itself. This is the longest of the notebooks, and the distance between the first notes and the final version is also the greatest. There is no Kirilov until the latest notes, and he is there briefly and sketchily; no passionless, remote, and terrifying Stavrogin from beginning to end; no redeemed Stepan Trofimovich Verkhovensky; and only a few hints as to what the metaphysical and political plots have to do with each other. Even the names are different: Stepan Trofimovich Verkhovensky is "Granovsky" until the very end; Peter is "the Student" briefly, and "Nechaev" until the very last notes; Liza is "the Heiress," "the Beauty," "the Fiancée," and "the Horsewoman," before she is Liza; Dasha is "the Ward" until the very end. Stavrogin never becomes Stavrogin, and except for a few late references to "Nicolas" and "Nicolas Vsevolodovich," he is "the Prince" throughout.

What we have from beginning to end is a romantic complication to which Dostoevsky returns again and again; Granovsky (Stepan) as aesthete, fool, and phrasemonger; Nechaev (Peter) as champion of destruction; Shatov as messianic nationalist; the Princess (Barbara Stavrogin) as friend-enemy of Granovsky and worshiper of fashions in ideas; the Ward (Dasha) as obedient and submissive servant to the Prince; and Liza as passionately hating and loving the Prince. Dostoevsky wastes most of his time on the romantic intrigue, the least time on Kirilov. Stavrogin came hardest, and Nechaev and Granovsky easiest.

As in the novel, Stepan Trofimovich is a liberal aesthete who worships ideas and beauty at the safe distance of luxury; he is intellectually and morally flabby—an idler, sponger, and fool. He is all these things in notes and novel, but in the novel he is redeemed at the end; in the notes he is not. When the center of intellectual influence passes from father to son in the novel, something changes in Stepan Verkhovensky. Unlike his benefactress, Mrs. Stavrogin, unlike the Virginskys and the Liputins, and unlike most of the town, he refuses to "go over" to Peter's side. When he is betrayed by his son, his benefactress, and his old cronies, something stiffens in his back and his will. He continues to mouth the same phrases, but some shadow of consciousness and responsibility falls across them. He is no wiser, but he is firmer. Betrayed and friendless, misunderstood and misunderstanding, Stepan Trofimovich begins his last quixotic journey in ignorance and hope. He remains foolish and self-serving, but some spark of recognition and repentance flickers faintly in his soul. It is too much to say, perhaps, that he is redeemed, but he is born before death into responsibility.

Yet there is almost nothing in the notes—from beginning to end and throughout variant after variant—to indicate that Dostoevsky meant Stepan Verkhovensky to emerge, no matter how slightly, a better man. He is always the fool, and never the hero. In the notes, as in the novel, Granovsky recognizes himself and his generation as the spiritual fathers of Nechaev's generation; but while there is recognition and even astonishment, there is no learning from suffering. The best that Dostoevsky can say is that he meant well: "Granovsky was truly pure, and ardently wished to do good, yet toward the end, he couldn't help playing a role and inevitably became a phraseur. And as if this wasn't enough, he became—"a fop." And, "Granovsky falls ill and dies. He makes an effort to comprehend all that has happened and what they (the socialists and all these people) might be striving for, but he can't. Dissension between him and his wife. He is not allowed to leave town." Even later in the notes: "Granovsky is not a genuine ideal. He is passé, self-destructive, full of false pride, a caricature." And as if this were not enough Dostoevsky gives him the indignity of dying from frustration and diarrhea.

For those of us who have asserted that Stepan Trofimovich is a better man at the end, the notes must give us pause. Something may have happened between notes and novel, and then nothing may have happened. The facts of the novel do not dispute the portrait of the notes, painted so often and so consistently. Stepan Trofimovich does battle with Peter and the forces of nihilism and radicalism, but in the name of abstract beauty; he confesses his wrong, calls himself the worst sort of swine, but in delirium and sickness; he admits that he has lied to Sophia Matveevna, but perhaps for effect. Stepan Trofimovich says the right things at the end, but the "right things" abstracted from soil and heart can be the wrong things. I am not sure, but the notes may help us to decide.

No such ambiguity attends the portrait of Nechaev-Peter in the notes. He is throughout contemptuous of others, arrogant, and insistently the apostle of destruction. He talks, but does not explain, acts but does not do. Almost everyone is fascinated by him, and he is fascinated only by Stavrogin. As in the novel, he tells us little about his program, and what we learn comes from the arguments of Granovsky and Shaposhnikov (Shatov) against the program. Nechaev promises nothing but the axe and revolution, but Granovsky and Shaposhnikov argue against the loss of personality, communality of living and loving, the submission of the individual will to the collective will, and the destruction of God, Church, and national identity. Granovsky argues from grounds of continuity of historical change; that is, he argues that change of any kind must be slow and concrete. His argument is, from one point of view, an argument to do nothing, which is thoroughly in keeping with his character. Shaposhnikov argues from grounds of national identity—that the people will not follow what goes against their inviolate nature. Nechaev does not argue back, because both national identity and the God that guarantees it are unreal to him, as is the culture Granovsky champions. He has no use for the concreteness of cultural continuity, and no use for the concreteness of the people's spiritual body. He is the passionate abstract man, a creature Dostoevsky learned to hate and to fear, and one we have become accustomed to in the twentieth century.

Dostoevsky was fascinated by Nechaev, in life and in these notes, and there was no doubt that he wanted to crush such petty monsters. Yet Nechaev-Peter is not a Virginsky or a Liputin. We can understand the Virginskys and the Liputins and we can laugh at them, but the laughter we feel for Peter is mixed with apprehension. Peter is funny and dangerous. We cannot dismiss Nechaev and we cannot dismiss Peter. Dostoevsky tries to do so repeatedly in the notes: he is appalled by Nechaev's ignorance of Russian reality, and he is contemptuous of his naïve belief that the changes he recommends will come forth automatically. In the last notes we have—written probably after the novel had begun to be serialized—we still find Dostoevsky repeating what he had said so often before: "All his clever cynicism notwithstanding, Verkhovensky was terribly stupid in believing that it would be possible to make everything collapse. With regard to this point, he was as much of a theoretician as Liputin." Peter in the final version may be incomprehensible, but he is not uncomprehending. He managed to convince others that everything was about to collapse, that the country was rife with secret councils of five, that his fingers touched a network of conspiracies and fellow revolutionaries—but he believed none of it. He did not believe in God, or socialism, or a new order, or the imminent collapse of anything. He had no aims, except the immediate, pure, reasonless, motiveless aim of power over others. He is Dostoevsky's Iago, awesome in evil because real.

Dostoevsky did not understand Nechaev, but he knew who he was. He did not understand Stavrogin, and did not know who he was. These notes are in large part a record of wrong Stavrogins, of trial upon trial of a different Prince (Stavrogin). The passionless, frightening, self-contained, silent Stavrogin who has passed beyond the monstrous dialectic of Kirilov, the messianic nationalism of Shatov, the aesthetic liberalism of Stepan Verkhovensky, and the romantic intrigues with Dasha, Liza, and Mary Shatov is not to be found in these notes. The Stavrogin of the novel has passed beyond words and passion, creation and destruction, faith and unfaith. His lips are sealed by the confidence that no word is worth speaking and no act is worth doing. About him is a babble of voices and a riot of action, and he alone seems to be meaning in his unmeaning. He is wise with the wisdom that wisdom is not wise, and strong in his faith that all faith can be shaken. Peter may be mysterious, but Stavrogin is mystery.

But the Prince of the notes is not mystery, and not calm. He talks, loves, propagandizes, philosophizes; he is passionate, jealous, spiteful, ambitious, and envious. Dostoevsky tries him out again and again in role after role, and none of them fit because Stavrogin will be beyond roles. Dostoevsky knows what he wants Shatov, Granovsky, and Nechaev to stand for; but he does not know what he wants the Prince to stand for. The Price is shallow and deep, desperate and hopeful, a believer and an atheist. He is:

A frivolous man, who does nothing but play the game of life, an elegant Nozdrev, who plays an awful lot of tricks on people, some of them noble and some dirty; and it is he who then suddenly shoots himself; in between, he listens to Golubov[15] (once).

Merely shallow and frivolous, but in the end he turns out to have been more profound than anyone else, and that's all there is to it.

Also, he is:

seeking the truth; he has found truth in the idea of Russia and Christianity.

He is cruel. Nechaev arouses his jealousy against Shaposhnikov.

Christian humility and self-condemnation.

He gets reconciled to his mother.

The Prince is also the ardent lover, seducer, jealous rival. In seemingly endless variants, Dostoevsky embroils him—and just as improbably, Shatov—in a romantic intrigue in which both are taken through role after role as competitive lovers. The romantic intrigue is in the final version, but it is there in vestigial form, scattered about in bits and pieces. Most readers will have trouble remembering it. It seems disconnected, skeletal, and faded in passion and purpose. In the notes and novel, Liza hates-loves the Prince-Stavrogin, the Prince seduces and ignores Liza and Dasha; the Princess–Barbara Stavrogin hastens to marry Dasha to Stepan-Granovsky; Mary Lebiadkin is the secret wife that everyone fears; and Captain Lebiadkin and Mary are killed with

---

[15] Konstantin E. Golubov, a churchman who wrote on religious, social, and political problems. Russian *émigrés* in London were interested in him, and Ogarev exchanged letters with him. His views are close to those of Shatov in the novel.

the Prince's consent. But in the final version something greater than love and passion has consumed Shatov's soul and cooled Stavrogin's heart. The secret marriage to Mary Lebiadkin still shakes the cowardly social heart of Barbara Stavrogin, but more is at stake in confessing the marriage than the romantic humiliation of Liza.

If it is difficult to think of the Prince as passionate lover, it may be even more difficult to think of him as the passionate defender of Russia against the West, Orthodoxy against godlessness, and Christ against the nonbelievers. In long monologues and dialogues the Prince exposits his views on the Russian idea and on the saving grace of Orthodoxy. First he is the expositor and seemingly the exponent, then the examiner, and finally the rejector. He is fascinated by Golubov and then by Nechaev. Nechaev offers him the axe, and Golubov the ideas "of humility and self-possession, also that God and the Kingdom of Heaven are within us, in self-possession, and that's where freedom is too." First he stands between them, and then they within him, and finally he beyond both.

The Prince's passionate defense of Orthodoxy and Russia are Dostoevsky's. They are insistent in Dostoevsky's biography and insistent in these notes. The Prince says: "The Earth has never *seen such* a gigantic idea as the one which is now taking shape here, in the East, and moving to take up the place of the European masses <*sic*> ~~which~~ to regenerate the world. . . . Orthodoxy, the true, and glorious, eternal creed of Christ and ~~regeneration~~ a full moral regeneration in His name. We are bringing the world the first paradise of the millenium." And in the note that follows: "Leaves for Petersburg and hangs himself in Skvoreshniki." Dostoevsky can give his ideas to the Prince, and the Prince can recite them passionately, but a line later the suicide negates what he recites. Dostoevsky may believe in what the Prince says, but the Prince cannot. Shatov can believe in them, but Shatov is a half-demented creature feeding on the leavings of Stavrogin; his spiritual life is as twisted as his social relations. The Prince cannot embody Dostoevsky's Christian beliefs in Russia and God, and Dostoevsky knows he cannot.

Dostoevsky apparently entertained the idea of bringing about the Prince's regeneration (a motive from the sketch of "The Life of a Great Sinner") by love or by faith. Throughout the notes we have references to the moral feat the Prince wishes to perform. In some versions it is marriage to the Ward (Dasha), and in some it is the path of Golubov and the monastery: regeneration by religious penance or by love. But the references to moral regeneration by love are always followed (as were those to regeneration by religion) by references to the Prince's shooting himself: "During his last visit (when <he presents> his conditions) he says, in a rapture, that he loves only her, that she is his salvation, and—an hour later he shoots himself." Dostoevsky cannot give regeneration by love to the Prince any more than he can give him regeneration by faith in Russia and Orthodoxy.

Dostoevsky comes to Stavrogin's character at the pace of a tortoise. He resists the real Stavrogin by evasions, twists, and wrong turns. He gives the Prince the wrong words, the wrong actions, the wrong loves, and the wrong feelings. Even at the very end, Stavrogin is explaining himself too much and his tone is all wrong—garrulous, superior, self-justifying. In late notes for the letter he writes to Dasha, he says the following:

> Unlike all of our young generation, I cannot welcome the reign of mediocrity, envious equality, stupidity coupled with a lack of individuality, the rejection of any kind of duty, or honor, of any obligations. I can't welcome the rejection of my country, just as I can't welcome those whose only goal is destruction, and who cynically reject any principle that might reunite them after their goal of total destruction has been realized, when the ~~rout~~ profanation and plunder of everything will have brought about the moment when it will no longer be possible to continue life even with the small supply of products and things left intact in the general destruction of the old order. They say that they want to work—they won't. They say that they want to create a new society. They haven't got the bonds ~~to create one~~ for a new society, but they give no thought to these things. They do not think! But their doctrines have all become so complex as to divert them from thinking altogether. The golden mean. No. I am not a democrat.

Somewhere between this and the final version Dostoevsky knew it was all wrong, just as somewhere between his plans for the first published version and the publication of subsequent versions Dostoevsky came to realize that "Stavrogin's Confession" was all wrong. Whatever the correct interpretation of that enigmatic chapter may be, it shows us a Stavrogin who is still struggling and failing with the temptations of repentance and pride. But the Stavrogin of the final version is beyond moral struggle, and only the possible loss of self-control threatens his glacial calm.

Long before Dostoevsky knew what Stavrogin was, he knew that he was everything; and one can trace out the systematic and relentless growth in importance of the Prince. Even while he is seducing and philosophizing, he is insisting on being, whether in doctrine or love, the pivot of character and relationship. Little by little Dostoevsky comes to see that the vital connection is not between the Prince and the Ward, or the Prince and Liza, or the Prince and Golubov, or the Prince and the monastery—but only between the Prince and Nechaev. In the fall of 1870, not long before the beginning of publication, Dostoevsky says and apparently perceives the following:

Most Important

The Prince and Nechaev are tied to each other by mutual secrets which they accidentally share.

Yet Nechaev is concealing a good many things from him (though he is tempted to initiate him, seeing his colossal stature. He is studying him.)

A short time later, in section V, Dostoevsky is firm that the novel has to do with Nechaev and the Prince: "Therefore, the most important thing about the novel is: The relationship between Nechaev and the Prince."

These are the hints that in consciousness—long before he did in fact—Dostoevsky had recognized that the structure of his novel depended upon "the relationship between Nechaev and the Prince." The metaphysical and political plots come together when Peter and Stavrogin come together. Stavrogin does not believe in the dialectics of Kirilov or the messianic nationalism of Shatov, and Peter believes neither the "bright hopes" of Virginsky or the Fourieristic dreams of Liputin. Peter destroys the world about him, and Stavrogin destroys the world within him. They are body and soul, noise and silence, destruction and unfaith.

One of the strongest impressions one is left with from these notes is how wrong Dostoevsky was in so many things. He comes to his characters and to their relationships by twists, turns, circlings, retreats, byways, and wrong ways. Sometimes he barely comes to them, and in a few cases he does not come to them at all. The reader will be exasperated with the endless rehearsals of Stavrogin's and Shatov's rivalry in love and seduction, astonished by Stavrogin's defense of faith and Christ, and skeptical of Dostoevsky's appraisal of Nechaev as naïve and ignorant. Something of the same kind of indirection and misdirection is to be found in his rehearsal of the Idiot's character in passion and revenge in *The Notebooks for "the Idiot"* and in Dostoevsky's trials and mistrials about technical matters in *The Notebooks for "Crime and Punishment."*

Is the misdirection, miscalculation, and the trying and retrying of scenes wasted motion? Or does art—at least Dostoevsky's art—grow because misdirected? Something of a tug-of-war seems to ensue in these notes between what the characters want and what Dostoevsky wants. Many of the wrong starts, much of the pirouetting in place, many of the blind alleys come from the inertia of past works and the dessicating effect of the author's conscious intention and judgment. The notes for *The Possessed* read like a purging of old ideas, old situations, and worn-out intentions. It is as if the new can arise only when the old is invoked, confronted, and overcome; Dostoevsky's genius lies in large part in his ability to recognize what is wrong, and in larger part in his creative capacity to sacrifice what he wants for what must be. The Russian Formalists have told us that art in its very nature is made of indirection, purposive obstacles, and voluntary difficulties. Dostoevsky's notebooks seem to tell us the same thing may be true about the making of art as well as the nature of art.

IV

This edition is a translation of *The Notebooks of Dostoevsky,* edited by E. N. Konshina (Moscow, 1935), but with a number of important changes. The notes in this English edition are presented in a substantially different order from that of the Russian edition. In the Russian edition the notes follow the page order of Dostoevsky's notebooks. This would seem to be the natural thing to do, except for Dostoevsky's eccentric working habits. Dostoevsky jotted down notes on successive pages at widely different times; he would leave pages blank and then return to them with notes months and even years later. As one goes from page to page, one may be reading early, late, and middle notes in a bewildering and even chaotic order. In short, the paginal order does not represent the order in which Dostoevsky wrote the notes. The order in which the notes appear in the notebooks have only accident, haste, mood, and convenience to justify them. They preserve no context, no special groupings, and no significant associations.

The longer I worked with these notes the more distressed I became at the prospect of introducing the reader to the chaos and arbitrary associations of the paginal order, and the more convinced I became that the Russian editor had presented them in chaotic fidelity from excessive timidity and pedantry. Surely the chief value of notes of this kind lies in the illumination they shed on the creative process, and creative process means time order. The longer I brooded over this the more convinced I became that the notes could be put into an approximate chronological order. That is what I have done.

The task has not been as arbitrary as it might seem. Many of the notebook pages are dated; many more are easily identified in time by subject matter, name, and situation. There is, for example, a uniform evolution of names: Lebiadkin is Kartuzov in the early notes; Stepan Trofimovich Verkhovensky is Granovsky until the very last notes; Peter Verkhovensky is first "the Student," then "Nechaev" through most of the notes, and only "Peter" near the very end. Since different names change at different times, combinations of several names make identification even more precise: thus Nechaev-and-the-Lebiadkin-woman is later than Nechaev-and-Lebiadkin. Often, too, simple continuity permits one to put two or twenty pages in one chronological position, even though only one date may appear.

Except for notebook 3, the notebooks had large "chunks" that could be rearranged rather easily for approximate chronological order. Notebook 3, the longest, did not have such easily identifiable large sections, and it presented what seemed to be an impenetrable unchronological order: the time seemed to change every half-dozen pages. Fortunately, there are more dates and more continuity of dialogue in this notebook than in others. When I reached the point beyond which I would not pass into arbitrary choice, I found myself with less than one-sixth of the notebook undetermined in time and order. Half of these notes were about "Nechaev" and "Tikhon," and I grouped them accordingly by subject matter. Finally, a small number of pages remained, the chronological order of which I could not determine with any certainty and which, because of the miscellaneous character, could not be grouped about any subject. These notes have been presented in a separate section (XVII) as miscellaneous matter.

I should add that I have never cut up a notebook page, even though in a few cases some of the entries were easily identified as from more than one chronological period. It seemed wiser to preserve the whole notebook page and place it where the bulk of the material seemed to require it. Fortunately, such mixed pages are rare. I have retained the original notebook page numbers in the left-hand margin of the text, to permit the reader—if he so wishes—to identify the original order of the notebooks. A small portion of the material in the Russian edition has not been republished in this version because the material had no direct bearing on *The Possessed.* The appendix notes to early and vaguely related works, which appear on pages 355–91 of the Russian edition, have not been included in this edition, except for a small part of the notes to "Kartuzov" which appears in section II, "Early Anticipations of *The Possessed.*" From the main text, only pages 12 and 13 (notes for *The Eternal Husband*) and page 19 (notes for an early story about a young man) from notebook 1/10 have been eliminated. These three pages seemed to have only the most remote connection with *The Possessed.* Portions of rough drafts for chapters 9 and 10 of part II and chapter 2 of part III, published in *F. M. Dostoevsky, materialy i issledovaniia,* ed. A. S. Dolinin (1935), have also not been included in this edition because such rough drafts are so close to the final version as to be substantially different in character from these notes. Finally, in the introductory comments that precede each section, I explain which notebook pages are included in the section, and comment further on the reasons for the order I have given.

In the preparation of this text, the original notebook divisions have been discarded since they served no useful purpose, but the text has been divided into eighteen sections. The principle of division is always in some way time, but also subject matter and the natural divisions of the unity of some variant, dialogue, or scenic entity. These editorial devices have been used in the preparation of the manuscript: crossed-out material has been crossed out in the text, illegible words have been indicated by (. . .), and incomplete words or phrases by <. . .>. Illegible words are always few in number, and it seems pedantic and unilluminating to specify the number of words that are illegible. Angle brackets are also used for material inserted by the editor and the translator. Unspaced dots in the text are Dostoevsky's. Numbers in the left-hand margin—as mentioned before—refer to the original pagination of the notebooks. All italics are Dostoevsky's, and large and small capitals are approximations of devices of emphasis used by him. Dates with a slanted line between the two sets of numbers, as "June 18/30," refer to the twelve-day difference in time between the nineteenth-century Russian calendar and the Western calendar. References to the text of *The Possessed* are given in this form: Part II, Chapter 3:4, where the "3:4" refers to chapter and sub-chapter, thus permitting reference to all editions. Some changes have been made in Dostoevsky's punctuation. Obvious oversights on Dostoevsky's part, such as the lack of end parentheses and quotation marks for direct discourse, have been supplied, and adjustments of Russian punctuation conventions to conform to English conventions have been made. Every effort has been made to preserve significant departures from convention and important personal eccentricities.

As editor I have supervised the translation and the preparation of the manuscript, compiled the footnotes, and written the introduction and the eighteen interchapter introductions. Victor Terras has done the translation, the notes indicated by asterisks, which refer to matters of translation, and compiled the index. We hope we have done a service to the understanding and honor of Dostoevsky.

EDWARD WASIOLEK

I
Autobiographical Notes

Notebook pages: 54, 56, 41, 42, 60, 61, 62, 59, 58, 57, 53 from notebook 1/10.

These notes date from August, 1869, to October, 1870. They consist of two plans for novels, a record of two dreams Dostoevsky experienced, a record of fits he suffered from August, 1869, to October, 1870, and the rough draft of a letter to *The Russian Messenger* dated October 1, 1870.

"The idea of a novel," dated February 16/28, 1870, has something of a thinly veiled authorial vengeance upon Dostoevsky's competitors and critics. An old downtrodden writer who has endured miserable working conditions suddenly surprises everyone with brilliant work and achieves fame and money. Dostoevsky had complained in letters more than once that untoward working conditions, especially of time and money, prevented him from achieving his best work.

The fleeting thought found on notebook page 56 is a sketch for an unrealized novel. Its central character is a passionate woman, who in a variety of ways stimulates both lovers and husband to violent action. The interest in the piece lies in the reference to the Tropman case, which also permits us to date the sketch as no earlier than January, 1870. Tropman was a celebrated murderer who killed five children and their parents in cold blood in France, from the motive of robbery. He was caught and guillotined on January 7/19, 1870.

The notes on the dreams, dated June, 1870, and the record of fits are fascinating raw material for the psychologist and for the biographer of Dostoevsky. In both dreams Dostoevsky is persuaded that there is something wrong with him. The sense of impending harm increases in severity and concreteness as we go regressively from the dream about the brother to the dream about the father and the ancestors. The father seems to be the source of harm; it is he who points out to Dostoevsky that something is wrong (in the form of a growth under his nipple) and it is he who is "very glad" after pointing it out. Something like psychological displacement seems to be working when the doctor confirms the father's words and assures Dostoevsky that he has only a few days to live. For Dostoevsky, the waking reality seems to confirm the ominous dream: he actually feels a painful mark under the nipple; his lungs are full of phlegm; his breathing is difficult; he has an attack of hemorrhoids; his digestion is not good; and he has a hemorrhage in the stomach.

The record of fits Dostoevsky experienced from August 3, 1869, to October 22, 1870, is fascinating direct autobiographical evidence as to the nature, symptoms, effects, and feelings that accompanied his attacks. It may come as a surprise to the reader to know that the fits were of such frequency—on the average about every three weeks—that most of them came, thankfully, at night, that the effects lasted five, six, or seven days, clouding Dostoevsky's memory and brain and leaving him restless, nervous, and unable to work.

The record also provides us with an account of Dostoevsky's desperate psychical and physical condition at this time: his money is short; his daughter Liuba is sick; his fits increase in frequency and duration; the weather is hot and unbearable; and like some historical background for his desperate personal situation, two armies of three hundred thousand men face each other on the Franco-Prussian frontier. When Dostoevsky says of the impending war between the Prussians and the French, "Something's got to give! Probably tomorrow or the day after tomorrow a decisive encounter will take place," one feels that he is also thinking of his own situation, that in some way his own desperate situation is confirmed by history itself. There is also something hallucinatory about the interweaving of the record of fits and personal and public events. He tries to connect the timing of his fits and Tropman's execution and, at times, the fits and the phases of the moon. He seems to imply or wants to believe that what is happening to him is somehow connected with things beyond him.

---

4 MARVELOUS IDEA. KEEP IN MIND.

Idea of a novel, February 16/28, 1870.

A novelist (a writer), in his old age, and mainly on account of his fits of illness, has seen his faculties grow dull, and himself sink into poverty. Realizing his failings, he prefers to cease writing and accept the lot of poverty. A wife and daughter. All his life he has been writing to order. Now, he no longer considers himself equal to his former peers, but rather feels that he is in their debt. To the critics, whom he still calls *scoundrels* under his breath (below all, it would seem; yet consequently, above all), he tells episodes from his earlier life, as if for the edification of children, etc. Public lectures. How he had many ideas, literary and other. A tone of apparent self-irony, yet to himself: "Why, it really is so." How his children, and his wife, and the M<iliuk>ovs think little of him. How Turgenev, Goncharov, Pleshcheev,[1] Aksakov[2] let him have it, how he quarrels with Saltykov. How he suddenly, without telling anybody, proceeds to write an excellent work. Fame and money.—etc. etc. N.B. A PROMISING THEME—well, granted, I won't compare it to Count L. Tolstoi or Mr. Turgenev (N.B. never simply Turgenev, without a "Mr."); or even the other Count Tolstoi;[3] but the realist Pisemsky[4]—that's a different matter! For that is French vaudeville posing as Russian realism.

N.B. About the transience of life, and tales—a poetic representation, somewhat like *Oblomov's Dream*,[5] of Christ—(and later, to himself: "This is worth a good 200 roubles per sixteen pages, and I'm letting them have it for nothing, while they think that they are doing me a favor.")

About trends and ideas in literature.

6 A FLEETING THOUGHT. A Field Marshal, with his pregnant mistress, comes to this provincial town. ~~The wife~~ (To entice her husband again.)

---

[1] Aleksey N. Pleschcheev (1825–93), a minor poet. He was a member of the Petrashevsky Circle in the late forties, and was arrested in 1849, along with Dostoevsky and others.

[2] Probably Sergei T. Aksakov (1791–1859), author of the famous *A Family Chronicle* (1856).

[3] Aleksei K. Tolstoy (1817–75), an important writer of satirical verse. His most famous creation, written in collaboration with two cousins, is *Kosma Prutkov.*

[4] Aleksey F. Pisemsky (1821–81), novelist and dramatist. His most famous work is *A Thousand Souls* (1858).

[5] A fragment from Goncharov's novel, *Oblomov.* The fragment appeared in 1849, almost a decade before the entire novel was published.

Her husband is a man of principles, self-improvement, children left at doorsteps. He isn't deceived by her charms, yet he is constant in his love for her. Having developed the desire to seduce her husband she becomes a victim of her own deception. The Prince is a finished man. Finally she wants to flee this temptation, for she has begun to yield to it. She drives the Prince out of his wits, and he is jealous of her husband, slaps his face, tries to kill him (but does not succeed). (N.B. She has been egging him on, even though she hasn't said it in so many words, but rather has been provoking his jealousy). But when he shoots her husband, she deserts the Prince—and once and for all embraces her husband, while the Prince kills himself. ? (N.B. Her husband takes her back, but no sooner has he accepted her than she again grows tired of him. With a schoolboy, with the Governor.)

The hermit—Mary of Egypt.

She induces the Prince to insult his mother. (She is making experiments with the Prince all the time.)

N.B. She seduces her husband to the point of actually giving herself to him.

N.B. She has just returned from abroad and would like to see a nihilist. A schoolteacher, who is a nihilist, shows up in town. (The murder of her husband; the Prince makes friends with the nihilists, and talks them into killing.)

She has witnessed Tropman's execution. Description of the execution. About how delightfully handsome he was.

N.B. Either the Teacher rejects her, i.e., he doesn't reject her, but fails to be seduced by her charms (even though he may have taken possession of her). Then she takes vengeance on him, and when she does (she kills him)—she is shedding tears.

The Prince is a tragic figure (in him, there lies *the seed* of the plot and of the events of the novel).

The wife, formerly the mistress of a field marshal, has been returned to her husband, a schoolteacher, by the latter, along with a handsome remuneration. She turns his head, makes him insult ~~her~~ his mother, kills the Field Marshal, forces her husband to fight a duel with a man who has insulted her (a young prince who had been her lover briefly), turns the whole province upside down, finally dies with her husband sobbing at her side.

60

41 *Notes* June 17/29 16/28 <1870>

The weather keeps changing; it is rainy and relatively cold. The money has not arrived, and I don't know if I'll get any at all. I've completed the fifth chapter of the novel.

~~In the evenings~~ at night (two ~~evenings~~ nights in a row) I can hardly work: the blood rushes to my head, I feel torpid, sleepy, I'm afraid of the bad consequences of working at night (a stroke, or something of that kind?).

Last night I saw my brother[6] in a dream. He had, it seemed, returned to life, but was living apart from his family. It seemed as if I was with him, having the feeling that there was something wrong with me: loss of ~~memory~~ consciousness, as after a fainting fit. ~~I don't think (...)~~ I went to a large nearby hospital to consult a doctor. My brother seemed to be kinder to me.

I woke up, went back to sleep, and saw what seemed to be a continuation of that dream: I see my father[7] (I haven't seen him in a dream for a long time). He pointed at my chest, under my right nipple, and said: "Everything is all right with you, *but here it is very bad.*" I took a look and there actually appeared to be some growth under my nipple. My father said: "*Don't unsettle your nerves.*" Then there was some kind of family celebration at my father's, and in came his old mother, and all our ancestors. He was very glad. From his words I concluded that I was in a very bad way. I showed my chest to another doctor, who said: "Yes, it is right there. You haven't long to live; *you have only a few days to live.*"

N.B. Having woken up in the morning, at 12 o'clock, I noticed, almost at the spot pointed out by my father, a mark the size of a hazelnut, which was extremely painful to the touch—as when you touch a painfully bruised spot. I had never had this before.

N.B. My lungs again are full of phlegm; I keep wheezing and find breathing difficult.

Altogether, this illness has continued for a year and a half, apparently getting worse. I'm becoming short-winded.

N.B. Apparently I am also having, right now, an attack of hemorrhoids. Pain in my stomach, as before a hemorrhage. My digestion is good.

---

[6] Mikhail M. Dostoevsky (1820–66). Dostoevsky was very close to his brother. They put out together the journal, *Time,* (1861–63), and briefly, *Epoch* (1864).

[7] Mikhail A. Dostoevsky (1789–1839), a military doctor. He was a cruel father, who was murdered by his own peasants and whom Dostoevsky remembered with ambivalent feelings. See Sigmund Freud's analysis of Dostoevsky's complicated relations with his father in the essay, "Dostoevsky and Parricide."

42 June ~~18/30~~ 17/29 <1870>, Wednesday.

Ania[8] has developed <a case of> ——. ——. She is weak, her nerves are shattered, she sleeps little? Is she really pregnant?

60 1)

Fits (1869)

Note. In Florence,[9] during the summer, infrequent and not very strong fits (rather, comparatively rare). At the same time, active open hemorrhoids.

August 3, a fit, in Florence, while leaving town.

August 10, a fit, in Prague,[10] while en route.

August 19, a fit, in Dresden.[11]

September 4, a fit, in Dresden. Very soon after the fit, while still in bed, a painful, literally unbearable pressure in my chest. A feeling that I might die of it. It passed after fomentation (dry, heated plates, and towels with hot ashes), in a half hour.

September 14. A fit at night, while in bed.

N.B.$_1$ Almost all of my fits come while in bed, in my sleep (during the first few hours of sleep, some time between three and four o'clock A.M.)

N.B.$_2$ Compared with my fits in the past (over the years), the series of fits which have occurred recently, since August 3, show an unprecedented increase in the frequency of these fits, as compared to anything I have experienced since I have had the disease; it seems that the disease is entering a new, malignant phase. Over the years, I think I wouldn't be wrong saying that the *median* interval between fits was constant at *three weeks* (that is just the median, or proportional median figure; i.e., there were

61 2)

intervals of six weeks, and of 10 days, but on the average it would come to three weeks).

---

8 Anna Grigorievna (maiden name, Snitkina) (1846–1918). Dostoevsky's second wife. She came to work for him as a stenographer when he was writing *The Gambler*. They were devoted to each other, and the marriage was close and happy.

9 Dostoevsky lived in Florence from December, 1868, to the middle of August, 1869.

10 Dostoevsky spent three days in Prague in 1869, looking unsuccessfully for a furnished apartment, and then left for Dresden.

11 Dostoevsky lived in Dresden from the winter of 1869–70 to July, 1871.

The present increase can be ascribed to the drastic change in climate between Florence and Dresden, to the strain of the trip, to my distraught nerves while en route and in Germany, etc.

September 30, at night, a fairly strong fit (after having worked at night).

1870. January 1/13, a fit, strong, after an indiscretion, at six o'clock in the morning, during the first hours of sleep. The interval between fits was of unprecedented length—three months and ten days. As a result of not being used to it so much, my ailing condition persists very long: it is already the fifth day after the fit, and my head still hasn't cleared up. The weather ~~is changing~~ has changed from fine (plus 2 or plus 3 degrees Réaumur) to a slush. The fit occurred during an almost full moon.

<January>7/19. A fit at 6 o'clock in the morning (the day and almost the hour of Tropman's execution). I did not feel it, awoke after 8 o'clock, with a feeling that I had had a fit. I had a headache and my body was aching all over. N.B. (Altogether, the aftereffects of my fits, i.e., nervousness, shortness of memory, an intensified and foggy, quasi-contemplative state, persist longer now than in previous years. They used to pass after three days, while now it may take six. Especially at night, by candlelight, an indefinite hypochondriac melancholy, and as if a red, bloody shade (not color) upon everything. Almost impossible to work during those days. (I am writing this note on the sixth day after the fit.) N.B. The weather is fine, snow flurries. The winter in Dresden is unusually mild this year.

February 10/January 29. At three o'clock A.M., a most violent fit, in the hall, in a waking state. I fell down and hurt my forehead. Not being conscious of anything and remembering nothing, I did, however, carry to my room a burning candle without damaging it a bit, shut the window, and only then did I become aware of the fact that I had had a fit. I awakened Ania and told her. She cried very much seeing my face.

3)

I began to calm her and suddenly I had another fit, while still awake, in Ania's room (Liuba[12] was carried to another room)—a quarter of

---

[12] Dostoevsky's five-month-old daughter. She was born in September, 1869, and died in 1926.

an hour after the first fit. When I awakened from it, I had a terrible headache, and for a long time I couldn't speak correctly; Ania stayed with me that night. (Mystic terror in the highest degree.) It is now already 4 days after the fit, and my head is still far from fresh; apparently my nerves are in a bad way; the rush of blood to my head must have been very strong. I can't even think of working; at night I experience a strong hypochondriac feeling. I fall asleep late, around 6 A.M. I go to bed after three o'clock, I can't earlier. All of last week we had a strong frost, around 10 degrees. It is a full moon now. At the time of the fit the moon was better than half full. (Light symptoms of open hemorrhoids at the time of the fit and before it.)

February 23/11. A fit, in my sleep, immediately after I had gone to bed, at 5:10 A.M., before dawn. I felt nothing, and only after awakening, at 11 o'clock A.M., I realized that I had had a fit. I am told that it was a light one; I think so myself, although now the aftereffects of my fits (i.e., a feeling of heaviness in my head or an outright headache, distraught nerves, a nervous laughter, and mystic melancholy) persist much longer than previously: for about five, six days, or even a week, I couldn't say that it was all over, or that my head was completely clear. ~~The phases of the moon,~~ no moon, it has grown much warmer, foggy, but in the daytime a bright sun. I am writing this on February 27, a Sunday. One can positively say that today is the first day of spring, such a fine day it is. Mentally, I have great worries, I'm getting no news, Liuba has fallen ill (God save her!).

Congestion of blood in my lower abdomen, constipated feeling, sleep with interruptions, not always pleasant dreams.

May, 1870. A fit while awake, after a day and a night en route, in H<ombur>g. I arrived, had dinner, went to the station, and having returned to my hotel at 4 o'clock P.M., at my room, I felt that I was having a fit and fell to the ground. Fortunately I only hurt the back of my head slightly; I had a lump there for about a week. After regaining consciousness I wasn't in possession of my full faculties for a while. I remember that I was wandering around in the hotel, telling people about my fit; among others, I told the owner of the hotel. I didn't lie down, but went back to the station. The fit was in general of the heavy variety, accompanied by mystic melancholy and nervous laughter. My nervousness contributed a lot to things going badly. During the entire time of my absence, all week long, I was hardly in my right mind, it seems. It was cold, damp, and rainy all the time. Incidentally, I caught a cold, and even now,

4)

two weeks later, I am still coughing. In general, it must be noted that I positively can't stand traveling distances of any length by railway: I have a fit every time. N.B. The fit occurred at the very beginning of a new moon. Now my health is in decent shape. Ania's nerves are quite distraught from breast-feeding; Liuba, thank God, is in good health (may the Lord have mercy and save both!). I have great worries. The hot months lie ahead, terribly strenuous work—the novel for *The Russian Messenger* (I put no trust in it). I have thought up a letter to N. Let it rest until September 1. Something's got to give! We shall be very short of money right until fall!

1870, July 13/1. A fit while asleep, toward morning, right after I had fallen asleep. I fell asleep and learned about it from Ania as late as half past twelve. It seemed to her that it was not a very strong fit. Today, July 17 (Sunday) my body hasn't been really aching *too much,* but my head still isn't clear, especially in the evening. Melancholy. In general, I notice that even fits of medium strength are now (i.e., the older I get) affecting my head, my brain, more noticeably than even the strongest fits used to in the past. My head won't clear up even in a whole week. The weather is hot; there was a full moon on the 13th; rare light, warm rainshowers. I am struggling with the 1st part of my novel, and I'm desperate. War has been declared. Ania is quite exhausted. Liuba is nervous and restless. N.B. Kashpirev sent the money two months later than promised. Our situation has hardly improved, even though the money has been sent. All my hope rests with the novel and my trip to K<issinge>n. I wonder about the war. It could give us a lot of trouble. God forbid!

July 25/13. A fit, in the morning, after I had fallen asleep; preceding it, terrible convulsions. The night before, an indiscretion. It is hot, and a cutting, most annoying breeze from the north. Liuba has been feverish all the time, a cough and sniffles; teething; now she is better, but her teeth are giving her trouble. Ania as before. Apparently no hope at all to go to Kissingen. The army has taken over all means of transportation. Even the mail doesn't come anymore. Yesterday, no newspapers from Berlin. The battle will probably be in a week. No money. Very anxious. Something's got to give.

I'm told that the fit was a light one, yet I'm aching all over, and I've got a headache.

58 5)

1) *The Search,* a short novel, November 21/9, 1869, 11 o'clock. P.M.

2) An existence in the process of radically breaking up. The gradual process of impoverishment. A man who incessantly swears to take revenge on those who are persecuting him, when luck finally smiles upon him, gives away the last thing he owns: "What's the use of taking revenge, anyway?"

July 16/28, 1870. A fit while asleep, toward morning, a few minutes after 8 o'clock. (The exact hour and minute of the beginning of a new moon.) Three days after the fit of July 25/13. I am told that I had a very strong rush of blood to my head; that my face turned blue. Now it is already August 3d; almost until today, my head failed to clear up. My mental condition was an agonizing one. On August 1, I acted stupidly at the reading room. I ascribe it directly to my mood after the fit. Terrible heat. Until today there has been a thunderstorm every day, but not today. The grasshoppers are chirping. No money. Liuba is in good health, Ania could be better. Two armies of three hundred thousand each are about to clash on the Rhine. Only yesterday they were facing each other, ready to attack any hour. Stocks are going down. Prices are up on everything. Neither side will be able to stand a long war. Yet they are prepared to keep fighting for a long time. Something's got to give! Probably tomorrow or the day after tomorrow a decisive encounter will take place.

August 7. Another fit. At night (6 o'clock in the morning). I was very much upset all day. (Today is the 11th, and I still can't get my head to clear up.) My novel is most definitely turning into a reject (terrible!). On the 6th of this month the French were routed; they are now gathering their forces in front of Metz and apparently they have lost their presence of mind and don't know how to maneuver; they are losing time.

September 2, 10 o'clock in the morning, in my sleep, of the strong variety. I went to bed toward morning, very late. Ania and Anna Nikolaevna[13] became ill. I had some rum with coffee. Ania is weakened by breast-feeding the child.

~~September 9~~

September 9, 1870. In the morning, just after 9 o'clock, a rather

---

[13] Anna Nikolaevna Snitkina, Dostoevsky's mother-in-law; she lived with the Dostoevskys in Dresden.

weak one. Liubochka is being weaned. Ania is quite worn out. Maybe one of these days I'll make a trip to Prague. The novel is progressing slowly, according to God's will. The money situation is bad. No reply from *Dawn*. Today is the 14th of September and possibly the <German> forces have reached Paris.[14]

7 6)

October 10/September 28, 1870. A fit, toward morning, immediately after I had gone to bed, ~~almost~~ in a waking state. I fell down by the small wardrobe and was lying on the floor. Ania had a good deal of trouble reviving me. A strong fit. I felt a chill. Things are bad. I haven't mailed any part of the novel as yet. We shall have to move. Taking care of Liuba is enough to exhaust Ania. Liuba is in good health, but she has acquired the habit of sleeping badly at night. The weather, for the first time this summer, is very cold. Paris is under siege.[15] In France, inertness as a consequence of their administrative system. No stable government. What will *The Russian Messenger* reply? My letter to Sonia[16] apparently got lost. I haven't answered Strakhov[17] yet. After 6 months of silence, I received today a letter from Maikov.[18]

October 16. A fit, toward morning, at our new flat, 6 days after the preceding fit. In my sleep, I didn't feel it. Of the weak variety. It took a long time for my head to clear up. Now (October 22) I have a stomach-ache for the third day. Yesterday I sent a letter to Katkov.[19] Today to Maikov and Strakhov. Ania is very thin and very melancholy. A hard life! What shall I hear from *The Russian Messenger?*

October 22. In the morning, while asleep (after 6 o'clock), a fit, and after I had fallen asleep, an hour later, another. Now it is the 26th, and I'm still utterly distraught and expect another fit any minute.

---

[14] The French army was crushed September 1 at Sedan and Napoleon III was taken prisoner.

[15] The siege of Paris lasted four and one-half months.

[16] Sophia A. Ivanova, Dostoevsky's favorite niece. Many of his letters are to this niece, the daughter of his sister, Vera Mikhailovna.

[17] Nikolay N. Strakhov (1828–96), critic and philosopher, conservative in view. He was the biographer and critic of the lives and works of Dostoevsky and Tolstoy.

[18] Apollon N. Maikov (1821–97), poet and close friend of Dostoevsky. At this time Dostoevsky wrote frequently to him. Maikov's most ambitious work was *Two Worlds* (1852), a tragedy on the subject of the struggle between Imperial Rome and early Christianity.

[19] Mikhail Nikiforovich Katkov (1818–87), editor of *The Russian Messenger* and a conservative force in nineteenth-century Russian journalism.

Now it is the night of Oct. 26/27. A storm outside. The last three ~~days~~ nights, aurora borealis. Ania is having a toothache. Liuba, thank God <is in good health>. No money. They had a fair here. I must do some writing, I've really fallen behind schedule.

53 October 1/September 19 <1870>

Dear Sir, Mikhail Nikiforovich:[20]

Since my last letter to you, I have been working with all my strength, and incessantly, yet it seems that I have again deceived you, i.e., I haven't sent you anything as yet. But I kept being frustrated in the execution of my plan, and having twice completed as much as 240 pages, I had to change my plan ~~twice~~ (not the idea of the novel, only the plan). Twice I had to re-do it from the very beginning. But now everything is well organized and has taken shape. I don't know if I shall succeed, yet the idea is a good one. This novel does mean a great deal to me.

Its length will be about 480 pages, ~~in two weeks~~ and it will consist of *three* major parts. Within two weeks after receipt of this letter, the editor of *The Russian Messenger* will receive the first two episodes of the 1st part, that is, one half of it, and by November 15 the entire 1st part. From then on, delivery will be made without further delays. Out of ~~almost~~ 240 pages written so far, 192 will probably be incorporated into the new version ~~of the novel~~. The success ~~of this novel~~ means a lot to me, and I do not want to let it suffer any harm, consciously at least.

Thus, it won't be possible ~~to make arrangements for~~ to print it before January first of next year. ~~If, by my earlier promise to send it in to be printed still this year~~ I beg you very much to forgive me that ~~again~~? I haven't kept my word ~~to the fullest~~ and haven't dispatched it earlier. I assure you that it did not depend on me. Yet I felt it to be necessary to advise you, in this letter, of the current state of affairs, ~~to wit~~ i.e., that I shall certainly deliver my work and that I won't fail you under any circumstances.

---

[20] Katkov. See Note 19.

II
Early Anticipation of The Possessed

This section is divided into two parts: notebook pages 1–8 from notebook 1/10 and pages 91–96 and 101–2 from notebook 1/4. The first part consists of notes written in 1869 when Dostoevsky was thinking of "Atheism" and "The Life of a Great Sinner"; the second part consists of notes for the unpublished story, "Kartuzov," the hero of which was a prototype for Captain Lebiadkin. These notes are undated but were written probably in late 1869 or early 1870.

In the first part there is no plot or coherent conception of a story. There are capsule characterizations, fragments of thoughts, floating motifs. There is a Usurer who strives abstractly and futilely for good deeds. The proud Prince has met the Usurer abroad; there is some secret between them, and they are in conflict over the Fiancée, whom the Usurer steals from the Prince. The Prince makes pregnant the Ward (an anticipation of Dasha), whom he abandons to the Usurer. Mary Lebiadkin of *The Possessed* is already portrayed in the lame girl, the daughter of a drunken beggar of a lieutenant; she has been raped by a convict, Kulishov (an early conception of Fedka); and Kulishov kills the lame girl and her father, presumably at the instigation of the Prince.

The Usurer is an unbeliever who hungers for and seeks truth and suffering; the Prince is "envious, aspiring to high human dignity without paying a price, proud without having a right to be, a pathetic figure." But at times they are not clearly distinguished from each other, for both hunger for life without knowing how to find it, and both in some of the variants shoot themselves.

There is no hint of a political plot in these notes, but the murder of the lame girl and her father by a convict in possible collaboration with the Prince clearly anticipates one of the central situations of the final version of *The Possessed*.

The notes on Kartuzov in the second part are a representative selection from a repetitive portrait published more fully in the appendix to the Russian edition of these notes. In the notes, Kartuzov is ambiguously foolish and pure, dignified and comic, a defender of the Amazon's (Horsewoman's) honor and something of a pest in his defense of her. The portrait degenerates by the time it reaches the final version, where Lebiadkin is a drunk, a mistreater of his sister, only a pest to Liza, and the pawn of people like Liputin. The love and defense of his lady, and the dignity, are still there, but both are distorted, eccentric, unpredictable. Lebiadkin is a comic buffoon, foolishly clutching shreds of dignity.

---

1 <The first page of this notebook has the following entry in the hand of Anna Grigorievna Dostoevsky: "This notebook of F. M. Dostoevsky is presented by me to my grandsons Fyodor and Andrey Dostoevsky, January 28, 1909. *Anna Dostoevsky.*">

Make a change in the novel about the boy[1] (a natural son in the family).

The Usurer[2] knows the Prince from their university days (change, and think about this novel).

Do over Kartuzov, the Count[3] <was> chased out—(a scandalous duel).[4]

The Usurer and the Prince each know about a certain dark affair of the other's, ~~and both~~ (what kind of affair, precisely?).

Both the Prince and *she* are dependent on him. He is a natural son, the Prince treats him arrogantly.

<The rest of the page is taken up by some arithmetic calculations.>

---

[1] The novel about the boy is from the projected "Life of a Great Sinner."

[2] Hero of the projected novel, "Atheism." This is a common character type in Dostoevsky's novels: Ptitsyn in *The Idiot,* Ipolit in his fantasies in *The Idiot,* and Arkady in *A Raw Youth* are examples.

[3] In early notes for the sketch Kartuzov, the Count is Kartuzov's rival for the hand of "the Beauty." Kartuzov is suspicious of his motives.

[4] The duel is a commonplace theme or situation for Dostoevsky; it is usually satirized. Examples are the Underground Man in his fantasies about getting even with Zverkov and company, and Stavrogin's duel with Gaganov's son, when he refuses to shoot back.

2 1) Lizaveta[5] <a crossed-out illegible word> Shchurov

2) Kartuzov

An Attempt of an Idea

3) Three people.

~~His father was a usurer, *not he.*~~

It wasn't his father who was killed, but his wife—(a fat woman whom he had married for her money).

Her husband had been living in slum tenements—I don't believe it.

With a pawner—he refuses to take advantage of the other man's wife.

He has been making hints about his sister to the Prince (from venom).

After a heart-to-heart talk with his fiancée, having conceived a sincere and profound idea, he spends the night at Maksim Ivanov's[6]—orgy and murder.

He wants to shoot himself.

The poet's adieu to life, and the unbeliever (a brilliant chapter).

The Usurer on God, nature, and life.

The *Fiancée*—she has come to see her friend, the wife of the dying poet-toiler.

~~The Fiancée~~

The Usurer says to his fiancée: "I would like to get rid of my property, and to seek trial and suffering, for I am not an atheist but a believer."

She replies: "If you will go, I shall be with you."

Then he, the unbeliever, as a reward for his doing that (for he is an atheist) decides to relinquish his property in a different way, i.e., to shoot himself. The trial for <the murder of> his wife saves him, and he goes to Siberia to suffer, with joy. (N.B. Even though he knows that someone else is guilty, not he.)

The 2d person, the Prince—envious, aspiring to high human dignity

---

[5] The same as "the Beauty," "the Fiancée," and "the Horsewoman." She is always a headstrong character who is the point of romantic contention between the teacher and the Prince and later between Nechaev and the Prince. The prototype of Liza.

[6] A real person, the chief of a band of murderers. Dostoevsky learned about him in connection with the von Sohn affair. Von Sohn was killed by Ivanov and his companions on November 8, 1869. See note 15 in section V.

without paying a price, proud without having a right to be it, a pathetic figure; in love with the Fiancée, who is stolen from him by the Usurer. (N.B. He has made a girl pregnant, and turned her over to the Schoolteacher.)

The Fiancée, a long-suffering victim of fatigue, melancholy, and boredom, she thirsts for real life and believes in it.

The 3d person, the Schoolteacher. Leaving babes on people's doorsteps; a simple, live, and grandiose feat.

3 "I admit that matter may exist, but how can I possibly know if matter is material?"

An underground idea for The Russian Messenger—~~December~~ November 14/2. <1869>

I~~?~~, my family, since childhood, Moscow. Everybody is in his debt. Growing up, Chermak,[7] the first and the last, accused of everything. Silent and morose, he supports the whole family. Everybody is dependent on him. He remains silent. Everybody feels oppressed. The girl whom he had loved (she opened her heart to him once) has married his brother. His brother loses his health. Everybody looks at him with trepidation. He keeps up his silence and his good works. For example, somebody slaps his face. He does not call him out. In the family, they won't dare to laugh. Give it a tragic finish.

<The rest of this page is taken up by arithmetic calculations.>

5 Badergasse 19.

The last attempt at realizing the idea of February 2/January 21.

The Usurer is the son of his father's first wife, from a poor family, brought up *aparte.* (Not a relative.)

The Prince met him abroad. (A very young sister, his mother, and her ward.)

The Usurer has a house in Moscow.

The Prince appears (1st, because the two had met abroad, both having attended the same university and also being, apparently, distantly related; 2d, because he is fascinated by the Usurer's intellectual leanings; and 3d, by the Usurer's inexplicable liaison, abroad, with the Beauty. They are sharing some secret, he thinks, as he finds it impossible to admit that any serious ties might exist between them).

---

[7] Leontii I. Chermak, a teacher in the school where Dostoevsky studied as a child from 1834 to 1837.

The Prince makes the Ward pregnant, leaving her with the Usurer, who places her in a slum tenement.

(The Usurer's idea and *secret:* "Self-education requires persistent work. Then you will get to love Nature and find God." But the Usurer does not love and continues being a Usurer [yet he would do an occasional good deed on the spur of the moment]. The fast—and, suddenly, at Maksim Ivanov's.)

It requires a tremendous effort, for I am ~~a usurer~~ addicted to usury and love of money.

? ? ?

The Beauty investigates and learns that he secretly does good deeds.

I shall shoot myself in 2½ hours.

A babe is left on the doorsteps.

Meanwhile, the Prince and the pregnant bride are for him.

He jumped from a railway carriage.

He pushed his father out.

The Prince saw it (or perhaps the Beauty did).

The Usurer himself.

Since that time ~~the bride~~ the Beauty keeps him under surveillance, and he knows that she does.

But she thinks that she only fancied to have seen it.

An Idea

N.B. The preliminary period of his life is described so that nobody could even have imagined that he would ever marry. And there, suddenly, he arrives with a wife, and keeps her locked up. Impossible to meet her.

The Atheist is married. Nobody knows why he got married, but he is terribly jealous and torments his wife.

His family at first hated his wife, but then the Cripple fell in love with her (they want to get her over on their side).

His wife is innocent and young, like a child. She is terribly afraid of him, fearing he may kill her. They have been telling her that he would kill her. Finally, she makes up her mind, and runs off to them from upstairs.

They actually refuse to turn her over to him (which shows that they are not really in bondage to him).

The rape of the ~~hunchback~~ Lame Girl who lives across the courtyard and is in love with him. She is well educated, the daughter of a drunken beggar of a lieutenant. She used to be jealous of his wife and hated her, when he was living with her and when he arrived with his wife. The anonymous letters were arranged by the Lame Girl to be sent. She takes up with Kulishov. She asserts, before witnesses, that she has seen him beating his father. But actually she only saw Kulishov and the Prince, but not *him*. It was Kulishov who raped and killed her. Back to the gate. (Before she was murdered, he had quarreled with her.) Kulishov uses this as an alibi. (There is a witness to the murder of the old man.) His wife also testifies that he was a frequent visitor there and that he had been despondent on these occasions. Kulishov does not actually live on a forged passport, but he knows various jailbirds and the *old* Raskolnik. He acts as an informer.

N.B. (Kulishov knows the ways of the entire family, including that they all owe him money, so that they will surely say "yes" to everything, and that his wife will also be inclined to inform.)

Kulishov wants to get some money from him. A scene showing them bargaining?

Seeing that he cannot prove his innocence, he goes? (?and confesses?). He is actually glad to get rid of everything. His wife. (There is some Tartar princeling who owed some money to the murdered captain; it is he who incited Kulishov to commit the murder. But the Prince disappears. It is *he* who has got the promissory notes; the Prince hasn't got all of them.)

?N.B. (Kulishov's death, through the Prince?)

The Lieutenant, who makes a living begging for alms in a genteel manner and who is the father of the Lame Girl, used to be a friend of the murdered Captain. They were in the same company and used to drink together. He swears that he will find the murderers. A phrasemonger. He is received by the family. He distributes petitions.

8 2)

He thought that he might escape despair by marrying.

But he had only jealousy and no passion.

Would gladly commit crimes.

One cannot live in this fashion, but where is one to go?

He has developed an idée fixe about self-control, after having experienced the torments of jealousy, and therefore he does not keep his wife from leaving him.

The Prince went to see *him* and has long since confessed his crime, which Kulishov does not know.

Yet when Kulishov proceeds to prove it, the Prince suddenly loses heart and fails to show up.

At this point the Prince receives an inheritance and wants to get married.

The idea of gradual self-perfection in the feats of the Saints fascinates him (yet he has no faith). He wants to perfect himself. (He seeks to perform a feat and stumbles immediately.) Self-perfection little by little.

1 KARTUZOV CONTINUED

N.B. Kartuzov is a poor conversationalist; he never finishes his sentences. He is never embarrassed, apparently he doesn't suspect that he is funny. He can be quite businesslike when necessary. He conducts himself well, strictly according to etiquette. But only to a certain point, so long as he can remain silent and is not obliged to do anything. But the moment it becomes necessary for him to make a movement or say a word, he often compromises himself by his very first gesture, and sometimes comes up with such antics as no one would have expected of him, leaving people nonplussed and eventually making them laugh.

N.B. Begin by drawing a picture of how Kartuzov becomes interested <in the Amazon>, and intrigue the reader by a description of his early moves: he is critical of the Amazon, he dresses himself up; he is with his friends, the jeweler, the governess; he gets to the point of hating; he raises his finger to the peak of his cap. *And suddenly he is in love—everything becomes clear.*

N.B. During the time when he still hates the Amazon something ~~happens~~ *must happen* that is more romantic than the <episode with the> jeweler. An encounter with the Amazon, he does *something* for her. She thanks him. Kartuzov leaves, jaded and in the grip of powerful emotions.

N.B. *A trait*: Kartuzov's habitual arrogance (though he can, on occasion, display enough simplicity: for instance, with his social inferiors his behavior is rather, or even most, acceptable). That is why his comrades find him amusing, but hateful as well. He tends to provoke taunts.

N.B. Present the figure of Kartuzov to the reader in a more comic, more mysterious, and more interesting light, right from the beginning. All of the savage and romantic moments, their truthfulness and realism notwithstanding, should be *drawn from nature* with a comical tinge.

N.B. But when Kartuzov is down with a fever, everybody is stunned,
2 as if they had not expected anything that serious. Everybody is hushed, and people now speak of him without derision, though still without

any particular sympathy. Incidentally, on the outside everybody continues to judge him with condescension, just as before.

N.B. Kartuzov is always abrupt (though softspoken and polite)—as on the occasion when he reads his poem about the cockroach. Sometimes when startled he would suddenly blush.

N.B. Kartuzov has been in Revel *before*. He pays visits to everybody. He is dry, softspoken, but polite.

N.B. It must be that he has rarely, *or perhaps never*, seen an Amazon <i.e., a lady on horseback>.

N.B. I had a terribly hard time trying to find out what he knew and what he didn't know. Verses about Pushkin, he blushed and kept silent, yet gave polite answers when asked. Little by little I noticed that he trusted me more than other people. I actually observed some attempts on his part to gain my friendship.

And immediately thereafter:

Revel is a seaside town, situated on a bay; people come here to bathe in the sea, etc. Everything briefly, à la Pushkin, from the very beginning, without psychological subtleties, in short phrases. *Learn how to write.*

N.B. Kartuzov brought me one (?) piece of official correspondence—<showing that he was> quite illiterate. He was terribly uneducated.

93 *Revel.*

A German town with a pretense to being knightly, which for some reason is very funny (even though it actually did, at one time, belong to some knights).

I accidentally belonged to, or to be exact, was connected without belonging to, a small group of officers in charge of coastal structures. There were among them several lively young men; yet Captain Kartuzov drew more attention than anyone else. He had been recently transferred in from some other fortress.

To the club.

There was no common tie between the visitors. There was no station used by all.

N.B. N.B. Kartuzov run over by the lady on horseback.

Prior to that he keeps reiterating that the Count is an *inveterate scoundrel.*

They play a practical joke on Kartuzov calling him to rescue a lady bather from drowning. Kartuzov rescues the beauty, carrying her out naked. (Kartuzov tells me: "How good it feels." Conversations about poetry.)

Kartuzov retorts that she is not going to bathe like everyone else, not out of a bath-house, but in some special fashion.

"Well, in some special fashion."

"Probably they've got their own bath-house, all lined with velvet."

"Why, the velvet will get wet."

"In a three-cornered hat, with a feather, and wearing a sword."

The Count: "Well, Captain, how come you turn up here?" Kartuzov is offended.

He used to visit <me?>, the jeweler; he breaks a teapot.

He suddenly comes to see me: "I want to write him a letter to tell him that he, the Count, is an inveterate scoundrel."

"Why that?"

"It just happens to be my opinion."

"You haven't the right to express it."

"Really?" he replies, quite surprised.

<"He is marrying her> for <her> money."

Then suddenly and for no obvious reason at all, he goes to see the Count, seeking a reconciliation. He sits at the Count's <for some time>. He leaves lost in thought.

He returns: "Is it true that you are marrying her for her money?"

Kartuzov leaves, red as a lobster.

Kartuzov suddenly sends <her> a letter. A scandal. I go to see Kartuzov to inquire about the matter. It is true. He shows me his verses. He swears that he won't leave her alone. Here then, Merder shows up. He swears once more.

~~To the Commandant~~

Respect.

The Count shouts: "Out of my way!" And <lashes him> with his horsewhip. The duel. Negotiations.

Here, <the matter goes>to the Commandant. Verses, arrest. She breaks her leg. (Naïve daydreams about his career in the service and the dowry.)

94 N.B. { A capital thing
Naïveté

In a private interview with her, he blurts out quite unabashedly: *"I am doing a heroic deed."*

She is quite amazed:

"What heroic deed?"

"Of selflessness; for you have lost a leg. Therefore, you are bound to appreciate it."

N.B. Whenever one would try to talk some sense into Kartuzov, he would listen in astonishment and then, suddenly, get sunk in reverie and remain lost in it.

N.B. *In Revel.* Kartuzov's letters used to be passed from hand to hand: he went to everybody for advice and showed them to everybody, under the seal of secrecy. In these letters he would write, most naïvely, about his successes in the service and about his salary.

Some officers offer to abduct her for him. A commission. A conference. Kartuzov is willing to listen, but does not approve of it.

(With his superior, a colonel. "What do you find in it?" <Somebody suggests> that he buy himself a bear. He walks his bear <through the streets>. He fires a shot from his pistol.

Somebody suggests that he go up with a balloon.

He is naïve like a child.

? N.B. N.B. Perhaps there really was a duel.

N.B. I call him away from the meeting of the "commission."

"Why, they are making fun of you."

"Really?"

"Come on! Why must you absolutely tell everybody everything?"

N.B. Allow me to pour forth my love,
Please deign to accept my proposal,
And, with your remaining limb, partake
Of legitimate pleasures.*

N.B. *A Question*: I ask him, in utter amazement: "Where have you been up to now, Captain? (i.e., where have you been serving, with whom have you been living, and how have you managed to survive to your present age without a catastrophe? For, let me tell you, you do need a nurse to take care of you. You just can't be left alone.)"

Kartuzov does not understand the question. He does, however, communicate, indifferently and incoherently, two or three features of his past life, which, incidentally, provide some *most significant* (i.e., awfully

---

* The first two lines are regular iambic tetrameters; the last two lines are irregular (no meter at all). The rhyme scheme is *abab*.

strange) glimpses <of his character>. The conversation is interrupted by someone else and is never taken up again.

5. N.B. *I* ask him if he really has any hope.

"No, no, I know that it is impossible for me. Impossible!"

"Why then are you writing her all these letters about your salary, your career in the service, your hopes, and even describing a flat in a little house?"

"Just so. ~~This is only a dream~~ Just for sport, and from the simplicity of my heart. I know myself that it is all in my imagination. Sure. ~~Yet my imagination gives me pleasure. I daydream all the time—but what if it is possible?~~"

"But why should you be sending her these letters?"

~~"Why not?" (astonishment)~~

"But all this is true; I am daydreaming myself all the time, and she ought to assume that this is all a product of my imagination."

"But she may not like it at all."

"I don't think so."

"But this is scandalous. You are defaming her."

"Why so? I let everybody know that I am in love, yet I raise no pretenses."

"It isn't decent. You are putting yourself into an improper position."

"How is that?"

"Why, they are taking you for a buffoon (AS A BUFFOON)."

"They are themselves buffoons. ~~But~~ Katerina Nikolaevna can't be making fun of me. And even if she might laugh, then with a kind of divine laughter. However, I wouldn't mind if she did make fun of me. Really, I am writing this sincerely. But what do I care: I don't give a damn for all of them.* Except of course Katerina Nikolaevna. And ~~if there has been some laughter~~ incidentally, I am convinced that this scoundrel (he is getting angry) has played a dirty trick on me; that's why they are laughing at me."

"No, listen, Platon Egorovich, anything can be turned into a joke."

Verses:

"I can't have any pretenses."**

---

* *naplevat' na vsekh,* literally, "I spit on all of them"; however, the Russian expression is merely an emphatic colloquialism meaning "I don't care."

** Iambic tetrameter.

N.B. He has written her, too, that the Count <wants to marry her> for her money.

N.B. He is a terrible daydreamer. For some time he comes to see me two days in a row to tell me about his daydreams: a flat, vases, rugs, several expensive pictures, a statue (bare posterior, a bacchante picking strawberries), and *besides I am doing good deeds.* ~~Etc.~~

N.B. ~~Why~~ Suddenly, this question: "Why should statues be nude?" N.B. (He comes, sits down, sits in silence for a while, asks the question, gets up, and leaves. He is smoking all the time while he is there.)—

N.B. Kartuzov is unchangingly satisfied with himself. After the beating, as well as during the duel, he is amazingly calm.—

N.B. What has struck him most is: *the Amazon.*

N.B. Nasty stories about the Count, told by some rogue. They leave Kartuzov stunned.

Kartuzov speaks French: "I understand, I understand everything."

N.B. A French mademoiselle shows up in Revel. Having learned about Kartuzov's love and his hatred for the Count, she invites Kartuzov over. Her story, riotously funny, serious, and impudently naïve: *Figurez-vous que ce monstre barbare soixante mille francs,*[8] and so on.

96 Kartuzov politely takes his leave of her, saying nothing. And later, in the course of a conversation, dryly and curtly: *"slut."*

Or: "Right. Too much of a slut."

N.B. He loathes spying, yet is caught spying himself. He goes to see the Count on the grounds that, "I am in love, so why shouldn't I find out if you really love her, or if you're just after her money?"

"Why then did you see the Frenchwoman?"

"How could I miss a chance to learn the truth, if I am ready to surrender my whole body for her slightest advantage. To get myself some peace of mind, I went to see the Frenchwoman."

He beats up the Frenchwoman.

"Il a surpris ma religion."[9]

---

[8] French: "Imagine this barbarous monster sixty thousand francs."
[9] French: "He has discovered my religion."

"Soixante mille roubles."[10]

N.B. Kartuzov is in an exalted mood after having been run over; he appears there in the morning, asking to be announced, breaks a cup, fails to give an answer to the Count, but blushes. Then, suddenly, he leaves.

He comes in an elated mood, a note to the Count.

All the remaining days he is in an elated mood and, when visiting me, inquires about vases (he has seen some vases at the Karmazins', and exaggerates, about the strawberry-picking bacchante. "Imagine I bought this at an auction!" (Good deeds.) (About his successes in the service.)

The Count, having run into him, shows him the note. Kartuzov is embarrassed, blushes, doesn't answer the other man's question, and walks by, saying: "Scoundrel!"

"Tell me, gentlemen, is he mad?"

The commanding officer of the detachment then has a word with Kartuzov; he very nearly uses abusive language.

The rogue, later that night, among the officers: "But gentlemen, he really is a scoundrel."—About a scandal with the newly arrived governess.

He also offers to introduce Kartuzov to the governess.

Meanwhile, there, he is told: "<The mistress> is not at home." But he barely notices it.

"Too much of a slut." ~~A casual conversation with me~~. The bear. He goes to see the Count, seeking a reconciliation. "You are a chosen one."

A casual conversation with me about "the slut," and then, suddenly, he hands me some verses and a letter—

I could hardly collect myself. Meder <*sic*> arrives on the scene (or wait a bit more with Meder).

Personally, to see the Commandant <. . .>. After the Commandant, the commanding officer of the detachment.

~~A letter to the Count telling him that he is a scoundrel—the horsewhip~~.

Then, the bear ~~and a second letter about his being a scoundrel~~. ~~Verses.~~

Evening.

Conversation about an abduction. (Kartuzov is calm and keeps smiling.) The balloon. The officers get to talk among themselves (his visit to the Commandant has become known).

---

10 French: "Sixty thousand roubles."

Next morning, to the Frenchwoman. And here then, the letter in which he calls him a scoundrel.

Prior to that, he had only seen him in order to apologize.

N.B. The Count had invited me over, before Kartuzov had called him a scoundrel (though not very politely, and not wanting to pay me a visit), and showed me Kartuzov's letter.

"He'll be stopped."

He keeps sitting at home, daydreaming.

He rarely tells about his daydreams:

"I'm making a voyage on a steamboat, as a Field Marshal."

"A <little?>boy."*

101 THE COCKROACH

N.B. "Nikifor represents nature, ~~but~~ let me observe one more thing: the cockroach is not complaining." ~~This fact~~

"Does he remain true to his character?"

Merzavtsev gave me a stern look.

"One does not remain true to one's character in a ~~rinsing~~ tub. However,—"

"Perhaps you would like to have some more tea?"

"No, thank you."

"And thanks to you, too."

"Verses are useless."

Kartuzov is stunned by <her loss of> a leg and by the question, "why fate?"

Kartuzov is being told: "You are like Don Quixote; you don't care though your damsel be married, you still love her faithfully."

Kartuzov: "Was their love really so strong?"

~~A question of nobility~~

2d question: "Can anyone die of a noble heart?"

---

* *M. mal'chik,* in which *M.* may stand for *Malen'ky,* "little."

The Count has cleaned out a local Baron Osten at cards—and a duel on account of that.

A slap in the face (Kartuzov got involved).

The Result
The main, firmly marked essence of Kartuzov:

1) Kartuzov falls in love *immediately and abruptly,* by a process which makes it appear as if inevitable, oriental fashion, as if it just had to happen. This actually is neither infatuation nor love, but merely *inescapable and unavoidable adoration.* It began with the side saddle, quite literally so, for it was on account of the saddle (i.e., the beauty <of it>) that Kartuzov came to ascribe to her every kind of perfection, moral as well as physical, up to and including the highest ideal; moreover, once he has ascribed these *to her,* Kartuzov not only does not doubt the reality of such ideal perfection, but actually cannot doubt it; in fact he couldn't admit that there might be even the slightest shadow of a doubt! With him, this is not some kind of an opinion, or conclusion, or conviction, but rather a sort of faith, or even something higher than faith—something like a positive fact, which is so tangible and positive that it not only becomes quite impossible to question it, but even as much as, for instance, living in a house with four trees in the front yard, and not knowing whether there are three or four trees there after having lived there for a year; or living in Vevey and admiring the mountains on the other side of the lake without knowing or even without ever having asked oneself what the contours of these mountains were like, etc. A perfectly Quixotic conviction, with the difference that Don Quixote at least created *a question* for himself from ~~that~~ his conviction, for otherwise he wouldn't have found it necessary to ride out and defend his conviction with his lance, whereas Kartuzov does not assume or has even once thought of the possibility that somebody might not agree with the idea of *her* perfection.

2 (Explain all this in the course of the narrative, *from the narrator's point of view.*)*

---

* *ot sebia,* literally "from oneself," but untranslatable. The antonym is *ot geroia,* "from the hero's point of view."

2) Kartuzov, having reached the highest stage of adoration, fails to see even the slightest indecency either about his adoration of her, or about his own actions, i.e., his verses, and specifically, (mainly) for the reason that he actually does not believe it to be possible that she might marry him, or admit even the slightest notion of equality *with her.* (Yet his verses she could accept, because he is a captain.) So that, whenever this matter would come up *accidentally,* he would actually admit, without any air of excitement or suffering, that he was unworthy of her. (He is so far out of her way and so much lower than *she,* that all of his antics, all kinds of verses appear to him as admissible, for who could ever place him on an equal footing with her?

N.B. (So that Merzavtsev's first love was a time of the highest happiness for him.) But it goes without saying that from here on everything that had anything to do with the Kramzins <*sic*> represented for Kartuzov a question of life and death; and so the idea emerges: SAVE MISS KARMAZIN!

N.B. Merzavtsev, who cares little about the other man's millions, is enthusiastic about the vases and pictures *at her house* (these, by the way, are nonexistent; he has made up everything himself).

Furthermore:

3) Actually, there isn't even any feeling of jealousy in him, nor does he suffer in the least from jealousy. He isn't in the least jealous of the Count; however, *a higher human calling,* concern, role, emerge in his mind in connection with the question: is the Count entirely worthy of her? That's why he goes to see the Frenchwoman, that's why he hates the Count, that's why he makes up with him again and is seen bustling about around him.

So that:

4) His main worry is not that the Count loves her (and is therefore his rival?), but rather, that the Count may *not be truly worthy of her,* and almost, that he does not love her enough. It is precisely because of this that Kartuzov is worried about the Count loving her *too little,* rather than *too much.* Having become reconciled to the Count it is he who blows the horn for him, singing the praises of the Count's merits, virtues, and future successes; his wealth, good looks; he addresses his verses to both of them. Finally, he befriends the Count, *hardly leaves him alone, enters* into his interests,* his favorite topic of conversation

---

* An untranslatable pun: *ne vykhodit ot nego, vkhodit v ego interesy,* literally, "he doesn't *go out* of his house, and *goes into* his interests."

with the Count being ~~his~~ the Count's future; with a dreamer's rapturous ecstasy he envisages the details of that future. However, although the Count finds Kartuzov and his sudden friendship ridiculous, he still cannot change him into a *clown* (which he would like to do very much), because Kartuzov behaves with great simplicity and dignity. (He is too clever not to understand Kartuzov, even though he is a wicked man at heart.) When the Count finally rejects him, rudely and in a fit of bad temper, Kartuzov leaves quietly, forgiving him.

However:

5) He will not forgive the Count the Frenchwoman who has suddenly appeared on the scene; he stirs up an affair; then, all the consequences and

6) *most important,* Kartuzov is going out of his mind at the very thought that he dared to yield to the Count's influence and propose *to her* when she was stricken by misfortune. He considers himself a scoundrel.

III
The Life of the Great Sinner

The dates of these notes go from December, 1869, to May, 1870, but most of them were written between December, 1869, and February, 1870. Only notebook page 19 has the later date of May 15/3, 1870. They comprise pages 8–22 from notebook 2.

Dostoevsky first conceived of "The Life of a Great Sinner" under the title of "Atheism" about December, 1868, and then reconceived and worked on it between December, 1869, and May, 1870. What we know of this famous unrealized novel comes from these notes and from various letters. Dostoevsky conceived of writing first three and then five separate novels unified about the experiences of a great sinner. He was probably influenced by the scope and success of *War and Peace,* which was published between 1866 and 1869.

Dostoevsky planned to take his hero in the thirties and forties through the suffering of childhood, boarding school, flight and complicity in murder, life in a monastery and the beneficent influence of Tikhon Zadonsky, exposure to the world and interest in various contemporary political and philosophical movements such as atheism and positivism, and finally, after much sin, cruelty, suffering, and ambivalent feeling, to a religious crisis and regeneration in love, humility, faith, and Christ.

Most of this development can be discerned in these notes, but not in that order. There is considerable emphasis on the miserable childhood the hero experiences: he is beaten, falsely accused, witnesses his stepmother's affair, and possibly his father's murder. The negative influence of reading fiction is taken up from time to time. Several times—probably at the boarding school—he astounds everyone inadvertently with a brilliant examination. For a time he roams about with a convict, Kulikov (a prototype of Fedka), and seems to be implicated in a murder. Under the influence of the monastery and Tikhon he learns something of self-control and humility, but what he learns is quickly

—though not finally—destroyed by his experiences in the world.

Whether in childhood, boarding school, the monastery, or in the contemporary world, the "great Sinner" is characterized by tumultuous passions and contradictory drives. He attempts to find what he is looking for in debauchery, in the accumulation of wealth, in science, art, and letters, and in the monastery. The characteristics Dostoevsky lists at the very beginning give us a schematic idea of his character and situation:

Accumulation of wealth.

Emerging powerful passions.

Strengthening one's will power and inner strength.

Boundless pride, and his struggle against vanity.

The prose of life and a passionate faith which keeps overcoming it.

So that everybody will bow before me, while I shall forgive.

So as to fear nothing. Sacrifice one's life.

The effect of debauchery, a cold horror. A desire to smear everybody with dirt.

The poetry of childhood.

Education and first ideals.

Secretly learns everything.

All alone, get ready for everything.

What drives him most of all is a desire for despotic power over others. The other passions—money, debauchery, knowledge, faith—are most likely forms of despotic power. Dostoevsky speaks of his "titanic idea of despotic power," and explains his isolation from his fellow man by his "dreams of power and of reaching exorbitant heights so as to be above everything." His visions of power reach the point of conceiving the dethroning of God. He forces Katia (the lame girl) to bow down before him, and declares: "I myself am God."

Dostoevsky's notes for "The Life of a Great Sinner" became source materials for *The Possessed, A Raw Youth,* and *The Brothers Karamazov.* Themes, situations, and types, which were later used in each, can be easily distinguished. The theme of the great sinner returning to the world is an adumbration of Dostoevsky's plans for Alyosha; the persistent temptation of the boy to accumulate wealth and power is one of the main themes of *A Raw Youth;* the search for firm ground on which to build one's life, and the failure to find it, is used in *The Possessed;* and the theme of dethroning God may be an anticipation of Kirilov's argument and of the Grand Inquisitor's credo and action.

---

8 December 20/8 <1869> THE LIFE OF A GREAT SINNER

Accumulation of wealth.

Emerging powerful passions.

Strengthening one's will power and inner strength.

Boundless pride, and his struggle against vanity.

The prose of life and a passionate faith which keeps overcoming it.

So that everybody will bow before me, while I shall forgive.

So as to fear nothing. Sacrifice one's life.

The effect of debauchery, a cold horror. A desire to smear everybody with dirt.

The poetry of childhood.

Education and first ideals.

Secretly learns everything.

All alone, get ready for everything.

(All the time he is tirelessly preparing himself for something, even though he does not know for what—but strangely enough, it worries him very little *for what,* as if he were perfectly confident that it will come by itself.)

Either slavery or despotic power.

He believes. And that is all. His disbelief appears for the first time in a strange episode, and takes shape only when he has come to the monastery.

The Lame Girl. Katia. Brother Misha. The stolen money. He suffers the punishment. Fearlessness. The cornfield. "Don't cut my throat, uncle dear!" Love for Kulikov.[1] Johann. Brutilov. The Frenchman Pougaut. Upbraids Brutilov. Studies. *Albert* the diver. Chibaut. Holy Communion. *Albert* does not believe in God. Old folk. He secretly loves many things and keeps it a secret. He is called a monster, and he acts like one. N.B. A passionate desire to shock everybody by his out-

---

[1] The prototype of Fedka in the final version; a variant of Kulishov.

rageous actions? But not out of vanity. Alone. Old folk. Songs. Thérèse-Philosophe.[2] Johann. Brien, Brutilov, his brother, *Albert*. Friends; he torments his friend, rejects him. His friend is a quiet, kindly, and honest boy who makes him blush. Self-education through self-torture, and accumulation of money.—Humboldt.[3]

He is told immediately that he is not their brother. He meets Kulikov. The Doctor's wife. She appears to him in a kind of halo. A passionate desire to soil himself, to dirty himself in her eyes, rather than to make a favorable impression. It happens. Thievery. He is being accused, he fails to assert his innocence, but the matter is cleared up anyway. His stepbrother is the thief.

A lack of respect for the people around him, but not as yet rationally, but *solely because they elicit in him a feeling of revulsion*. A strong and permanent trait. Plenty of revulsion. "I am eating grapes." He is beaten and whipped for showing his revulsion. He merely becomes more secretive and hates even more strongly. Haughty contempt for his tormentors, and the quickness with which he condemns people. The extraordinary quickness with which he condemns people suggests a strong and passionate exclusiveness. He begins to feel that ~~it is necessary~~ these quick condemnations are no good, and that he must strengthen his will power with regard to this circumstance.

The beginnings of breadth.

"That's a lie, mon Mouchoir."

Arkashka and French conversation.

Arkashka, Brutilov, and he are apart from the crowd.

Mother's children at Souchard's[4] and at Chermak's (their feeling of revulsion, caused by stupidity).

N.B. Only Brutilov and his story at Souchard's; only two chapters —ending with his striking Souchard. The beginning of *Albert*'s story.

~~In the country~~ The boarding school. At home—unjust punishment. The examination.

In the country. Selflessness: Katia.

In the city and at the boarding school, he astounds people with his

---

[2] Reference to an erotic book entitled *Thérèse-philosophe ou mémoires pour servir à l'histoire de D. Dirray et de Mlle Eradice la Haye*. Written about 1748, reputedly by Montigny.

[3] Alexander Humboldt (1769–1859), naturalist and encyclopedist. Dostoevsky does not have in mind his more famous brother, Wilhelm Humboldt, the philologist.

[4] Nikolay I. Souchard, Dostoevsky's childhood French teacher.

brutality. ~~Kulikov.~~ *Lambert.*[5] Feats—to flee with Katia. Kulikov, with him. The murder.

He forgives nothing false or insincere, and senselessly, attacks immediately with his fists.

For a long time he didn't believe Katia, he then put her to a test, and finally frightened her with the shame of it.

Willpower is his principal goal.

After Kulikov, he immediately proceeds to make inquiries about the Lame Girl. That's where he is caught.

In the country, the Doctor's wife falls in love with him.

Catches her with her lover.

The Doctor's wife, Alfonsky—characters.

9 At the old folks. Reading Karamzin[6] with the old man. Arabian tales. About Suvorov, etc. About interest. He insults the young "old woman." "Apologize!" "I won't." Used to lock them up. Death. Anna and Vasilisa flee. They've told Vasilisa. The last Holy Communion. The first Confession. A feeling of revulsion: "Is there a God?" The Bible and reading.—

January 2 <1870>

Breaks a mirror on purpose.

Decides to remain silent and doesn't say a word.

Reverend Mother: "Why are you presenting yourself as a sacrificial victim?" (An ideal and a strange creature.)

Alfonsky the father—(words addressed to his son, and inquiries).

A feeling of destructiveness.

Voluptuousness (as for this, he wants to wait until he has got money).

And the titanic idea of despotic power—(the spontaneity of his emotions) reveals itself so powerfully that he feels incapable of adjusting to these people.

"How many sciences must one master?" (in a talk with Vanka).

He is surprised at himself, conducts experiments with himself, and likes to probe the abysses of his mind.

N.B. Flight with the little girl and encounter with the bandit Kulikov immediately after changing from Souchard to Chermak. (A fact

---

[5] A character in *A Raw Youth.*

[6] Nikolay M. Karamzin (1766–1826). His works were favorite reading in the Dostoevsky household. He is a celebrated Russian man of letters. His best-known tale is *Poor Liza* (1792) and his most influential work is *History of the Russian State* (1818).

which has a shattering impact and, to a certain extent, bewilders him, so that he feels a natural urge to retire into his shell and think things over, so as to settle his thoughts upon something definite. (He then settles on money after all.) N.B.

So far he has not given any thought to God.

After the experience with Kulikov he *seems* to have turned more quiet both at home and at school (to think things over and FIND HIMSELF, to get settled).

Yet he is unsociable and uncommunicative. His silence is broken a year and a half later, when he makes a confession about Kulikov. And, of course, it couldn't have been any other way, for he remembers, and has guilty knowledge of so horrible a thing that he must, for instance, look at all the other children as though they were completely alien to him, as though they were something from which he has been carried away as if on wings to entirely different parts, for better or for worse. Sometimes he is tormented by the blood. But also,

what is most important:

It isn't this alone which isolates him from everybody else, but even more so his dreams of power and of reaching exorbitant heights so as to be above everything.

THE MOST IMPORTANT—The idea of the first part—The fluctuations, the insatiability of his idea. He is merely preparing himself for his career, yet is strangely *confident* that all will come by itself, that money solves *all* problems.—An instinctive feeling of superiority, power, and strength. The search for a firm foothold. At any rate, he is a most unusual individual.

(He is terribly fascinated by something—*Hamlet* for instance.)

The inhabitants of the moon.[7]

N.B. He is displaced from his lofty heights by becoming aware of the sciences, poetry, etc., that is, in the sense that these things are higher and better, so that in these fields, too, he must be higher and better than everybody else.

Or better: not one thought about what he ought to be, or what his

---

[7] Probably a reference to the popular book which Belinsky reviewed briefly in 1836: *About the Inhabitants of the Moon and Other Remarkable Discoveries, Made by the Astronomer Sir John Hershel During his Stay at the Cape of Hope.* This is a translation from the German, but Belinsky's review does not give the German title or author. See Belinsky, *Polnoe sobranie sochinenii,* vol. 2 (Moscow, 1953), p. 226.

calling might be, diverts him from the accumulation of great wealth.

The ultimate goal of money and the accumulation of wealth invariably dispels his doubts.

Pictures (cows, tigers, horses, etc.)

About a horse gone wild, or a fire.

(He sells to servants—)

His father gives him a flogging. A complete break. "I don't consider you to be my father."

He sells to servants, and is held in general contempt for that, but <. . .>

He finds a billfold—the respect which he secures once and for all through the examination—he almost gives in.

But then, the incident involving Katia's disgrace, and thereafter a hellish orgy with *Albert,* crime and blasphemy, and confession of the murder committed together with Kulikov—*straight into the abyss.* The monastery.

Although money does give him a terribly *steady* focus and provides him with an answer to *all* his questions, this very *focus* vacillates on occasion ~~and he~~ (poetry and a good many other things), and he sees no way out. It is precisely this *vacillating* condition that gives substance to this novel.

Strengthening his will power, enduring wounds and burns as well as pride, that is what sustains him. He wants to be ready for anything.

He decides to make his money honestly. He wavers over the billfold. N.B. Since there are many things which on occasion *move* his heart, he flings himself into a spree of debauchery in a terrible fit of rage and pride. THAT IS THE MAIN THING.

His alienation is also due to the fact that everybody looks upon him as an eccentric, with derision, or with fear.

A bashed-in head *(pantalons en haut),*[8] sick. Later, Chermak leaves him alone. (Mango.)

N.B. He has, for instance, come to the rational conclusion that one need not be *dishonest,* that it will be *even easier* to make money *honestly,* because the rich, anyway, have every possible privilege to commit all kinds of wrongs.

He and *Albert* tear off a star from the crown <of an icon> and escape undetected (it was *his* idea), but when *Albert* starts blaspheming, he goes at him with his fists. Yet later, in court, he freely declares himself to be an atheist.

---

[8] French: "raised trousers."

Idea: one might get even higher in one's pursuit of power if one were to use flattery, as does von Brien.

"But no," he thinks, "I want to reach the same goal without flattery ~~I myself~~."

"I myself am God," and he forces Katia to bow before him in worship.

He does God knows what with her. "I'll start loving you when you've done everything I've told you."

In his fantastic vagaries, boundless dreams, to the point of dethroning God and putting himself in His stead (Kulikov has had a strong influence).

A PROBLEM, *memento*. 1st act. Early childhood.

2d) The family, Souchard, running away, and Kulikov.

3) Chermak—the examination.

4) In the country and Katia, the orgy with *Albert*.

Find the common proportional.

20 childhood
20 the monastery
40 before the exile
20 the Female and Satan
40 feats

A feeling of revulsion toward people ever since he first became conscious of himself as a child (due to the passionate temperament of his proud and despotic nature; also, from contempt).

"I'll take it by assault, I won't stoop to Brien's flattery and craftiness."

And this, too, out of a feeling of revulsion for people and out of contempt for them, since his earliest childhood.

"Ah, if only I'd be willing to play the part of a sycophant such as Brien—there's no telling what I might accomplish!"

And sometimes he begins to reason in this way: "Shouldn't I become a sycophant after all?" (He discusses this point with the lame girl.) "This, too, requires fortitude of spirit—*to be able to stand it being a sycophant*. But no, I don't want to, it is repulsive—and besides, I'll have money going for me, so that willy-nilly, whether they want it or not, they'll all have to come to me and bow before me."

He displays great fortitude of spirit in his encounter with Kulikov, who does not cut his throat but lets him go, but <an illegible crossed-out word> the deserter they kill together.

35 years ago, he was born in 1835.

If anybody had overheard his thoughts, he probably would have died; yet he reveals everything to the Lame Girl.

Whatever he has read, he passes on, after his own fashion, to the Lame Girl.

"A slap in the face is the greatest insult." With blood—

The first articulate thought, and the importance of money.

The Lame Girl keeps everything *he* tells her a secret, and strangely enough, she does so of her own accord, without his having told her, ~~having understood~~ having tactfully understood it herself, so that most of the time he won't even tell her that she ought to keep it a secret.

The Lame Girl won't agree to become an atheist. He does not beat her for that.

13 Only one, but detailed, psychological analysis regarding how works of fiction affect a child, etc. *A Hero of Our Time.*

A child's indignation at the guests who visit with them, at the indiscretions and impertinences which they allow themselves (Uvar<ov?>). "How can they dare?" the child thinks.

The old folks' downfall.

Theater. "Sit on my lap."

He is flogged for showing his revulsion.

When he and the Lame Girl move in with the Alfonskys, he tells her that <she may talk?> about Gogol and, from among our <...>, nothing about their travels.

He has read an awful lot (Walter Scott, etc.)

At the Alfonskys', they are not treated as brothers. They let him know that.

He pretends to be brutish, backward, and stupid.

With the servants.

The Alfonsky woman provokes the idea that <...> not together with the children.

At Souchard's. Alfonsky flogs him. It turns out to be in vain. The Alfonsky woman had made it up; he runs away. With Kulikov. He is caught.

The visitor: "Call him in." Interrogates him. Sincere ideas.

The visitor is surprised.

The house is on fire, or something—illness.

Alfonsky makes speeches.

At Chermak's. Development, reading, the examination.

After the examination, Alfonsky causes to fall in love. Alfonsky questions him. For the Lame Girl. With Katia. The cornfield. Domestic scenes.

Alfonsky, his friend, a slap in the face.

In Moscow, *Lambert—*

On classical education at Chermak's Herr Thayder).

January 27

He is struck by the fact that all these people (adults) absolutely believe in their own nonsense, and that they are much more stupid and worthless than might appear from the outside.

(One of the *learned* visitors takes a tumble, as he takes to drinking and carousing with the gypsy girls at Maryina Roshcha.)[9]

A period of disbelief in God. N.B. Absolutely bring in how he was affected by the Gospel. He is in agreement with the Gospel.

The main thing is at this point his own *I* and his own interests. As to philosophical questions, they interest him insofar as they concern him personally.

FEBRUARY 22. START SENDING. *January 27.*

February 10
15
February 22

I

Squeeze all this into 64 pages *(maximum).*

One ought to sense in every line: "I know what I am writing, and I am writing it for a good reason."

FIRST PAGES. 1) Tone, 2) insert the ideas artistically and concisely.

N.B. *Tone* (the narrative is a *vita*—i.e., even though it comes from an author's pen, it is concise, not sparing of explications, yet presenting some things in scenic form. (Here, harmony is of the essence.) Matter-of-factness of the narrative, sometimes to the point of Gil Blas.[10] At spectacular and scenically impressive junctures, *it may appear* that there is little reason to attach much value to this trait.

Yet it is also important that the dominant idea of the *vita* be apparent, i.e., even though the whole dominant idea may never be ex-

---

[9] A suburb of Moscow.

[10] A novel by Alain René Le Sage (1668–1747). *Gil Blas* is his most famous work. It came out in four volumes from 1715 to 1735, and is a controversial novel of manners.

plained in so many words, and though it may remain something of a mystery, the reader still ought to know at all times that this idea is a pious one, also that the vita is deemed to be a work of importance, so much so that it was worth starting it with the childhood. Also, the selection of the subject matter of the narrative, and the facts which appear in it should, as if continually, convey a certain *something;* and, also continually, the man of the future is to be exhibited for everyone to see, and to be placed on a pedestal.

"When I grow up."

1) They caught a mouse.

The Lame Girl.

Old folk.

(The nurse, washing, an order on his neck—and retire.)

Anna and Vasilisa ran away.

The last Holy Communion (the Italian takes the money from his pocket)—the first idea.

The teacher (drunk).

The first Confession: "What has he got in those little boxes and in the cup? Is there a God?"

Convert the Devil.

Beating the Lame Girl.

The dead man by the fence.

They've sold Vasilisa.—

Interest payments and conversations with the visitor.

Readings. About Suvorov. Arabian tales. Daydreams. Umnov[11] and Gogol (the Lame Girl laughs).

The old man and woman grow more decrepit every day. He has been locking them up. Got drunk. He and another boy go stealing. Gave him a bad beating. *Fighting with older boys.* Full debauchery. ~~Teased the lady. They~~

He beats the Lame Girl, trying to force her to fight with the boys. She tries to leave, but is given a sound thrashing and begins to cry.

Dreaming of great will power. Umnov (peeping at nudes, having designs upon the Lame Girl).

N.B. When the old man and woman die he is 11 years old, and the Lame Girl ten.

Alfonsky—the old man and woman. Death. He harangues the Lame Girl on how she ought to conduct herself.

---

[11] Childhood friend of Dostoevsky's.

Prior to that: They were teasing a lady—attacked her, they were dragged into the house to be given a flogging.—

He is afraid to complain. (He is afraid himself, yet he beats up the boy.)

The first clash; he attacks the gentleman with the decoration and beats him with his fists: "I'll never be afraid of anything."

"I'll learn not to be afraid."

He cuts himself for a test.

Instruction in fuck<ing> from another boy *(Thérèse-Philosophe*—beats him up for that, but keeps the book).

Begins to save money.

He is saving money (tells the Lame Girl about it).

The Lame Girl had come to live with the Alfonsky's before he did. No sooner he gets there than he begins to question her about things. (Directives to her: "Don't tell anybody about Gogol, or anything that is *our business.*")

1st part. The boy is wild, but he does an awful lot of thinking about himself.

The main thing, Nota-bene: He started to save money with only a vague idea why, but this idea has been growing stronger all the time and is proven to have been correct as the action continues. But the principal impetus was provided by his moving in with Alfonsky.

II

The Lame Girl: "What if I tell them that you said you'd be king?" (or something ridiculous). He cuts her up for that.

What do he and the Lame Girl talk about? About all of his daydreams. "When I grow up I SHALL NOT MARRY YOU, BUT SOMEONE ELSE." So that it won't be necessary to say that he was daydreaming about such-and-such, but only that he went to see the Lame Girl and told her such-and-such.

About what he's going to be and about money. *He used to beat her because his money wasn't increasing as fast as he'd have liked it to.*

He used to tell her about reading Karamzin, fairy tales, etc. The young woman, also the old woman and others, taught him French and German. They used to go to other children to learn from them (there, they were being laughed at).

He beats the Lame Girl for not being enthusiastic enough about Karamzin.

He knows the whole Bible, and tells her about.

World history, geography poorly.

(Daydreams about travels, <reading Captain> Cook[12] with the Lame Girl.)

They read some novels.

(N.B. He is very well developed mentally and knows a good deal. He knows Gogol and Pushkin.)

He meets Umnov who proves to him that he knows more than he does. Upon his return home, he tells the Lame Girl that Umnov is a fool who knows nothing; he gives the Lame Girl a beating, and from here on seeks Umnov's company.

He never shows any tenderness for the Lame Girl, not until that one time when he carries her in his arms.

"Why won't you do this—cut it out; I don't wish that you learn together with my children."

Whenever the oldsters would get very drunk and could not stand on their feet, the Lame Girl would cry over them. In the beginning, he would beat her for that, but later he no longer did.

They've killed a goose.

The Bible. Jacob bows three times. Gets it mixed up with the Bible. The Lame Girl laughs.

He has acquired a habit of beating her; he won't kiss her.

(N.B. The Lame Girl did not freeze to death. Somebody found her. But she disappears from the Alfonskys' place.)

One incessant thought, ever since he can remember himself: "What will become of me, and how shall I get all these things done?"

Later, doubts: Is power alone worth everything else, and could it be that one may be a slave and still stronger than everybody?

He begins to train his will power.

Passions take hold of him.

He and *Lambert*—a perfect picture of depravity. Yet *Lambert* is intoxicated with it and finds that there is nothing higher. The frivolity typical of his nationality.

If *he* embarks upon debauchery with irresistible desire, he does it also with fear. He is struck by the emptiness, sordidness, and absurdity of debauchery. He quits everything, and after some terrible crimes, remorsefully turns himself in.

---

[12] James Cook (1728–79), English navigator.

1

Osip the lackey—at first, he is taken into the house; he amuses them with his tales and with his jolly disposition. *Alfonsky* had flogged Osip's brother to death, and later, takes Osip to the recruiting station. That's where Osip makes his escape (he is the same person as Kulishov). They kill Orlov. They part. Kulishov (Osip) lets him go.

A year and a half later his stepmother complains about Alfonsky's faithlessness. He openly keeps a mistress. It is Osip's sister. (That's why he had Osip's brother flogged to death.) Alfonsky is killed by his peasants. (?)

Outline of the novel. Alfonsky's highborn wife (the hero's stepmother), at the time when she was still languishing away as a spinster, used to have a suitor (an officer or somebody, a teacher).

But she got married to Alfonsky. Dissatisfied with and insulted by Alfonsky, ~~she~~ (she used to slap her paramour's face) she developed a liaison with her former lover who somehow appeared on the scene. The boy saw them kissing. "You can tell it to your father," but later asked him not to. The boy kept quiet; but Alfonsky knows that his son knows that he has been cuckolded and that his stepmother has a lover. Back in the country, he raises a fuss about the Lame Girl. He cruelly makes fun of Katia. The mother is quite beside herself as she takes Katia's side. In the city, he is with *Lambert,* etc.

Here N.B. N.B. ~~(It could be~~ *It could be* that Alfonsky was killed by his peasants when he started fooling around, and the boy may have been a witness,—and—

(Might also invent something about his stepmother's affair with her lover, and to what extent and degree the boy was *involved* in their romance.)

Alfonsky does have a benefactor, who is precisely his greatest enemy because he is his benefactor. All the favors which he receives from him wound his pride, while the other man can't live without playing the role of benefactor, yet demands three yards of gratitude for an inch of his favors. Each is humiliating himself; they are humiliating each other; and they hate each other almost pathologically.

2

The boy's extraordinary pride is the cause of his not being able to feel either pity or contempt for these people. He can't even feel very indignant about them. Neither can he sympathize with his father or with his mother. Quite inadvertently, he does brilliantly at the examination—he had actually meant to show himself to be an idiot. He is deeply contemptuous of himself for not having restrained himself, but having made a show of his brilliance.

The dangerous and extreme thought that he would become an exceptional man took possession of him even while he was still a child. He thinks about it all the time. Wisdom, cunning, education—all this he wants to acquire as future means of becoming an exceptional man. Again, it appears to him that money certainly ought to be useful to have, as its power can be applied in any possible situation, and so he decides to concentrate on it:

The sciences appear terribly difficult to him.

Then again, it appears to him that, even if he won't turn out to be something extraordinary, but on the contrary, most ordinary, in that case, money would still give him everything, i.e., power and the right to despise people.

And finally, he reproaches himself and is tormented by his conscience for having wanted to be extraordinary in such a *base* way. However, he doesn't know himself what he is going to be.

The pure ideal of a free man occasionally flashes across his mind; all of this at the boarding school.

He makes friends with Osip; about the Khlysts; they all but sleep together.

Umnov; knows Gogol by heart.

May 15/3 <1870>

19

The Main Idea

After the monastery and Tikhon, the Great Sinner, together with Tikhon, returns into the world to become *the greatest of men.* He is convinced that he will be the greatest of men. And he behaves quite accordingly: he is the proudest of the proud and treats people with extreme arrogance. Yet the form of his future greatness remains quite undefined, a circumstance which perfectly befits his youth. But he has (and that is the main thing) acquired *through Tikhon* the idea (the conviction) that in order to conquer the whole world one must only conquer onself. He has not chosen a career as yet, but there isn't any time for that either: he is beginning to observe himself in a profound manner. But there are also contradictions: 1) gold (hoarding it) (a family to take care of); the idea of hoarding wealth is insinuated to him by the Usurer, a terrible man, an antithesis to Tikhon; 2) education (Comte,[13] atheism, friends); education—ideas and philosophy torment him; however, he masters what is essential about them. Suddenly, youth and debauchery. A great moral feat and terrible crimes. Selflessness. Mad pride. Out of pride he becomes an anchorite and a wanderer. Travels all over Russia. (A romance, love. Thirst of humility and so forth, etc., etc.

N.B. (A rich canvas.)

Fall and resurrection.

An extraordinary man—but what has he done and what has he accomplished?

Traits. Out of pride and boundless arrogance toward people, he becomes kindly and gracious toward everybody—precisely because he is already immeasurably higher than everyone else.

N.B. He wants to shoot himself (somebody has left a babe at the doorstep).

He ends up running an orphanage at his place and becomes a man like Gas.[14] He becomes more and more transfigured.

He dies confessing his crime.

January 1, 1870

N.B. A type entirely contrary to the ~~rotten through and through~~ scion of that noble family of Counts, degenerate to the point of swinishness, which Tolstoi has depicted in *Childhood* and *Adolescence.* This is simply a primitive type, subconsciously agitated by his own primitive strength, a strength which is completely spontaneous and ignorant of any basis of support. Such primitive types are frequently either Stenka Razin's[15] or Danilo Filippovich's,[16] or they become full-

[13] Auguste Comte (1798–1857), French mathematician and philosopher; the founder of "Positivism."

[14] Probably Fyodor Petrovich Gaaz (1780–1853), an old prison doctor, famed for his unselfishness and self-sacrifice in behalf of prisoners.

[15] Stepan Timofeevich Razin (Stenka Razin), birth unknown, died in 1671. He was a Don Cossack who led a peasant uprising against the Russian autocracy in 1667–71.

[16] A peasant, the half-legendary founder of the "Khlysty"—a religious sect that arose in the middle of the seventeenth century. By the middle of the nineteenth century they had disintegrated and no longer functioned as a unified group. They were distinguished by the belief in eternal rebirth and the materialization of the holy spirit. They whipped themselves (Russian word Khlyst means "whip") to drive demons from their bodies.

fledged Khlysts or Skoptsy.[17] This is an extraordinary, innate power, hard to bear for those who possess it, a power which asks for and seeks a foundation to stand on and a cause to lead, a power which greatly suffers if it is exposed to the storms of life, yet cannot help stirring up storms before it finds its peace. He finally comes to rest in Christ, but his whole life is all storm and disorder. (The masses of our people live instinctively and harmoniously, *peacefully* in their native way; however the moment ~~a ferment~~ a movement appears in it, i.e., a simple function of life does take place within them, these types will invariably emerge from among them.) This immense, instinctive force, seeking nothing but peace, yet agitated to the point of suffering, does in the course of its searchings and wanderings veer into monstrous deviations and experiments, until it will finally come to rest upon so powerful an idea as to be fully proportional to their ~~their~~ instinctive animal strength, an idea which is strong enough to ~~pacify~~ organize finally this force and to calm it down to a balmy quiet.

---

[17] The "Skoptsy" were a religious sect that arose in the 1770's. A separation from the "Khlysty," their main belief consisted in the doctrine that the only way to salvation was by battle with the flesh and by emasculation.

IV
The Earliest Variant, "Envy"

These notes constitute in all probability the earliest variant of the plot of *The Possessed.* They were written near the end of 1869 and no later than February, 1870. They comprise notebook pages 20–27 of notebook 1/10.

The structure as conceived at this early date concerns the characters of a teacher (a prototype of Shatov) and A.B., the Prince (a prototype of Stavrogin). The Teacher is morally beautiful, and it is this moral beauty that the Prince comes to hate and yet to envy. The drama of hate and envy is embodied in a romantic situation: the Prince makes pregnant a poor ward, refuses to marry her (because of his high station), and attempts to marry her off to the impoverished, slightly ridiculous Teacher for various sums of money. There is some reference to the Teacher and the Ward falling in love with each other, and to the attraction the Beauty, the Prince's fiancée, feels for the Teacher. The Prince attempts to compete in moral beauty with the Teacher by marrying the Ward. When the Teacher is not impressed by his magnanimity, the Prince slaps the Teacher. Dostoevsky says: "The Prince marries the Ward—to show off." The Prince's attempts to outdo the Teach in moral beauty remind us of the Usurer's unsuccessful attempts (in the previous section) to do good deeds, as well as of many references in other works to good deeds corrupted by pride: Ipolit in *The Idiot,* the Idiot (in the notes), and even the Underground Man are examples.

One aspect of the final version of *The Possessed* is partly discernible here: the romantic complication of Stavrogin, Dasha, and Liza. Dasha's submissive love is portrayed in the unmurmuring obedience of the Ward; Liza is adumbrated in the Beauty (Horsewoman); Kartuzov (Lebiadkin) is already attached to the Beauty and is busy conniving to protect his attachment. Barbara Stavrogin's attempt to marry off Dasha to Stepan Trofimovich Verkhovensky to cover up her son's affair is anticipated in the attempt by the Prince to marry off the

Ward to the Teacher for a sum of money. But there is no political plot (although there is one mention of Nechaev), and the Prince's character, as well as the romantic complication, are vastly different in the final version. The Prince is characterized in the following way: "A.B. is brilliant, envious, proud, ~~generous~~ base, and everything. *Without* any self-control, and actually without suspecting that this may be necessary." The Prince envies moral magnanimity; Stavrogin fears it; the Prince lacks self-control, and Stavrogin is corrupted by too much. Stavrogin has passed beyond envy, passion, turmoil, and into a fearful passionless world that Dostoevsky does not discern at this time.

---

21 1)

ENVY

N.B. *Characters are the only thing that matters.*

This is the story:

Prince A.B. He has a mother, an important lady, and a sister. (They have returned from abroad.) *The Ward.* A little brother and a little sister.

Large landowners ~~(V—v)~~ after the fashion of V—v (N.B. The desire to play the role of large landowners)—they've got money. They are well to do.

Their neighbors have also returned from abroad. A beautiful daughter who is a rich heiress. A.B.'s mother (a despot herself, she obeys her despotic son) has her eye on the beautiful daughter for A.B.

The Ward is an orphan, poor, with very wicked aunts and uncle (mauvais genre).

A.B. becomes involved with her, stupidly, inadvertently. He is passionate, proud, and leads an irregular life.

The Ward's character—she is still a child, but lively, given to mockery, truthful, with a big heart, yet (strangely)—a timid child.

She is pregnant. The important lady is appalled. Hide it from her sisters. The girl submitted absolutely without offering resistance, and without any display of coquetry. Somehow, strangely, she submitted. A.B. says that he is sorry. But how could he marry her? Naturally a marriage is out of the question. *She* doesn't even think of marriage herself, doesn't even consider it a possibility.

Our noblemen are lackeys.

0 2)

Meanwhile a large group of people has gathered in this rural countryside. There is a neighbor, a general. A law suit and a settlement with him. Another neighbor, a beautiful woman. And various minor neighbors.

The Teacher has been recommended. A meek and timid character. Terribly absent-minded and strange. Partly a nihilist, he doesn't believe in God. A citizen. Rapid-firing rifles. Tried his luck in the service. A fool.

N.B. Another neighbor, a nihilist, very wealthy, with students. The Teacher observes that all nihilists are terribly fond of making some money for themselves. (The proclamations. Nechaev appears in passing; have the Teacher killed (?).

N.B. ~~The Teacher~~ A.B. prepares to play a role.

At first he makes fun of the Teacher. ("How is he with children?" The water carrier, and so forth.) The Teacher is laughing at himself, yet A.B. is ultimately impressed by the fact that he conducts himself with dignity. 2,000 lost.

The Ward is the *first* to laugh at the Teacher.

She gives no thought to the affair, but there, suddenly, she finds herself pregnant.

The General, who has lost his wife, proposes marriage to the Ward. She rebuffs him (but suddenly, her pregnancy). The Mother scolds her, "Why did you refuse him?" as she is still unaware that the Ward has a liaison with her son.

N.B. The Teacher meanwhile, typically for him, has gotten ready to make up and to think up a few extra details to round out the picture.

The affair has come to light. Scenes between A.B. and his mother. Though there really is no cause for making scenes. A.B. says to her: "Why those fainting fits? You aren't concerned about the moral part of it, are you? And, of course, there is no chance of a marriage."

N.B. A.B. respects the Teacher, but in his own way.

She must be removed, of course. Pretend that she must join a sick aunt. The whole affair has greatly affected *her*. She seems astonished, and at the same time her milieu has changed for her from one of luxury to one of abomination—which makes her sad. And also, she experiences for the first time a feeling of humiliation, although, once again, she has no claim at all on marriage.

The idea to offer her to the Teacher. They do. (For covering up the disgrace and for expeditious action, 15,000.*) He blushes, but says nothing about the 15,000 in the beginning. *She* accepts him, laughing.

The Teacher goes to see her, a friendship develops, he is courting her. *She* even begins to reveal her innermost thoughts to him, about Christ, about God, and about science. She listens. "You are a good man." But suddenly she begins to cry. He timidly comes forward with this proposition: "What if without those 15,000?" "Why didn't you speak up?" "I love you." (Humility, etc.)

Finally it reaches the stage where she says: "I love you too." But he can see that she doesn't.

22 3)

Think up many more details

In the meantime, the Teacher, whom everybody held to be a coward, repeatedly displays extraordinary strength of character, daring, and courage. The fire. An argument with some neighbor about something. A slap in the face (in the presence of the Beauty). The Teacher can see that *she*, too, already despises him that night for having had his face slapped. He calls out that gentleman. The latter offers him 300 roubles. Prince A.B. offers to act as his second. *This* makes the duel possible. He firmly faces the shot, but refuses to fire himself. The Beauty is fascinated and develops a passion for him.

N.B. *The most important.* Kartuzov, a neighbor, who is writing verses to the Beauty.

The Teacher, seeing how mortified she is (and, to make things worse, A.B. who has quarreled with the Beauty and, in his pride, wants to do a generous act), decides to marry *her.*

(Build up the character of A.B. and the struggle of a peculiar kind of pride. Partly beautiful, but also cowardly.)

N.B. He has visited the Ward even before, when she was all by herself.

To his mother's horror he marries the Ward. The latter rejects the Teacher.

Her *parting* from the Teacher. (She is unhappy.)

---

* Literally, "to save her belly, expeditiously."

He leaves, penniless and with only one little suitcase.

? (He is murdered en route?)

More briefly. Everything depends *on form,* however. Create forms. Sharply define the characters. Work some more on this plot.

The most important. The *Prince's* character—A.B.? Proud, in a special way; hates the Teacher (ever more and more).

N.B. Define the character of the Beauty and the nature of her relations with the Teacher. (The Beauty has a nihilist girl friend.)

4)

Question: Is it necessary to write this novel? N.B.

Idea. The Teacher, more and more so through the entire novel, keeps growing in beauty. He starts out by being funny and ends up by presenting a perfect *ideal* of beauty. A.B. is brilliant, envious, proud ~~generous,~~ base, and everything. *Without any* self-control, and actually without suspecting that this may be necessary. For instance, he is capable of understanding generosity, aesthetically so-to-speak, and of developing a feeling for it; but this feeling he takes for generosity itself —and is desperate about how generosity won't come to him gratis and without any effort on his part.

2) The Teacher explains this to him.

"What then, should I do?" And, having posed this question, decides to perform a moral feat—to marry the girl, thus giving everybody a scare.

The Teacher goes to see him and asks him outright to retract his promise (A.B., on the other hand, even before that visit, is indignant that the Teacher not only fails to show any admiration for his moral feat, but actually receives the news about it with a rather equivocal expression). They quarrel. A punch in the face. She remains unhappy.

(A hermit and God's fool.)

(*An idea.* A.B. is constantly (more and more so as the novel goes along) envious of the Teacher. He actually felt offended *for himself* when he refused those 15,000. The Beauty starts a flirt with the Teacher. A rendez-vous. ~~A.B. hits him.~~ Here, a duel with another man. A.B. is envious of the Teacher's superiority. A heart-to-heart talk between A.B. and the Teacher, during which the latter plainly shows him, who is so proud of himself, that he actually despises him, however, without anger, but rather with pity. Here then, A.B. makes up his mind to perform his moral feat. As they part, he strikes the Teacher. The latter leaves without saying a word.

A.B. may shoot himself (?)

N.B. (IN GENERAL, THERE IS A LOT OF WORK TO BE DONE ON THE CHARACTER OF A.B.)

(A.B. receives instruction from the Teacher. Cries on his shoulder. Nobody knows that, it is a secret. He tells him (lets him know) that he shouldn't dare to make their relationship public. He is terribly haughty with the Teacher. The disappearance of 2,000. ~~When~~ He sees clearly that the Teacher has stolen the Beauty from him (that's where the 2,000 enter the picture). Confesses to him.)

And suddenly, in a fit of hurt pride, he makes this decision: "*I, too,* shall perform a moral feat." He marries the girl. But when the Teacher leaves—*he strikes him.*

He does not say a word.

N.B. The provincial capital is only 7 versts away. Many acquaintances in town.

24 N.B. The Beauty lives in town, only ~~4~~ 3 versts away.

The Teacher arrives: he enters, sits down, and talks about education. "Do tell *the truth.*" A holiday. Visitors. Among them, Kartuzov. Kartuzov's verses. Kartuzov meets the Teacher; they remain standing at the door together for quite some time; their acquaintanceship. Glad to meet an educated man. (N.B. Compose all these little episodes, and get the reader interested in the Teacher.)

The Prince's steward is a nihilist; 10 loads ~~?~~. A meeting at the nihilists'. The Teacher gets into an argument.

One or two weeks at their place. During this time, show them all, as well as all of their society, *through little stories.* (The Governor, intrigues, petty slights. The Teacher manages to show himself in a mysterious and most interesting light. Think up some anecdotes.)

Kartuzov.

The Ward is laughing at him. A storm is brewing at the house.

NAUSEA.

Some incident involving the Teacher where he behaves in a striking manner. The Beauty notices him.

The General proposes to the Ward. Refusal.

The General or something. The incident involving the Teacher. He insults him—A.B., in the presence of the Beauty; also insults the Teacher.

The Ward leaves. The offer to the Teacher. (Kartuzov starts meddling in the Prince's affair with the Ward, as he is looking after the interests of the K–zin woman). The Teacher tries to talk some sense into Kartuzov.

Her trysts with the Teacher continue, and finally—no need of those 15,000, because I love <her>.

Meanwhile the Teacher gets a slap in the face—on account of the Beauty (because of Kartuzov, somehow through the Polish Count).

(The Prince is jealous of that Count. The Beauty makes fun of the Prince. She infuriates both the Count and the Prince by flirting with the Teacher. That's where the horsewhip enters the picture.—The challenge. (Kartuzov) 300 rubles. The duel, he won't fire.

The Beauty almost surrenders herself to the Teacher ~~a moment~~. One such moment.

5 In his offer to the Teacher, the Prince demands full secrecy, and that he take the blame.

The Prince, smarting with envy and jealousy against both the Count and the Teacher, and thinking that the Beauty is taunting him to get even for his having failed to propose to her, suddenly suffers a full affront as he sees that she is completely surrendering herself to the Teacher. The Teacher won't take her. Joseph makes his escape.

The Prince leaves her for the reason of her having wanted to surrender herself to the Teacher. ~~He goes to see the Teacher.~~ He meets the Ward. Goes to see the Teacher. Repents and sheds tears. And the next day, he performs his moral feat, in order to take *the other woman* away from the Teacher.

The Teacher is relieved of his position.

As he is taking his leave, the Prince suddenly strikes him, unintentionally, from a morbid impulse. The Ward rushes to the Teacher's side. (She saw the blow he struck him with his fist.) "Let us leave—I do not love him." They leave. They are happy.

The Prince marries the Ward—to show off.

Kartuzov is the guardian of the Beauty's honor. He won't propose himself because he is no match. But he can always write verses, for he is too insignificant—He hates both the Count and the Prince.

The Beauty is related to the Governor.

The Count's steward is a nihilist, and there is a whole den of nihilists there. The nihilists make certain proposals to the Teacher.

The Prince is angry at not having been properly appreciated in some quarters.

The Prince is insulted by the Governor. Yet the Governor, being a relative of the Beauty's, makes overtures to the Prince and cultivates his friendship with him, expecting a proposal on his part (the Count, concerning counterfeit money).

The Prince *earlier* (in the beginning) insults the Teacher and asks his forgiveness. Since then, hatred.

27 1)

Variation. The Teacher, somewhere and somehow, falls in love with the Ward and proposes to her. She refuses.

The Prince disgraces <her>, and the General is refused also. The proposal had been made, and *accepted,* long before. The Teacher returns, having completed his studies. In the interval, a mistake, and the Teacher arrives after it has happened.

The Beauty. Nausea. The Beauty becomes interested in the Teacher (yet, at the same time, she is expecting the Prince's proposal). The Beauty brings along the Count as her hanger-on.

Suddenly, the Teacher is being attacked in society; he behaves quietly, yet marvelously well. The Beauty is fascinated.

The Teacher pays a visit to some friends in town. He gets all the inside information. (He has his mother living.)

The Prince makes him an offer.

She and the Teacher get together. She laughs.

Conversations. He recovers his spiritual happiness—the role of a Christian. The Teacher himself moves around, keeping his eyes and ears open all along.

Events in town. People begin to notice the Teacher. (A hero.) The Beauty is interested.

The quarrel with the Count. The Teacher behaves with dignity. The Beauty surrenders herself. Joseph.

The Prince envies the Teacher. Some dealings between the Prince and the Teacher even in the very beginning. The confession. The Beauty jilts him. The Prince performs his feat—he strikes the Teacher.

N.B. The Prince and his family (the Prince's mother) consider themselves to be the Teacher's benefactors. The thing is that the Prince had met the Teacher long before, abroad; on one occasion he had blushed in his presence on account of an important matter (make up something here), and he has been hating him ever since, trying to double his own good deeds <to him>.

He doesn't *fully* realize that he hates the Teacher, although sometimes he does. He has committed several blunders: on occasion, he would express his remorse before the Teacher, even though preserving his *superiority* and being convinced that this *superiority* has not been broken; suddenly, with that keen mind of his, he would see that it had been broken. And that's where he began to hate him. In a word:

An altercation has been going on between them for a long time (even though the Teacher hasn't noticed it), and their relationship has been clouded by *envy* and *hatred*. In the Prince's case, this envy is naturally the result of a feeling of inferiority (which is to say that his is a noble spirit); but he can't stand it.

N.B. The Prince has developed a theory of "the eroded generation and the immaturity of the high nobility." He is an enemy of the Count's. He is very intelligent.

N.B. Early in the novel, let the Prince appear to be the hero of the novel and an ideal figure, and carry on in this fashion up to the very point where he strikes the other man with his fist.

2)

The Teacher arrives in town, not as a teacher but as a free man: to see his mother, who is ill, some business in connection with his tiny estate, and to get together with his fiancée (he has made the acquaintance of the Prince's family abroad; his mother and sister have told him every little detail). Strange and absent-minded: no sooner had he arrived than anecdotes about his strange behavior were heard all over town. (Make up some anecdotes, something about his clash with the General.) In a word, a big event about town, with the Teacher mixed up in it. The Ward rejects him and makes fun of him when he comes to see her. The Prince treats him condescendingly as his protegé. The Teacher is run over by a woman on horseback[1] through his own fault (let's say he was crushed—anyway, it is a *big* event through *which* he is established romantically). And when the horsewoman takes notice of him—the Prince makes him <that> offer and personally takes him to the Ward's in his carriage.

A Christian. The word of a Christian.

(A story with an explanation of all the inside details. For instance, why the Prince both fears and despises the Teacher, etc.)

---

[1] The same as the Beauty or the Fiancée; Liza in the final version.

The 2d part at the Ward's in ~~the country~~ town—Trysts in the evening (a resurrected and strange love between him and the Ward). Meanwhile, the Horsewoman's passion.

Thereupon, a clash with the Horsewoman and some really big event (such as a duel).

3) The Prince abandons the Horsewoman, quits the whole affair, and proposes marriage.

The characters of the Prince and the Teacher are what matters most.

Still another variation (perhaps):

The Teacher has been living in town with his mother a full year before the arrival of the Prince's family. A year earlier, abroad, the Ward had given him her word; he is expecting her arrival, and the Prince's. (He has met the Prince before.) Meanwhile, during this one year he has done, one by one, many a strange thing about town (children). All in all, three abandoned children and two grown-up orphans. The Ward, immediately upon her arrival, jilts him. Along with the rest of the party, the Horsewoman also returns from abroad.

N.B. She arrives a little later. Everybody considers that the Horsewoman is tied by her word to the Prince (only the Prince and herself; they both still act very independently, considering themselves at liberty; for *the final word* has never been uttered between them), and here now, on top of everything else, she brings along with her a certain Polish count. Also, Captain Kartuzov appears on the scene (he has obtained a position in town).

V
The Student and Granovsky

There is one date in this section, January 24/12, 1870, but there is no assurance that it applies to anything but the immediate context. Nevertheless, the evidence is strong that these notes were written in January and February of 1870, as evidenced by the early variant names, the situations, and the continuity of analyses and dialogues. There is one exception to this, the first notebook page of this section (6), which was written in December, 1869. These notes comprise notebook pages 6 and 23–35 of notebook 2.

In large part, these notes are an extended confrontation between Granovsky (the named used for Stepan Trofimovich Verkhovensky in all but the very late notes) and the Student (the very early name of Peter Verkhovensky, who is called by the name of his historical prototype, Nechaev, throughout most of the notes). Both Granovsky and the Student are portrayed essentially as they are in the final version. As in the final version, the Student is contemptuous of everyone around him, scandalously disrespectful of his father, and holds easy sway over the Princess (Barbara Stavrogin). He considers his father to be a fool and a sponger, and he tells him so; and, as in the final version, Granovsky is hard put to defend himself.

Granovsky, here as there, is an abstract liberal who worships ideas at the safe distance of luxury and idleness. He is a poseur, bavard, and an ineffectual aesthete. There is no hint in these notes that he will grow in stature when he recognizes himself as the spiritual father to his son, and his generation as the progenitors of the monsters of the sixties. Indeed, he does explicitly recognize himself and his kind as the fathers of the nihilists, and though there is astonishment, there is no learning from suffering. Fool he is and fool he remains. The best that Dostoevsky can say about him is that his intentions are pure: "Granovsky was truly pure, and ardently wished to do good, yet toward the end he couldn't help playing a role and inevitably became a phraseur. As if this wasn't enough, he became—a fop." He conceives of Granovsky's end in this way: "Granovsky falls ill and dies. He makes an effort to comprehend all that has happened and what they (the socialists and all these people) might be striving for, but he can't. Dissension between him and his wife. He is not allowed to leave town."

The Student's ideology is one of contempt, impatience, and ridicule for all those who would prop up the existing regime, or who would dream of reform or of other systems. He is no ideologue; ideas for him are useless and harmful. This explains why he is as contemptuous of Chernyshevsky and Dobroliubov, the political thinkers of his generation, as he is of Belinsky and Hertsen, the thinkers of Granovsky's generation. They are all useless, because they think and to think is to dream and to spin fantasies. Destruction alone matters. Something of Peter Verkhovensky's perversity and mystery is already here; Dostoevsky himself seems appalled by the Student's ignorance of Russian reality, and by the naïveté of his views about the Russian people. Yet he seems fascinated by the Student's singleness of passion and purpose. To be sure, there is little of the political plot that is so important in the final version: there are a few references to the spreading of sedition, to uprisings, and to the spreading of disorder by the counterfeiting of money. Peter Verkhovensky is here in the Student's character; the political pamphlet and the political murder are not yet here. But the idea of "murder" of some kind is already here, though Dostoevsky is not sure whose murder, by whom, and for what.

For the most part Dostoevsky thinks of the action as turning on romantic complications, as he will do throughout most of the notes. The most frequent variant of the romantic complication is the following: Shaposhnikov (Shatov) makes Granovsky's wife pregnant; the Prince is in love with Granovsky's wife, and slaps Shaposhnikov's face from jealousy, or he is rumored to have killed Shaposhnikov. The Prince has also dishonored Shaposhnikov's sister, who in some variants kills herself; such dishonoring is an added cause for enmity between the two men. There is a hint that the Student connives to use the enmity for his own ends, but nothing more than a hint is given. Liza (here called the Beauty) is present in a few notes as a helper and perhaps mistress of the Student. The Prince is also in love with the Beauty, and thrashes the

Student for his interest in her, thus providing the Student with a cause to implicate the Prince in Shaposhnikov's murder.

It is interesting, from a technical point of view, that Dostoevsky's grasp of character is firmer than his grasp of plot. The characters of Granovsky (Stepan Trofimovich), Shaposhnikov (Shatov), the Student (Peter Verkhovensky), and the Princess (Barbara Stavrogin) are all essentially those of the final version. The action and its structured disposition (what the Russians call "siuzhet") is fragmentary, halting, in part arbitrary, and often abstract. For Dostoevsky, the direction of creative movement is clear: character makes action and not action, character, Aristotle notwithstanding.

---

6 The Prince says: "I want to be above all movements and vacillations; I'm all alone and I live for myself; and doesn't your own morality amount to much the same thing?"

Or, the Prince plays an indifferent *role*.

Or, the Prince is himself a member of the nihilist organization.

<Part of this page is taken up by arithmetic calculations.>

Nothing authoritative.

The germs of the most powerful physical passions.

A tendency toward boundless despotism and an unshakable faith in his own authority. Move mountains. Glad to put his power to a test.

Struggle is his second nature. But a quiet, not a turbulent one.

His strength makes him loathe any lie.

~~"This is no whim."~~

"~~I consider it unnecessary to discuss my financial condition. But in order to accomplish anything at all, I shall need a certain amount of money~~."

"~~I have an idea."~~

~~"By December 1~~."

~~"For this, I am requesting an advance of one thousand rubles."~~

"~~I don't feel too strongly obliged not to be bothering you with a further suggestion~~."

~~"You can rely on me~~."

~~"If you will find."~~

~~"All this is made even clearer by the fact that it is I who have taken the initiative, offering to become a collaborator."~~

~~"If you will find my suggestion feasible, please contact Vasily V. so as to find out what his decision might be."~~

"~~Let me know beforehand~~"

~~"By spring—move to different quarters."~~

23 *Shouldn't the story be told in the first person?* Jan. 24/12 <1870.>[1]

The Slavophiles are a gentleman's fancy. Their opinion of Pushkin (the poverty of Russian literature).[2] Kireevsky's words about the icon.[3]

La propriété c'est le vol.[4]

> Blazing love's grenade
> Burst in Ignat's chest
> And again the One-armed, in terrible pain,
> Set out on his rounds of Sevastopol.*[5]

1) The Prince.

24 T. N. Granovsky

A portrait of a pure and idealistic Westernizer in his full splendor.

Perhaps he is living (in Moscow) in a provincial capital.

Characteristic traits. That aimlessness and lack of firmness in his views and in his emotions, which have dominated his whole life, used to cause him suffering before, but *have now become his second nature* (his son makes fun of this tendency)—

Married for the third time. (A most characteristic trait.)

He thirsts to be persecuted and likes to talk about the persecutions he has suffered in the past.

A man of the forties, he remembers those years well and is in touch with survivors ("I and Timofei Granovsky").

---

[1] This line refers to "The Life of a Great Sinner."

[2] This undoubtedly refers to three articles on Pushkin by I. V. Kireevsky, "Something of the Character of Pushkin's Poetry," "A Survey of Russian Letters for 1829," and "A Survey of Russian Letters for 1831."

[3] Ivan V. Kireevsky (1806–56), his brother Peter Kireevsky, and Alexey S. Khomiakov were the most important Slavophiles. Alexander Hertsen recounts in *My Past and My Thoughts* a story told by Kireevsky about how he was deeply impressed by an icon.

[4] French: "Property is theft." This is Proudhon's (Pierre-Joseph Proudhon [1809–65]) famous formula, from his work "Qu'est-ce que la propriété ou recherches sur le principe du droit et du gouvernement" (1840).

* In verse: iambic tetrameter with feminine rhymes *(aabb)*.

[5] A poem by Lebiadkin-Kartuzov.

A spot on the wall.

His name has once been famous (two-three articles, one monograph, a Spanish travelogue[6]—a note on the Crimean War, in manuscript,[7] passed on from hand to hand and responsible for the persecutions he has suffered). Without being conscious of it, he places himself on a pedestal, as a sort of holy relic to be worshiped by pilgrims. Loves it. Often speaks without pronouns.

He is actually honest, pure, and considers himself an oracle of profound wisdom. Instability of opinions.

A great poet, something of a rhetorician.

Has gained a thorough, penetrating understanding of Russian life.

Shuns nihilism and fails to understand it.

55 years of age. Literary memoirs. Belinsky, Granovsky, Hertsen[8]—(A and B, "What made you talk to such a fool?")[9] Turgenev, etc.

Likes champagne.

The role of ~~Polinka~~ Saks.[10]

Likes to write lachrymose letters. Used to shed tears at such-and-such, and at such-and-such place.

"Leave me God, and art. You can have Christ."

---

[6] Reference to Botkin's (Vassily P. Botkin, 1811–69) *Letters about Spain* (1847). Botkin was a critic, representative of a minor current of opposition to the ruling social criticism of the time.

[7] Reference to Boris N. Chicherin's (1828–1904) unpublished article "The Eastern Question from the Russian Point of View," written in the middle fifties and circulated in manuscript form. Published finally in 1907. Chicherin was a proponent of *laissez-faire* economics.

[8] Alexander I. Hertsen (1812–70), famous Russian *émigre* revolutionary. His most famous works are *My Past and My Thoughts, From the Other Shore,* and *The Bell,* a weekly newspaper founded and published in England (1857–61).

[9] This is a reference to an anecdote told to Dostoevsky by Hertsen about Belinsky. Belinsky re-creates an argument between A and B. A, representing Belinsky, is very intelligent, and B, representing his opponent, is very stupid. When Belinsky finished telling Hertsen about the argument, Hertsen said that it was very good, but added, "Why did you waste your time arguing with such a fool?" The argument between A and B is to be found in Belinsky's collected works under the title, "Conversation between Mr. A and Mr. B."

[10] Hero of Alexander V. Druzhinin's (1824–64) novel, *Polinka Saks.* When his wife falls in love with another person, Saks sacrifices his rights as a husband and offers her perfect freedom and separation. References to "Saks" are made a number of times, and Dostoevsky obviously wishes to associate Stepan Trofimovich Verkhovensky with the same liberal gestures. But he changed his mind, and in the novel the only reference we have to *Polinka Saks* occurs on the morning that Liza leaves Stavrogin. As she flees Stavrogin and tries to avoid seeing Mavriky Nikolaevich, Peter asks her if she has ever read *Polinka Saks* (Part III, chapter 3:6).

The stupidity of frankness: He has grasped the essence of the Madonna.

"No, I am now a natural enemy of nihilism."

"Did he ever receive people kinder than these?"

"Probably not, for these are precisely the most cruel."

Christ failed to understand women.[11]

George Sand[12] and idols are apparent constantly despite his serious airs.

He is truly a poet. *Dies irae,* the Golden Age, Greek gods.

Devote an inspired chapter to him. He has arranged his financial affairs quite well.

Little portraits. Little memoirs,

(etc., in the same vein.)

His son is being educated abroad.

Portrait of his young wife (four months pregnant).

N.B. (He sheds tears about all his wives, yet keeps getting married all the time.)

"I can't resign myself to it, I have that melancholy feeling all the time."

He is clever and witty.

The Princess had been working on both Shatov and Granovsky, but she succeeded in getting her hands on Granovsky only. But she established connections with a number of writers, Goncharov among others. In Petersburg, she wanted to gather some nihilists around herself, but nothing came of it. The Great Writer, one great critic who, however, was drunk much too often.

25 *Shaposhnikov.*

2) Shaposhnikov is in town. Acquainted with his wife. *Granovsky* has heard something before.

Conversations with Shaposhnikov. (Shaposhnikov is a student who

---

[11] Stepan Trofimovich says in Part I, chapter 1:9, "The very fact that Christianity has failed to understand women is enough, as George Sand has so splendidly shown in one of her great novels."

[12] See quotation in note 11 for reference to George Sand in the final version. Dostoevsky gives us an account of his thoughts and feelings about George Sand in *The Diary of a Writer* (June, 1876).

has been involved in student disorders.) Now he is no longer a student, he has a mother, ~~children~~ (foundling children).

Shaposhnikov—*a truly native type*. His convictions—that Slavophilism is a gentleman's fancy. The nihilists are the sons of country squires. Nobody in Russia knows who he is. We have lost sight of Russia. We can't recognize our own peculiar nature, nor do we know how to deal independently with the West.

This is not a matter of convictions: this is a matter of the ultimate results of Peter the Great's reforms. He decided that his Russians must become Europeans by decree, and 150 years later he's finally got them, his Europeans. To be sure, they've become alienated from their own people and yet haven't become attached to any other nation—because the others are all national, whereas we deny nationality on principle, wanting to be just Europeans, although there just isn't such a thing as a European.

"Get things done!" He rails against the Westernizers. Granovsky argues hotly, and with pleasure. A poetic soirée.

The Student[13] appears (with the intention of spreading counterfeit money, proclamations, and <conspiratorial> threesomes). His arrival makes Shaposhnikov happy. He embarrasses his father with his nihilism, his gibes, and his paradoxes. Plain and outspoken. "Rebuild the world."

He invites Shaposhnikov to participate. The latter was foolish enough to attend some of their meetings. Talked back to them. Inadvertently mentions it to Granovsky.

Granovsky discusses this with the Student.

The Student rebukes him for having revealed the matter to Granovsky.

Shaposhnikov hotly replies that he does not consider himself tied by anything (inform the police in ¼ hour, Colonel Mezhuev, Granovsky says that he would not have informed the police).

(For six months to Solovki <monastery>.)

The Student is in town and moves around in society. (*Bazarov.*)[14] Shaposhnikov (has come to take a close look at the Prince who has dishonored his sister).

A poetic portrait of Shaposhnikov's sister; she drowns herself.

---

[13] An early name for Nechaev and Peter Verkhovensky.

[14] The main character in Turgenev's *Fathers and Sons* (1861).

The Student incites the threesome to kill Shaposhnikov. They kill him.

This is preceded by:

A most important conversation with ~~his father~~ Granovsky about their definitive opinions. *The Student,* who has been defeating his father on every score, defeats him this time as well, and moreover, tells him that his wife is pregnant with Shaposhnikov's child (Laughs at *Polinka Saks.*)

(Or, for instance: "If you wouldn't have these persecutions to your credit, you'd be most unhappy." Or, vague statements. Laughs in a grotesque fashion.)

His theory: At present, the structure is shaking, von Sohn,[15] 8000 versts of railway tracks.

Credit is shaken, so is morality. Keep shaking it by means of counterfeit money and false news—anything. (A passionate and brilliant picture.)

A son has killed his mother.

"Is it true?"

~~The Student~~ "Why, they wanted to kill you also. A piece of jewelry."

Shaposhnikov asserts that the reforms are acting strongly and are having a revolutionizing effect. When the waves will subside, the ruble will become steady also.

"But when is it going to become steady?"

"As soon as we shall take a national course in every respect, and most of all in our reforms, as soon as we shall become aware of this."

"Which means never," says *the Student.*

Granovsky and his wife. She finally snaps out that she had no intention whatever to betray him, but that she is in fact bored with him. (This is toward the beginning; this is also when he has his verbal duels with Shaposhnikov.)

"You are demanding the impossible from Russia."

26 Hint of a plot. The Prince—the Ward—a sister or fiancée of Shaposhnikov's. The Beauty.—The Prince refuses and gets *Granovsky* in-

---

[15] Von Sohn was the victim of a sensational and vicious murder that took place in St. Petersburg. Von Sohn was lured into a dive on the pretext of being provided with a fifteen-year-old girl. He was murdered by a gang headed by Maxim Ivanov, and robbed. His body was stuffed into a trunk and sent to Moscow. The baggage ticket was burned. Further murders were planned, but one of the gang confessed and the first murder was discovered.

volved in the affair (who participates with his bits of advice). A quarrel between Shaposhnikov and the Prince. The Prince fears that they might tell the Beauty. The murder is put down to him.

The Student, as he departs from the scene, actually makes fun of Granovsky, telling him that he will be implicated.

Simply and powerfully.

The Ward is ~~the fiancée~~ *Shaposhnikov's* sister. The Prince, Granovsky's elegant friend, fearing a scandal draws in Granovsky as a mediator. Shaposhnikov declares that neither he nor she want to create a scandal—and that, if *the Prince* would ask for her hand now, he would be rejected. One night, (she and the Student are discussing children, marriage, and nihilism), and later ~~she says~~ she goes to the garden, where she meets the Prince to exchange reminiscences with him. She starts telling *Shaposhnikov* about their love, how they met—details, etc. She can't bear it and throws herself into the water. But she begins to scream and is pulled out. She dies, however. Shaposhnikov stays alive. To kill the Prince. Granovsky is afraid of that. This is water on *the Student's* mill. Having killed Shaposhnikov, they accuse the Prince.

Granovsky is himself caught with counterfeit money.

The Student is in hiding. Granovsky is shown the proclamations. They are looking for him. One night ~~he~~ the Student turns up, before making his final escape.

The Student's theories. "You have made something private out of nihilism, in order to turn your backs on a general, universal, and natural phenomenon. You have become frightened and have retreated, clinging to God, art, and science. As soon as God is abolished, a new era will begin for mankind."

(N.B. He has come for a short time only, en route to a different province. *Granovsky* does not know where he is heading.)

~~Education~~

One of the murderers, Uspensky, was in love with Shaposhnikov's sister. After having killed Shaposhnikov, he feels the pangs of conscience and confesses, at first only to Granovsky (can this be true?).

(N.B. The murderers have spread a story about a meeting between Shaposhnikov and the Prince, and that somebody even heard how the latter killed him, in self-defence. Everybody has heard about it, yet nobody knows for sure.)

But what has Granovsky to do with this story?

He is there for the purpose of letting *two generations of what really are the same Westernizers,* those of pure vintage and the nihilists, meet each other. Shaposhnikov, however, is a new man. (Morose, simple, strong, and as of late, impetuous.)

N.B. *The Prince slaps Shaposhnikov's face.* (The Prince is a large landowner.) Shaposhnikov endures the insult. Granovsky is surprised that he does, almost nonplussed, but later he is very nearly convinced that Shaposhnikov has vowed to kill the Prince, and tells his son about it. That's where the latter has a bright idea. (The little Priest.)

The Student's theory as outlined to Granovsky: "You would have done exactly the same thing if you hadn't stopped on your way."

"But your feelings, where have you left your feelings?"

N.B. The Student fascinates even Granovsky in a serious way. ~~The Student~~ (Perhaps the little Priest comes to see the Student. The old Raskolnik.)

Granovsky is afraid that his son may have brought subversive characters to his house.

27 Not his fiancée, but his sister.

The Student's idea: "All this just won't work, and so its better to destroy it all, down to the root, and try the other way."

WORK OUT AS CONCISE AS POSSIBLE A PLAN OF THE NARRATIVE.

Granovsky is to a certain extent dependent upon the Princess, as well as receiving a pension (from the Smirnov[16] woman).

(The Student says to him: "Why certainly, since you are receiving a pension from them!")

Granovsky traveled abroad with the Prince as his tutor-governor.

Dinner at the Princess's. Granovsky and the Princess are ancient and perennial friends, yet theirs is a peculiar friendship: each has come to know the other through years of experience, and each knows the other's

---

[16] Aleksandra Osipovna Smirnov-Rossett (1810–82), possibly a prototype for Barbara Stavrogin. Many of Gogol's letters in *Selected Passages from Correspondence with Friends* are addressed to her.

shortcomings. Each also esteems the other's virtues. A strong friendship, even a very warm one. If either of them were to die, the other might not survive the blow (at least that's what people close to them say about their friendship, and they believe it themselves.) The Princess is somewhat more finical, ~~capricious~~ and colder; Granovsky more sensitive and capricious. Such great friendship notwithstanding, they both practically ~~observe~~ observe the etiquette of alternate visits. Granovsky feels (rightly) that, on occasion, the Princess simply gets tired of him while, on other occasions, she needs him so badly she's almost hysterical about it ("to fling all kinds of slops at him," as *the Student* puts it, "for one needs a friend to empty one's slop-buckets.")

"She is supporting you."

For Granovsky is more inclined to observe etiquette. He forgives the Princess her aristocratism and has resigned himself to the notion that she considers him much her inferior. The Princess, in turn, considers herself obliged to recognize his authority as a great man. Granovsky won't pay a visit to the Princess when she hasn't been around for a long time. He even preens his presence before her, and strikes a pose which is not without a tinge of enamoration. Occasionally, the Princess allows herself pointed, peevish, and slighting gibes at Granovsky, although she knows only too well that he is very touchy and would not stand for it; yet she can't refuse herself this pleasure—so disgusted is she with her friend at times ("That's precisely what you need a friend for, to pour out your slops at him," says the Student, "and besides, she is supporting you, isn't she?"). "How do you think friendship will be arranged in the society of the future?" "Why, there won't be any friendship, rather ~~everybody will understand~~ relationships between people will be clarified without any trouble at all, according to strictly scientific natural definitions." "So people will be mere pawns?" "Quite the contrary, but ~~knowing~~ having found out exactly what precisely is natural and necessary according to human nature, they will quit reproaching a man for these things as if they were shortcomings and vices, or quarrel with him, or slight him because of them. You won't need any kind of love then, least of all Christian love, but only knowledge, science."

He is jealous of *the Student* and delivers a tirade to regain his authority with the Princess, who has started to scoff at him. Recalling this at home, he tells himself: "Could I really have felt satisfied with this kind of friendship?" He looks at his wife and says: "Here is my refuge and my hope from now on!" Right there, though, suspicions and rumors that Shaposhnikov is his wife's lover.

At dinner, the Student is reserved, taciturn, and addresses the Prin-

cess with only the slightest trace of mockery, but without a shade of arrogance. He avoids any discussion of important topics, yet gladly talks about minor things, not in the least disconcerted by the fact that he may appear something short of refined. It gets to the point where the Princess takes offense at his considering her intellectually incapable of discussing serious subjects and therefore avoiding them in her presence. He eats with good appetite.—"Mark you well," he later tells his father, when the latter takes him to task for not discussing any serious topics (such as nihilism) with her, "let's say you have started to talk about something intellectual, and she has responded enthusiastically, still, the moment your son comes around and begins to talk about Prince Pyotr Ivanovich, and that his second ~~daughter~~ niece may be about to get married, she'll quit everything and let you know all too clearly
28 that the last bit of news about Prince P. M. is much dearer to her than all your intellectual talk. All of them are like that, but you had to insist on being so smart and approaching things from a different angle."

"Besides, it seems that you've taken care of your affairs very nicely now, what with taking a wife at 60 and getting some money on top of it."

"I haven't even touched the money which Maria Alekseevna[17] brought me, the money is hers, and I'm very glad that she will be left with a substantial sum after my death." "Sure, sure! Why, they couldn't help giving you the money," says the Student.

"But anyway, she is supporting you, and you are her dependent. You're exchanging letters, you are flirting with each other; I really haven't read your letters."

"You are not writing these letters for friendship, but for posterity, for you do consider yourself a great man, don't you?"

At dinner, Granovsky: "Little Pisarev." "Why little?" From—. ("He resembles Pisarev.") Pisarev used to be at the Princess's. (Pisarev who got beaten.)

The Student. He is very polite all the time, yet he is absent-minded and pays absolutely no attention to the Princess's coquetry. Suddenly he calls his father: *"a whining civic-minded old woman."*

At dinner, *the Student,* though in passing only, expresses a very momentous and important idea, but fails to go on with it or try to develop it, as if he hadn't noticed (~~perhaps~~ *he actually had not noticed*) what he

---

[17] Apparently an early name for Granovsky's wife. As such an early name for Dasha.

had said, even though he arouses everybody's curiosity. Instead, he turns to the pies. He looks down on everybody, as if this were quite natural, and later, when summoned by his father, declares to the latter: "These are all lies, all your friendship, and emotions, and coquetry, and letters, and her toilette, and her princely rank. And, inasmuch as I don't take any of this seriously, I reacted to the whole business by being bored. Granted, all these things are needed now, but they surely will go out one day, won't they?"

N.B. The Princess has heard of nihilists and has seen some (Pisarev), but she would like to have a Bazarov with her, not to argue with him or to convert him, but just to hear, from his own mouth, some of his opinions (on art, on friendship), and to have a look at him as he'd strike his pose *à la Bazarov*.

The Student, on the contrary, pulls off this trick of presenting himself as a most indifferent, very calm and pedestrian mediocrity. He quickly starts to bore people, but suddenly, toward the end of the dinner party, as the conversation gets around to the subject of manners, he says that a Russian nobleman is a lackey when abroad (the way he dresses, his obsequiousness, being obliged to talk of interests that are alien to him, and not having either a face or an interest of his own); also, <he calls his father> "a whining civic-minded old woman."

(It is the Princess who is the most important person in the house, yet *the Student* addresses mostly the Prince during the dinner party, and acts as if he were taking scant notice of the Princess.)

The Student laughs at phalansteries where people will be dancing and singing while mowing hay.

"Why, you have no love even for your own cause?," says Granovsky.

"All this love is nothing but vanity," replies the other.

"As far as distribution of labor is concerned," he says, "I am going to abolish it, while they would like to develop it further."

"Don't tell me that you aren't vain yourself," says Granovsky, "haven't you been telling people about having escaped from the casemates <of the secret police>, and what not."[18]

"Why, you are getting caustic with me—don't be angry," he then added in a somewhat milder tone, "I do see, it offends you that I'm not paying due tribute to the fame which you enjoy in these parts and you

---

[18] A reference to rumors the real Nechaev spread—to inflate his reputation—that he had been imprisoned by the St. Petersburg police and had escaped from their clutches.

felt the sting from the very beginning. Yet I also realize that it couldn't be any other way; you are a mummy which can't possibly be awakened to a new life. All your life you've acted in this manner, and so you must remain what you are. (They would have you killed, but I vetoed it, because, I said, there was no need to kill you, you'd become scared anyway, and there might even be an uproar about you; but now everything has turned out all right; you just keep still, and stick to your role, and keep repeating the same words.)"

The Beauty has brought the proclamations with her.

During dinner, at the Princess's, about the proclamations.

29 In the beginning, *the Student* appears to be so small, ~~modest~~ unimportant, silent that Granovsky says to his wife, with chagrin, that his son, alas, would hardly set the world on fire. There is a dinner party at the Princess's. Then suddenly, a report that they are still looking <. . .> (even prior to that, discussions about socialism with his father, which he enters reluctantly). The Student gives his replies reluctantly, as if merely out of politeness; not condescendingly, or disdainfully, but indifferently, which ever so much more ~~offends~~ inflames Granovsky's vanity. ~~Having shown inadvertently~~ But when he sees that his son is making judgments ~~and has opinions of his own~~ he remarks to him, during a conversation: "I can see *that you are qualified after all to make your own judgments.*" But when Granovsky realizes that his son actually has definite views of things, even he is astonished by this fact, and he tries to embroil him in a debate. ~~The latter sharply~~ (Here then, Granovsky's monologue.) The Student, abruptly and fragmentarily outlines some sardonic opinions, the one about the whining old woman being among them. But when this is followed by a barrage of facts, Granovsky is frightened and finally learns, in the course of a definitive exchange of opinions, what kind of a man his son is.

(Bazarov was created by a man of the forties, and without any affectation, which means that a man of the forties could not create Bazarov without distorting the truth.)

"In what sense then, is he unnatural?"

"He has been placed on a pedestal, that's what is unnatural about him."

"Little Pisarev."

"Why do you say, 'little Pisarev'?"

"Pisarev wasn't very tall, but he wasn't very short either, was he?"

"Did I say 'little'?" (As if himself surprised, and after a second thought:) "I don't know why this word escaped me—yet it seems that it fits Pisarev well. I'm not speaking of his stature, or anything in particular, he merely appeared small to me in a general way, my entire impression of him was one of something small..."

"Come on now, and you are really a ~~big~~ giant yourself, aren't you?" (the Student suddenly said).

"I used to like Pisarev very much," said the Princess.—

~~Vissarion~~ The late Belinsky[19] would abuse Christ in the vilest terms, yet he couldn't have hurt a fly.

"Oh yes, when it came to reality and understanding real things Belinsky was very weak indeed. Turgenev has rightly said of him that he knew very little even in the field of scholarly learning, yet that, at the same time, he had a better understanding of things than anybody else. You are laughing, as if you wanted to say: 'Come on now, how much understanding did everybody else have?' My friend, I do not pretend that I know the details of real life. I was just talking about Belinsky. I remember the writer D.,[20] then still almost a boy, whom Belinsky was trying to convert to atheism. When D. would raise any objections in Christ's defense, he would abuse Christ in the vilest terms. ~~To me~~ 'Why, every time I curse a little he will make such a mournful, crushed face,' Belinsky would say pointing at D. and laughing in a most good-natured, innocent manner. Once this D. met Belinsky at the railway station which was just then under construction. 'I can't wait calmly, I have decided to take a walk to this place every day to have a look at the railway.' Oh, if the poor dear had only known with what eyes many people, including those who were building it, looked at this railway in those days! Belinsky used to say: 'I am not like everybody else, why, I am so painfully concerned with this thing. They'll bury me all right, but some day they'll find out whom they buried.' D. walked along with him and they began to talk about the railway of the future, about heated railway carriages, finally about the fuel problem in Moscow, where the price of firewood was going higher and higher. ~~And with increased~~ 'And in the future, when all the various railway lines will meet in Moscow, prices will be so much higher yet. Probably they'll be hauling fire-

---

19 This reminiscence about Belinsky (under the name of Granovsky) appears in Dostoevsky's *The Diary of a Writer* (1873) in an article entitled "Old People."

20 Dostoevsky himself.

wood to Moscow by railway, from the wooded parts of the country.' Upon which Belinsky laughed uproariously at such poor knowledge of reality: 'Why, he is going to haul firewood by train!' The very thought appeared absurd to him. Imagine, he actually believed that railways would be for passengers only and that, as far as freight was concerned, only the most refined and precious *articles de Paris* would be transported by railway. So much for his knowledge of reality. Yet he had more understanding than anyone else."

"Must be then, that everybody else really understood a fat lot—"

"My friend, I have been out of touch with affairs...Presently, I don't want any part in them, nor can I..."

"What do you think you'd be good for, anyway?"

The Beauty shows her favor to the Student and invites him to her house. The Prince introduces him to———There is a scene between her and the Student, who tells her bluntly that he hasn't got time to waste on love.

"You've been brought up badly, you've got vile manners..."

"Oh, I wasn't even listening to you, what is it you were saying?"

Granovsky is angry and starts some kind of a tirade.

"Never mind, it's all nonsense anyway," the Student cuts in, "better tell me (and he asks him about a most vital matter regarding the relationship between Shaposhnikov and his wife, dropping a strange hint as he does)..." Then he begins to laugh, and leaves.

On the following day, when challenged by Granovsky, he says: "Oh, *this* is none of my business; I asked this question with something else in mind."

Inform the police: "Taking the case of Karakozov,[21] and knowing about his intentions two hours ahead of time, would you have informed the police?" (a question addressed to Shaposhnikov).

Granovsky says "no," but keeps hedging on his answer, trying to qualify it.

"Even if you weren't yourself involved in the conspiracy, but having, somehow, learned about the intentions of the conspirators?"

---

[21] Dmitry V. Karakozov (1840–66), who attempted the murder of Alexander II on April 21, 1866. The attempt failed and he was arrested and then condemned to death. He was hanged on September 3, 1866.

"No, I would not have informed the police."

Shaposhnikov: "For my part, I'm going to inform the police. Why, this is unnatural. You are not using your own reason, or feeling your own emotions, or following your own rules—"

The Student: "Shaposhnikov at least has the courage of his convictions, while you are a windbag even in this respect."

After Granovsky has repeated many times that his son will not set the world on fire, he hears that his son is a favorite of the Beauty's and that the Princess is planning a special dinner party to invite Granovsky and *the Student* with the intention of bringing him together with the Beauty. Granovsky feels not only surprised but a bit jealous too, it seems. The Student says: "Admit that you're already jealous of the favors this magpie is showing me (because you are a hanger-on of hers) and envious of my success." Granovsky feels outraged, and that very night shines at the party by delivering his improvisation. He is in a state of rapture.

Upon returning home he says to his son: "Such are my convictions; I don't know how I discovered in myself that source of inspiration which has been dry for so long. But my grief, and the outrage I have suffered from you have called it forth. You have heard me. That is the whole of me."

"If that's really the whole of you," the Student replies, "you are simply a whining civic-minded old woman, like the rest of you people. But it appears to me that you are not only an old woman, but you also envy me, and that this is why you were blabbing so much today. Well, enough. Maybe I won't be around for some time, don't ask anybody about me."

"How can you talk to me in this way?"

"Why, isn't it the truth?" ~~Isn't it the truth~~

The Princess summons Granovsky and tells him about certain rumors concerning counterfeit money and proclamations. She also shows him a proclamation.

Granovsky goes to see his son. They have a talk, and here for the first time they get to speak seriously of their respective ideologies. The son defeats him on every score, and tells him about his wife (an informer). "Go away and don't meddle in my affairs."

That same night, the girl drowns herself.

On the third day, the murder.

Granovsky thinks that it is the Prince.

But the Princess calls him over and tells him ~~every little bit~~ about her son ~~?~~ Where is he? That same night his son shows up. "Is it true?" The son laughs and says that it has been decided to have him, Granovsky killed also. He also makes it definitely clear to him that Shaposhnikov has made his wife pregnant. "Play the role of Saks."

Uspensky informs the police, and meanwhile Granovsky makes a scene to his wife.

Uspensky tells him that all that talk about her being pregnant is nonsense, that he used to know Shaposhnikov well and that ~~him with~~ he loved the girl who drowned herself. But most important, that the murder was committed by Nechaev and the officer who had embezzled some official funds and was already wanted by the authorities.

The Princess talks about Granóvsky. Strangely enough, they don't seem to resemble each other at all. Granovsky even now, at 57, is a handsome man, with the mane of a lion, aquiline eyes, of tall stature, with that thoughtful expression on his face, those majestic gestures—while the other looks exactly like that cherub painted on the ceiling ~~and has a perfectly stupid face to boot.~~ Nevertheless, there is a resemblance also: the cherub would suddenly take on an exceedingly clever and serious expression—just as his father, while Granovsky's face would suddenly burst into some sort of laughter, turn terribly banal and change very suddenly from a lion into that ~~ceiling~~ cherub on the ceiling, the very image of his son.

32 Granovsky was truly pure, and ardently wished to do good, yet toward the end he couldn't help playing a role and inevitably became a phraseur. And as if this wasn't enough, he became—a fop—

La vertu à nous ce n'est pas l'innocence...[22] (in his inspired after dinner speech at the Princess's).

The Student says: "The sciences, too, are superfluous. I'm not too erudite myself, nor am I a Westernizer, and I certainly have nothing against Russia. Why, it's even better here. It's simply that I am <in favor of tearing everything> up by the roots."

Shaposhnikov speaks about landowners and divinity students, and about how Belinsky and Granovsky simply *hated* Russia. (N.B. In more detail and more to the point about hatred for Russia.)

---

[22] French: "Innocence for us is not virtue."

Granovsky (answers him:) "Oh, if you only knew how they loved Russia."

Shaposhnikov: "They loved themselves and used to whimper about themselves only."

Shaposhnikov says: "The sons of country squires, and all sorts of mediocrity, idleness, aversion to hard work, a disposition to loafing, easy work, and first and foremost—the fact that the sons of country squires are an uprooted class—"

"You sure are . . . embittered," remarks *the Student.*

"What is it they are? Their boldness in tackling problems, etc."

Shaposhnikov: "Nothing in particular, just a bunch of gophers, or something."

The Student says: "Victor Hugo speaks about the last terrible war, and then—songs, art, and so forth. An old windbag, and nothing else. ~~And Chernyshevsky, too, is a windbag.~~"

Granovsky: "You even haven't got the excuse of a Utopia,[23] like Chernyshevsky, Dobroliubov."

"They are windbags, too—we are the last and the best of the lot."

After the last parting words, about his wife and her being pregnant:

Granovsky: "I don't believe it, I don't believe it!"

"Sure, sure. No husband ever believes it. Why, even your vanity and ~~vaingloriousness~~ won't let you, and your vaingloriousness—(are you taking pictures?)."

"Leave me~~, cursed~~ you are no longer my son, your hands are blood-stained! I ~~am going to die~~ am having a stroke, and I'm going to die."

"Well, you may go on living for a while yet, but suit yourself... Still, what a phrase-mongering, lachrymose old woman you really are, let me tell you this much."

"Monster! If it is true, as that unfortunate man (Shaposhnikov) has claimed, that yours is the product of my own uprooted generation, that it is we who in due course engendered the Utopists of about 8 years ago, and after them ~~you and that~~ *in due progression* you, in that case, tell

[23] Probably a reference to the utopian vision that appears in Chernyshevsky's *What Is To Be Done?*

me, what will they be like who will replace you, and whom I may yet have the misfortune of seeing in my lifetime?"

"Why, they will not be like me, who did after all speak up in favor of leaving you alive when the question of having you strangled or not came up; they will certainly start with you, and perhaps rightly so."

After dinner, at the Princess's, the latter asks Granovsky to deliver a defense of poetry. He speaks marvelously well (a whole small chapter).

"No, you are still useful, Andrei Nikolaevich,"[24] says the Princess—

"I—I..."—and here comes that improvisation in which Granovsky pours forth everything that has been dormant in him.

"Yes, you are right, he is a coward," says his wife to Shaposhnikov.

"It isn't that he is a coward, but he has no ground under his feet."

33 "Well, you will find solace in tears. I once read a book by Parthenios the Monk about his pilgrimage to Mount Athos,[25] and it said in that book that Nicholas the Monk had the gift of tears. Well, that's what you are, Nicholas the Monk who had the gift of tears."

N.B. *The most important thing.* After *the Student's* initial appearance, when his father, having introduced him to the Princess, has become convinced that his son won't set the world on fire, there follows directly the whole story about the Prince and Shaposhnikov's sister, and about Shaposhnikov himself. (The Beauty has not arrived yet, and so she couldn't have invited the Student to her place so as to destroy Granovsky's illusion that his son won't set the world on fire.) Later *he* is suddenly developed in full, and the first part of the finale transpires, then a rapid finale. (Shaposhnikov's death, the calumny against the wife, etc.)

Before the Beauty's arrival, the Student occasionally drops a slight hint about the Princess, the Prince—and there is even a debate at Granovsky's who, in Shaposhnikov's presence, refutes socialism. During the debate, the Student keeps laughing things off, but inserts a few serious

---

[24] An early name for Granovsky.

[25] A reference to an important book Dostoevsky had read: *The Legend of the Wanderings across Russia, Moldavia, Turkey, and the Holy Hills of the Monk Parfeny.* The scene about Semyon Iakovlevich in *The Possessed* is taken from this book.

remarks also—not many though—and on the main point, until the discussion drifts on to the subject of denunciations. Later, Granovsky when alone with his son inadvertently mentions the enmity that exists between Shaposhnikov and the Prince. The Student listens intently and leaves silently.

Here now, the Beauty who has arrived only three days earlier, sends an invitation to *the Student.* A soirée—after which he makes that statement to his father about his being a whining old woman, and also drops his first hint about <his wife's> pregnancy.

That same night, Shaposhnikov's death.

On the next day, the girl drowns herself.

On the third day, the Princess, quite alarmed, summons the father to tell him that it was all his son's fault.

~~"Could this be true?"~~

The next day, Uspensky.

That night: "Could this be true?" *The Student* leaves, and the curse.

Granovsky falls ill and dies. He makes an effort to comprehend all that has happened and what they (the socialists and all these people) might be striving for, but he can't. Dissension between him and his wife. He is not allowed to leave town.

With the Beauty's arrival in town, the romantic strain in *the Student's* character becomes apparent. He completely disavows her, and so does the insulted Prince, who gives the Student so bad a thrashing he's black and blue all over. He has known for a long time that the Beauty loves him and is jealous of him.

N.B. (Develop the story of the Beauty and the Student.)

The most important

The Student says: Actually, I am not concerned with the people or with getting to know the people. I know that it is now possible to spread sedition among the people, and that is all there is to it.

In discussing the people he suddenly displays, in a certain matter, a glaring and strange (absolutely essential that it be strange, and that it strike the eye with its absurdity) ignorance and unawareness. It is pointed out to him, with ridicule; but most remarkably, he isn't in the least embarrassed, nor does he waver, and even his vanity isn't touched. He takes it terribly coolly and casually. "Perhaps it is so," he says, "but it doesn't matter at all, for this is not the point; the point is that it is now possible to spread sedition, and that's what I'm going to do."

He is told that he won't be able to spread sedition, not knowing the people. Also, that the proclamations are simply preposterous.

"That's nonsense," he answers, "give me a quarter of an hour and let me just talk to the people, without censorship, and they will follow me right away."

When assured that the people are a lot more solid than that, he says:
34 "Why, this is nonsense!" And he points out facts—robberies, incendiarism, von Sohn, "and in any case, you can see for yourselves that this thing is still undecided, and <I see that> you've stopped making comments." ("The people were taken in by the Golden Charter, so why shouldn't they be taken in by a proclamation?")

Sometimes he displays a frightful ignorance. He doesn't even pay attention to his father's serious objections (for instance, regarding the fact that human nature is not wholly known to us, and that reason represents no more than $1/20$ of the whole man), nor does he attempt or even want to argue the point. He actually admits outright that he doesn't know much about these things, but adds that this is not the point.

He is perfectly bland in his ignorance.

As to his father's speech at the Princess's, he hasn't even heard about it.

But nevertheless, he completely crushes his father ("you can't argue with him," says the father).

He knows nothing at all about the problems involving Slavophiles and Westernizers, not even in an approximate way; all he has heard is that there exist some kind of Slavophiles and Westernizers, but that *it is all nonsense anyway*, and quite beside the point.

He can't even spell correctly.

N.B. When his father shows concern that he may be arrested, he says to him: "Don't you worry about me, I'll give them the slip."

"Maybe I'll give them the slip a lot more easily than you think."

"I'm engaged in this business, because it has to be done. Every cause must naturally take its beginning from this (from destruction); this I know, and this is why I ~~am doing~~ have started it. I don't care what it is going to lead to, yet I know that this is how it must be started; and the rest is all so much idle talk."

"It only corrupts, and takes time."

"All these reforms, adjustments, and improvements—they are all a lot of nonsense. The more you improve and reform, the worse it is; for by so doing you artificially prolong the life of something which must in any case die and be destroyed. The sooner, the better; the earlier you start, the better (first of all, God, kinship, family, etc.) One must destroy everything in order to erect a new structure; it is quite absurd to keep propping up the old building with props."

"Very well, assuming now you know that sooner or later you must die, why won't you then shoot yourself right now, the sooner, the better?"

"Solely because I don't want to, yet, and because there is this business to be taken care of."

"I am no genius, nor do I want to be one. But I know what is to be done right now, and I'm doing it. You used to know it, too, but you ~~cry~~ do nothing but cry. Whereas we aren't crying, but simply doing."

They took the key to understanding, but haven't entered themselves, nor will they allow others to enter—"[26]

"How true. That's a good one. But where does it say so?"

"That is in the Gospel. Can it be that you really didn't know that either?" (He didn't.)

"An eye for an eye, and a tooth for a tooth, as in the Gospel."

"You wretch, this is not from the Gospel."

Nota bene. Mention that proclamations have appeared in this town even before, that such material had also been in evidence. Also, there were those fires three years earlier, counterfeit money had been circulated, etc.

The Student is asked by his father: "Is it true that you have something to do with the Beauty?"

Previous unpleasantness with his son—"You were married three times, weren't you?" Some instance in which he absolutely misunderstands a contemporary phenomenon of popular life, and his perplexity regarding recent reforms. (April issue of "Dawn.") His contempt for

[26] A free quotation from Luke 11:52.

Vanka—Belinsky. Iskander, "A" and "B." Poorly managed roads, 80,000 children, von Sohn, confusion created by lawyers—freed 4 o'clock because of mitigating circumstances, commits a new theft at 7. Society, attuned to everything new, is credulous, while the peasants already tend to believe the uncommon, rather than the common. He takes offense at the fact that Russia is happy. Proclamation: destroy the churches, the family—we'll convince them that it comes from the Tsar (Granovsky's note).

35 Previous unpleasantness with the son, but he had not seen him in the last three years. He is at his flat, waiting for his son (the thing is that he arrived in town a week ago). The Student has previously been in the civil service, while Uspensky, his accomplice, is a secondary school teacher.

Shaposhnikov asserts that we have not, so far, developed an independent view of Europe. ("Not that there is such a great need of it," says Granovsky.)

During the dinner party at the Princess's, Granovsky makes fun of his son (he envies him) for the levity of the latter's views on human happiness and love: "You do not know life, nor its great goals, nor the manifestations of human nature. A man will never reconcile himself so easily to the loss of his love and happiness, and he will consider it base and even degrading to forget so soon the woman whom he has lost and to replace her with another; much rather, he will dream of full happiness only in conjunction with irretrievable love."

"Why, there you are, telling me that you have such a hard time forgetting," says the son, "yet you are married to your third wife."

Granovsky blushes: "Does this mean that I have forgotten them? And, while it is true that I have remarried, it was after an exceedingly long interval in each case, when the heart had gotten tired and weary of suffering, even though the old wound would remain open forever."

"Etc., etc. Yet in the end you did remarry and your only justification is that it was after a long interval. ~~Well, as far as I am concerned, the shorter So then, this~~ But no matter if the interval is ~~long~~ large or small, you still arrive at the same result, just as any other person with only a light memory—well, ~~as far as I'm concerned~~ it is obvious that the shorter the interval the better."

"Nor is a long interval any kind of virtue to be shown off for people to see. You are just made that way. If this weren't so, a person who digests more slowly would deserve more respect than one who sh—s in due time."

Or: "if this isn't so, the slower the digestive process, the more respect one owes a person."

Granovsky, who is at first only superficially arguing with his son, says laughingly, laughing at the Russian people: "Let the authors of these proclamations spend some money and print them on silver paper, in golden letters and with vermilion ornaments, and let them say in the heading that this is a Golden Charter from the Tsar—why, the people will destroy their churches as well as their families, having learned that this comes from the Tsar."

"Tiens! ~~why~~ c'est une idée!"[27]

---

[27] French: "Say, that's an idea."

VI
The Romantic Complications

These notes were written in all probability in February, 1870. There are two dates mentioned: February 16 and 18. The notes comprise notebook pages 36–55 of notebook 2.

The fragments of the romantic complication given in the previous section are developed here at great length. The Ward is at its center. She is either to be married to Granovsky or is married to him. The Prince is passionately in love with her, and in one version marries her. Shaposhnikov is either her brother—and hence concerned with her honor—or he is himself having an affair with her. The Student's part in the romantic intrigue is to needle his father with revelations that Shaposhnikov is having an affair with his wife, or to work on the Prince's jealousy by telling him of Shaposhnikov's liaison with the Ward. In some of the notes it seems that the Student wants to move the Prince to murder Shaposhnikov, or at least to move him to a public display of anger at Shaposhnikov, so that the murder may be blamed on him. Kirilov has not been born yet and will not appear until late in the writing process; but the idea of murdering Shaposhnikov (Shatov) and blaming the murder on someone else is there.

The Fiancée or Beauty (Liza) is by family agreement destined for the Prince, but neither one likes the other. She encourages the Student's attentions and cooperates in his conspiracy. She is appalled by the murder of Shaposhnikov, but in some of the notes, she admires the Student all the more because of the murder.

Dostoevsky returns again and again to the romantic intrigue, but the complications seem to motivate very little and to serve less. Dostoevsky doubtlessly wanted to use the rivalry for the Ward's hand as a vehicle to bring out the essential nature of those involved. In reality, the intrigue serves as something of a hindrance, warring against the nature of someone like Shaposhnikov, and preventing the development of the Prince's character. Shaposhnikov is already the Shatov of the final version in many respects: the ardent nationalist, the man of the soil, and the restless, though ineffectual, seeker of beauty and truth. We are told: "Shaposhnikov is the restless type, the product of a collision between a bookish world and reality, a man who has embraced his faith with passion, yet does not know what to do. Much beauty." Yet we are asked to think of him as the lover of the Ward and the romantic rival of the Prince.

Similarly, the character of the Prince is still something of a mystery for Dostoevsky, and he is far from the compelling and frightening figure he will be in the final version. Much of what is said about him is required by his role in the romantic intrigue: he is jealous, at times petty (he tells Granovsky that his son is having an affair with his wife), and passionate and angry (he slaps Shaposhnikov because of his liaison with the Ward). He is largely what the intrigue requires, and it does not require the chilling metaphysics of Stavrogin.

Only Granovsky and his son continue to breathe easily in the amorous complication: the son because he can turn any situation to his profit, and the father because as victim and fool the romantic intrigue is the appropriate vehicle to bring out these qualties: Shaposhnikov and the Prince cuckold him, the son ridicules and intrigues against him, and the Princess welcomes the indignities he suffers. Never does Dostoevsky seem harder on him: for Dostoevsky he is a windbag and a fool who meets his end by dying from diarrhea. Dostoevsky says: "Granovsky is not a genuine ideal. He is passé, self-destructive, full of false pride, a caricature."

The persistence of the romantic intrigue as the core through which the central characters reveal their essential natures explains, I think, something about the final version. The romantic complication is there in vestigial form. Liza is in love with Stavrogin, and Stavrogin in some way is particularly attached to the Ward; Barbara Stavrogin does want to marry Stavrogin to Liza, and Dasha to Stepan Trofimovich. But I will venture to say that the average reader has a hard time remembering the amorous complications. They seem disconnected, skeletal, and faded in passion and purpose. It seems, in short, largely irrelevant to the real purpose of Stavrogin, Shatov, and Dostoevsky. The Shatov of the final version has no romantic liaisons, nor can we imagine him having any, and the Stavrogin of the final version slaps no faces from romantic jealousy. They have other things to do, and what they are has yet to appear in the notes.

---

36 *Granovsky* used to tell stories about Belinsky and about Iskander.

He was at a loss to decide what was going on—8,000 children, etc., and seemed to be glad.

An instance of a profound lack of understanding for some fact of popular life.

~~The Beauty~~ The Ward—*only has a miscarriage*—The Prince slaps Shaposhnikov's face. The latter bears it.

He proposed to the Ward. She refuses.

T. N. Granovsky
He and Shaposhnikov
His wife enters: "I have been to your place."

Notabene: Make the beginning entertaining, as brief and rich in events as ever possible, so that all the *personae* are juxtaposed as naturally as possible, and romantically as possible; also, so that all express themselves as fully as possible.

??? Do not introduce Shaposhnikov's sister, for the sake of brevity, and replace her by a different personage.

Granovsky's wife comes from the Princess's household (it is she who is the Ward.).

The Prince fell in love with her. The Princess, during the Prince's absence, married her off to Granovsky. The Student Shaposhnikov consoles her. The Prince does not like that. Meanwhile the Beauty arrives. The Prince continues to love Granovsky's wife and is struggling with his passion. The Beauty is somehow assigned to him by family agreement. She is the daughter of the General and his wife.[1] The Prince is getting ready to meet her in a haughty manner, with a tinge of ridicule, and with an air of gracefully borne inevitability. Now, the Beauty has previously met *the Student* abroad, and suddenly—upon meeting him at the Princess's—says: "Oh, it is you." Everybody is sur-

---

1 In the final version Liza is not the daughter of General Drozdov; he is her stepfather.

prised, and the Prince no less than everybody else. In the meantime, the Prince suddenly slaps Shaposhnikov's face, who bears it. The Prince asks his forgiveness in Granovsky's presence. ~~He~~ But Shaposhnikov says that he doesn't need it.

Meanwhile the Beauty offers to elope with the Student.

~~During the second soirée~~ But at dinner Granovsky realizes that his son is stupid.

But the Prince informs Granovsky ~~that~~ in a condescending manner and facetiously that his son is trying to steal his bride. "They've had a rendezvous, I know—" Granovsky has a serious talk with his son, whereas up to this point he has only been arguing with him in a condescending way.

A soirée at the General's and the Beauty's.

Granovsky's wife attends it. Granovsky feels piqued—His son and Granovsky's improvisation.

!N.B.! The Prince always ~~was~~ hated Shaposhnikov, but after that sudden slap in the face Granovsky is perplexed. However, his son has this explanation for him: "Why, it is Shaposhnikov who is giving solace to your wife, and the Prince is jealous of Shaposhnikov."

Almost better?

February 5 <1870>

N.B. Some kind of a scandal at the Beauty's soirée—where *the Student* is clearly the favorite. The Princess is alarmed.

Even earlier, the Student drops a hint about Shaposhnikov to his father.

7 Granovsky

Shaposhnikov and Granovsky and wife

Enter the Prince. He discusses Granovsky's son—surprised. Granovsky's wife asks about the arrival of the Beauty. The Prince invites them to dinner for the next day. And he brings along his son. "I only saw him the day before yesterday."

The son shows up—"for just a minute ." He disappears—everybody is invited to dinner.

~~Granovsky and son~~ At dinner, "so this is you!"

The Prince had thought that he was going to meet the Beauty with condescension, but now it turns out that it is she who treats him with condescension (she is a nihilist).

Gossip about Granovsky's wife, supported by his son.

The murder of Shaposhnikov (she flees with ?the Student).

The Beauty quarrels with her father about being forced to marry the Prince, and also tells the Princess openly that ~~the Prince~~ the Prince has a liaison with Mme. Granovsky and that he is jealous of Shaposhnikov who apparently has stolen Granovsky's wife from the Prince and is now her fortunate lover.

An affair is brewing. ~~Granovsky~~ The Princess has a showdown with Granovsky, but there, suddenly, the murder of Shaposhnikov.

N.B. *The Student* leaves town before the murder of Shaposhnikov, but after the murder he shows up in Granovsky's garden demanding that the latter remain silent. "You have ruined the reputation of my wife!"

The Prince is passionately and hopelessly in love with Granovsky's wife. She is keeping him at a distance. He is jealous of Shaposhnikov. The arrival of his bride makes the Prince even more anxious to have a heart-to-heart talk (about something) with Granovsky's wife. (N.B. Granovsky's wife still loves the Prince, and has confided this fact to Shaposhnikov). In the meantime, *the Student* puts together his version of the story *(fully convinced of its truthfulness)* and informs the Prince that Mme. Granovsky really has a liaison with Shaposhnikov. The Prince slaps his face when he meets him, etc.

At first, the Student is very mild and not talkative, so that his father actually makes fun of him (he certainly won't set the world on fire, *thou* and *you*). Here then, some characteristic little stories.) (A conspiracy of the y<oung> people ?.) But suddenly, an argument with his father, (Meanwhile, proclamations, etc.) and *rumors* (from the Princess and the Prince) that *the Student* ~~is stealing the other man's bride (who has begun to talk openly and boldly to her father, the General)~~ and that Shaposhnikov is making good progress in a certain undertaking of his, etc.; also, that the Beauty is sharing his opinions. Here then, the debate about poetry and Granovsky's tirade. In the evening, Granovsky's argument with the Student, and the latter's revelation about Granovsky's wife. (Disdainful attitude toward his father: "Why, I wasn't even listening.") (At this stage the Beauty *begins to talk* to her parents.) The Princess and Granovsky, and concerning his wife's relations with Shaposhnikov. On the same day, the slap in the face. Although Granovsky has turned his son out of his house only the day before, he goes to see him for an explanation. For the first time, <the son puts up> an insolent argument: "that slut," etc. The son departs (i.e., he pretends that he is leaving town). Granovsky and his wife, the tragedy at his house. On the third day, Shaposhnikov's death. Rumors. The Student shows up in the garden. Leaves the nihilist girl with him and departs. Granovsky has diarrhea, etc.

The Princess invites him together with his son.—"My son? But he isn't here yet." "How is that possible? I met him only a moment ago and even told him that I'm coming here." "Strange." At this point the Student rings the doorbell.

The Prince has been absent himself, and has just arrived. (N.B. Granovsky does not relish his visits, but never shows it.)

The Beauty also arrives at the same time (as both the Student and the Prince).

The Prince speaks condescendingly of his bride. He is actually irritated by the prospect of having to meet her.

3 N.B. Granovsky tells Shaposhnikov about his son, not knowing that they are acquainted and in touch with each other.

Granovsky.

Granovsky and Shaposhnikov (partly about his son and the proclamations). The proclamation.

Enter the Prince—he hasn't seen his bride as yet, since she, too, has arrived only in the morning. He tells him that he has met his son. Surprise.

Enter the son. A few strange words. The son leaves. (Shaposhnikov and the Prince exchange biting remarks on the street corner. Shaposhnikov is walking along by himself when suddenly the Student appears from behind a corner, laughing, and joins Shaposhnikov as they walk on together. But one can see that something has been going on between them. (There is an air of mystery about whatever they are discussing.)

The Princess. Her attitude toward Granovsky. Toward the bride (toward Granovsky's wife) ~~She went to see the General~~ She sends the Prince over to the General. The Prince meets his bride (N.B. she goes on horseback, or something of that kind). She has pushed the Prince to the wall (the Prince is a major landowner, yet he also needs some money).

There is a proclamation at the Princess's.

Dinner. The Princess, the Student, and Granovsky have come earlier—and suddenly the bride walks up to the Student. *The Student* is accidentally pushed into the foreground (some kind of provocative act —"A whimpering civic-minded old woman," or something of that sort; about recent political affairs, about nihilists).

After dinner, a committee meeting, and Shaposhnikov.

(N.B. The Prince has written a letter to Mme. Granovsky. He is asking her for a rendezvous. Shaposhnikov knows about the letter. He demands an explanation from the Prince, etc.)

The sojourn of the nihilist. A visit to the General's house, and to the Beauty; gossiping about Shaposhnikov and the Prince. Rumors: the Father feels piqued, has a showdown with his son. Meanwhile, money, the proclamations, etc. Soirée at the General's. (The General is acquainted with Granovsky.) At the General's party, Granovsky's speech about art and about himself.

The son: "I wasn't even listening." Quarrel. About Granovsky's wife. He walks up to the house—and the Prince and Shaposhnikov are there. The Prince slaps Shaposhnikov's face in the presence of both Granovsky and *the Student.*

Granovsky is embarrassed—his son embarrasses him even more. ("I won't be around for some time.")

In the morning, the affair at the General's house. The Beauty refuses —and the Prince refuses too. The Princess summons Granovsky. Various bits of information received by the Princess about the rumors. ~~Granovsky~~

Granovsky goes to see his son. A showdown and a quarrel. (Shaposhnikov and Mme. Granovsky—Mme. Granovsky tells Shaposhnikov that she loves the Prince). Here now, the rendezvous between the Student and the Beauty. Shaposhnikov is an informer. She has come to Shaposhnikov's flat almost in a fit of despair (the slap in the face, and her sisterly love for Shaposhnikov, and her love for the Prince).

Immediately after she is gone, Shaposhnikov goes to the park (the printing press).

In the park, they are waiting for Shaposhnikov. He comes, and they kill him.

Granovsky and his wife. The Princess sends for Granovsky. This is he—three days. The Student shows up at night—A final showdown—The bride flees, but shows up again. ~~The Prince~~ The Student rejects her, is cursed by his father, and leaves. The Prince meets his bride and takes her home.

Granovsky dies of diarrhea. Holy Communion—The Prince and Granovsky's wife in perspective.

N.B. More details about the Student's actions regarding Shaposhnikov and the conspiracy, also about the fact that Shaposhnikov is about to turn informer (he himself tells Granovsky's wife about his intentions as he takes leave of her).

(A curious tête-à-tête between the Student and the Bride.)

In more detail: the conspirators (about the Student and the Bride: do it over again, with some new additions).

N.B. *The most important.* (When Granovsky's wife was about to get married to him, she rejected Shaposhnikov's proposal, or he rejected her, for some romantic reason, something in that vein. Couldn't Shaposhnikov's wife be presented as an alcoholic?)

The Prince says: "I never possessed firmness of character."

The Beauty says: "I've decided to put an end to all this nonsense."

Her father the General is desperate and, after an unsuccessful attempt at being severe, begins to ply her with entreaties. "You are not an animal"—a lecture on the differences between animals. She says: "You are making a fool out of yourself." (Perhaps she is by nature gay and disposed to laughter.) *Perhaps* she participates wholeheartedly in the murder of Shaposhnikov. Get a bishop for the entreaties. Yet *the Student* meets her with composure. The General writes a letter to Granovsky about liberalism (illiterate). Granovsky replies—Eloquence and tears—

Shaposhnikov tells Granovsky's wife that he is greatly concerned *about a certain affair,* and that he wants to report it to the authorities.—

Granovsky has a brother, a retired lieutenant colonel. A freethinker and liberal, dissipated but extremely honest. When liberalism raises its ultimate demands—he is utterly scared and appalled by his nephew. He is in love with ~~the Beauty~~ the Governor's wife or the Beauty and writes poetry. He is at odds with his brother (Granovsky) and looks down on him. He indignantly rebuffs his nephew when the latter slanders Mme. Granovsky. He does not like Shaposhnikov, but helps the latter's (drunken) wife. He has started to help the family and quits being angry with Shaposhnikov. ("It would be indecent and tactless for me to be angry with him, while I'm helping him.") At first he engages in some freethinking with his nephew, and enjoys it; but later he is horrified. Behaves oddly about town. Harpagon, *The Bear*. Muddle-headed letters.

40 The Student's *associates.* The honest and fiery Uspensky,
—the fool Zaitsev and his sister,
—a schoolteacher, bitter at everything and everybody,
—a little scoundrel,
—a man who is completely and honestly convinced of everything, including that two million heads <must fall>, and that one ought better to start hanging and burning right away, and forget about the law.
Blasphemy and sacrilege in church.)

About the rebellion of December 14 as a senseless undertaking, which wouldn't have stood up for as much as two hours. N.B. "They are complaining—but didn't they go for it themselves?" (the Colonel's opinion).

The Colonel asserts that the Russian soldier possessed a high and a firm spirit even before, without gymnastics.

Let even the slave be like a free man (St. Paul)[2]—an opinion stated to Granovsky by Shaposhnikov. Granovsky fails to understand.

~~When the nephew[3] is invited to the Princess's, he teases the Colonel that the latter is envious of him. (Whereas the Colonel, on the contrary, is as happy as a puppy and takes offense at his nephew's supposition that he is (1) envious, and (2) desirous of a visit with the Princess. "She'd be all too glad to invite me, but she won't, because she knows that I'll turn her down rudely.")~~

~~The Colonel is supporting his sister, mother of the Student. When the Student arrives in town, the old lady immediately changes her loyalty, deserting the Colonel and becoming utterly devoted to her son. She tells her son a lot of things about the Colonel, presenting him as a monster of cruelty. Her son eventually abandons her, leaving her with the Colonel. She learns about the murder of Shaposhnikov, sews a sack for the body (though she is cursing her son): "They've gone quite mad." She sews the sack and disposes of the body, while praising the deceased. "I am his godmother. I wonder what his old mother, Natalia Petrovna, will be doing now." She curses him definitively when he is disrespectful and makes fun of her. She hates the Colonel because he is in love with~~

---

[2] A free quotation from I Corinthians 7:22.
[3] Nechaev or Peter Verkhovensky.

~~the Beauty (poetry). He reports it to her son. She is glad to hear that the Prince has broken with the Beauty. She has designs for her son.~~

(N.B. Shaposhnikov is the brother of Mme. Granovsky?)?

~~*Granovsky* had supported his brother (who is his enemy) while the latter was in the service, and also his nephew (*the Student*) whom he brought up at his expense. The Student's mother is particularly hostile to Granovsky.~~

Shaposhnikov is the brother of Granovsky's wife. He has no mother. He hates the Prince. He keeps watching his sister, who takes offense at that, but still loves her brother. She has a firm relationship with the Prince.

The Lieutenant Colonel, a malicious and low jester, ridicules his brother and the latter's friendship with the Princess behind their backs, and also speaks ill of her, precisely because she is a benefactress. And the Princess absolutely insists on being everybody's benefactress. The brother is a madcap. He covets the Beauty, slanders Mrs. Granovsky. *The Student* has no mercy on him, and eventually exposes him outright as the scoundrel he is, without showing him any compassion.

"When I look at his face," says Granovsky several times, trying to nettle his nephew (which the latter immediately acknowledges).

The book by Flerovsky (*Dawn,* No. 1, section "Criticism").[4]

Granovsky says: "To the pen from the card table, and to the card table from the pen. And there is a set time for high and for low tide."[5]

Shaposhnikov immediately chimes in:

"Chatsky, being the narrowminded fool that he is, doesn't even realize how very stupid he sounds saying this. He yells, 'a carriage for me, a carriage!,' indignant because he is ~~was~~ unable to see for himself that even in the Moscow of his time one could do better than 'to the pen from the card table, and to the card table from the pen.' He is a gentleman and a landowner, and nothing exists for him except his own little circle. That's why he becomes so despondent about life in the higher circles of Moscow ~~because~~, as if nothing existed in Russia beside that way of life. Like all Russian progressives, he overlooks the Russian people. Overlooks it the more, the more progressive he is. The more one is a gentleman and a progressive, the more one hates—not

---

[4] *The Situation of the Working Class in Russia; Observations and Researches* (1869).

[5] A quotation from Griboedov's (1795–1828) *Woe from Wit.*

conditions in Russia, but the Russian people. About the Russian people, ~~he thought~~ its religion, its history, its customs, its destiny, and its huge numbers, he thinks only in terms of rent received. The Decembrists, and the poets, and professors, and liberals, and all the reformers until the time of the Emancipator-Tsar thought exactly in the same way. They collected rent, spent it living in Paris, attending Cousin's[6] lectures, and ended up becoming Catholics, like Chadaev[7] or Gagarin.[8] If they happened to be freethinkers, they would end up hating Russia after the fashion of Belinsky *e tutti quanti*. But what is worst of all, a Chatsky couldn't even imagine that there existed in Russia another world beside that of Moscow ~~a real~~ because he was himself a Moscow gentleman and landowner. How infinitely more clever ~~than he~~ than this fool of a Muscovite was the man who simply played cards. Let him be stupid—at least he has a kind heart. Let him be short-witted—at least his thoughts have some originality. Back in those days, all these tirades against Moscow were at least original. But what about you, what about you ? who are repeating this stuff today? Oh, if you only knew
42 how badly you've fallen behind even the Muscovites of those days, and I mean both those who spent their time playing cards and those who were in the service! And you consider yourselves progressives! Anyone who becomes a captive of organized liberalism is *eo ipso* behind times. The form of liberalism must always be original ~~As soon as it becomes organized, liberalism immediately becomes stagnated and degenerates~~, a new one for each generation. I'm not speaking of substance, I'm speaking of form. This is a symptom. A liberalism that has ended up being antinational and nurturing a personal hatred against Russia is all stagnation and confusion, though you don't realize it, having long been taking all this to be the most progressive and the loftiest. And don't forget either that it was the Tsar, and not you, who freed the people. This idea was ~~already~~ in the minds of ~~former~~ Tsars, but it never entered the mind of the Decembrist Chatsky.

My God, they have never realized that the Tsars have been more

---

[6] Victor Cousin (1792–1867), French philospher, opponent of Condillac's sensationalism.

[7] Pyotr I. Chadaev (1791–1856), Russian liberal thinker. He wrote his *Philosophical Letters* in 1829–30. The first of the letters was published in 1836 in *Teleskop*. As a consequence, he was put under arrest and forbidden to publish. In notes for "The Life of a Great Sinner" his name is used as a prototype for the hero.

[8] Prince Ivan S. Gagarin (1814–82). He went to France in 1843, converted to Catholicism, and became a Jesuit.

liberal and more progressive than they, and not only that, because the Tsars always went along with the people, even under Biron.[9] Whereas they, on the contrary, used to be placed under public tutelage on account of their cruel treatment of the peasantry—and why? Because they were so wicked? Not at all, but simply because they wouldn't dare to take a more original view of Russia—because they mistook their own Moscow society for all of Russia. I bet you that the Decembrists would have definitely freed the Russian people, and without delay, but also definitely without their land—for which the people would have definitely and without delay wrung their necks,* thus proving to them that Russia consists of more than just their own Moscow society—to their very great surprise. What then? Why, even without their heads they wouldn't have been able to understand a thing, notwithstanding the fact that it was precisely their heads which, more than anything else, impeded their understanding. No Sir, this is a schism. Ever since Peter the Great we've had two schisms—the upper and the lower."

"And certainly the people would have done well, for it was certainly their heads which, more than anything else, impeded their understanding."

"This... isn't so..." observed Granovsky, assuming a dignified air, "I cannot of course give you an answer to this and, for that matter, I don't know who can; not because I actually can't, but because my hands are tied." (Which leaves Shaposhnikov nonplussed;** he smiles venomously.)

Here! N.B.

It all starts out by Granovsky being terribly afraid that he won't be invited. In front of Shaposhnikov, he gives himself independent airs. Enter the Prince.

The Prince, having sat there for a while listening to the irritable Shaposhnikov and the pedantic Granovsky, asks him to have dinner at his house the next day, with his wife and nephew. Astonishment about the nephew having already arrived.

---

[9] Ernest I. Biron (1690–1772). He had great influence on the Empress Anna Ivanovna. Her ten year reign has come to be known as "Bironovshchina." He was exiled after her death.

* Literally, "twisted off their heads," thus permitting a pun in the next sentence.

** Since the Russian text leaves it open whether Shaposhnikov is the subject or the object of this sentence, the translation might also read: "Shaposhnikov has left him nonplussed."

Enter the nephew. Biting remarks aimed at Granovsky. (He considers himself immeasurably superior to Granovsky, does so naïvely and quite sincerely; can't help finding him ridiculous. Avidly listens to gossip.)

The next day, at the Princess's, he displays his bad manners and makes fun of everybody. The Prince finally stops him. They quarrel. Whereas the Bride shows herself most favorably disposed toward the Nephew. On the following day, she has a showdown with the Prince.

Before the dinner party, Granovsky is terribly afraid of his nephew's raillery at tomorrow's dinner.

44 *The last, February 16* <1870>

Granovsky the bridegroom's nameday. He has a slightly swollen cheek and doesn't feel quite well. *He is toying with a piece of jewelry.* All the time he is meaning to get down to work. A letter from his son, and he is afraid. He awaits the Princess's impending visit with trepidation. To keep up appearances, he is carrying on a lively conversation with the bilious Shaposhnikov. Everybody arrives at the same time. The Princess asks Shaposhnikov to keep talking. He has received a proclamation. The Prince mentions his son. Granovsky (and everybody else) is surprised that his son has already arrived. Must be he has stopped at his brother's. Enter the son: about the brother, about poetry, "I'm looking at him, that elegant snivel."

"I'd give him a failing mark."

Granovsky, throughout the novel, is constantly bickering with his son about leadership*; then suddenly realizes that his son hasn't been joking at all, but on the contrary, doing things all along.

The guests are leaving. Granovsky's son and Shaposhnikov are staying. The Prince. A comic situation. "Business—really, why should we discuss it here?" They leave. (Along the way, the Prince with his fiancée.) At his brother's, *Shaposhnikov* and *The Student.* They make fun of his brother, and a confidential talk. *Shaposhnikov* refuses. (The Student speaks ill of the Bride in the brother's presence, and in Shaposhnikov's eyes he begins to take shape as a person suspicious of everyone, and a cad. Shaposhnikov ~~who is employed as a private tutor~~ has a

---

* The Russian word, *verkhovenstvo,* is significant in that it contains the key to the symbolism of the name *Verkhovensky.* Note that *verkhovenstvo* is a rather rare word.

mother and a drunken wife at home. Shaposhnikov has fallen in love with the Ward.)

The relationship between the Prince and Shaposhnikov ought to be revealed by the narrator.

Shaposhnikov hasn't even declared his love (but the Prince is still jealous). As to the Prince, it is assumed that there isn't anything doing at all. *The Student* tries to calm the Prince down.

The 2d part reveals all the relationships in which the Bride is involved (there is a soirée at their place). Dinner at the Princess's. She has a heart-to-heart talk with the Prince. Stormy sessions with the generals of the house. She sees a lot of *the Student,* the main reason for this being ostensibly that she has brought the proclamations with her. But *the Student* does not respond and does not pay any attention to her. She sends the Prince over to *the Student in that certain* matter. It gives him a scare: "She hasn't blabbed out the secret, has she?" She does blab it all out to Shaposhnikov when the Student fails to come and see her. Shaposhnikov tells everything to the Student, who is very angry. Meeting with the teachers. (The first is easy.)

Meanwhile in town, rumors about proclamations. Projects of arson. The Prince penetrates into these affairs, being against them.

2. Meanwhile there is a soirée at the Princess's. Granovsky's tirade on poetry. *The Student* teases him about his marrying *the Prince's sins.* (He also teases the Prince saying that he has heard about his sins from Shaposhnikov. The Prince slaps Shaposhnikov's face. Gossip.)

3. Shaposhnikov, after having had his face slapped, openly protests at the final meeting. (He has been arguing against it even before, in conversations with the Bride and with the Prince.)

3d part. Shaposhnikov wants to inform the police. The murder. The Beauty comes running to the Student, who sends her away and leaves all by himself. The Prince suddenly marries Granovsky's fiancée.

Granovsky—diarrhea.

3 *Shaposhnikov* and *the Prince* exchange caustic remarks to the utmost limit.

The proclamation, an act of sacrilege, and *the fire.* (After the fire Shaposhnikov wants to inform the police.)

N.B. Granovsky is ideally in favor of incendiarism. "If you really want to act, then act." Shaposhnikov tells him about himself (confesses)—

Here, *the most important*—father and son quarrel, open clashes at the various parties.

However, the son still manages to instill in Granovsky a feeling of shame about his marriage, which leads to an argument between Granovsky and the Princess. Yet Granovsky *still* strikes a pose and, with ostensible magnanimity says *that he won't believe it.* "If you don't believe it, then why are you raising all this fuss, and whimpering so much?" says the Princess. The princess also complains to Granovsky that the Beauty has become involved with the Student. This causes Granovsky to take a more respectful view of his son, whom he now admires and envies. His son openly tells him all these things.

Yet ~~Colonel~~ Miliukov already knows, and has spread it all around, that today Granovsky has been "polishing up the old horse's teeth."

Not a general, but a colonel, *her* stepfather, who has married her old mother for her money. Rabid liberalism (her mother remains silent for the time being). Makes up to both the Student and the Prince. (~~The Student~~ The Colonel has noticed the Student's attitude toward *her;* he is paying court to *her* because she rules over her mother.)

Captain Kartuzov—a Sevastopolian, a cousin of Granovsky's. A son of Anna's sister.*

Granovsky is talking about his wedding: "This isn't a settled matter, it is a delicate matter."

46 *February 18* <1870>

The Princess has just had a heart-to-heart talk with Granovsky. Little is being said openly, yet both Shaposhnikov and the Prince know about it. The Ward is willing. The Prince loves her silently, but has never declared his love. Early in the novel the Prince is undecided as to how he ought to act; but it seems that he is inclined to give in. The notion that his mother is marrying off the Ward to Granovsky greatly astonishes him: up to this point he has been silently, yet most terribly, jealous of Shaposhnikov. Whereas the Ward, wishing to avoid any damage to the Prince's career, has failed to dispel his notions regarding Shaposhnikov. Yet she would avidly have listened to the Prince declaring to her his love, even though she has made up her mind not to do anything that might damage his career. But the Prince is proud, dis-

* Or, "A son of his sister Anna."

trustful, terribly shy, sickly, and very much under his mother's thumb. He hates Shaposhnikov all the time. The Student has managed to find out about that hatred of his.

The Prince has been away for a long time, about three months, deceived by the Ward's false confession, ~~made~~ made in a state of vexation, that she loves Shaposhnikov. He hasn't been home (in 6 months) all summer. When he returns in August, he suddenly learns about her betrothal to Granovsky.

Meanwhile the Beauty and her family have returned from abroad after a 1½ year stay. (A year earlier, the Princess was abroad also; she returned half a year before them.) The two mothers (childhood friends) had fixed the wedding. The Prince and the Beauty know about this decision. The Prince and his fiancée had stayed abroad longer. The Beauty still won't say either "yes" or "no." Two weeks before the Prince's return, when the Beauty had just arrived, the two mothers had again been discussing the matter (they were expecting the Prince), and the Beauty had learned about Granovsky. ~~(M.~~ She goes horseback riding with her stepfather.)

In the meantime the Beauty has met the Student abroad. Actually they had become acquainted while the Prince was still with her. Having returned herself, the Beauty tells the Prince immediately upon his arrival that "he is late" (she says nothing of the Student, but the Prince guesses it himself, finding her very strange) .

N.B. The Prince hadn't suggested anything to the Beauty; it is she who *(tactlessly)* writes him that he has come too late. The Prince explains his position to her, but she isn't at all embarrassed and shocks the Prince with her conceit and liberal nonsense.

The Prince announces the Student's arrival, and Granovsky, too, has received a letter and shows that he is worried (there had been an argument before). Granovsky is ashamed of his relatives and is worried about them. His sisters had been sent away and were receiving a pension. But later, he is proud of his son's successes and bickers with him about erudition.

At Granovsky's nameday party the Princess accidentally reveals the betrothal of Granovsky and his bride. *(Actually, she was only planning it.)* Shaposhnikov, the Prince, and the Beauty are all present. The Ward has a fit. Granovsky's son appears on the scene. Impertinences. Everybody is amazed by the way the Beauty treats him.

During that same soirée the Bride turns down the Prince's proposal.

Granovsky on poetry.

47 The Student ~~talks~~ has a showdown with Shaposhnikov.

Contacts with Uspensky.

Shaposhnikov declares to the Prince ~~and assures~~ that the Ward has never loved him, but that she loves him, the Prince.

The Tragic Mother has a heart-to-heart talk with her daughter and the Colonel—~~Shaposhnikov~~ The Student is getting chummy with the Colonel, who is making up to the Student ~~because~~ in order to ~~his daughter~~ please his daughter.

A break between mother and daughter.

A break between the Prince and the Princess—a big argument, they lock themselves in their rooms. Then, to the Captain. A terrible scandal.

The betrothal has been set to take place at the Princess's. It doesn't come off. The son makes fun of his father. Granovsky plays the magnanimous.

The Princess breaks with Granovsky for his having given in. Rumors about his son. (In town, proclamations, acts of sacrilege, arson.)

Granovsky has a showdown with his son.

The Beauty suddenly reveals to her mother that she is going to marry Granovsky's son.

Granovsky treats his son with respect.

The murder of Shaposhnikov, who had wanted to report everything to the police.

The Student escapes, having frightened both the Colonel and Granovsky.

Granovsky's death.

Both *the Student* and the Beauty are inhuman and ruthless to their families, and even to each other. The Governor failed to take any action against *the Student up to that point* because he did not want to antagonize the Princess.

The Captain gets spat at and laughed at, as she flees with *the Student.* The Captain finds out about everything, including Shaposhnikov's death. He informs the police and goes out of his mind. The Captain is arrested.

~~The Prince leaves.~~ The Chronicler visits him in the hospital. The cockroach.*

The Prince marries the Ward.

N.B. The Prince makes friends with the Captain from that very

---

* Or, conceivably, a person named Tarakanov.

moment when the Captain learns that the Beauty has rejected his proposal.

The Prince befriends Shaposhnikov and the Captain, but not in public.

{The novel has the form of an epic poem about how Granovsky wanted to get married, but didn't.

{Or, an explanatory account of how *all this* happened. Start with the proclamations. All in the form of a *narrative*—as simple and concise as possible.

From a provincial chronicle. Start from how everybody is discussing this whole business, and how so-and-so-many were carried away by it all, and how people were wondering about many things, such as broken-up marriages, and suicides, and how we could possibly have such an *échevelée*[10] literature. Just as they are saying God knows what about the last days of Timofei N. Granovsky (it is known for a positive fact now that the Princess had been paying him a pension). Whereas actually, everything happened quite simply.

At odds with the Governor. The Governor is out of town at first, but then he arrives and introduces doubly severe measures. He starts with the Captain (who happens to be the most innocent of the lot), while completely overlooking the Student. Some people have actually claimed that he really overlooked him on purpose.

On the day of the nameday party (the first day of the novel) the Captain is frustrated also.

I was the only other person present at Granovsky's during his passionate exchange with Shaposhnikov. And altogether, whenever I am giving an account of conversations which took place between just two persons, don't pay any attention to this: ~~I know~~ Either I have positive facts, or I am, perhaps, *inventing* them myself, but in any case, I can assure you that everything is true.

The system which I have adopted is that of a *chronicle.*

Thus, for instance, Nechaev enters. Here, what his face looks like will be given, and what kind of an impression he made on me. They used to say that he had a wart somewhere—but nothing of the kind; but if, as they say, an agent of the police actually let him slip across the border, this isn't surprising at all—particularly if it is true that he

---

10 French: "disordered."

was so clever at disguising himself: really, there was nothing special about him.

Even the opinion regarding police agents.

(Whereas the Beauty, poor fugitive who had followed Shaposhnikov, did get stopped. ? She had fled with the Captain. The Captain was brought back (Ushakov[11] had reported everything to the police). (The Prince paid him a visit.)

N.B. (A description of the fire, for instance: "Can you imagine that, at the time I... It started at Nikola's place, a wooden shed being the first building on fire—he is a local merchant.")

About Ushakov—quick-tempered and fervent (he lets slip the secret <of the conspiracy> during a conversation—this I shall report in his own words).

I have also talked to the Student.

All in all, the Student's opinions and doctrines were such—(two million heads, etc.) Whereas Ushakov went even further, etc.

N.B. Whenever the meetings of the conspirators are mentioned, the Chronicler adds this note: "It is possible that they had more meetings —of course they did—I don't know, but presumably the actual course of events was this..." (And here then, often in the form of a narrative, the details of how Nechaev talked them into accepting his ideas, how the Beauty smuggled the proclamations across the border, how the Captain is guilty of nothing at all, how Timofei Nikolaevich Granovsky initially agreed with their ideas, but eventually funked out disgracefully, about the Princess's thoughtlessness, about the Tragic Mother's suspicions, how the Prince apparently knew everything, how they fabricated a false accusation to implicate the Prince, how the Student aroused the Prince's jealousy, while telling his father (Granovsky) that the Prince was going to kill *Shaposhnikov*—(which is why Timofei Nikolaevich came up with his absurd accusation of the Prince in Shaposhnikov's death), how he later got scared and died of diarrhea.

N.B. Or, the Chronicler reports, in his narrative, the argument between Shaposhnikov and Granovsky. Not the whole conversation, but in the manner of *narrator's comment,* so that the Chronicler says: "Shaposhnikov's opinion was such-and-such (about Chatsky)."

---

[11] First reference and sketch of Shigalyov.

N.B. When he speaks about Granovsky in general, as he describes him in the beginning of his narrative, he has this comment: "Unfortunately, our contemporary public must be reminded even of people of this calibre. Why is it that we tend to skim along our present so lightly, while altogether forgetting our past?"

The Student talks his father into believing that he is covering up for the Prince's sins and causes him to quarrel with the Princess (he has his reasons for doing it).

??? What reasons?? N.B.

In the middle or in the end of the novel, the Chronicler himself makes this comment: "Altogether then, the Student had this end in mind; however, this is based on Ushakov's testimony. I know nothing about their affairs in Switzerland, yet I believe to have defined correctly the essence of this movement, its philosophy, the meaning behind its actions: I can vouch for that."

"Granovsky has gotten a little out of hand and, I'll have to admit it, he's been having altercations with the Princess."

I know for sure that he was afraid the Princess might not come to see him: "She has brought up the subject of this marriage herself, and now she has quit seeing me."

N.B. "I am writing this for you—since you have expressed your desire to learn about these events."

Shaposhnikov says: "We can have neither family, nor familial virtues, because a family cannot be cosmopolitan and is destroyed the very moment it is severed from its native land. And we have cursed our native land; in fact, we deserve credit if we are merely indifferent toward it."

Granovsky being chewed out by the Governor, a comical figure.

Nechaev is a man who can't be put out of his countenance by aristocratic condescension. The Princess reads his character, and is making up to Nechaev.

The Princess used to play a role in town, especially while a relative of hers was governor. But now, *for no good reason at all*, she has an altercation with the Governor, a mild-mannered man of average social background. (The Governor unwittingly shares Granovsky's fate.) Nevertheless, the Princess had never actually formed a party—there wasn't a good enough reason for it, and moreover, there was nobody available to be recruited into such a party.

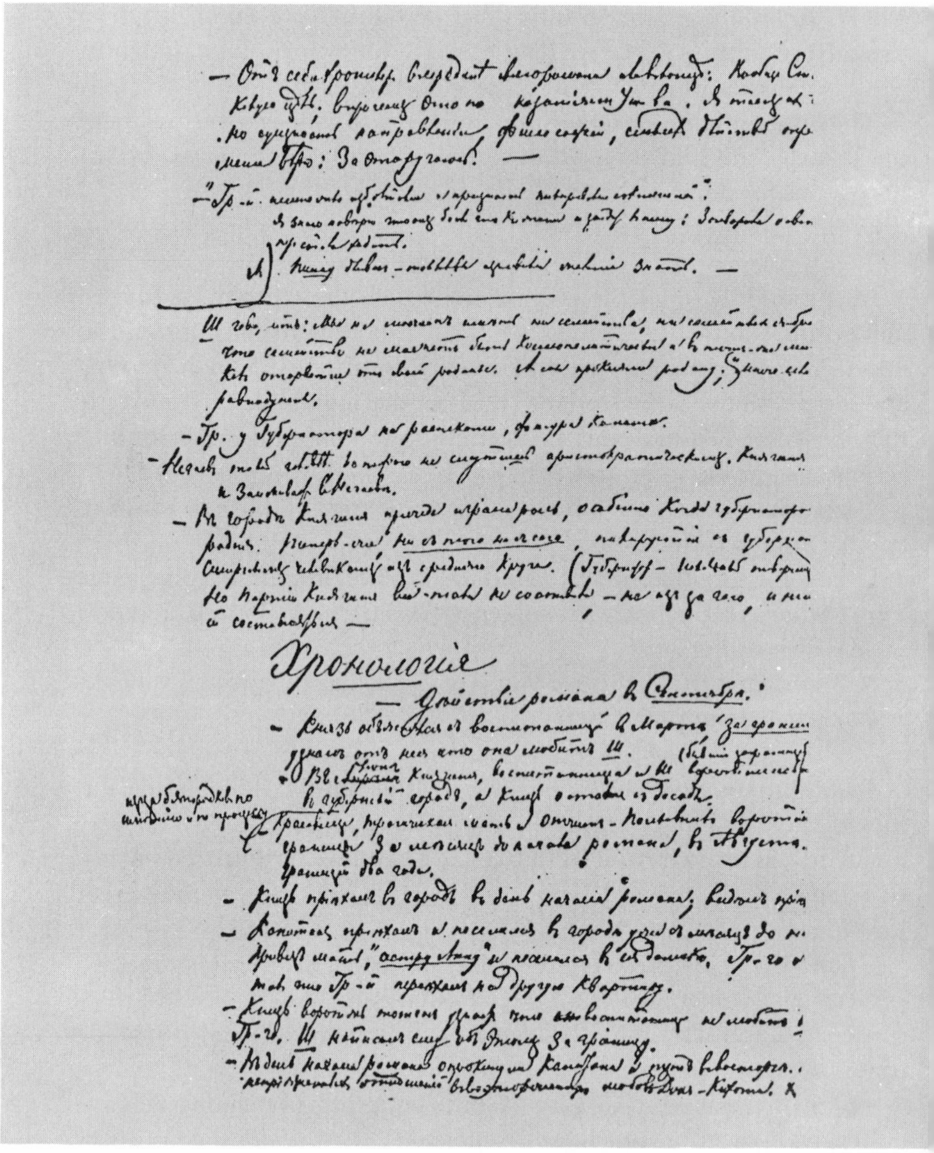

Notebook Page 49, Notebook 2

The page is representative of Dostoevsky's even and orderly handwriting. The reader can see the various devices Dostoevsky used for emphasis and reflection: underlinings, the capitalization and isolation of the word "chronology" in the middle of the page, and the frequent use of a line drawn to separate comments (expressed in these notes by spacing).

Chronology

The action of the novel takes place in *September*.

The Prince had that heart-to-heart talk with the Ward in March, *abroad*. That's when he learned that she loved Shaposhnikov.

In ~~April~~ June the Princess, the Ward, and Shaposhnikov (who had been abroad for half a year) returned from abroad to this provincial town, while the Prince stayed behind, vexed.

Because of some trouble concerning his estate, and also a lawsuit.

The Beauty, the Tragic Mother, and her stepfather the Colonel returned from abroad a month before the beginning of the novel, in August. They had been abroad for two years.

The Prince arrives in town on the day when the action of the novel begins; he has met Granovsky's son, who has also just arrived.

The Captain has come to town and established residence there a month or so prior to the beginning of the novel. He has brought with him his mother and his "*sister Anna*," and is living in her cottage. Granovsky is greatly troubled by this, so that he moves to a different flat.

The Prince, upon his return, immediately learns that ~~he~~ the Ward does not love Shaposhnikov, but that she has, in the meantime, become engaged to Granovsky. Shaposhnikov had written him about that while he was still abroad.

On the day when the novel begins, the Captain has been virtually knocked over <by some happy news> and is beside himself with delight. A change from hostility to enthusiastic, Quixotic love.

Begin to explain this change, say, in the second part, through the Chronicler, *leaving everything as is*, and with psychological thoroughness. Then, put it all together and connect it with the rest of the action. But in the first part, give a mere sketchy outline of the Captain, yet absolutely present him as an oddball.

After the Prince returns, the Princess immediately makes plans for a betrothal. But the Beauty, as early as the first day, politely informs him in a letter: "You have arrived too late." The Prince, even abroad, had never been very close to her, much to the displeasure of his mother, who had imagined that, having stayed abroad, he would be with and around the Beauty all the time. Simultaneously, she has decided to carry out an old project of hers: get the Ward married to Granovsky. She knows and senses that her son loves the Ward. She has a heart-to-heart talk with him and says: "This simply cannot be!" Psychologically, on this mother-son relationship.

Everything happened by accident.

Shaposhnikov has an alcoholic wife. Shaposhnikov treats her in a Christian manner: forgiving and admonishing her. She is jealous of the Ward. When the latter comes to see Shaposhnikov (on the occasion that she has been, accidentally and falsely, declared to be ~~the wife~~ the fiancée of Granovsky) and cries in his presence, Shaposhnikov's wife tells the Prince (who is jealous of Shaposhnikov) and Granovsky about it. Granovsky makes a scene, meaning that he displays a noble disbelief. "Then why have you raised a scandal in the first place?" says the Princess to him.

The Student, on the other hand, in his cynicism is convinced that the Ward had her good reasons to visit with Shaposhnikov, and that the two have a liaison going.

But the Prince who, while still abroad, received a letter from Shaposhnikov about the actual state of affairs and who, moreover, on the very first day of the novel is given a complete explanation by Shaposhnikov at the latter's flat, is still indignant when he hears that the Ward has visited Shaposhnikov. He strikes Shaposhnikov.

First the Student derives a cynical pleasure from spreading the news (which he believes to be true) about the Ward's liaison with Shaposhnikov, and secondly, finds it expedient, *in the interest of the cause,* to embroil the Prince with Shaposhnikov, so that the murder would be ascribed to him.

N.B. The Student does not go into hiding prior to the murder, because he thinks that the Prince will be suspected. (He hasn't wound up his business with the factory workers as yet.) But ~~about the Prince~~ the murder affair takes a different turn, and then the Student makes his escape.

The Student does not want to marry the Beauty at all. He reveals to his father that the Ward has a liaison with Shaposhnikov, and that she had one with the Prince before. Granovsky inadvertently blabs this out to the Princess, who demands an explanation. She won't believe it, but she still persecutes the Ward. The latter declares that she won't become Granovsky's wife (after their engagement). The Princess is furious; she says that she <the Ward> will yet be ~~betrothed~~ Granovsky's wife. Yet she is glad that she can now at least tell her son, that is the Prince, that his beloved has an affair going with Shaposhnikov. Hence the slap in the face. But the Prince won't believe it; he has a showdown with the Ward. (It might be that the foolish, cruel, but generous, Beauty helps the Prince in discovering the truth, namely, that the Ward has always loved him, the Prince, but has been concealing it.) Definitive showdown between the Prince and the Ward; they vow that they love each other. The Captain (the Beauty is already at his place), Shaposhnikov, and the Prince are triumphant about ~~the wedding~~ the new wedding. *The Student* is also there, and suddenly Shaposhnikov is murdered. The Beauty has no knowledge of it, she is shocked, but flees, following *the Student,* and is arrested. Whereas *the Student* has made a fool of everybody, including the Beauty.

N.B. The Beauty did not initially know about the murder of Shaposhnikov; it shocks her, but it also instils in her (her anemic little brain is at fault here) even more admiration for *the Student.* As for the fact that *the Student* has abandoned her, it positively fills her with even more awe for him.

1) When the Beauty has run off to the Captain and a scandal is brewing in town, everybody thinks that Nechaev wants to marry her, and this is how this bit of news reaches the Governor: the Tragic Mother complains to the Governor. Yet Nechaev remains aloof, so that the Beauty is bewildered and sad. But not very much so, for she is a frivolous creature. Therefore the Prince, 2) has a serious talk with Nechaev. as does Granovsky, which merely throws both of them off: if he isn't staying to lead his intrigue to a successful end and marry, then to what other end? But later Nechaev, who is at first evasive about the whole thing, realizes (it is the Chronicler himself who reaches this conclusion) that a would-be elopement with the Beauty will divert people's attention from his real aims, and he begins to support this notion himself.

Chronicler's comment: Nechaev was actually so naïve that it was really Uspensky who first gave him this idea. 3) And even after it has been suggested to him, he still continues to make excuses and tries to laugh it off, for he despises everybody so much that he considers it superfluous to put up appearances for their sake. Yet the more he jokes about it, and shows his indifference, the more they believe him.

Obviously, chance has been favoring him.

Chronicler's comment: Earlier, there wasn't a chance to write a novel here in Russia, but now, what with publicity (yet it is my opinion that the new order, too, is conducive to the emergence of the most romantic *échevelées* stories).

Mazurik ?,* Akimov with buckshot, Golubenko <is killed> by the women—poisons, daggers, drowning—

A question about the Student: is he really sharp, or isn't he? He is going to be a really sharp one some day, but he isn't right now, he's still a youngster. Only chance and our milieu helped him to achieve his success.

What does *the Student's* intrigue actually amount to?

Why, there really isn't much of an intrigue either. He has, first of all, his cause: proclamations, the factory workers, fires, threesomes, etc. Golubov—

But, in order to get these things going, he must stay in town for a certain time, and he knows that he is being watched and that he may get caught (for he is organizing and setting up "the cause").

Therefore, with the inherent tact of the organizer, he studies the locality, personalities, makes notes, gets to know people who cross his way, and their interests (this, he really enjoys doing). Finally, he understands perfectly well that, having become involved in these interests, he is diverting people's attention from his other, *truly important* activities. When Nechaev has brought in Miliukov with the fire, he is perfectly at ease. He tells them so himself. He is so successful in this respect that up to the very moment of his departure nobody asks him: "What is it you are doing in town?" (Except perhaps, occasionally, Granovsky.) Nor do people notice his connections with the schoolteachers and with Uspensky. The Governor himself, seeing him at the Princess's and in her company (as well as at the house of that rich heiress, the Beauty), is convinced that he has come to these parts to settle down, to start a career, and to marry the Ward. (The Governor, and so everybody in town, *at first* thought that *the Student* had entered the Princess's employ, having struck up an acquaintance with her abroad, and that, having enmeshed that oddball and idiot, the Prince, in this friendship with him, he was now, in compliance with the Princess's instructions, trying to talk him into marrying the heiress.)

Everybody in town, including the Governor, believes those rumors about Shaposhnikov and his liaison with the Ward, and blame him for it. As for Granovsky, they just laugh at him. They assume that *the Student* is running the whole show. Later, when the Beauty runs off to the Captain, the whole town immediately "*figures out*" that she hasn't

---

* This could be a surname; but dialectally, *mazurik* means "crook, jailbird."

run away to the Captain at all, that the Captain is only a dupe, that it is actually the Student who has enticed her to get married to him, and everybody says that he is "quite a guy." Even the Governor has words of praise for him and invites him over. The Governor, of course, is very glad that the Princess has been made a fool of (the Tragic Mother and the Bishop have complained to the Governor).

All this the Chronicler explains in his own comments, midway through the novel, supporting it by specific traits:

N.B. Perhaps he will eventually become a man of action, but right now he is still too young. Shame on the milieu. *The Student* is nobody's fool, but he is handicapped, most of all, by his arrogance and nihilistic superciliousness toward people. He does not care to learn about reality. (Anecdotes, based on rumors, about how those very same factory workers made a fool out of him, while he left them, confident that there were going to be barricades after the French fashion. As for Uspensky, he never even suspected that the man had a heart and that he might turn informer.)

Like other nihilists, he never bothers to become concerned with questions of decency, or lack of it. It does not interest him in the least, and neither do other such fine details. The only thing that matters, he thinks, is that *one must* act now, failing to realize that even a man of action ought to at least look around himself once before beginning to act.

And this is an amazing fact: The Student was so incapable of conducting a farsighted intrigue that he never even suspected it might be a good idea to make some diversionary maneuvers, and was so contemptuous of everybody in his way that he actually did not take any special precautions and committed a multitude of blunders (describe these, the blunders, that is).

The Princess and Granovsky both have a hunch regarding *the Student's* criminal intentions (on account of the fires and the proclamations, among other things; the Prince, too, has a pretty good idea, but he is the silent type; the Colonel-stepfather is stupid enough not to notice anything at all).

He has no idea at all.

As regards Shaposhnikov, he is not a man of action either, just another windbag. He knows that himself, yet he also despises Nechaev's efficiency, for it is based on nothing but stupidity, total ignorance, and on his being unfamiliar with reality. Meanwhile Granovsky talks a lot about action, saying: "If it's got to be fires, let it be fires; if it's got to be action, let's act!" N.B. (This puts him into a comical situation, for he is saying this in front of his son, not suspecting at all that it is his own son and "those good-for-nothing Uspenskys" who have set these fires. Later, consumed by shame and fear, he dies of diarrhea.)

While Shaposhnikov says to himself: "I'll show you how to get things done. I may be a windbag, but even I can get a thing done: *I'll turn you in!*" (he says this both to himself, and out loud). ~~But~~ Nechaev has enough sense to realize that Shaposhnikov is the one person capable of such action, and immediately decides to kill him.

In the Student's opinion, Uspensky is merely a person quite incapable of action, which is why he turned informer.

Granovsky dies (it is a shame to have to admit it) more from fear than from regret, or even hurt vanity.

The main idea, however (that is, the pathos of the novel), is focused in the Prince and the Ward—*new people* who have stood the test and who decide to start a *new* and regenerated life. The Prince discusses this with Shaposhnikov right before the latter's death. He expresses ideas to this effect before the Ward, the Princess, and Granovsky. The Prince wants to work (that proud Prince!), a notion which breaks his mother's heart.

Granovsky has been the Prince's tutor and has brought him up on *those* principles. But now, upon his mother's request, he is dissuading him himself: "Mais distinguons."

The Prince has a strong character, and a stubborn character, but an impressionable, melancholy, and shy soul. The Princess understands him, Granovsky does not. The Princess and Granovsky talk a lot about the Prince, and disagree about him.

53 At the improvised engagement party, Granovsky strikes the poetic pose of a father before the Ward (on February 20, the first day of the novel).

But the Ward hesitates to refute this from the very first word, because everybody was avoiding saying that one important word.

Later, Granovsky plays the role of the magnanimous man who is returning the Ward her liberty, etc. Here, though, she cuts him short, pointing out that he never did have any rights to her.

The Ward has a very firm character, yet she is also tender and generous. Immoderately proud. Later she explains everything to the Prince: ~~proud~~ she has loved him, yet concealed it, out of pride, for he hadn't told her that he loves her. (Also, from pride, and because of the question: will he have the strength to keep his vow?) Later, he failed to declare his love because he was jealous of Shaposhnikov.

The Prince tells her: "I am a plain man, and not famous, but we shall be worthy and fine people. Besides, now I really know my strength. However, we'll have to approach mother delicately."

N.B. *Problem*: (Adorn and build up this couple—the Prince and the Ward. That's where we run into trouble. The Prince is preparing himself to become a Justice of the Peace.)

More poetry.

? N.B. (For instance, tell how Uspensky gets to talk about how a non-Russian will start to save money, and how the purpose of saving money is to save enough—the Prince is listening, smiles, but remains silent.)

The Prince, for instance, never gets into arguments with the atheists, although he passionately believes in God. He is stubborn and independent in the extreme.

Generally speaking, toward the end of the novel, no one suspects that the Prince will reveal so much strength of character and so much passion.

Tomorrow, make an outline of all the characters, i.e., the Prince and the Ward—a modest ideal and genuinely good people.

Granovsky is not a genuine ideal. He is passé, self-destructive, full of false pride, a caricature.

Shaposhnikov is the restless type, the product of a collision between a bookish world and reality, a man who has embraced his faith with passion, yet does not know what to do. Much beauty.

2) He wanted to kill the Ward. And suffered from it. Later, it is precisely for this reason that it is thought the Prince may have killed Shaposhnikov. Actually, the Prince had been down on his knees before him, begging his forgiveness.—

3) The Prince is an aristocrat who says: "I hate and despise them all."

All in all, create the portrait of the Prince.

He has lost his estate: "I'm not shedding any tears over my lost estate, but neither will I relinquish what is mine."

4) Have self-respect and be scrupulously honest; be a true Prince.

? N.B. He has informed the police about "the one who bites."

etc., to everyone his epithet, but first and foremost *about the Prince,* two or three major traits.

(It goes without saying that he is no ideal, being jealous, stubborn, proud and persistent, taciturn and sickly, i.e., melancholy (tragic, many doubts). Even his desire to marry the Ward wasn't, God knows, strong, for he was fully aware of his character and knew that she wouldn't be able to stand it. He had been on friendly terms with her two years earlier, but later their friendship broke up. Toward the end, in a showdown with her, he demands full submission on her part. He had not acted earlier, nor shown his real worth, because he was still trying to get the right angle on things.)

54 On the relationship between the Prince and Nechaev: both have partially understood the Prince. Nechaev tells Uspensky that one must beware of the Prince.

The Prince, in terribly proud and stubborn fashion, expresses his will before his mother. Even she had not expected this much. Everybody had been thinking that he was under her thumb, and now he suddenly reveals his real self, yet with human feeling, and sensibly.

The Princess, in considering the marriage between her son and the Beauty, had counted on her son's prudence and practical sense, his lack of poetic feeling, more than on anything else.

Yet that's just what he is: a poet; he bitterly loathes all atheists, and *believes* in an embittered way.

He would like to become a muzhik and join the Raskolniki.

He manages his estates. But there is nothing to manage.

N.B. The Princess was actually inclined to disbelieve that the Prince could love the Ward—he is much too unpoetical and prudent for that. But there was one fact that made her think better of it, and put a doubt into her mind. So then, she immediately decides to play it safe and get the Ward married to Granovsky.

The Prince has been in Petersburg during those past two months (there are some claims pending against him in court).

Shaposhnikov had written to him in Petersburg, not abroad.

The Prince has perfectly well-rounded and long-settled ideas about people and events. Granovsky doesn't even suspect what the Prince's opinion of him might be. He keeps silent, then suddenly, on a certain occasion, corrects Granovsky when the latter quotes from a book. The Prince has formed an equally correct conception of the events that are taking place around him.

In a serious discussion with Shaposhnikov, *he makes his views on things and on people completely clear.* "I shall be a plain, honest, and new man" (?). He frightens Shaposhnikov with the fervor and hidden fire of his soul, also with his hidden scars, from prolonged savage and gloomy silence. He is a man who is capable of anything—there *are* such people among us.

He avoids discussing Nechaev with Shaposhnikov, and only listens to Shaposhnikov.

The Prince is having a close look at Nechaev and begins to worry—(what's needed here is poetry). The burnt-down town troubles him. *He decides to make up even with Shaposhnikov in order to* have a sincere talk with him about his suspicions. "I knew that I was at fault, yet I didn't ask your forgiveness. Shame was holding me back." He is a loyal citizen in the highest degree. (It isn't true at all that he wants to be *only* a simple and good family man.)

N.B. Although Nechaev at one time begins to suspect the Prince he ultimately fails to consider him, both out of contempt for him and from his general thoughtlessness.

When the Prince is publicly charged with the murder of Shaposhnikov, the Prince immediately guesses the whole truth, goes to see Uspensky, induces him to confess, and in a forceful manner submits the whole case to the Governor.

And generally, it is the Prince who discovers the whole plot. It is the Prince also, who speaks of the boyar party.

The Princess has been raving about the boyar party for some time and takes up with Nechaev because nihilists and boyars tend to come to terms. She is convinced that the Prince, too, is a boyar.

And when Granovsky is about to "return her liberty" to the Ward (he is trying to strike a noble pose when things have gotten to where he can't do anything else!) the Princess, then still at the height of her nihilist leanings, is willing to set Granovsky's son on his own father in order to humiliate him (thus avenging herself for their friendship of many years). N.B. Here the Chronicler inserts, on his own part, a tirade on hatred bred by beneficence, and how this happens quite often. To exalt his son. So, when Granovsky starts his tirade about poetry and the Madonna of Raphael, she says bluntly: "Why, this is all nonsense, nonsense! And they've simply made up that Madonna, too!"—

N.B. The Tragic Mother cuts down the Princess in terrible fashion when the Beauty has run off to the Captain.

N.B. Like a madhouse—the doctors are biting each other. The cause of it is the depth of economic and social change, and the disorganized nature of this process.—

5 *Granovsky*

N.B. "Wasn't Granovsky's speech about the Madonna marvelous? Surely he had this *morceau* worked out beforehand."

The Princess tells Granovsky, during her nihilist period: "We've both been smothering each other with praise; our whole friendship has been based on mutual flattery."

Well, that certainly was not true: Granovsky did love the Princess. Perhaps because he had gotten used to her, and because he was such a sniveling weakling.

Granovsky actually stooped so low as to first exchange caustic remarks and eventually quarrel with his son, like when the Princess set one on the other for her own amusement.

What is terrible is that I exist.

Granovsky had understood the happiness and depth of life immeasurably more loftily than many others, but he had grown shallow, and terribly lazy. He was a poet, and profound in his inspiration, yet in him, as in all men of his kind, the seed had fallen upon sand. A good parallel to his character could be found in his physiognomy, which could change so rapidly and so unexpectedly.

Finding himself at the short end of an argument with his son, at the Princess's, Granovsky begins to cry.

Later, when everything has changed and the Beauty has run away, all her nihilism is gone and she again rushes to Granovsky. All her nihilism is gone. He turns up his nose first, but then recovers his composure and plays the magnanimous.

VII
Shaposhnikov and Granovsky against Nechaev

These notes were written in late February, at approximately the same time as those of the previous section. One will notice, however, that the Student is now called Nechaev, which he will be called until the very late notes.

These notes consist largely of arguments by Granovsky and Shaposhnikov against Nechaev's program. Nechaev himself tells us almost nothing about his program, and what we learn of it comes largely from what Granovsky and Shaposhnikov attribute to it: the loss of personality, communality of living and loving, the submission of the individual will to the collective will, and the destruction of God, the Church, national identity, and marriage. Most of these specifics—more positively put forth—were taken by Dostoevsky from the commonplace pronouncements of radical critics, and most of them are to be found in the works of Chernyshevsky. The historical Nechaev is close to the way he appears in these notes: someone who promises nothing but the principle of the axe and the revolution.

Granovsky argues against Nechaev's "program" on grounds of historical and cultural continuity; Shaposhnikov on grounds of essential national identity, which has been lost by the intellectuals, but preserved in the people. According to Granovsky, even a just program of such dimensions takes centuries to be accepted; and only ignorance and madness can believe that men will go automatically and unquestioningly into Godlessness, communality, and the loss of individuality. Shaposhnikov's scorn for Nechaev's program is even more heated and devastating: it is not history and culture that will prevent Nechaev from instituting his program, but the essential nature of the Russian people, who—forgotten and discounted by the intelligentsia—have preserved a knowledge of what is true and will reject what is false.

Shaposhnikov's ideas about national identity are close to those that Shatov will enunciate in the final version, and they are close to what Dostoevsky himself believed in. Despite the fact that Belinsky is damned in these notes and elsewhere, much of what Shaposhnikov says—and what Dostoevsky believed in—flows from Belinsky's own statements on national identity (*narodnost'*). Writing in the 1830's, Belinsky believed that Russian national identity—and a literature to express it—was imminent, and he believed that such national identity came to birth in history and not in the arbitrary constructions of men's minds. Appollon Grigoriev, whose ideas were close to those of Dostoevsky, recognized the kinship of his views on national identity, as the concrete manifestation of the absolute in time and national fabric, to those of Belinsky and generously acknowledged his debt to Belinsky. Inspired by some personal animus against the great Russian critic, Dostoevsky was unable to do so.

Nechaev remains impassive and immovable before the rhetoric and arguments of Granovsky and Shaposhnikov. Alienated from the historical and cultural concreteness that Granovsky champions, and the universal and religious concreteness that Shaposhnikov (and Dostoevsky) champions, Nechaev–Peter Verkhovensky is the passionate abstract man—a terror Dostoevsky learned to fear in his encounter with him in these notebooks, and which we have learned to fear in the political arena of the twentieth century.

---

56 *Shaposhnikov, Granovsky, Nechaev.*
The Arabs.

Shaposhnikov says that we (Russians) no longer feel like being duped, and this is why our liberals call us reactionaries. And who is it our dear little liberals support, thinking up stories about Tashkentians:[1] who but those from whom they can obtain promotions and money, those from whom they may *get* something. Though not all of them think up stories about Tashkentians; there are those who are simply stupid.

---

[1] This phrase is a reference to M. E. Saltykov-Shchedrin's (1826–89) satire, *Gentlemen of Tashkent* (1869–72).

It is those, those precisely ~~whom they support~~, who are in such a comical situation: they are actually supporting despotism and abuse, though they aren't aware of it at all and sincerely believe that they are liberals!

Shaposhnikov says: "Why, this happened only ten years ago."

Nechaev: "Well ~~anyway~~, that is too far back; ancient history (and seriously so)."

Uspensky initially prides himself with their having killed Shaposhnikov, and is full of enthusiasm, but later he suddenly collapses and begins to cry.

Granovsky—he finally agrees to become a nihilist and says: "I am a nihilist." He has a serious talk with Uspensky, for he is afraid of his son; he drives over to Uspensky's place.

Rumors to the effect that Turgenev is a nihilist, and the Princess is now really ~~out of her mind~~ in a whirl.

?Arrival of the Great Writer.

Marko-Vovchok (the Artels).

Granovsky is told this: "Our generation was too literary. In our day an active (progressive) man could be nothing but a littérateur, or an observer of literature. The present generation is more inclined toward action. ("Ideas picked up in the streets!" replies Granovsky.)

Shaposhnikov, Nechaev, the Princess, Granovsky.

Shaposhnikov faces a situation where he must become a police spy (on spying, Karakozov).

Uspensky's wife has died. In our country, a policeman who is making an arrest is probably trembling with politeness as he makes his arrest, so as to appear more liberal. (<If the contrary is true,> this would be somewhere out in the sticks, or else if the policeman happens to be a ruffian.) And indeed, he is all trembling with politeness—because his head is utterly empty.

Nechaev: "In antigovernment proclamations—the more you lie, the more honest you appear. That's a trick used by Hertsen."

Shaposhnikov: "And by the Jesuits."

Nechaev: "The Jesuits are an extraordinarily clever Order and, once you've brought it up, there's a lot of truth in what they're doing. That's the only way to survive in this world."

The Princess (with fervor): "I have always thought so!"

"Think, and you'll get nowhere; so better make up your mind without thinking, with a blow of the axe—that's your whole low-down program."

QUESTIONS AND ANSWERS.

Granovsky:

"You are offering us happiness. Now, granted that you are perfectly right about the ultimate goal of your strivings (which is an absurd notion, but I'll let it pass for the moment), your very own proclamation shows how exceedingly immature and frivolous your minds are, and consequently, how very poorly suited for reaching that goal of yours. Don't you realize that such a regeneration of man as you are suggesting cannot take place, either individually or socially, anywhere nearly as easily or as quickly as you are confident it will? For you say that everything will be taken care of by the axe, and through pillage, whereas actually centuries won't be enough to make man renounce God, his love of Christ, his love and feeling of responsibility for his children, his individuality, and his desire to maintain it. For example, the social and legal provisions for security within the framework of the state have been worked out in the course of millennia, and yet, how very unsatisfactory are they everywhere, even today! In actual practice, even a universal and vital necessity such as this is developed and becomes established so very slowly! And therefore, though what is already there and what has been established may be most unsatisfactory indeed, man will not easily give it up, which is also why he won't follow you: for though it may be bad enough, and little enough, it is still something, while you have nothing at all to offer. For you declare outright that everything is going to be run according to a contract based on nothing but mutual love, so that nobody will have any kind of personal guarantee whatever, unless the matter might concern the collective. To evade further questions you assert that there won't be any injustice either, ~~and therefore~~ in that new society of yours, so that consequently no guarantees will be needed. But only a madman can make such an assertion, without ever having tried it out, and without any other foundation. ~~Individuality~~ What is your guarantee? But now, if man won't renounce ~~even~~ this so easily, how then is he going to renounce his children, his love for them, God, and his freedom? You are not answering a single one of the questions that trouble mankind, you are simply pushing them aside. Yet, if you won't give an answer to these questions, how are you going to solve them? And therefore, how could everybody follow you and be instantaneously transformed into your new society? Those who will follow you are merely a bunch of thoughtless people, and some scoundrels to whom you are opening up a perspective of robbery. And if this can be created in centuries only, how can you take it upon yourself to create it in a few days (as you are literally claiming yourselves)? And aren't you really accepting much too lightly the responsibility for the streams of blood which you are intending to shed? It is difficult to build up a thing. You are breaking it up, because this is the easiest thing to do."

"No responsibility whatever. We are simply risking our heads. The society of the future will be created by the people, after universal destruction, and the sooner the better."

"This is a goal men have been pursuing for centuries; this you can't deny. And you want to reach it in a few days, which only shows your stupidity. And everybody, seeing ~~your~~ this stupidity ~~and vileness,~~ will refuse to follow you."

"However, first of all, the people will refuse to fight not knowing for what, as a result of which all the fighting, burning, and looting will be done by a bunch of secret scoundrels. For the people couldn't possibly accept your program: abolition of private property, individuality, God, and the family. I repeat—even if your program were a just one, it could be carried out only in the course of centuries, centuries of peaceful practical study and development. The people, even if carried away at first by the rioting and looting, will nevertheless quiet down very quickly and set up something different, after their own taste, and probably a good deal worse."

"Granted. But even this will be good enough, if only the old order will perish. A new one will arise, albeit with flaws of its own, an order established by the people, but certainly a little bit better than the old. When people will become aware of its flaws, we or our successors will again overthrow it, and so on, until finally our program will be accepted in its entirety. Yet even our very first effort will have attained an important goal in that the principle of the axe and of revolution will become accepted as a result of it."

"But why are you so sure that your program is infallible? What if it is all stuff and nonsense, and complete, preposterous ignorance of human nature in general and of the Russian people in particular? For you cannot prove it in any way, save by your own ratiocinations about what seems to be right to you? But perhaps you are simply being foolish, and this is why things look to you as they do? Why should everybody turn himself into a fool just to qualify as your follower? But ~~you if~~ you even refuse to think. ~~Everybody who is against~~ You say that who is not with you is against you, and doom to death everyone whose opinions do not square with yours, forgetting that a discussion does, if nothing else, at least keep things moving. And with how much hatred are you going to deny the right to exist of those who will eventually go into action against you, their convictions being different from yours?"

"This is all nonsense and trivial detail!"

"But if you don't know for sure whether your program is founded on truth, aren't you burdening your conscience with criminal destruction?"

"We believe that our program is founded on truth and that everyone accepting it will be happy. That's why we are willing to shed blood, because this blood will be the price of happiness."

"You can believe in God, but in life you need facts."

"And what if it won't buy happiness?"

"We are sure it will, and that's all we care to know."

"Wretches! I'm only glad that you haven't a chance to succeed, because you do not know the people. Granted you'll succeed in organizing some cases of robbery, arson, murder, and debauchery; granted you may even stir up a rebellion; yet the people as a whole will immediately hang all of you and will refuse to accept your program, because it is against nature and, besides, based on total ignorance of the Russian people. Social man will never relinquish to you his faith, or his family, nor will he willingly enter that prison which you are offering him in your program, nor will he exchange his personal freedom for such servitude as you are preparing for him... Also, the people won't surrender their Tsar-Emancipator to you."

Shaposhnikov says: "Man needs unhappiness as well as happiness, and a lot of it, too."

"You want to cut throats and loot, because that is the simplest thing to do. This doctrine, through no accident, appeared in France after the communists had failed spectacularly everywhere and had turned out to be mere good-for-nothing mischief mongers."

59 "Whence comes this family name?"[2]

"This, I say, is an indiscreet question."

"Fieldmarshal-General Dyrochkin."*

"One can't help admitting..."

"It would be best of all to join a band of robbers."

"Be virtuous."

---

[2] The schoolgirl in Part II, chapter 7:2 of *The Possessed* asks "How did the family arise?" and Stavrogin answers, "I think the answer to this question wouldn't be quite discreet."

* *dyrochka,* "little hole," with an obvious obscene connotation.

"What about virtue?"

"Virtue won't cover up..."

"Right you are, it won't."

"Why won't they call on Dyrochkin if they want to save Russia?"

"Why, naturally! Then everybody would be taking off his hat—'There's Dyrochkin for you, yes sir!' "

"Eh no, that they won't know..."

Dyrochkin.

Nikchorydov.*

"Your ancestors succeeded through their actions, you do it by the euphonic quality <of your name>."

"Listen, they used to say these things in the olden days, and the most clever people ~~?~~..."

Uspensky's mother has learned about the murder of Shaposhnikov and wants to inform the police (a tragic figure). Uspensky begs her not to do it. He informs the Committee about her, they say that she must be killed. He implores them to spare her, then goes to the police and confesses the crime.

Shaposhnikov.

"It is impossible to talk to you. ~~But yourself~~ It's you who reject any discussion and want to simply exterminate the opposition. But if this is so, you leave them with no other initiative but to exterminate you."

"Fine with us; a war is a war."

"If this is so, don't complain! Why then, are you sniveling in your proclamations about so-and-so having been put in prison, and so-and-so having been hauled off to a stockade?"

"In so doing we are addressing ourselves to the people, asking for their sympathy. The people will make their own decision as to whom they will join, you or us."

"That is, they will decide which of us they should pity more?"

"Precisely."

"Crooks and arsonists will join you, the people won't. ~~And so~~ But mark you well, even the crooks aren't joining you because you have their sympathy, but because they can use you as their fellow-arsonists.

---

* An anagram of *Dyrochkin.*

Which means that they will betray you after your very first failure."

Granovsky.

All of the above is what Shaposhnikov has to say in refuting <the Student>. But later, Granovsky goes into a more sophisticated analysis of the problem, for instance, concerning the question as to how an individual will feel living in the collective, in dormitories, whether he will feel jealous, or whether he will be able to stand jokes on himself.

Granovsky.

N.B. "You say that the Committee can give freedom and security to the inventor. But how do you know that the Committee will always guess correctly? It may, as long as things don't go beyond boots, footwear. But in cases where the invention in question will amount to discovering America or the rotation of the Earth, it will surely go wrong, and surely go against the member of the collective. In that case, he will have only the following choice in your society: either renounce his idea forever, or starve to death."

Granovsky.

Granovsky says: "Still, one can't help being surprised at the extraordinary amount of stupidity found in Russia."

The Prince says: "Why, these are only school drop-outs who understand nothing at all either about society or about the people."

Granovsky: "Who have, however, received, and are still receiving plenty of support, and whose ranks are being eagerly joined, granted, only by boys and girls, yet certainly not by ten-yar-olds, but by young people of twenty and older, at which age it is quite unforgivable to be that stupid."

Shaposhnikov: "For goodness' sake! Why, everybody in our country is that stupid, including educated men of 60! Whole newspapers, journals, serious people, even some professors and executives, favor the idea of breaking up Russia and alienating our frontier lands! Isn't that equally stupid? Did not you yourself consider it to be a disgraceful act of informership when he asked you that categoric question: 'Would you have informed the police on Karakozov if you had known within ¼ hour of his attempt what his intentions were?' "

Granovsky: "Yes, there is really some kind of *cercle vicieux*[3] here."

62 "Haven't you been telling us how various littérateurs, or literary

---

[3] French: "vicious circle."

gentlemen (the A—vs), were, together with Belinsky, discussing such-and-such or such-and-such detail of the society of the future? It all started with you and your age. So you were more clever then, weren't you? Isn't the notion that all the nations of the West ought to be national and that they must be respected for being just that, also that the specific nature of the national development of each of them should be recognized and regarded with reverence, whereas the Russians alone must under no condition be themselves and it would be wrong to assume, even ideally, that they may have their own specific traits, isn't that notion even more stupid than what these punks are writing in their proclamations? Why, in actuality, they are resting upon your very own reasoning. It is you who have started this whole mess. ~~The basis~~ The basis of everything is the failure of these people to recognize and to take cognizance of Russia and her independence—and it is you who have been preaching just that.

Now, as for these punks, it is they and nobody else who, by virtue of their program of action, have created a state of war between themselves and society. Therefore, they must not act surprised, or complain, when society is going to exterminate them (. . .). They say that they won't be stopped by moral scruples, but will kill and burn. Why then, shouldn't they be treated likewise? After they get through butchering the government, they will give people just a few days to turn over everything they own to them, and to renounce it forever, and to sign up with one of their collectives, as shoemakers or something. I'd say that everybody who is against it ought to treat them just as unceremoniously. In my opinion, it ought to be made clear to the people what they want, whereupon the people will promptly start killing them off. The people won't rise with them, but there will be plenty of crooks and fools who will, and there may be a lot of trouble in store. So that's why everybody can and should defend himself."

Shaposhnikov says at *the meeting*: "I'm ashamed to sign such a program (a few days, and everybody a shoemaker), ten-year-old boys ought to be more clever than that. You are fully convinced, judging by the tone of your program, that everybody will be greatly impressed by your élan, give up their wives, children, property, and churches, and follow you, to rob, murder, and set fires. One can see from your words that you are fully convinced that the people hate the Tsar and thirst for the hour when he will be killed, and that they are eagerly waiting for the moment when they can give up everything they possess and join you. So convinced are you of all this, that you have already begun to rob and set fires, and to commit murder in cold blood. You are so childish as not even to be aware of the simple fact—leaving everything else aside—that the people, too, possess self-esteem, and so you really believe that they'll give up everything and come running to you, punks that you are. You are so brainless and stupid as to seriously believe that you have made a great discovery, quite oblivious of the fact that mankind would have realized this idea long ago, if it had only been the truth, and would have never suffered for a thousand years, waiting for you to come and save them. You are not ashamed ~~to announce~~ to lie the way you are lying in your proclamations, distorting facts, and asserting most naïvely that this is Jesuitical, and that the Jesuits were clever men; and that you'll act exactly the way they used to, not suspecting at all that any such lie or distortion of facts is liable to be exposed much sooner than you'd ever expect, and that society will recognize you for what you are, deliberate liars, refusing to follow you. Punks that you are, you believe that this doesn't matter at all and that, on the contrary, everybody will find the way you're lying most attractive, and will cast away everything he's held ~~sacred~~ holy and loved—God, their wives, children, order, good manners—and will come running after you, solely because you murder and set fires, not knowing yourselves why. You haven't been ashamed to tell a nation of 80 million people, in writing, that you are giving them just a few days to turn over to you their property, to give up their children, to desecrate their churches, and to sign up for your collectives as shoemakers. You are convinced that everybody hates churches, considers marriage* a burden, and is eagerly waiting to move into an aluminum palace, where people will be dancing (by the way, what about working?) and taking their common wives and husbands to separate chambers.

You have no idea that such childish views on serious things do properly identify you as what you are—punks, who ought to be given a good flogging. Also, you have so little respect for society that you haven't even bothered to edit your own proclamation a little more carefully. The public, having realized that Russia, in your schemes, is seen to be acting altogether childishly, giving up everything and becoming totally regenerated in a matter of days, will be amazed by your stupidity, but realizing that you are scoundrels besides, will eliminate you as dangerous lunatics, and severely so. But alas, it seems that practically *nobody* is any wiser than you are, and that all this has happened because

---

* The text reads *drakami,* "brawls, brawling"; however, it is obvious that the editor has misread (or misprinted) *drakami* for *brakami,* "marriages."

we have become uprooted, and because we haven't been living our own kind of life, but an alien kind, and under foreign tutelage all along."

"That's true, how true! Alas! Maybe you're really more clever than the rest of them—"

3 *Shaposhnikov*

"There is too little that's dear to the heart about that life of ours spent under tutelage for anybody to stand up for it. There has been a good deal of depravity and frivolity. If people were to work out their own lives, if they were to create life under hardships, yet independently, with all its misfortunes and struggles, with all its burdens, yet also with all the joys that come with a struggle successfully completed, and, most important of all, with a lot of hard work, I repeat, working hard themselves, and not just getting by under administrative tutelage, then they actually would create their own facts of life, then they would accumulate much experience and many dear memories, precious traditions of struggle and of hard work, and the memory of these experiences and events would be dear to all, as would be the memory of their past leaders; and so would be the leaders of the present, who would be esteemed highly and who would have an influence upon everybody; and society would not respond to their call so frivolously as it actually does today to all kinds of trash, and to stupid and depraved, soulless punks. What a lesson! That Holstein [German] tutelage! My God, what a lesson. There is no people, no nation in all of Europe that couldn't save itself by its own innate forces; even at the very height of a revolution, even while still on the barricades, they proclaim order, and death to thieves, rapists, and arsonists. And you, facing a great nation of eighty million, ~~by robbery~~ hope to create a following and to arouse people's sympathy by dangling before them the lure of arson, murder, and regicide. This means, evidently, that this society places no value at all on all that has happened in its history so far, and that it finds life under administrative tutelage very much to its liking! ~~I have been saying a lot~~ That's what you have degenerated into! And you, you actually imagine, to this very moment, that the people haven't turned their backs on you completely, I say completely! Why won't you try to place them under tutelage once more? No, it is in entirely too Holsteinian a manner that you've been looking at the people!"

"Squire's sons or divinity students, i.e., the most uprooted of all classes."

And then, immediately, the Chronicler makes this comment:

These were Shaposhnikov's words, spoken in a state of frenzy, yet with perhaps a grain of solid truth in his words. In truth, this tutelage over, and alienation from, the people has created a situation where society, firstly, holds nothing precious and considers nothing worth standing up for; and secondly, seeing how the people, at the same time, hold on to their own precious way of life, and are willing to stand up for it, and live such a full life—all this gives society an ultimate reason to hate the people, precisely because they live a full life. I can understand now the things Shaposhnikov used to say about the hatred which Belinsky and his like, as well as all of our Westernizers, have always felt for the people. And if they are going to deny it, obviously they simply aren't aware of it. That's precisely how it was: they thought that they hated while loving, and actually said so. They weren't even ashamed of their own extreme squeamishness toward the people, whenever they came into practical contact with them. (Theoretically, they did love the people.)

The Princess.

Granovsky says: "Weren't the people under tutelage too, like everybody else: Yet you say that they have retained their own, that they have remained the Russian people, that they did not degenerate under tutelage, and that they do not hate Russia."

Shaposhnikov: "The people were exempt from the German reform from the very beginning; they were given up for hopeless. They were even allowed to keep wearing their beards. ~~It was deemed necessary to convert~~ The people weren't considered essential at the time, but were looked upon as raw material, and as payers of the poll tax. Sure, they were closely guarded, but as to their internal, proper life, it was left to them in its entirety; and though the people had to suffer a lot, they finally ended up by loving their own suffering. Whereas the entire upper class of Russia ended up being transformed into Germans and, uprooted, got to love everything German and to hate and despise everything of their own. That's how it was everywhere: in Lithuania, in exactly the same way, native Russians got to hate their own people."

The people were *immediately* exempt from the reform, at its very beginning, as it was deemed preferable to look upon them as mere raw material.

64 ~~How can~~

Shaposhnikov says: "Belinsky, as an adjutant to some ~~German~~ emancipated woman, like say, M-me Högg,[4] running errands in the feminist cause."

The Princess or Shaposhnikov: "Let the nihilists score any kind of success, and you'll be the first to apologize to him."

"You are rejecting God and Christ, without giving any thought to how, without Christ, everything in the world will become sordid and sinful. You are condemning Christ and making fun of God, but what about yourselves, for instance? What sort of an example are you presenting yourselves: how petty, corrupt, greedy, and vain you are! ~~And meanwhile~~ By getting rid of Christ you are getting rid of mankind's unattainable ideal of beauty and goodness. What have you got to substitute for it?"

Granovsky: "Granted, though this is still debatable—but what prevents you from revering God as an ideal of perfection and moral beauty, while refusing to believe in a Godlike Christ?"

Shaposhnikov: "All the while disbelieving that the word was at the same time made flesh, i.e., that the ideal was there in the flesh, and so, not unattainable, but attainable to all mankind. Indeed, can mankind get by at all without this comforting thought? Isn't this precisely why Christ came down to Earth, to tell mankind that ~~even it~~ the nature of the human spirit as they knew it might ~~actually~~ appear in such heavenly brilliance, and ~~actually~~ indeed in the flesh, and not only in a mere daydream or ideal, this being both natural as well as possible. The followers of Christ, who deified this epiphany of the flesh, bore witness, under the most cruel tortures, that to carry within oneself this flesh, to emulate the perfection of this image, and to believe in it in the flesh, means great happiness indeed."

And thus, Earth has its justification.

"Others, seeing what happiness this flesh can give the moment man begins to have part in it and, in fact, attain a likeness of its beauty, were full of wonder ~~terror~~, and thunderstruck, and ended up by wanting themselves to partake of such happiness, and became Christians ~~and also accepted~~, and were themselves ready to suffer torture with joy. The whole point is that the word had truly "been made flesh." Therein lies the whole faith and the whole consolation of mankind, which it

---

[4] Madame Högg was the founder of a woman's boarding school in Geneva. She was the wife of a well-known German political activist in the sixties. This remark about Belinsky was written by Dostoevsky in almost the same words in a letter to A. N. Maikov, December 11/23, 1868. He also used it for *The Diary of a Writer* (1873), chapter 2.

will never renounce. And you are intent upon depriving it of just this very thing. By the way, you will be able to take it away only if you can succeed in coming up with something better than Christ. Show us!"

Shaposhnikov—Golubov, of a family of house serfs, a ward and godchild of the Princess's, self-taught (secondary school), thickset in every sense (he has not completed his education, and has been expelled from the university). Accompanied the Princess abroad. Married for 4 years already—embittered, etc. Golubov's ideas and teachings in many respects.

Granovsky, in the beginning, has this to say about the proclamations, and even about the fires: "To tell the truth, I cannot take this for a serious matter at all." Later, he loses heart and dies of diarrhea.

The Princess is a freethinker, and in the Student's company—an atheist. Tells the Little Priest to his face that she sees no need for either the Church, or for the sacraments of the Church. (The character of the Little Priest.)

The Great Writer says: "Why certainly I do not believe in God..." (Turgenev).

Granovsky tells about the Great Writer: "~~Oh, my mother~~ He was screaming 'Oh, my mother!' when he was in that train accident."[5]

The Great Writer has been at the Governor's, but has failed to pay a prior visit to the Princess, which throws her into a fit of fever. Granovsky, too, is scared to death that the Great Writer may not come to see him. Finally, he comes to attend a soirée at the Princess's. He apologizes to the Student and declares that he has always been a nihilist.

---

[5] A reference to Turgenev's behavior during a fire on a boat traveling to Germany. See his story, "Fire at Sea."

VIII
The Prince between Nechaev and Golubov

These notes were written in the latter part of February, 1870. They comprise pages 65–77 of notebook 2.

The characters of Granovsky and Shaposhnikov are portrayed here as elsewhere with consistency and uniformity: Shaposhnikov is always the champion of native Russian roots and for a long time the improbable lover and consoler of the Ward; Granovsky is always the abstract liberal and aesthete, the butt of his son's jokes, and the secretly grudging recipient of the Princess's economic favors. The romantic intrigue continues to be the core of the dramatic situation, and what little there is of the political conspiracy is ancillary to the romantic intrigue. An outline of the plot on notebook page 74 makes this graphically clear. The central thrust of the plot is the betrothal of the Heiress (Beauty, Fiancée, Liza) to the Prince, the refusal of the Heiress (in other versions the refusal by the Prince or the mutual refusal), the rivalry of Shaposhnikov and the Prince for the hand of the Ward, the Ward's refusal to go through with a betrothal to Granovsky, and the murder of Shaposhnikov. The political plot comes out peripherally, vaguely, and fragmentarily; there are nihilistic activity, Nechaev's machinations, fires, and proclamations, but there is no coherent conspiracy or clear relationship of political events to the romantic intrigue.

Dostoevsky knows fairly well what he wants Shatov, Granovsky, and Nechaev to stand for; but he does not know what the Prince stands for. He is shallow and deep, cruel and honest, desperate and hopeful, a believer and atheist. He is:

A frivolous man, who does nothing but play the game of life, an elegant Nozdrev,[1] who plays an awful lot of tricks on people, some of

[1] A character from Gogol's *Dead Souls,* an amusing con artist.

them noble and some dirty; and it is he who then suddenly shoots himself; in between, he listens to Golubov (once.).

Merely shallow and frivolous, but in the end he turns out to have been more profound than anyone else, and that's all there is to it.

And he is

seeking the truth; he has found truth in the idea of Russia and Christianity.

He is cruel. Nechaev arouses his jealousy against Shaposhnikov.

Christian humility and self-condemnation.

He gets reconciled to his mother.

The quotations are not contradictory, but they point to the wide possibilities open for the Prince's character. Perhaps the following quotation is the most significant:

The Prince: sincere, cruel, determined, hating the existent order, progress, and contemporary people (becomes involved with Nechaev), with Golubov (to become a monk), in the end offers to marry her.

The Prince is disgusted with the world about him and with himself as part of that world; he wants something other than what is; he wants to be a "new man." He says: "We must become new men; we must be honest." But what kind of "new man?" A Nechaev or a Golubov? Nihilism or creation? Destruction or the monastery? Dostoevsky places the Prince between them, and obviously between the contradictory impulses within himself. This is a familiar doubling, and it is not satisfactory for Dostoevsky. Finally, he was to place Stavrogin beyond both poles.

---

65 N.B. *February 26.* There is a persistent rumor that the Prince has seduced the Ward, and that Granovsky has agreed to marry her. *The Student* also believes this story.

~~Shaposhnikov got married in the absence~~

Nechaev. He has also come to arrange a deal with Golubov concerning a secret printing press belonging to some Free Old Believers.

Shaposhnikov, after the trip abroad, has been refused access to the Princess's house (suspicion of a liaison with the Ward, and he has made up with his drunken wife, and with his mother).

Make it so the Prince has never declared his feelings to the Ward. Never. Even in their childhood he was always exceedingly haughty toward her. (It is the Princess who is from a grand family, not he.) ~~Abroad~~ Yet he had known for a long time that she loved him. And altogether, he would view people with suspicion, and haughtily. He took her love for a young girl's trivial and ridiculous infatuation. On a certain occasion abroad, however, he caused her passion to flare up, though he had said nothing in particular. But suddenly, seeing that he had ignited her passion, he decided to stay abroad. At the time, the Heiress still appealed to him very much (later, after he had decided to stay abroad, he became disappointed in her). He returns to Russia, his will hardened like iron, and with a secret vow to break with the old way of life, even if his mother would disinherit him. (At first he gets to be on close terms with Nechaev, later with Shaposhnikov, and finally, through the latter, with Golubov.)

Having carefully studied the Ward through the entire duration of the novel, and having witnessed how she rejected Granovsky, and also how she was actually ejected from his mother's house, knowing the secret of her heart, he suddenly offers her his hand in marriage. "Leave everything, break with people entirely"—a pact with her, and he amazes her by the firmness of his decisions.

Shaposhnikov is watching him closely. He also believes that the Prince has committed the seduction. He demands satisfaction from the Prince.

5 They meet at Granovsky's, as if by accident. On that very day, the Prince has given a good thrashing to Uspensky, for the article. They've bowled over the Captain's cousin. The Great Writer is in town. He has paid a visit to the Princess, but not to Granovsky. He arrives late. The Prince enters and announces that he has met Granovsky's son. Suddenly, the son. (Shaposhnikov has tried several times to cut in.) Granovsky's engagement. The Captain leaves, rattling his sabre. Poetry. On this occasion, Granovsky on poetry. "No, you aren't dead yet!" His son: "You are a whimpering old woman." The Great Poet: "I am a nihilist." The Beauty also announces her presence. Granovsky

on fires and other subjects. The guests depart: The Beauty has a heart-to-heart talk with the Prince, and Granovsky's son with Shaposhnikov (the Beauty gives a sign to Granovsky's son). The Colonel has received orders to apprehend Granovsky's son.

A quarrel with mother.

~~Next morning~~

Shaposhnikov with his family (his drunken wife). A serious talk between Shaposhnikov and the Prince. The Ward at Shaposhnikov's, crying. The Student sees it.

The Captain and his actions. The Captain makes friends with the Student.

The Student makes friends with the Princess. The Princess turns nihilist. (Here, the Great Writer, too, has some influence on her.)

The Beauty's blasphemy, her mother calls the Bishop. The Beauty quarrels with the Governor's wife. Her flight to the Captain.

~~Nechaev~~ *The Student* IN THE FORM OF A HERO OF OUR TIME.

The Prince announces that he is going to marry the Ward.

Granovsky, at several soirées, displays indulgence for love.

The Prince used to know *the Student* well even while still abroad etc.

~~N.B.? Nechaev is only the son (*son*) of sister Anna, and harasses Granovsky.~~

~~The Prince~~ It is revealed that the Prince has returned to Russia having previously accepted a steward's position, which fact greatly infuriates the Princess.

The Captain keeps proposing to everybody. The Princess is thinking of marrying off <the Ward> to the Captain, if Granovsky won't have her.

Granovsky doesn't want to get married and sharply refuses the offer. The Princess is angry with him. Suddenly, during the soirée at his house, the betrothal (...). The Prince, having arrived, refuses to marry the Beauty. On the very day of the Prince's arrival, the Ward hurriedly gives her consent. But she has overestimated her strength. That evening, seeing Granovsky's coquetry, she refuses to go on with their engagement and runs off to Shaposhnikov, to tell him about the Prince.

(She also ran to Granovsky who promptly makes a messy scene to show off his sensitivity.)

But then she ran off.

(Shaposhnikov with his mother, Golubov with his drunken wife.)

Intrigue and idea. The young girl is dying of love for the Prince (he knows, and she knows that he knows, and has written him a letter), but he has never given her an answer. She gladly accepts the Princess's offer regarding Granovsky. But subsequently she doesn't have the strength to go through with it (and she goes to Shaposhnikov, her friend). Shaposhnikov has a serious talk with the Prince. Meanwhile people begin to talk about her having rendezvous with Shaposhnikov. The Prince is furious, and everybody believes it, including Granovsky, who promptly makes a scene. But when told that she actually loves the Prince, Granovsky tries to bring the Prince together with her (unsuccessfully, though).

Granovsky: "Bakunin[2] is an old, rotten bagful of mad nonsense; It would be easy for him to carry children even to the privy."

The Student: "And it would not be easy for you?"

Or:

1) Granovsky, introduction.

2) Granovsky is expecting his son, who is preceded by a certain notoriety.

3) An accidental betrothal (caused by the Prince's arrival on the day of Granovsky's son's).

4) Granovsky has a frank talk with his son: "You have come at a good time. I'm about to get married, etc." Later, connect everything with the son, as well as with Granovsky's relationship with his son (everything originates from him—like from the Hero of Our Time).

Rumors about the arrival of the Great Writer are causing Granovsky some worry. The Great Writer appears in the 3d part.

WHERE IS THE TRAGEDY OF IT?

Or:

The Prince is hopelessly and desperately (to the point where he

---

[2] Mikhail A. Bakunin (1814–76), an important *émigré* Russian revolutionary and competitor of Marx for control of the International. Leonid Grossman has advanced the hypothesis that Bakunin was a prototype of Stavrogin, but there is nothing in the notes to support this thesis. See Grossman's *Tvorchestvo Dostoevskogo* (Moscow, 1928), pp. 214–311.

could commit a crime) in love (that's where you have the tragedy), and there is tragedy also in the fact that a new type of people appear on the scene.

The Ward is in love with Shaposhnikov, who is married (a tragic figure, he amuses his wife by cracking his fingers—a tragic and loftily Christian figure).

The Prince hates everything and everybody and finally joins *Nechaev,* in order to kill Shaposhnikov.

The Ward curses the murderer, and only later finds out that this was a political murder.

Granovsky's influence, and it is he who has been made a fool of.

The Student says this about Russia: Why, a lot can be done here! Why is it that they say there's nothing to be done in Russia? Only a man who doesn't know Russia can say such a thing. Firstly, there's socialism everywhere, and secondly (secondly—nowhere is destroying things so easy as it is in Russia).

Shaposhnikov speaks against the people (about the French proletariat), *O ma mère que je venère.*[3]

The Prince dislikes everything that is sham—sham democracy, Granovsky, sham love. He finally offers ~~the Beauty~~ the Ward these conditions: to renounce his inheritance, and all pleasures, to go and live in poverty, to work hard. She accepts it.

Initially he had been preaching that the stick was the best remedy against democracy.

He had clashes with Shaposhnikov and with Golubov. He gave a thrashing to Shaposhnikov; he also thrashed Uspensky, for a newspaper article.

He is seeking the truth; he has found truth in the ideal of Russia and Christianity.

He is cruel. Nechaev arouses his jealousy against Shaposhnikov.

Christian humility and self-condemnation.

He gets reconciled to his mother.

He blames himself for having, like the others, wished Shaposhnikov dead.

68 A conversation between the Princess and her son (the Prince) in the course of which the Princess wants to prove to her son that Nechaev is

---

[3] French: "O, my mother, whom I venerate."

right. Good for large landowners. The notions of feudal aristocracy and of nihilism keep popping up in her head in a completely haphazard way.

Shaposhnikov must be a tragic figure.

The Prince: sincere, cruel, determined, hating the existent order, progress, and contemporary people (becomes involved with Nechaev), with Golubov (to become a monk), in the end offers to marry her. (Self-condemnation.) Firmly announces his decision to his mother. Says to his bride: "We must become new men; we must be honest."

Irony, defense in the form of aggression. Hatred. A pure character. A new form of boyar. Terribly proud. "To be honest, get saved as quickly as possible, and start a new breed of men."—

Nevertheless, Shaposhnikov is weak, yet a phrasemonger. The Prince is not a phrasemonger, and strong.

N.B. A brilliant figure, but lift the edge a little.—

Shaposhnikov asks the Prince, in writing and orally, upon his arrival: "Could it be true, and what is it you want to do?" Shaposhnikov, who earlier had had his face slapped.

The Prince replies that it is the truth, but that he knows himself what he must do.—?— She doesn't want to herself, out of hurt pride (having been abandoned in such a condition), and goes to see Granovsky. The Prince bears all this with irony, listens to what Nechaev has to say, becomes an adherent of Golubov and Shaposhnikov (Golubov is restraining Shaposhnikov). The Prince, proudly and to their faces, accuses them all, including *her*. He is shocked by their humility and by their question to him: "And you, are you any better than they are?" Yet this very question keeps bothering him, too; he actually returned from abroad with this doubt in his mind, with this process of being changed into a new man already active within him. Sometimes he would suggest to her the most formidable prospects and conditions regarding their future life; then again, he would himself laugh it all off. To become men of a new type, to begin with one's own transformation. "I am not a genius, yet I have discovered something new, something no one before me ever discovered in Russia: self-improvement."

THE PRINCE IS EMBITTERED, sick with pride; he contradicts Shaposhnikov and is hostile toward him; out of a vengeful sense of pride, he laughs at the Ward's escapade with Granovsky; he is greatly impressed by Golubov, though he won't admit it; he is dissatisfied with everything and has secretly made up his mind to end it all (he despises himself most of all). Shaposhnikov's death leaves him thunderstruck. He tells his mother about the hard conditions which he has offered the Ward. (Some kind of a sensational story in between.) "Let's leave, let's run away, let's begin to work on a new type of man; we aren't ready yet (those other people are right, too, and so are all the rest of them, because none of them are any good), we must start all over again."

The Prince at Golubov's: "I'm trying to correct the first thing (about those who are uprooted from the soil)—I believe."

Golubov: "And the last thing, too! This is the first and the last. Nothing else is needed, all is contained in this one thing."

70 *The Monastery.*—"May God give us a good night, and to all wild animals likewise."*

(N.B. Read carefully some descriptions of wild animals. Humboldt, Buffon,[4] Russians.)

Science is service to God.

About the bear—

About his first love and how he became a monk—(chastity).

About who Satan might be?

Anikita goes to see Chadaev in order to appeal to his conscience. He calls Tikhon, who comes, argues with him, and later asks his forgiveness.

On bugs and on the cosmic joy of *living nature:* Tikhon's inspired tales.

Friendship with a boy who is bold enough to annoy Tikhon with his pranks. (He is possessed by a demon.)

Tikhon learns about Thérèse-Philosophe.

He gives him his blessings, both for his fall and for his redemption.

Tikhon's illuminating stories about life and earthly joy. About his family, father, mother, and brothers. Tikhon's exceedingly naïve, and therefore touching, stories about his minor sins toward members of his family, regarding pride, vanity, and making fun of them ("how I would do everything so very much differently now," says Tikhon).

---

* In Russian, the phrase is rhymed and clearly in the nature of a proverbial saying, conceivably in the style of an apocryphal saint's life.

[4] Georges-Luis Leclerc de Buffon (1707–88), French naturalist and author of *L'Histoire naturelle* (1749–89).

N.B. The very fact that he has become involved with that boy is touching.

Tikhon's story about his first love, about children. To live the life of a monk is lower, for one ought to have children, yet also higher, if one has a calling for it.

Thérèse-Philosophe embarrasses Tikhon. "Why, I had thought that my will was already well tempered." He observes obedience toward the boy, and does what he tells him to do.

N.B. (Loftily, vigorously, and touchingly.)

Tikhon tells one lady that she is both a traitress to Russia and a miscreant before her own children. How they lose their childlike souls even in childhood. Their studies, though accurate (Leo Tolstoi, Turgenev), reveal to them, as it were, a life that is not our own. Only Pushkin is a true Russian.

Occasionally, the boy has base thoughts regarding Tikhon: "He is so funny, he is so ignorant, he is so weak and helpless, he comes begging me for advice." But in the end he realizes that Tikhon is basically strong, pure like a child, that he is incapable of harboring an evil thought, that it is impossible to embarrass him, and that therefore all his actions are bright and beautiful.

Tikhon. On humility (on the great power of humility). All about humility and free will.

On forgiving a criminal guilty of an unforgivable crime (that this is the torture which torments man more than anything else).

Granovsky says to the Ward: "Why, why didn't you come to see me?" (He is jealous seeing that, in her desperation, the Ward has chosen the Prince or Shaposhnikov to seek refuge with). "And why didn't you confide in me? I would have found a way, surely I would have found a way to reassure you and to make you happy." (I.e., he would have played the role of Saks[5] beautifully and with éclat.)

~~Finally, the face of Nikolai Vsevolodovich, whom his guest was apparently trying to irritate by the impertinence of his "naïve" remarks, only too obviously prepared ad hoc beforehand, assumed an air of mild curiosity.~~

Finally, the features of Nikolai Vsevolodovich's face, which bore a contemptuously calm and even ~~a little bit~~ mocking expression in spite

[5] See section v, note 10.

of his guest's ~~apparent~~ obvious and concerted desire ~~to elicit~~ in to irritate his host, for some unknown reason, by the impertinence of his ~~only too obviously~~ crudely "naïve" remarks prepared beforehand and ad hoc, assumed an air of mild curiosity.

72 The Prince—an attractive figure, most handsome (under a surface of frivolity, he is deeply shocked and thinks a great deal), a sceptic and a Don Juan, but only out of desperation.

After his return to Russia, he offers his hand to the Ward in a most chivalrous manner, but is rejected.

A discussion with Shaposhnikov whom he asks to forgive him the slap in the face.

That night, at Granovsky's engagement party—what with his flirting with the Horsewoman and the unexpectedness of the betrothal, he drives the Ward to desperation—

With the Governor's wife—he creates an overwhelming impression on her, and leaves town with her. A scandal.

He falls in love with and, so it seems, intrigues the Beautiful Horsewoman—(her character, boring), but the Horsewoman rejects him and surrenders herself to the Nihilist.

Meanwhile, Granovsky's wedding. The Ward comes running to him in despair (he accepts her; scandal at Granovsky's). Shaposhnikov insists that he keep his promise.

But inasmuch as the affair with the Governor's wife has, in the meantime, taken its course, the Governor's wife, upon learning that the Prince is carrying on with the Ward, in a fit of mad jealousy decides to flee.

He flees with her. The Ward is left alone, Shaposhnikov is murdered. Nechaev abandons the Beauty, Granovsky dies, and the Prince, after having perpetuated one final disgraceful act, ~~and~~*...(N.B.? shoots himself). The Ward is left alone.

(Only Golubov is able to move and to fascinate him.)

"But since I have dared to say that I (...)."

if unhappily

Playing with his life

~~3~~ Idea: Playing with his life—waving his arms and closing his eyes,

---

* *i po*—could conceivably be extended to *i povesilsia,* "and hangs himself."

and spinning around in the slough so as to see nothing of it. Once he'll catch a glimpse of it, he will shoot himself.

Don Juan, but a conscious one, otherwise we are a race <...>.
Live as long as there's life.

Variant.
The Ward secretly loved the Prince, but he never made any advances.
Proud relationships: The Ward and Shaposhnikov know that he knows about her love and that he keeps silent and does not want to say the word "I love" (actually, he did say it once, turning his head just to fight his own boredom)—yet the Ward comes running to him and he surrenders (or rather, he finds the notion of cuckolding Granovsky to be a pleasant one).
He talks Granovsky into acquiescing to it and flees with the Ward ~~but then he grabs the Governor's wife and abandons the Ward.~~
Shaposhnikov intervenes, but is murdered.
The Governor's wife surrenders herself to him, and he leaves town with her, while the Ward is left alone.

N.B. A frivolous man, who does nothing but play the game of life, an elegant Nozdrev, who plays an awful lot of tricks on people, some of them noble and some dirty; and it is he who then suddenly shoots himself; in between, he listens to Golubov (once).
Merely shallow and frivolous, but in the end he turns out to have been more profound than anyone else, and that's all there is to it.
N.B. ??? (What will finally come of this?)
An elegant Nozdrev is an expression coined by Granovsky. His arrogance causes him not to be ashamed of Shaposhnikov; he actually admires his own frivolity. Erudite. "But when do you find the time to study?" says Granovsky, "What talent, what great talent!"
He is a sceptic and makes fun of everybody, yet he does it in a supercilious, careless manner.
Absolute indifference toward all kinds of civic affairs. Nothing but sensuous intoxication. ~~Cosmopolitan~~
A cosmopolitan cannot be an honest man at the same time (Shaposhnikov is convinced that this is so).

1) Is matter material?

2) We have a good deal of self-esteem, yet nobody has any respect for his own opinions.

The Prince, Shaposhnikov, Granovsky, the Princess.

The Last Days of T. N. Granovsky

Granovsky. He hates the Princess for the good she has done him and for his own baseness in accepting it. He speaks ill of her behind her back, in epigrams and insinuations, yet also with a good deal of cowardliness. The Chronicler pretends, on his part, that he feels very sorry, as a Christian should, about this blemish upon an otherwise great character. He finds excuses for Granovsky, saying that this is all very natural (virtues, idleness, Durov, and an unshakable sense of honor). Whereas the Princess, due to her innate lack of generosity, used to indulge in too many taunts. Such then, are these atheists, yet they are clever people; it might seem that they ought to be able to see their own weaknesses, their insignificance, and their baseness.

Granovsky has long since quit talking to the Princess as to a friend, or discussing with her his own concealed and lofty ideas (i.e., "incessant words of praise addressed to himself," as the Princess once put it). A new court has developed around him: Uspensky, Shaposhnikov, Golubov. At first he treats them with condescension, like a teacher, but eventually he realizes that they are all quite his equals and that they actually are looking upon him as on a ruin.

N.B. (Later, it turns out that each of them has his own, specific reason to be visiting with him. However, earlier they had all been more respectful toward him.)

Yet there were occasions when Granovsky actually did reach real heights of thought (when in grief, and sincere), so with the Prince and with Shaposhnikov. But this would happen only on occasion.

N.B. *The most important.* Granovsky lacks a sense of humor, appreciation of the irony and of the comic element in art and in life—and so, inevitably, he is a narrow-minded man.

(Of the pathetic school of ~~Racine, Corneille~~ French Classicism.)

Absolutely make *Granovsky* brilliant, attractive, and likable, without concealing, however, his faults.

Eventually, Granovsky renounces the Ward in the Prince's favor, yet he does so only after having drained from her every bit of shyness, embarrassment, etc., and, having thoroughly enjoyed all of it, he then strikes the pose of surprised victim. He joins their hands. At first he fails to understand the Prince (he has not seen him in a long time), but later he gets the idea. He has actually been thinking all the time that he is being forced to seal the Prince's sins by marrying the Ward. He hears her confession first, then the Prince's. He dreams of Polia Saks and, contrary to the Princess's wish, joins their hands.

Granovsky talks of bowing before the icon—in Kireevsky's words. Shaposhnikov says that this is a typically aristocratic remark. It means as much as that he does not himself believe. Consequently, he is just another dilettante, and not really with the people.

Shaposhnikov says that it is a sign of being separated from the soil and uprooted, as a man becomes inclined to love women of other nationalities, i.e., when foreign women get to be dearer to him than his own kind. Parisian and Italian women for Russian aristocrats. Greek and Turkish women for Russian poets, Englishwomen for Russian critics (N.B. Granovsky repeats Strakhov's opinion about Englishwomen).[6] The influence of Polish Catholic wives on our government officials and generals. A native woman of his own kind ought to appeal to a man more than any other woman. It is the sign of a strong nation if its citizens love and respect *their own* native women most. That's where you have your bonds of kinship, individuality, and family.

N.B. Granovsky's first wife was German, his second wife Polish.

On the day when the novel begins, Granovsky is at the Governor's. They've made an elephant out of a trifling incident with a police sergeant. The Governor's young and timid wife, caricatured by the Princess. Yet the Great Writer pays her a visit before he sees anyone else, and ignores the Princess, who is so frustrated she gets a fever. Then, as if it had been planned that way, Granovsky is in this accident with the Governor's wife's carriage and the police sergeant. The Governor, awkwardly, has a summons sent to Granovsky. An angered husband gives him a piece of his mind. Granovsky's dexterous and witty reply, witnessed by the Great Writer. The Governor apologizes and pays a visit to Granovsky, who does not receive him. Hereafter Granovsky is in fashion and it becomes a kind of obligatory demonstration to pay a visit to Granovsky. A soirée is improvised. (The Great Writer proclaims himself a nihilist; the Princess is shocked for the first time, but she stands up for Granovsky.) Something like a semi-engagement.

There haven't been any fires as yet, but the neighboring town has

---

[6] References to N. Strakhov's article, "The Woman Question" *(Dawn,* 1870, Book II). The article is a review of John Stuart Mill's *The Subjection of Women* (1869).

burned down, and somewhere in the vicinity the peasants are rioting.

1st part. Fires, the performance. Rumors about Granovsky's marriage, etc. Arrival of his son. The Great Writer.

2d part. Nechaev is a success all around, the Heiress's refusal. The Prince proudly and haughtily proposes to the Ward, who rejects him. Shaposhnikov and the Prince have already had a serious talk before. It was Shaposhnikov who had called him home, telling him in a letter that Granovsky had been asked to marry the Ward.

3d part. All the nihilists and the Governor.* The engagement party at Granovsky's. She couldn't make herself go through with it, runs away to Shaposhnikov, while there is a fire burning in town. (Quarrels between the Tragic Mother[7] and the Nihilist Girl, blasphemy, the Bishop, and the flight of the Nihilist Girl.)[8]

4th part.—The murder of Shaposhnikov, first steps toward solving it. Granovsky, cuckolded and sick with diarrhea. The Prince is charged with the crime, but exposes the whole affair, along with Uspensky and Golubov. He marries the Ward. "Cut oneself off from this society."

The Prince has returned to Russia with his thoughts concealed, yet with firm intentions. He hates lies. Sickly.

The Prince arrives and immediately has a showdown with Shaposhnikov. He has decided to propose. He goes home, makes his proposal, is rejected. The Princess tells him about Granovsky. The Prince goes to see the Beauty. Rejection, on horseback, the Captain is put out.

Simultaneously, Granovsky's affair at the Governor's (the Great Writer has promised to pay a visit).

Soirée at Granovsky's. Shaposhnikov with Granovsky, Uspensky; the Prince has brought news about Granovsky's son. The Princess, the Captain with Granovsky's son, the Great Writer (the Beauty is also among those present). A vehement debate about the fires and about nihilism. Granovsky delivers a tirade on the Madonna and on Christ. A sudden betrothal.

Granovsky remarks that democracy in the West has already enervated science. There are no great synthetic ideas any more, just particular

---

* Could conceivably also mean: "They are all nihilists, even the Governor."

[7] The mother of Liza, Praskovia Petrovna Drozdova.

[8] Liza.

specialties. And, as if this weren't enough, there is already some sermonizing going on on the part of the Socialists, to the effect that great knowledge and the sciences are manifestations of aristocratism, and harmful to equality.

Golubov says: "Paradise on earth. It exists right now, and the world was created perfect. Everything in this world is enjoyment—if it is normal and lawful, but only under that condition. God created the world and the law and, moreover, he has performed a miracle by showing us the law through Christ, as a living example and formula. Which is to mean that unhappiness ~~and abnormality~~ comes solely from abnormality, from noncompliance with the law. For instance, marriage is both a paradise and, at the same time, absolutely real, if husband and wife love only each other and are united by their mutual love in <*sic*> their children. Upon the slightest deviation from the law, marriage becomes a misfortune. It is on these grounds that the socialists call marriage absurd and stupid, ignoring the fact that the absurdity comes from their their own deviations from, and ignorance of, the law. ~~But that~~ These deviations may be diverse, yet they are all caused by a lack of self-control. A man who has 10 children and no fortune considers himself unhappy because he is unable to cope with his lascivious desires and stoops so low as to be moaning about certain privations. Self-control amounts to discipline, and discipline is in the Church. You are saying that a slave is not free. But Christ says that even a slave can be free in the very highest degree, while being a slave. You are saying that a man who has 10 children and only one course for dinner is unhappy, because he hasn't got two, and you are asking: 'What if he won't have even that one course, which happens often?' Whereas I say, yes, he is unhappy then, but again because of his general lack of self-control, and because of his ignorance of the law. Believe me, if everybody would reach the heights of self-control, there would not be any unhappy marriages, or any hungry children. And so the law has been given, stated, and embodied alive. If you haven't obeyed it, that's your misfortune. The ant heap certainly won't save you."

~~The One-armed of Sevastopol~~
~~Is again in the grasp of deep torment~~,
~~As the grenade of ardent love~~
~~Exploded in Ignat's chest.~~

~~Is this really so much~~
~~worse than "I love you like~~
~~the gloss on my sabre..."~~

~~She was flying along (GALLOPING) on her horse,~~
~~While I was prostrate in amorous sleep.~~
~~She jumped across me,~~

~~And I jumped up as if I had been burnt~~—
~~—Oh God, what did I see!~~
~~But this must be a dream, must be a dream!~~
~~I did not tell anybody,~~
~~Oh God, what did I see!~~
~~Of course it's a dream, of course it's a dream!~~[9]*

What follows is indecent, and I suggested that he shouldn't.

Part 1

Granovsky and his son are in the forefront. Granovsky fails to recognize himself in his son. Meanwhile nihilism engulfs the city. He argues with Shaposhnikov. "You are the progenitors." The murder of Shaposhnikov.

N.B. *Most important.* Granovsky has written the Prince a letter about the prospective match and has quarreled with the Princess. Shaposhnikov is married.

But *the most important,* Granovsky and his son are in the forefront.

Pathetic elements—the sickly Prince and the Ward. THE NEW, MORE SIMPLY.

Granovsky is preparing to get married, yet he is afraid of his son: "What is my son going to say about it?"

The Princess is Granovsky's benefactress. He proposes to the Ward, fearing the Prince. (The idea to arrange this match belonged to the Princess, who had become afraid of her son.)

The Prince returns home (?summoned by the Ward's brother). He goes directly to Shaposhnikov, of his own accord, without an invitation. The Prince proudly gives Shaposhnikov his word that he will propose, and does so. He is rejected. "Isn't it somewhat early?" He is amazed by that. (Earlier, he had slapped Shaposhnikov's face.) The Princess is triumphant.

The Prince, laughingly, pays a visit to the Heiress, who takes him aback by rejecting his proposal before he has ever proposed. However, they go horseback riding together and run over the Captain (drop in at Granovsky's on horseback).

Meanwhile Granovsky has his own troubles with the Governor, and all the consequences of that affair, i.e., the soirée.

Soirée at Granovsky's (prior to which he is with Shaposhnikov:

---

[9] Poetry dedicated to Liza by Captain Lebiadkin.
* Iambic tetrameter, rhyme scheme *abaab.*

"What is my son going to say?" also, about nihilism). Shaposhnikov has met his son abroad. The Great Writer, the Captain and Granovsky's son, Granovsky's tirade. The Prince *(Shaposhnikov)* poses the question about informing the police, they drink champagne. The stage is set.

The Prince loves the Ward for her pride. (He is at fault.)

More links.

(N.B. Granovsky shows his sensitivity before his son, the Prince, his fiancée, Shaposhnikov. Meanwhile his son is gaining social prestige all over town. This is also where the Beauty is to be introduced into the circle. Nothing comes of the Prince's courtship of the Beauty. The Prince listens to Shaposhnikov attentively and mockingly. He also meets Golubov.) Nechaev at Shaposhnikov's and at Golubov's.

3) They are all nihilists: the Prince's escapade (which establishes loudly and clearly, his character absolutely in connection with his love affair with the Ward, humbling). ~~The Beauty runs away from <her?> engagement party—(many scandals)~~ At the engagement party, Granovsky joins the hands of the Prince and the fiancée. Prior to ~~this~~ the betrothal, blasphemy, the Bishop, the Great Writer, a quarrel, the betrothal, the Beauty runs away to the Captain, that is, to Nechaev.

4) The final meeting. Shaposhnikov's death verdict. The plot is about to be exposed, everybody is scared.

Idea: The Prince is guilty before Shaposhnikov's sister and slaps Shaposhnikov's face. Later, Shaposhnikov's sister refuses (which suits the Princess fine, as she arranges things for Granovsky). Shaposhnikov's sister demands that he apologize to Shaposhnikov. (...) ~~The sister~~ The Ward—she does not say anything right away, but postpones it until later that night. That night, at Granovsky's, everything is decided. Shaposhnikov forgives everything (the Prince asks his forgiveness, but only after he has already been forgiven). He gives his word, right there, at Granovsky's. The Prince feels like a fool, and insulted.

Granovsky, in the course of the novel, seeks to persuade the Prince to forgive.

The Prince meets Nechaev and discusses moral regeneration with him.

He tearfully begs Shaposhnikov's forgiveness. (Shaposhnikov and his sister, it seems, do indeed despise him very much. Everybody in town knows that he was the seducer.)

In the course of the novel, the Prince's decision is frustrated, which is what accounts for the pathos of the novel.

The whole town also knows that the Beauty has rejected the Prince.

N.B. (The Prince will be penniless if he marries and goes against his mother's will.)

Even before, the Princess tells Granovsky that she is afraid of her son. He replies that he knew the Prince as so delicate. She replies by calling him a fool.

76 Shaposhnikov is married. A drunken wife. The Princess, pointing at her: "Your future kin!"

The Prince has returned from abroad with firmly established views on things.

1) *Or, another idea!* Nechaev gets the Prince involved in the murder, making him the murderer. (Which means he is as stupid as Bezobrazov.[10]

2) Or, the Prince is much the stronger and nails Nechaev, who wants to make a murderer out of him.

~~3) Or, the Prince is actually tempted to commit the murder; but the murder is then committed rather without his having any part in it, due to the thoughtlessness of Nechaev who fails to heed Uspensky's advice (the latter is the first to repent). The Prince is thunderstruck, repents, and accuses himself. Whereas the Ward goes over to the side of the murdered man's wife.~~

~~4) The Prince is passionately in love with the Ward, yet at the same time: "I am being insulted by a serf of mine!"~~

~~His hatred of nihilism and liberalism. There is no reconciliation, but he does become intimate with Nechaev~~.

~~The Princess in a comical situation—while remaining an aristocrat, she becomes a nihilist: "They are right." But most of all, she does it to spite Granovsky—to tease him~~.

~~The Prince is passionately in love with the Ward and is deeply hurt by her refusal.~~

~~The Ward is in tears. She is with her brother, who would like to reassure her and yet fears the Prince, a terrible and deranged character~~.

~~Or: The Prince is being facetious with the Beauty all the time.~~
~~He half laughs at Granovsky.~~
~~Formidable and elegant himself~~.

---

[10] Probably Vladimir P. Bezobrazov (1828–89), economist and geographer, a moderate champion of peaceful reform.

~~And finally he is captivated by Shaposhnikov, and says: "Forgive me."~~

~~N.B. He The crisis which leads to a change to enthusiasm continues throughout the novel~~.

~~Because of the laughter (he restrains himself). A passionate nature.~~

~~He finally surrenders, to the Beauty.~~

~~But he could nail Nechaev.~~

~~Generally, rather a serious character, serious to the point of curiosity~~. ~~He has returned from abroad with thoughts and with questions that fascinate him ever so much more since they are new to him. Some people consider him a nihilist (his mother, for instance), and he does have, in general, the reputation of a nihilist. Only Granovsky sees that he is not a nihilist (but what is he?) Sometimes he thinks that He thinks that he is a presumptuous young fool (Bezobrazov), which is what many of them are. The Prince is always laughing, which irks Granovsky. Granovsky finally comes to think that the Prince is in Nechaev's hands~~. ~~On some rare occasions Granovsky is impressed by flare-ups of a serious or tender temperament in the Prince. A most serious discussion. A profound trait: the Prince likes to listen a lot, and with great attention~~. ~~Nevertheless, his mother fears him all the time. At one time it looks as if Nechaev had him under control (i.e., Nechaev thinks that this is so), but very soon even the carefree Nechaev realizes that it isn't so~~. ~~However, he still wants to get the Prince involved in the murder (according to the advice and warnings of Uspensky). But Nechaev, though frivolous and happy-go-lucky, can be very clever indeed when the situation demands it: he suddenly realizes that he won't succeed in getting the Prince involved in the murder, that this just isn't in the cards, that the Prince has been merely listening, keeping silent, and watching; also, that he may be very well of one mind with Shaposhnikov. And so he immediately decides to go through with the assassination according to a different plan, that is, avoiding the Prince. Some suspicions~~ do nevertheless fall on the Prince. But here the Prince quickly takes the initiative and exposes himself.

He immediately masters the situation and wins over Uspensky, who makes a confession. He goes directly to the Ward, revealing all his deep love; yet he presents his conditions, which she accepts with enthusiasm. A new type of people, ~~new~~ life regenerated! Break the idols and burn the bridges. If necessary, he is ready to forfeit his inheritance; but his mother, trembling from fear acquiesces. He frightens the Governor and the Great Writer. He generously shows his compassion for the Beauty, whom he had earlier rejected rudely and abruptly, because of a frivolous act of hers. (At first they would laugh together; she thought that he was a nihilist and took it into her head *to play* with him; he very rudely severed relations with her, but he was actually wrong, for it hadn't been lewdness at all on her part, as it had appeared to him, but her thoughtless and yet deliberately conscientious persuasions.) Altogether, he realizes that it isn't easy at all to be an honest man, and especially a *new* man, that it just isn't enough to have enthusiasm. This he also tells the Ward when he eventually offers her his conditions. "I won't become a *new* man myself," he says, "for I lack originality, but I have finally found a few precious ideas and I'm sticking to them. But before there can be any regeneration and resurrection, there must be self-control; and that's where I need you, for you will save me with your gentle temperament." "I," he says, "used to condemn nihilism and was its bitter enemy, but now I see that I am more guilty than anyone else, and worse than anyone else; we, the gentry, have severed our ties with the soil, which is why we must be regenerated before anyone else; the curse weighs heavier upon us than on anyone else, and it is from us that everything originated."

~~With~~ He could listen to Shaposhnikov, yet he noticed in him a great deal of hatred, which is why he always looked down on him to a certain extent. But he listens to Golubov with respect. Faith and Orthodoxy.

He accepts a position as steward with the Governor, which shocks his mother. (But he still gives a horsewhipping to Uspensky).

In a word, it finally turns out that he has been in his right mind all along; but not in a calm and collected way, but under the spell of his crisis. At one time he wanted to become a monk (Pavel Prussky).[11]

In any case he is a gentleman.

If somebody had slapped his face, he would have called him out but failed to fire a shot, out of contempt.

He begged Shaposhnikov forgiveness, in secret and with tears.

He used to listen to Nechaev attentively, and toward the end begins to watch him closely. The fire gave him a shock. He worked at the fire.

His reputation in town and everywhere (still from the past, when he was still an adolescent) is that of a depraved, disgraceful, brazenly abusive man. (There is a government clerk whom he had beaten up, a husband married to a girl whom he had seduced. The Governor's wife

---

[11] A church figure (1821–93), an Old Believer, teacher of Golubov.

thinks he is a Melmoth.[12] He is momentarily attracted by the Governor's wife. She writes him a letter. He acts nobly toward her.)

The Governor hates him because of his wife, and actually has a serious exchange of words with him.

The Governor's brother insults him. A slap in the face, a brawl.

In the novel, he is the judge of nihilism.

He says to Golubov: "I am eagerly watching Nechaev to find out where he gets such strength of conviction and composure from. I am fascinated by Nechaev."

That's why the Ward thinks: "How could such a man marry me?"

The Governor has just only arrived at his office when the Prince comes in too. The Governor thinks that he has come to see his wife rather than him, and is embarrassed.

The Beauty's blasphemy suddenly hurts him so much it makes him sick—and all of a sudden a hidden nook of his inner convictions has shown itself.

He is initially cruel and cold toward her because he is, firstly, proud, and secondly, hates all affectation and insincerity. "Marry a whore—what's the difference!" There is such a woman in town.

Golubov says: "You need more humility; consider yourself as being nothing, only then you will be saved, and gain peace."

Shaposhnikov also used to preach humility and died a fiery enthusiast. Shaposhnikov belonged to the society of the axe, and disturbed (...).

Letters, December 23, to Pasha.[13]
" 9, to Pasha.

No. 763
December 11/23, 1869.

---

[12] A reference to Charles Robert Mathurin's (1782–1835) *Melmoth the Wanderer* (1820). A Gothic tale in four volumes.

[13] Pavel A. Isaev (1848–1900), stepson from Dostoevsky's first marriage. Frequent addressee of Dostoevsky's letters.

IX
The Prince in Search of Faith

These notes were written in March, 1870, except that notebook page 6 was written at various times from December, 1869, to March, 1870, and notebook page 62 of notebook 3 was written on April 10/March 29, 1870. It was pasted by hand—and probably in error—by Dostoevsky's wife in notebook 3. The rest of the pages are from notebook 2.

The core of this section is the development of the Prince's character. He is presented as a driven but rootless person. His desire for grounds for a new life is the motive for connecting him with Shatov (called this for the first time), Nechaev, Golubov, and Granovsky. Each of these four represents different grounds for belief. The beliefs of Shatov, Granovsky, and Nechaev have been reviewed before, and in essential outline have not changed. Golubov, who does not appear in the final version of the novel, is the positive believer, with ideas close to those of Dostoevsky: "Golubov's ideas are those of humility and self-possession, also that God and the Kingdom of Heaven are within us, in self-possession, and that's where freedom is too." He represents in more positive form Shatov's ideas, and in the final version his ideas are merged with those of Shatov.

As in the previous section, but perhaps more insistently, Dostoevsky entertains the possibility of the Prince's salvation by way of Golubov. More than once, he speaks of the Prince as a "new man," but after every attempt at the regeneration of the Prince—whether by religious penance or love for the Ward—Dostoevsky adds: "Immediately thereafter he shoot himself." Consider also: "He is attracted by the Ward and even tries to convince himself that he is in love with her (His conditions regarding becoming a new man; all of these conditions are infinitely difficult.) Immediately thereafter he shoots himself." And, "During his last visit (when <he presents> his conditions) he says, in a rapture, that he loves only her, that she is his salvation, and—an hour later he shoots himself."

It is clear that one of the ways by which the Prince is to be regenerated is by love for the Ward; and this is Dostoevsky's attempt to reconcile and to connect dramatically the rapidly growing stature and complexity of the Prince to the romantic plot that has so persistently been put forth. Similarly, Dostoevsky attempts to involve the Prince in the political narrative by the attraction he feels for Nechaev's strength of conviction. The Prince apparently informs on Nechaev and the conspiracy from some attempt to regenerate himself. But after exposing the conspiracy, he kills himself.

The Prince who tries to find "grounds" for belief and for life in religion, politics, and love is not the Stavrogin of the final version, but the Prince who fails to find such grounds is Stavrogin, at least in embryo.

Continuation from the end. The nameday of T. N. Granovsky may, it seems, serve directly as the beginning and as the basis of my chronicle: it is pregnant with events. Granovsky had written the Prince a letter after all. Here is where the chapter ends. This is why the Princess got angry with him and didn't want to attend his nameday party that evening. She was still afraid of those rumors about the Prince, and of his resolute character, and so she wanted to make sure that the marriage would come off before his return. There had been negotiations with Granovsky, but nothing in the open as yet. Suddenly the Prince arrives, being actually quite inclined to stir up an affair. He asks that Shatov be summoned (earlier, he had slapped his face, solely for his stupidity). He asks the Ward, in the presence of Shatov and his own mother, to explain once and for all: "Where is the root of this affair, an affair which is now taking a vile turn." He reads Granovsky's letter to them. She blushes. The Princess is furious: "Why, that old woman did write you after all." The other woman declares that nothing has happened between them and that she is raising no claims whatever. The Prince declares that if he considered himself capable of making someone happy, etc. She is indignant. She suggests asking Shatov's forgiveness. But he declines, considering himself guilty. Then, a conversation: "So you are marrying the old man." A compassionate glance, a few words about <what happened> abroad. He leaves together with Shatov; a few words, the latter keeps his eyes fixed to the ground and seems in a hurry to pass him.

The Prince goes to see the Beauty. Taking a ride with her stepfather. A conversation. A refusal before there has been a proposal. About Nechaev. "I'll pay a visit to Nechaev." They then have a go at the Captain[1] (he is the one who writes verse, i.e., he has already started to write). They pay a visit to the Captain. He is out of his mind. She has learned from the Captain that Nechaev is staying with him, though he isn't in at the moment. "Let's go and see Granovsky." Meanwhile, there is another affair going on, involving Granovsky—truly, a day of many affairs. ~~About how~~ The Great Writer.

Shatov at Granovsky's in the evening, Uspensky, conversation, "I haven't cleaned the old horse's teeth." Guests. Shatov is about to leave, but stays on. The Prince announces Nechaev. The Captain and Nechaev. A quick engagement. The Great Writer. "I am a nihilist." On poetry and the Madonna. (*Some kind of occurrence.*) (Nechaev is listening to Shatov, while Shatov isn't even aware that Nechaev is a member of the same organization.)

Nechaev and the Prince are friends. Nechaev has come also because of Golubov.

Course of Events

Granovsky—a personage.

The engagement, a mistake—a letter to the Prince, and one to his son.

The son arrives—description of his first adventures (N.B. however, incognito). Shatov and the Prince have gotten to know each other.

Arrival at the Prince's, account of what the Prince has come to. The Great Writer, the Governor.

Granovsky's nameday. Shatov—(Shatov, too, is incognito.)

Meanwhile in town, proclamations, fires, etc.

As a narrative, it will come off in fine fashion, without the slightest unevenness.

Most important, it is a chronicle.

N.B. Even that conversation at Granovsky's nameday party ought to be presented in narrative form, like, "here's what he said then."

(What is most important about those people is their faith in the coming of a golden age. It requires an unshakable faith to reach a decision to destroy everything. Actually the decision is to destroy everything only because this is the easiest and the least difficult solution.)

---

[1] Lebiadkin, who in earlier notes is called Kartuzov and Merzavtsev.

N.B. Kulishov, and Nechaev has his cheeks slapped, which doesn't affect him in the least.

? Nechaev is slapped by <Liza's> stepfather, or by the Prince (rather?). No consequences of any kind, and Nechaev isn't a bit embarrassed.

? The Governor's brother[2] spits in the Prince's face (unjustly so). A challenge. The Prince won't fire, for reason of his profound contempt.

N.B. Don't explain who Nechaev is, perhaps right until the third part. That's it; he's Granovsky's son! That ought to leave the reader nonplussed!

3 Nechaev must absolutely make up a story about how Granovsky "is marrying the sins of the Prince," and in the end he succeeds in embarrassing Granovsky: "I won't believe it!" But the Princess is furious: "If you didn't believe it, you wouldn't be so greatly worried about it!"

The Princess is furious that Granovsky has written a letter to the Prince prior to his engagement. (She wanted to marry him off.) "But why, then, did he write that letter? Could it be that he has some doubts himself?" thinks the Princess and is furious.

N.B. *Among the principals,* Granovsky quickly realizes (from the end of the 2d part, where his son proves to him that he has been envious of him and also makes up the story *about the sins of the Prince*) that he has blundered and that his fiancée loves the Prince. He interrogates his fiancée, brings her together with the Prince—that's what the conversation with the Prince is for—yet he has failed to analyze the Prince correctly. The Prince, only toward the end, dictates his conditions to her.

N.B. Present the Prince as an enemy of nihilism and liberalism, and as a haughty aristocrat.

Nechaev's clique: Uspensky (enthusiastic, the novel *What Is to Be Done?*).[3]

Zaitsev[4] (an idiot, as far as I can remember him) and M—v (rebellion

---

[2] Not in the final version. Stavrogin fights a duel with the son of Gaganov, whom Stavrogin pulled about by the nose.

[3] *What Is to Be Done?* An enormously popular novel by N. G. Chernyshevsky (1863). Generations of revolutionaries worshiped it, and especially the hero Rakhmetov. Dostoevsky satirizes the novel in *Notes from the Underground.*

[4] Varfolomei A. Zaitsev (1842–82), man of letters, critic, publicist. A follower of Bakunin, he worked for *The Russian Word* from 1863 to 1866, and emigrated in 1869. Prototype in part of Virginsky and in part of Shigalyov.

for its own sake, scepticism, an urge toward movement; he speaks of our Slavic brothers; scepticism everywhere, he is very clever, but restless and untidy. He and Uspensky are the first to start the conflagration). One might add *a fourth man*[5] (a pickpocket and windbag).

March 7 <1870>. N.B. The Prince has been <all along> a man given to debauchery, and a haughty aristocrat. He has shown himself earlier as a bitter enemy of the emancipation of serfs, and as their oppressor (manure). N.B. This is a man possessed by *an idea.* This idea grips him and gains mastery over him; however, its action is qualified by the fact that it does not so much rule over his mind as it does *become embodied* in his person, becoming a part of his nature, always with suffering and anxiety. And, once it has become lodged in his nature, it demands to be transformed into action without delay.

Now, first of all, he has returned to town after a long period of absence.

Meanwhile there has been a change in his convictions. To change one's convictions means, in his case, to experience a complete change in one's life, so that he actually returns home with the secret intention at least to renounce his inheritance, and to break all ties. ~~From~~ He has suddenly become a terrible sceptic, distrustful, and inclined to assume the worst—a phenomenon consistent with a strong character. To make a decision for him means to burn all bridges and do what is to be done. This kind of a person may well experience doubt before he makes up his mind, as long as he isn't quite convinced; but once he has begun to doubt, his passionate nature will turn him into a sceptic to the point of cynicism.

He loves the Ward (though not very much, but merely having retained some pleasant memories of her from their stay abroad)—and relinquishes her. He breaks with the Beauty. He seeks support for his convictions from Shatov and Golubov. Also from Nechaev. He is even willing to listen to Granovsky. As a result of all this, Golubov's ideas gain a stronger hold on him, while he rejects everything else.

Golubov's ideas are those of humility and self-possession, also that God and the Kingdom of Heaven are within us, in self-possession, and that's where freedom is, too. He didn't expect to meet Golubov. Hav-

---

[5] The fourth man became Liamshin. He resembles Aleksei Kuznetsov, one of the murderers of Ivanov. At the trial he admitted that he lost his head at the time of the murder, but Dostoevsky could not have known this fact since the trial proceedings were not published until 1871.

ing met him, he is thunderstruck, awed, and wholeheartedly submits to his influence.

(N.B. He takes a lot from Shatov, yet rejects him as a whole.)

He has arrived in town because, among other things, he has heard of Nechaev and would like *to investigate* him. He has made up his mind *to apprehend and turn him over to the authorities,* but before, he would like to find out what he has got to say.

4 And so it turns out that the Prince is a romantic and mysterious figure. He visits with everybody, listens to everybody—in order to grow firmer in his own convictions. But the reader won't know that before the very dénouement. Here, suddenly, he becomes enamored of the Ward...

Having rejected her in the morning, he takes a close look at her in the evening, at Granovsky's, then falls in love. (N.B. A romantic episode is of the essence. Their love will be such that the Ward will, at one moment, think that he loves her, and the next moment, that he doesn't. In this fluctuation there lies the sweetness of the love affair.) It ends with conditions for the Ward, and his proposal to burn all bridges and to start as new people.

? He seems to be a little crazy.

? The Princess has actually received letters to the effect that her son has apparently lost his mind to some small degree, and she even confers with Granovsky about this. These two take some measures accordingly.

(In this letter from Petersburg about his madness, some facts ought to be presented.)

He comes out for sacrilege.

He puts up with a slap in the face

He stands up for the Ward when she is insulted by somebody and surprises her by this action.

He decides to turn in Nechaev, but the latter manages to slip away, while Shatov is murdered.

It is he who discovers that Shatov has been murdered.

He also detects the fire and plays a hero's role during the fire.

Until the very end he never expresses any of his ideas. *A new man.*

The Prince, in his effort to investigate *everything,* even pretends to be a nihilist, makes friends with Nechaev and tries to elicit some information from him. He is struck by the fire and by the blasphemy. He decides to turn them in and goes to see Shatov, asking him to join him, but Shatov is hesitant about informing the police. The Prince views his indecision with derision. Right after which Shatov is murdered. Then the Prince immediately makes the whole affair public, apprehending Uspensky and M—v.

~~The Prince~~ *Definitive:*

However, the Prince has no particular ideas. All he has is a loathing of contemporary man, with whom he has decided to break. Nothing but outright loathing, for he has already realized his own rootlessness. But no ideas. Shatov says that Nechaev is entirely a product of ideas. The Prince believes him. A persistent desire to become *a new man.* "I haven't got any particular ideas, but I want to act if act I must." He listens to everybody, including Golubov, agrees with almost everybody, listens to them, but never states his own opinion.

4) He is attracted by the Ward and even tries to convince himself that he is in love with her. (His conditions regarding becoming a new man; all of these conditions are infinitely difficult.) Immediately thereafter he shoots himself.

It is precisely because he sees the power of his conviction that he is attracted by Nechaev.

He is attracted by Golubov, and it is only in desperation that he leaves him.

He is attracted by Granovsky, finds him ludicrous, and rejects him.

5) Our whole generation has turned out to be worthless and useless.

"One must not drive things too far."

"I can't reconcile <these ideas> so cheaply."

6) "I opened my eyes and I saw too much—I couldn't stand that rootlessness of ours."

7) The Prince's last confession, before he shoots himself, in the form of a letter.

"I used to know these fools (Nechaev), and I was with them, but I always believed them to be fools."

8) The Little Priest: he defends God and later admits that he doesn't himself believe.

He does not believe in God either, because he does not believe in his soil, or in his nation.

3R "Why, certainly I don't believe in God," he says. Shatov explains to him that no cosmopolitan can possibly believe in God.

To live on the soil, to be with one's people, means to believe precisely that all mankind will be saved through this very people, and the ultimate idea brought to the whole world, and with it the Kingdom of Heaven.

"I can't force myself to believe."

"Understandably so," says Shatov, "for if you were actually a Russian, you would be believing without even knowing it yourself; you wouldn't even reason about it but would simply think that it couldn't be any other way, and this without any presumption but with humility, as is true of any Russian."

"Does every Russian actually believe in this?"

"Absolutely."

"But aren't only muzhiks true Russians according to your definition? And does the muzhik really believe that all mankind will be saved through him?"

"Absolutely. Haven't you really noticed that either? Of course he isn't even thinking of this, nor could this sort of question ever enter his mind; yet if such a question were suddenly to enter his mind, no matter in what form this might happen, 2) he certainly would have to think in this and in no other way. Man is for him only a Russian man, God is for him only a Russian God, and only a Russian custom is for him a custom."

3) "This is separatism, fanaticism!"

"Not at all! The French and the English think in exactly the same fashion, or even more strictly and more exclusively so than the Russians, who are a mild-mannered people, 4) exceedingly mild—a distinctive quality of the Russian race, i.e., a mildness to the point of being conciliatory toward, and tolerant of, anything foreign, etc."

Knowledge of foreign languages.

N.B. *March 2* <1870>. Our recent fires and other strange developments in our, i.e., S—a province notwithstanding, I shall begin my narrative with T. N. Granovsky.

(Bring in Shatov at this point.)

He had no sense of humor, but <was a master of> the exposé.

Timofei Nikolaevich[6] did not understand nihilism and used to argue about it with Shatov. Yet these are digressions, of which many are needed; also, introduce as many particular events as required (he is expecting his son like a frightened mouse), then all of a sudden bring in a truly promising plot. Finish it with some major event and a lot of noise.

Enter Nechaev. His physiognomy.

---

[6] This is the name and patronymic of Granovsky, who is more frequently referred to by his surname.

2d. What was the reason of Nechaev's success? His first steps were such-and-such (although I do not, of course, know everything). What is he?

Nechaev. He suspects baseness everywhere, and this includes the Beauty. As for the Beauty, he failed to notice even the slightest bit of enthusiasm about her (her action).

The Beauty, as she comes running to the Captain, breathes a peculiar kind of poetry.

Nechaev lets his father know that he thinks the father is definitely jealous of him, of his successes, and that this is why he has been exchanging caustic remarks with his son.

The Princess, acting as a mediator between them, takes the son's side.

THE PRINCE SHOOTS HIMSELF.

5 An argument between the Prince and Granovsky.

The Prince argues that things have reached a point where a nobleman means nothing in Russia, while Granovsky asserts that the nobleman is everything, for the elements of civilization and leadership are concentrated in him. (It is the Prince's idea that he is still rootless, and a cosmopolitan, and consequently *naught.*)

Stavrogin.

During his first exchange of words with the Ward, which takes place immediately after his return, he says to her, in the presence of his mother and her brother (Shatov): "If any frivolous or thoughtless word may have fallen at one time so as to evoke certain thoughts in your mind, please forgive me—and take pity on me" (i.e., the gist of it is that he is incapable of love, and to be pitied for not being able to fall in love with such a wonderful girl as she is). He is mocking her, yet he also says it in a touching way, and looks hungrily at her. During the soirée at Granovsky's he had been eyeing her with mockery, and had embarrassed and tortured her. In the course of the novel, he comes to see her several times, sometimes in an almost passionate mood, yet every time he leaves almost laughing. He worries her terribly. During his last visit (when he proposes his conditions) he says, in rapture, that he loves only her, that she is his salvation, and—an hour later he shoots himself. He leaves his confession with her.

"Why won't you just simply live (look, I'm living, am I not?)," people tell the Prince.

"Why, this is the most difficult thing of all," he replies.

The Prince does something really mean in town (to the Governor's wife, or to the Beauty).

March 11 <1870>

The final image of the Prince.

The Prince arrives having made up his mind, and having resolved all his doubts.

He is a *new man*. He breaks with the two girls and intends to break definitively with his mother. He is full of a mad, deeply rooted energy, says very little, displays a derisive and sceptical countenance, like a man who is in possession of a definitive solution of all problems as well as of *the* idea. He is willing to listen to everyone for a time, and has little to say in return. In private, he thinks of Granovsky with condescending derision; is struck by a certain sickly air about Shatov and sees quite clearly the latter's bookishness and hopelessness; he follows Nechaev's moves and listens to his words with astonishment and curiosity, as he would like very much to find an answer to this question: what could it be that gives people so firm a foundation? (N.B. There had been some earlier ties with Nechaev.) Only Golubov gives him a real shock. Yet he admits to him, with enthusiasm (but briefly, in two-three words), that this is entirely like his own idea, his own convictions arrived at after a long search. He ~~wants to~~ has come to town to make amends for his past errors, injustices, etc. Absolutely. He makes peace with those whom he had insulted, endures a slap in the face. He defends blasphemy, locates the murderers, and, finally, solemnly declares to the Ward that he loves him <*sic*>, announcing his conditions. They mean that henceforward he will be a true Russian, and that one must believe even in what he once said at Golubov's (that Russia and the Russian idea will save mankind). He prays before icons, etc. He is in town all the time, displaying his new convictions with the most savage energy, much to the amazement of his mother. He tells the Ward that he has been watching her, that he has become convinced that he loves her and that they will be resurrected together, if only she would share his convictions. And then he suddenly shoots himself. (A mysterious personage, declared insane.)

The Prince loves the Beauty, incessant quarrels with her (bored), various demands.

He feels that he is unfair to his fiancée, decides to break the engagement, endures a slap in the face, steals Granovsky's fiancée. To her:

"We shall go alone," to Golubov: "I don't believe." He informs the police and shoots himself.

The Prince says with mocking condescension: "I do not believe in God, but I hope to be an honest man. I do not like those who say that they are for the people; there is a good deal of insincerity connected with that; we have already placed too many wreaths upon their lousy heads. You are saying that we, the upper class, have become alienated from the people and that we have betrayed them; whereas I consider myself to be, no less than the people, an independent social unit, and I shall retort by saying that it is I who have been betrayed, and not the other way round. Leave me alone, I'm all by myself. I'm an egoist and want to live my own egoistic life."

"Oh, my Prince, why are you saying that? If you weren't talking about it, but would simply live your own egoistic life, you might manage to live it out somehow; but now you are talking about it—and so you won't live it out."

1 March 15 <1870>.—The Prince is a person who is easily bored. A product of this Russian age. He looks down on people and knows how to remain independent, i.e., he keeps away from the gentry, as well as from the Westernizers, and from the nihilists, and from Golubov. Yet there remains for him the question: what is he himself? The answer for him is "*Nothing*." He is very intelligent and therefore realizes that he is in fact not a Russian. He avoids the issue by believing that *he does not find it necessary to be a Russian,* but when shown the absurdity of what he has said he shields himself behind an evasive phrase—that he is an independent.

Insofar as he is outside of all parties he can see and hear everything altogether dispassionately (remaining very much aloof himself). He takes a very close look at Nechaev and Golubov, and passes judgment on Granovsky.

But his character is a lofty one, and it causes him dissatisfaction and agony to be nothing in particular. He finds no solid basis whatsoever within himself and is bored.

When the Beauty deceives him, LEAVES HIM, HE ACTS LIKE A DESPOT WITH HER ~~he finds~~ abandons himself sentimentally, HE FINDS A GENEROUS EXPLANATION, he finds within himself the strength to accept the fact that she has left him, and suddenly sees, to his own surprise, that he actually did not need any strength for that, for he feels no pain (but only hurt pride, and he is above that), because he actually never did love her. Shatov proves to him that he actually can't love at all, because he is an universal man, and only men with a nationality possess the gift of being able to love.

Then he takes notice of the Ward and realizes that he has been wrong. He takes her away from Granovsky and insists that they get married. That's settled.

A slap in the face and a duel without a shot.

At the same time, out of indignation, he becomes involved in the Nechaev affair, informs the police, and exposes it.

But having exposed it, he feels that ~~he became involved~~ he became involved for no good reason, laughs at himself, and regrets having done it.

He feels that he does not love the Ward. Leaves for his country estate. Asks her forgiveness in a letter, for having carried her away (actually it was he who was carried away, his last self-delusion and self-deception). But he is bored and he won't make her happy. Then he shoots himself.

Before he does, he goes to see Golubov for the last time.

He says: "I wonder why I can't live like other people—like my mother, like the Count, like Granovsky, the Governor, the Great Writer?"

(Answer: because he is superior to them.)

But the author's idea is this: to present a man who realizes that he has nothing to stand on.

April 10/March 29, 1870

1)

No need to introduce Golubov.

WITHOUT GOLUBOV

It turns out that the Prince is the main hero of the novel. He makes friends with Shatov, causes him to become an enthusiastic follower of his doctrine, while not believing in it himself.

He just observes everything, remaining indifferent to everything, even to the murder of Shatov, of which he has knowledge.

N.B. (There remains this problem: Was he actually serious, and himself full of enthusiasm, when he talked to Shatov? Shatov was urging him to start acting.) The Prince listens sceptically and says: "I do not believe. I was only talking." He even writes Shatov a letter about this.

For a moment he thought of the Ward, became intimate with her, revealed to her that he was a citizen of the Canton of Uri—

He gets to ~~ponder~~ regret that he has aroused the Ward's emotions. Offers her his hand.

He shoots himself. A letter to her: "Forgive me. Perhaps I'm really mad. I am leaving everything to you."

Such then, are his relations with Shatov.

The Chronicler, on his part, adds: "It might also be that he was only laughing at Shatov."

"I am bored!"

No need to introduce Golubov.

Should Shatov slap the Prince's face before or after "I believe in nothing"? A question!

I'd say before??? But perhaps not.

Then the Prince suddenly (after "I believe in nothing") begins to treat Shatov with contempt and with derision.

He is interested in everything including Captain Merzavtsev, "and why didn't they report it," and the Ward, and ~~rapes~~ seduces a 13-year-old, which creates an uproar. (It just happened, by chance, a passing fancy.)

The Ward, in an exalted state, is ready to flee with him if must be to Uri (he has her)? He wants to marry her. Death.

But he is gentle, modest, quiet, boundlessly proud, and bestially cruel. (Sickness), shoots himself.

He visited the Ward a few times, but stopped seeing her (every time he'd visit her the Princess would nearly go out of her mind). Granovsky.

AND SO, THE WHOLE PATHOS OF THE NOVEL LIES IN THE PRINCE; HE IS THE HERO. All the rest moves around him, like a kaleidoscope. He also supersedes Golubov. A boundlessly lofty figure.

"I'm afraid that I may be hating someone here."

A meeting with her former husband, with the woman he had seduced. Plays tricks on them.

He emerges from the affair with pride and originality.

"What is worst of all, I don't believe myself."

Shatov says: "How can it be that you don't believe! How can you, if this is so, feel so strongly about Russia?"

"Perhaps it is because I hate her so very strongly," replies the Prince.

Shatov: "Were you really dissimulating?"

The Prince: "Maybe I wasn't. No, I wasn't dissimulating. I am bored! Perhaps I was dissimulating after all! How do I know?"

Occasionally he would complain, all of a sudden: "I am bored!"

S. S. "Alabama": "I'll get there!" (Dream).

X

The Prince in Defense of the Russian Idea

These notes run from about the third week in May, 1870, to the middle of June, 1870. They comprise pages 18–24, 108, and 123–45 of notebook 3.

A great part of the notes in this section consist of long speeches the Prince makes expositing his views on religion, Russia, and the contemporary world. The Prince appears as the defender of Orthodoxy, Russian nationalism, and Christ, and the bitter critic of liberalism and the West. Russia's salvation, as well as the world's, lies in moral and not quantitative measures; economic principles must come after moral principles; and if one were to follow Christ in humility, according to the Prince, all the complex problems of politics, individual happiness, and economics—even monetary reform—would be automatically solved. His speeches are delivered with the passion of Shatov, and they are probably made under the influence of Golubov. An example of his vehemence and the content of his views is the following:

Russia is no more and no less than the embodiment of Orthodoxy (a slave, and yet free). . . . We have reached the last stage of our submission to Europe, to civilization, to the curse of Peter's reform. Intellectual irresponsibility—(socialism, communism, baseness)—but we shall eventually grasp this not only with our vigorous vitality (as we did finally grasp <. . .> i.e., immediately and alive, but also with our intellect; we shall smash those European fetters which have been clinging to us for so long, and they will break like cobwebs; and we shall all realize, finally, that the world, the terrestrial globe, the Earth has never *seen such* a gigantic idea as the one which is now taking shape here, in the East, and moving to take up the place of the European masses <*sic*> ~~which~~ to regenerate the world. Europe will ~~either~~ flow into our waters as a living stream, ~~or~~ and the part of it which is dead and doomed to die will serve as ethnographic material for us. We are bringing the world the only thing we can give it, which is, however, the only thing it needs: Orthodoxy, the true and glorious, eternal creed of Christ and ~~regeneration~~ a full moral regeneration in his name. We are bringing the world the first paradise of the millennium.

The note that follows this impassioned speech is the following: "Leaves for Petersburg and hangs himself in Skvoreshniki."

When one reads how passionately Dostoevsky wanted to give the Prince his ideas of the Russian Christ, one recognizes how hard it must have been for him to give up this temptation. To most of us, what Dostoevsky puts forth here as positive doctrine boils down to a repeti-ive and somewhat irrational hatred of the West and a fantasy of the Russian people as in some way the incarnate spirit of true Christianity. The ideas are barely respectable in abstract form: they appear at best as the fervid and hallucinatory emanations of his characters. They are iterations of deep desires, expressed in feverish snatches and remnants —unanalyzed, mystical, and irrational. Dostoevsky can give them to the Prince, and the Prince can recite them passionately, but immediately after, a line about suicide negates what he recites. Dostoevsky may believe in what the Prince says, but the Prince cannot. Shatov can believe in it, but Shatov is half-demented creature feeding on worn-out learnings of Stavrogin; his spiritual life is as twisted as are his social relations.

One marvels at the time and patience and space that the distinguished Russian critic Grossman—and many after him—devoted to making a case for Bakunin as a prototype for Stavrogin, when the notes suggest nothing of the kind. Nechaev is, of course, the prototype for Peter Verkhovensky, but much of Dostoevsky's sketchy knowledge of Nechaev was filled out by his special knowledge of Chernyshevsky. When Nechaev says "All this love is nothing but self-love" and "The higher your love, the more self-love you obviously have," he is echoing almost literally what Chernyshevsky said in "The Anthropological Principle." And when Nechaev says, "There are no scoundrels. There are those pressed by circumstances, all according to the laws of nature," he was saying what Chernyshevsky said in almost the same words in "A Russian Gentleman at a Rendez-Vous."

Granovsky, now occasionally called Stepan Trofimovich, continues to be the same abstract liberal, sentimentally remembering his friendships with liberals of the forties, given to fine and unneeded distinctions, idle, garrulous, and ineffective. What is missing here and elsewhere are glimmers of the better side of Stepan Trofimovich that leads to his spiritual growth in the latter part of the novel, as a consequence of his conflict with his son and his loss of Barbara Stavrogin's respect. There is just one comment of the Chronicler that seems ambiguously to be about Uspensky (in part a prototype of Virginsky), but in content can refer only to Stepan Trofimovich. Dostoevsky has been talking about Stepan Trofimovich and continues to talk about him, and the word "Uspensky" can only be the random interruption of reflection. Dostoevsky says: "Uspensky. Incidentally, we loved him and even respected him—for his purity, and we are now sorry about the misfortunes that have befallen him. I want to make it plain that there was a lot more substances to that man than the comical nature of the dénouement might suggest." We do not have a better Stepan Trofimovich in this quotation, but we do have the possibility of a better Stepan Trofimovich.

---

130 *Granovsky:* "Shakespeare was a man chosen ~~by God~~ by the Creator and anointed a prophet who would (OPEN TO THE WORLD) reveal before the world the mystery of man."

The Prince and Shatov. N.B. Leave this vile race to others to take care of. N.B. Develop, as clearly as possible, the idea that our liberals are really the most backward reactionaries, and that the *national* party ~~alone~~ is our guarantee of strength and of the future.

N.B. Note the Idea

The Prince and Nechaev.

The Prince: "Our entire administration, taken as a body, in its entirety, ~~in relation to~~ is in relation to Russia nothing but—effrontery."

Nechaev (with a guffaw): "Did you say effrontery?"

The Prince: "Yes, effrontery, contempt and effrontery."

Nechaev: "Ahem, I shall not, of course, defend or praise your administration. But you know, as I've been looking around, learning a thing there during these months (because, you know, I don't really know much about Russia, ~~because~~ nor do I have to, because it's all coming to an end anyway, up by the roots)—well anyway, as I was learning a thing here and a thing there, I began to realize that it isn't really so bad at all, I mean the administration, because it is not pursuing any practical goal, but much rather the triumph of an idea, not any practical end, mind you, but the integrity and triumph of an idea. Of course I don't give a damn what idea exactly; let them have any kind of idea they want ~~because it is all going to be destroyed anyway, up by the roots~~, but they certainly have achieved a pattern of UNIFIED concerted action. ~~Unification~~ They've done it! They have found a way to do it. I guess they've got it ever since Peter the Great, ~~and in the main~~ it is really German. What I am talking about is not how the thing has been done, i.e., right or wrong, fruitful or stillborn, useful or harmful, but that it has been done after a certain pattern. And haven't they achieved extraordinary results, judge for yourself: they've got one law contradicting the other all the time, because these laws are passed needlessly and inefficiently, and for no other but ~~their own~~ administrative purposes, yet what is the outcome? Everything goes just fine, and there isn't a word of protest. To be sure, it is somewhat deadening, but...don't you think it is even better, really, if things are a little on the dead side? What do you think? Hasn't a higher goal been accomplished, eh? Any excessive ~~bustling~~ plenitude of life is ~~always~~ harmful. We might actually take this over from them, ~~in the future, I mean, their manner~~ their manner, keep it in mind for the future. Incidentally, I am sure they've gotten it from the Germans. Lately they have been taking over a lot from the French, who are masters in their own right, ~~but~~ though theirs is a different goal, and you know what, actually an almost unconscious one: everything for the sake of Paris, for Paris is a great idea. You know, had there not been ~~a Revolution~~ in Paris—I won't say 'in France'!—that Revolution of 1789, there wouldn't have been any so-called emancipation of peasants in this country, I swear it. ~~We've~~ emancipated them precisely because we got to be 'quite a bit' ashamed before the Germans, and so we didn't do the real thing, but just the form, nothing but the form... And you know what, as far as form is concerned, that German influence has been a good deal stronger than those two hundred years of the Tartar yoke, isn't it so?"

The Prince: "Why, you are a Slavophile!"

Nechaev: "Ha-ha-ha!"

"How do you mean, form? So you don't recognize that the peasants have been really emancipated and say that it is in form only?"

"All right, they have been emancipated ~~though~~; I didn't mean it literally when I said ~~that~~ it was in form only. You know what, even here they have actually blundered in the heat of the moment. Now they are bitterly complaining that, though it was done in form only, it really wasn't done in form only as much as it ought to have been, and so they regret it, they are greatly annoyed by it, and they want to change it. As far as I'm concerned, I really do not care: it doesn't interest me in the least, whether the peasants are free, or not free, whether things are going well, or whether they are all fouled up. You know: the worse, the better. Let the Serno-Solovievich[1] brothers worry about that, and retrogrades such as Chernyshevsky! We have a different idea, and you know what. ~~In my opinion everything ought to be pulled up by the roots.~~

131 N.B. The Princess was sitting under the Madonna. You'll ask: "How do you know that?" What if I heard it from Stepan Trofimovich himself? Later, he cried, but that's the kind of man he was.

N.B. NOTA BENE, MOST IMPORTANT:

Don't forget to mention, in the right place, that there had been

PROCLAMATIONS

"I am beginning to see the light, I'm beginning to see the light, only now I am beginning to understand!" the Princess used to say after having fallen under Nechaev's influence.

Nechaev talks a lot about *charity*, and among other things, that charity corrupts people without ever accomplishing its end. The pleasure of giving charity is an arrogant one, it is the satisfaction which a rich man gets from his wealth, from his power, and from comparing his own ~~power~~ importance to that of the recipient of his charity. It corrupts both him who gives and him who receives, and besides—it does not accomplish its end. Charity merely contributes to the growth of

---

[1] Nikolay Aleksandrovich Serno-Solovievich (1834–66) emigrated in 1860 and was in contact with Hertsen and Ogarev. He returned to Russia in 1861, and was arrested for revolutionary activities in 1862, at the same time as Chernyshevsky. He died in Siberia.

pauperism, as it creates a class of idle loafers who hope to live on charity. Like gamblers around a roulette table, they crowd around the givers of charity, hoping to be among the winners. But, tell me, who ever won at roulette ~~except by accident~~ ? Meanwhile, the few wretched pennies which are thrown to them aren't enough for even one tenth of these people. In our new society nobody will be poor…

"Oho! Even a new society. But what about politics?"

Granovsky: "Why won't you leave the initiative to me! ~~Give me~~ Leave me a chance to satisfy a need of my heart, let me give freely when I feel compassion… Leave me my personal freedom."

Nechaev: "Come on, tell me how much have you given away in your lifetime? ~~If~~ Eighty copecks or so, no more, try to remember it right! Try to remember, when was the last time you gave alms? About two years ago, or even four, am I not right? … Definitely, charity should be outlawed even under the present social structure; ~~because~~ you are shouting about charity while actually slowing up things… No, you are much too corrupt."

N.B. Regarding the disorders after the lectures on Othello. (As a result of a proclamation.) It has been observed more than once that some of our officials like ~~to show their power~~ to so-to-speak make a captive out of a private citizen within the confines of their particular jurisdiction. "~~Look here~~ Look here, you, I'll show you how much power I have!"—and he'll show him, especially when bitten by the bug. Any postal official, any ticket agent on the railroad may look at you as if he were Jupiter, i.e., the emperor himself. I'm told that a certain county official seized the sermon of a visiting clergyman for alleged freethinking, while the church service was actually in process, pointing out ~~those passages as freethinking~~ as freethinking certain texts from the Fathers of the Church and from ~~the sermons~~ contemporary ~~bishops~~ prelates of the Church, and summoned the clergyman to his office demanding an explanation. I am also told about that drunken deacon of one of our most important and representative churches abroad, who on his own initiative ejected, i.e., kicked out from his church an English family, causing the ladies to faint in the process, and this right before the start of a ~~great~~ solemn Lenten mass, and under the pretext that "foreigners have no business loitering about Russian churches, and that ~~they have been assigned~~ they should come at the prescribed hours." I am writing "drunken deacon" out of tact, for if he wasn't drunk that would make it ever so much worse for us. The deacon's superior, a pastor of strong missionary zeal, I am told, was highly pleased with such disposition regarding foreign heterodox flock, and put up a strong defense for his extra-diocesan subordinate.

132 ## About the Beauty

N.B. *Important:*

The Beauty decided to pay a visit to Granovsky and told the Prince about it in the morning, during their first meeting. He was slightly astonished when she told him that she found this to be the most important thing to do at the moment, and also about her telling him this after such a long separation...

The Beauty actually did go to see Granovsky, which surprised even the Princess.

As a result of this wilful act, there broke out, on the next day, a serious storm at the General's house.

N.B. Granovsky, in his pursuit of personal initiative in the field of charity, had spent perhaps eighty copecks altogether, but certainly not more.

Yet I am not out to expose any private shortcomings, for that is senseless.

N.B. The conclusion of the first two chapters:

...Such then was the man the tragedy of whose MELANCHOLY end we witnessed with our own eyes... However, at the time when our narrative begins, the mutual relationships between him and the Princess were becoming ever more complicated due to various circumstances ... namely, the following:

N.B. THE FIRST TWO CHAPTERS—a poignant bareness and rapidity of conclusions. Naïveté and naïve wit.

Should I try it?

A poem: Enter a young man who is eating certain herbs... he explains to a fairy that he is "sucking suffering."

The Governor, in a conversation with Nechaev (about God), agrees with Nechaev and mentions that religion is, however, necessary for the people, i.e., one among a number of ~~such~~ truths which everybody knows for what they are and which have been squeezed empty by civilization.

Conspect: The muzhiks are coming.
Thought that it was revenge.
Took a closer look at Russian life.
Enjoyed the flogging.
This is barbarity!!
In general, political convictions. A Republic.
He preferred freedom.

He was inclined toward the United States of America, Tocqueville.[2]

A Fourierist; but later, when more Fourierists appeared on the scene in Russia. The United States of America. Partition Russia.

In her heart, she was building an image of Stavrogin.

He was a bit of a freethinker and used to make fun of religion. (Think up some examples of such mockery.)

A short epic poem of his was printed abroad—his fame grew, he was full of pride, but kept protesting.

Granovsky with the Governor: "I have set about my lectures on Shakespeare, and I have started with Othello, issuing from a firm conviction that a literary interpretation of Othello cannot be immediately conducive to rebellion."

The Governor: "Rebellion? That is, how do you mean that?"

Granovsky: "My meaning was an absolutely conservative one."

The Great Writer, coming to his rescue:

"Your Excellency has at his command a battery and a batallion of troops, and in little more than three days you could have ~~gathered~~ a contingent of almost a full division, plus a regiment of hussars—in case there is a rebellion. And even if, against all expectations, our obstetricians, incidentally half of them ladies, should conduct a demonstration, and if they should, at the conclusion of the lecture, choose to erect barricades, Your Excellency would still have at your disposal a full battery, ready to fire."

Granovsky. His relationship with his wife; at times, ludicrous, pedantic, and naïve posing, at times a weak and tender man, then again a husband who notices that his wife is clever, lofty spirited, and noble.

---

[2] Alexis De Tocqueville (1805–59), French statesman and writer, whose extremely perceptive observations on America are found in his *Democracy in America.*

He tells her anecdotes about himself, about his misfortunes, like Raisky or Grigory Kositsky. The Petersburg side. All of a sudden he begins to pose as Saks, feigning unselfishness, then suddenly says: "Yes, it is actually true that I married you for your money. My whole life is ruined, my whole life has been despicable." She gives him encouragement (her lofty spirit). He tells her about his son, how he used to cherish him—how he knows more and *is worth* more than his son. "You are the only one left to me whose respect I can earn (on my knees)—that is all I want from here on." And immediately thereafter, again desperation. "Oh, my God, how they all know nothing at all," and how he knows more than anybody. About the Prince—but there she cuts him short and once and for all forbids him to talk about it. But for that, he would have dearly liked to play the role of Saks.

"I am ashamed that I married you. I can't support you. Your money has been spent to pay my debt to my son. We depend on her (the Princess). Yet let us flee, let us leave."

He seeks to justify himself regarding Fedka, etc., and so on, and so on.

N.B. In a word, make him a more lively figure (but where?)

Reserve a place for him. Don't bring in any intimate details in the beginning. Everything in its proper place, objectively, by using external facts, and everything in its right turn, never rushing ahead of things.

N.B. ABSOLUTELY.

The Prince, in a conversation with Shatov, mentions among other things that France will be in a war as a result of military despotism, ~~war~~ a civil war. But should Napoleon live on for at least several more years, or if in case of Napoleon's death his successor should stay on but for a few days so that the regents could secure the throne for themselves, it might be deemed advantageous, and in the interest of improving the moral of the army and securing its loyalty, to start an external war; for a successful war would make the army loyal to them for a long time.

N.B. If Granovsky is not married yet, make it so that he is pouting at the Princess, with some grimacing at his own interesting condition, that is, getting the feel of his role of a bridegroom. The Princess senses that and is so furious with him that there are moments when she actually loathes him.

The Captain suddenly seems to have some money. (Besides, he has inherited an estate nearby.) So he has resigned his commission and is looking for a place.*

May 23 <1870> FINAL REMARKS

Use a fast moving narrative.

The Tragic Mother had been insinuating to the Princess that the Prince may have *a weakness* for the Ward. ~~Guffaw~~ The Beauty has herself confirmed this to *her* mother.

In connection with this, the Princess immediately took the Ward back to Russia with her, and eventually married her off to Granovsky.

All in all, it was done much too hurriedly.

This hurriedness made people think that Granovsky had married the Ward because she was pregnant. (Most of all, Miliukov, who writes anonymous letters to Granovsky and to the Prince.)

Both of these anonymous letters were actually printed in the letters-to-the-editor section of a Petersburg paper—"well, there is this Prince, about to return from abroad—i.e., in our town there are ~~rumors~~ two anonymous letters making the rounds." This created a lot of hubbub and scandal. There was a good deal of talk even at the Governor's: so that to the Princess, who had been at odds with the Governor's wife anyway, this scandal was terribly upsetting. One tended to agree with Granovsky that it was Shatov who had written the two anonymous letters. But the Ward stood up for Shatov, and things didn't get as far as a complete break, just a frank talk between him and Granovsky. Yet, only the devil knows why, Granovsky then wrote a letter to the Prince.

And so did Shatov.

The Princess found out that Granovsky had sent that letter—she had written one herself—and yet she almost quarrelled with Granovsky for his having written to her son. "So you don't believe me?" (The whole past was coming back, though it had been coming back all the time even before.) She reproached him about the money and even about his relatives.

"And there you are, that relative of yours, that Captain, has also made a scandal—he has been in town only for a month, so I'm told by the Governor's secretary, and already he slapped his face the other day."

"He was walking a bear, and frightened the Governor's wife."

---

* Ambiguous: could mean "place to live" or "employment."

"He writes poetry, and his poems are all over town. The Tragic Mother has been complaining, which means that people will be laughing." The Princess is annoyed: "Try to quiet down your brother. Because of him, I have quarreled with Granovsky."

Yet Granovsky (precisely because of the scandalous rumors in town about his marriage) is pouting, although the Princess is in no way responsible for these rumors. The Princess, also, is angry and comes
135 to make him account for the letter he has written to the Prince. Granovsky's wife is also quite excited by it all.

By what he has written. They almost quarrel, but here Granovsky shows his civic courage as he stands up for the Polish priest, and the Great Writer arrives in town. (The Captain is suddenly shouting something about a spy.) ~~The Princess~~ Granovsky is summoned before the Governor on his nameday. The Princess, who had been angry at him, suddenly returns him to her good graces, gives him her blessings on the occasion of his feat of courage and for <his verbal duel with> the Great Writer. Granovsky leaves, and the Princess discovers that the Prince has returned home.

(N.B. Here, all kinds of strange characters enter the novel.)

A mild showdown between the Prince and his mother; he goes to see the Beauty, then the Governor's wife. The Beauty is with the Colonel; the Captain is bowled over by them. Meanwhile Granovsky is at his house, with Shatov being present there—Miliukov and the Prince.

136 The Captain, the Polish priest, Granovsky, the Governor, here, "betraying your country."

Nechaev, knowing the Captain for the fool he is, is staying at his place on purpose.

N.B. The Princess has also received a proclamation (Miliukov secretly spread them about). The Princess is outraged by the proclamations and is the first to discuss them at Granovsky's party.

N.B. The Captain makes a remark on the word *family* <rod> in Polish.* He develops a violent dislike for the Polish priest.

N.B. The Beauty (for the first time, as far as Granovsky and the

---

* The Russian word *rod* has several different meanings. The allusion here may be to the fact that Polish *rodzina,* "family," is a homonym of Russian *rodina,* "fatherland."

Princess are concerned) reveals at Granovsky's party that she is not only acquainted with Nechaev, but that they are actually good friends. Her behavior toward him is unusual—it seems strange to everybody, and respectful.

N.B. Granovsky talks and talks... "I wasn't even listening," says Nechaev. The Great Writer didn't attend the Princess's soirée. (He did send a note.)

N.B. A REMARKABLE VARIANT: Shouldn't I make Shatov *not the brother* of Granovsky's wife, but a former admirer of hers (now married to a nihilist woman)? But only Nechaev talks about her love for Shatov (and even he is just teasing Granovsky, who hears about it for the first time). The Prince also knows about it. He also knows that the Ward used to like Shatov a good deal, but never loved him. Through the entire novel, the relationship between Shatov and the Ward is a remote one. Yet Nechaev manages to make a whole story out of it. Nechaev concocts a story about Shatov and the Ward, just as he does about the Prince and Granovsky's wife.

It is obvious that Shatov's slapping the Prince's face is even more in character in this case.

Shatov has written a letter to the Prince. (He has always been firmly convinced that ~~the Prince~~ the Ward is in love with the Prince, and in his letter he is reproaching him, senselessly and *quite out of proportion,* of course.)

Shatov is accused of having written those anonymous letters, but it was actually Miliukov who wrote them.

He is also accused of spreading proclamations (surely, it is said, he is only pretending to be a Slavophile; the Governor is accusing him; his flat is searched).

THE CAPTAIN—insert a story regarding Shatov and Granovsky's wife. A tirade on the Russian soldier, to the effect that his was a lofty and a firm spirit even before. (That's Shatov talking at Granovsky's.) The Prince remembers that, and in his *discussions* with Shatov he tells him about the freedom which a man can have even while he is being flogged (St. Paul). All this, and such profound understanding altogether arouses Shatov's enthusiasm.

1) "It is that same, flogged Russian soldier who displayed such a lofty spirit defending Sevastopol."

N.B. "When I say this, you fools, I'm not defending flogging; on the contrary, I conclude from this very fact how senseless these floggings are, 2) if they are to sustain the discipline of men whose spirit is so strong. I'm all in favor of introducing literacy and different relations between officers and men; but not because corporal punishment would lower the spirit of our soldiers, for their spirit 3) has always been a lofty one, but because a man of such lofty spirit should not be flogged with rods."

135 4) "But as for flogging as such, it never did debase the soldier, or his spirit, though it did debase the spirit of those (and for a long time to come) who were responsible for the flogging. What I'm saying is based on facts." (Shatov is saying this at Granovsky's.)

...~~In part~~ "In part, also, because it is national. In part also because no floggings could ever debase a lofty spirit." (This, the Prince is telling Shatov.) He concludes from this that the spirit of the Russian people is an exceedingly lofty one.

Granovsky, arguing in favor of fires: "If you want to act, act." HERE.

A SPECIAL NOTE: 1) *the Prince*: *I am bored*.—2) The Prince has arrived and, though the Princess had herself sent him a letter asking him to return (though there had also been letters by other parties, such as Granovsky and Shatov), she nevertheless finds it somewhat strange that he has come. His mother (and several other persons) are anxious to find the principal reason for his return. N.B. There is no principal reason, just *an indistinct attraction*. Yet everybody (and especially his mother) is shocked, for some time, by the fact that the Prince, shortly after his return, completes the sale of his estate and has a deed of purchase made out at the Land Office, even though it appears that he is not in need of money. The purchaser (a merchant) arrives from Petersburg and buys the estate for a little over ¼ of its actual value. Some people (including his mother) believe that the sale of this estate was the reason for the Prince's return. N.B.

N.B. Granovsky's relatives (sisters) had been moved out of sight, and were receiving a pension from the Princess. And so were his aunts. When the Captain returns, it is learned that they haven't been receiving their pension for a long time (the Princess had forgotten about it). Granovsky is ashamed of these poor relatives, 1) because they are poor and rather too much the plain old-fashioned type, having spent almost their entire lives <in the country>, and 2) because it now turns out that he hasn't been helping them at all, in spite of the fact that he has been telling people, including his son, quite often that he was supporting them. His son keeps rubbing this under his nose, among other things: "You kept telling me that you were helping them, yet you were lying all the time."

N.B. Those anonymous letters were (from Miliukov) addressed to Granovsky, saying that the Prince was coming back to take possession of ~~his own~~ what was lawfully his own, namely his wife, for Granovsky had accepted money for marrying her.

? ? ?

A REMARKABLE VARIANT

Perhaps it is all right to let Granovsky be married.

? The Ward only once, in the mountains of Switzerland, had a scene with the Prince, a scene which left her with a scar in her heart for the rest of her life. That's why the Princess was in such a hurry to marry her off.

The Princess, having learned about it, immediately married her off to Granovsky.

Inasmuch as nobody in town knows why the Prince has returned, *everybody* thinks that he did because he was greatly angered by Granovsky's marrying the Ward.

However, the principal scandalmonger is Nechaev.

A showdown after the scene at Granovsky's—Nechaev says: "I thought that this was the proper way." Shatov smiles—but later, without uttering a word, slaps his face.

The Prince always keeps aloof from Granovsky's wife; a pure and lofty relationship. He remembers, however, that scene in the mountains.

However, he has come mainly for the Beauty's sake, as well as knowing a thing or two about Nechaev's plans; and, in reality, due to his *excited condition* prior to his departure to Uri (he is mad).

After Granovsky's death—having never before said as much as a word about his love to the Ward (now a widow), he suddenly offers his hand, never thinking that he might be rejected; extremely confident, but respectful to the point of ecstasy.

Incredible warmth and tenderness.

The Ward accepts, directly and without a word, for the Prince has been her ideal all along.

Suddenly, Uri.

The episode with the citizen of the Canton of Uri.

N.B. It is precisely through the Prince's delicacy toward the Ward, and his behavior with regard to the Beauty and Shatov, that his appeal and conquering charm should be explained. Altogether, the Prince must be shown to be an *extraordinary* man.

N.B. Granovsky expects his son with apprehension, because of his recent marriage, and because of the estate.

The Princess, too, seems to be afraid of her son (the Prince), as she is counting on the Beauty.

She reaches an agreement with Granovsky—but there the affair (with the anonymous letter) is launched by Nechaev.

Granovsky: "She doesn't say much, but she is a good wife."

Nechaev: "Why do you keep repeating that? It shows your disrespect for her."

Granovsky keeps holding her hand and looking at her.

Nechaev: "I think that she is bored with you."

Nechaev: "To be lecturing one's wife about the emancipation of women..."

"You *have no shame*, that's all.

N.B. Granovsky's appearance before the Governor is necessary so that he could, at the lecture, shout about the Captain: "You cheap spy!" Also, he struck the Polish priest—there was a scandal.

The Captain could insult the Governor's wife with the bear.

138 N.B. At the lecture arranged for the benefit of the Polish priest, Granovsky gives a talk on Othello:

"Oh, Iago, how sad am I, how sad."

Here then, he recalls Desdemona's face. "The clamor of so lofty and ennobled love" (he just couldn't do without remembering Desdemona's face)...

To be sure, Granovsky understood it very well himself, yet he was, in actual practice, a most abstract kind of egoist.

Shatov's idea about revaluating the ruble: "As soon as we take a national course." (Perhaps at the meeting of the Committee.)

"That is, never," says Miliukov.

Granovsky. This innocent man suddenly becomes a sceptic: "One needs a friend to pour out one's slops on him. (Friendship is a good thing, up to a certain point.)"

~~You have written~~

The Princess to Granovsky, reproachfully: "You've written me sentimental letters not for friendship, but for posterity, because you think that you are a great man."

"You wrote me about the poor, yet you've spent no more than eighty kopeks!" (Nechaev's words.)

"All this love is nothing but self-love," says Nechaev at dinner at the Princess's. "The higher your love, the more self-love you obviously have..."

"That's indeed so," says the General's wife.

"Friendship for pouring out your slops."

"I haven't been answering your letters, for you weren't really addressing yourself to me, but to posterity, for you are convinced that you are a great man."

A joyful fire was shining in the Princess's eyes; she was watching Granovsky intently.

"When I was talking about the Madonna, you were eyeing me ironically."

9 *About Granovsky*

N.B. *The most important*: Abstractness of thought, the abstractness of one's own life and of one's social position may be, in some persons, the cause of extraordinary cruelty toward people, as well as of a prejudiced view of people and of things. This is sometimes the case with men engaged in abstract speculation, even though theirs may be an extremely refined intellect, and their reflections of the most profound. In their judgments of things, events, and people whom they have to face, they are often malicious, cruel, injust, and onesided—even vengeful. On the other hand, a man with a practical attitude toward people, even if he is actually malicious, cruel, and depraved, an oppressor and a predator, almost invariably has more faith in people, places a higher value on them, is less arrogant toward them, ~~and if he has good~~ and if he has good qualities of the heart and of the mind, he can view people with more compassion, more justice, in a more many-sided and profound way, and is capable of forgiving them many things.

"Nothing is more stupid than to act from conviction, Mr. Shatov. Act by acting. At your first success, everybody will join you. Nowhere in Europe is the ground as fertile as in Russia. We have here awfully many empty heads, with nothing at all put into them as yet. Just put something before them, and they will follow you immediately."

General Main Plan of the Novel

(Definitive)

The Prince. N.B. (All these philosophical systems and doctrines (Positivism and Comte, etc.) have appeared before (some new fact, and there is a renaissance) and have suddenly disappeared in an awful hurry, without leaving a trace, and unnoticed by almost everybody. And not because they were refuted ~~etc~~, oh, no–simply because they did not satisfy anybody... Whereas other ideas (Christianity, etc.) suddenly spread all over the world, conquered it, and certainly not because they were proven to be true, but simply because they satisfied everyone's needs...)

The Prince. He touched upon Shakespeare, got to talk about him, brought in Russia for comparison, and suddenly said: "Oh, well, how and where could we compare ourselves to anything so colossal?" (Could be that he dropped this as a hint to Granovsky.)

...More and more often the Prince would come to see Shatov at night, and Shatov was catching fire more and more, his eyes were lighting up... And light up with a terrible fire did also the Prince's eyes. And strangely enough, as time went on, and with every new visit, he was becoming more of a mystery to Shatov! "What does he intend to do? What is on his mind? Why did he come here? True, he came here in response to my own letter, but that is such a trivial detail! Surely he has some colossal and definite goal, some ready project, and he will begin... What is it that he will begin? Here or anywhere. There's a Russian with a new idea. But what is his idea?" Etc.

N.B. The citizen of the canton of Uri was hanging on a ~~twine~~ string, hidden between a wardrobe and a chest of drawers.

The Chronicler, on his own part: You know what, I still don't consider this important (the nihilists, that is). No matter what you say, it is unimportant (humorously, briefly, and in apt phrases).

Shatov's speech at the public lecture... (N.B. Shatov was talked into giving a speech, on the grounds that, having slapped the Prince's face, he had become a celebrity.)

In the West, the old social order has fallen into decay. The French Revolution.

The whole 19th century, struggle and ferment. Not a political, but a social upheaval.

If one wants to smash society and civilization, one needs a substitute for them. The socialists have their passionate faith. It has been compared to the Christian faith.

To be sure, a great many swindlers have joined them too, and look how many fools have joined them since they went out into the streets.

Religion has degenerated in the West. Their world is painfully suffering for want of spiritual life. (About religion and the need for it; science cannot fill the vacuum left by faith.)

Socialism has been embraced not only by those who are hungry but also by those who are thirsting for a spiritual life.

Society is built by Morality and by Religion. Moral principles are derived from Religion. Aesthetic strivings must be ~~firm~~ firmly established, the concepts of good and evil.

If there is no Religion, another morality will be substituted for it.

In order to abolish the former morality, one would have to abolish the belief in the soul and the faith in God.

That's where everybody seems to be of one mind, as if there were a purpose behind it, for Catholicism, too, has abolished the faith in God, having perverted Christ.

Our people have rushed headlong into accepting what is ready-made. Western tutelage. If they only knew what cause these people are serving.

Here. N.B. Better if Shatov would develop this thought: "If they knew that they are serving the most inveterate obscurantism, while thinking they are liberals. That's what it means to rush into accepting what is ready-made."

There have never been such retrogrades.

Stupid, petty, ignorant little fools.

But Orthodoxy will save everything

(deafening applause).

Whereupon the crowd also applauds the nihilists and everybody indiscriminately (a scandal), etc.

N.B. Reforms ought to be sincere and irrevocable. Even if modified in time, or subject to further progress, they should never change on principle. (This is said by Granovsky, and such voice was never heard before among us.) Perhaps Granovsky says this at the Governor's, during his first visit.

N.B. The Prince's idea (in his conversations with Shatov) concerning the enormous importance of Orthodoxy and its new phase. The influence of the Vatican Oecumenic Council of Pope Pius IX.[3] (My entire view of Orthodoxy as the fullest and most real self-expression of Russia, with definitive poignancy.) A future war because of two religions (France and Russia, Russia and Europe). Indirectly, they may be convinced that the war has nothing to do with religion, yet in reality it will be a religious war. The *spirit* of that war and its inevitability will emerge from a conflict of religions, as well as from the struggle for a new idea.

N.B. Miliukov, having listened to *some* of the things said at Nechaev's, asks him: "~~But~~ Tell me, when do you think the coup will take place?"

Nechaev answers resolutely: "~~I think that certainly~~ By spring. Judging by some indications I assume that it will start in February. By May ~~everything~~, of course, it will be all over."

Miliukov. "No," says Miliukov, stunned and startled by Nechaev's unsoundness, and ~~consequently~~ also by the very fact that he has become involved with him, "No, I don't think that it will be all over by May."

Nechaev: "Ah! Is that what you think? And what are your reasons for being of such opinion?"

Miliukov: (about the immensity of Russia). He is greatly surprised.

Nechaev: "~~Oh, these are all trifles. There's nothing to be afraid of.~~ This shows that you haven't understood what is most important about
141 our plan. Believe me, that immense structure which frightens you is held together by phantoms. Didn't you recently, and most felicitously, develop the very same idea (in your lecture)? And now, when the time has come to act, you are afraid. Does this mean that you have no faith of your own convictions? To be sure, this is quite natural for those distrustful likes of you who are counted by the millions. That's why we are

[3] Held in 1870, this Council established the infallibility of the pope.

around, to give encouragement and unity to the distrustful. It is boldness that strikes the imagination. One must begin by capturing the very strongest imaginations; one must see to it that what even the strongest imagination could not have surmised would actually happen. Then, this million of ~~wavering~~ convinced, but vacillating, people will be amazed at first, then join us en masse, and follow us. Besides, you know: locally, the peasants will be prepared by proclamations; then, with the help of the factory workers, we shall capture the city; and, through our members who are with the Regiment, get the whole Regiment over to our side; if not the whole Regiment, then certainly the greater part of it. I know that they've got arms at E–ts. We shall capture the plant, and the arms. Within a month, there will be uprisings in three or four provinces, in addition to ours. We'll shout that Stepan Timofeevich <Razin> has risen from the dead and is bringing his people new freedom. Then—then—well, why am I talking about this, you know it all anyway."

Miliukov: "Yes, but..."

Nechaev: "On the contrary, no *but's* at all. However, I suggest that you think it over. As for myself, I have no time for you right now; and altogether, I simply haven't got the time. Lots to do. Good-bye. Tonight, if I get the time, I may tell you about a certain detail." (N.B. He is alluding to Shatov's murder. This is already after the fire.)

Nechaev leaves, being perfectly convinced that he will be back in two and a half months.

N.B. Shatov (in his public lecture): "...these men, at least, have been paid for pledging to murder and to outrage their mother (Russia). They know full well what they are doing; they are pointing a knife at the throat of their victim, saying: 'That ought to bring us some money.' And their employers pay them with alacrity ~~for the murder~~ so they will finish off their victim. These men are obviously in the employ of Russia's enemies. But these others (the newspapers), those vile, silly little creatures, those academic adolescents, our herd of Panurge[4] (Korsh), why are they ~~dancing~~ dancing to celebrate the matricide? They don't even have to be paid. They hate Russia from conviction, and at every word about Russia and the Slavs they break into a cannibalistic dance and violent abuse. Arse-displayers."

---

[4] The hero of Rabelais' novel *Pantagruel* (1534).

Nechaev and Miliukov. While discussing the possibility of the Governor being converted to their beliefs, Nechaev says:

"Of course, I could see that he was lying in order to keep up appearances and to pose as a liberal, and of course he didn't know ~~with~~ what ~~who~~ he was talking about. But still, if one would make a real effort, I'm sure he could be brought around. However, that's not the point and there's no use talking about it. What difference does it make if one or the other is for or against us, especially if he is one of those who will all come and join us of their own accord, provided only we are successful. They'll be *coming over to our side* according to the rate of our success."

"It isn't a matter of propaganda, it's our scheme of action that matters. The unheard of boldness of our actions will stun them, and they'll be joining us by the thousands upon our very first success. Moreover, our teaching has already reached the masses. Everybody seems to be prepared, after a fashion. Look for yourself. Everybody is talking about family and children, about religion—but what kind of husbands and fathers are they, and do they have any kind of serious faith in God? Either indifference, or vacillation. Both of which serve us well... Look if the Government is firm. The very fact that it is so much afraid of us." Shatov.

143 *Nechaev* says, in his speech at the meeting: "They (i.e., the Government) have started a lot of reforms, and have only done us a favor by so doing. Absolutely nobody except the Government has worked for us so hard, because through the vagueness and weakness of these reforms, through their distrust of themselves and of society in carrying out these reforms, they have produced in our society that unsteadiness, that vagueness, that confusion, that debility of conviction and of faith, which Shatov has pointed out to us. By rejecting the old they have confounded the reactionaries; while by failing to give the necessary reassurance, they have discouraged the progressives. Any reform must be firm, clear, and as far as this is possible, definite, sincere, and irreversible. ~~For every reform has~~ Whereas what they've got is the perfect ideal of the golden mean, something made a little weaker and a little more indefinite, with an effort to conceal this and to hide that ~~and to remove the traces~~ and what's the purpose of it all? It's ridiculous, really: it is all so as not to irritate the reactionaries and to ~~pacify~~ keep down the progressives, thinking that in this fashion both will lay low or at least not make too much fuss ~~"they'll get over it, they'll take it more calmly"~~, while in reality it is all so much nonsense and confusion. For the sup-
142 porters of the reforms and of the Government, feeling weak and dis-

couraged, and realizing that it is they, in the first place, whom the Government distrusts, as it conceals things from them and converts the whole *business* into a bureaucratic secret, will either become indifferent, or even bitter enemies. The reactionaries, on the other hand, who were initially the enemies of the reforms, the landowners and government officials hurt by the reforms, will not only fail to acquiesce, but quite on the contrary, turn into ever so much more ~~bitter~~ potent enemies; for seeing the weakness and the vacillating of the Government, and sensing that it is afraid, afraid of them, they will regain their courage, take heart, and turn into an opposition, now in deed, as well as in word. A reform ought to be sincere and irreversible. Unsteadiness, confusion, the fall of the idol, the decline of our faith and of our morality which, though they may have been fantastic, yet had been standing firm and were supported by our entire social structure. This unsteadiness will penetrate into the lower classes and will leave the whole ocean of our common people agitated. It isn't easy to raise waves upon the ocean, but once you've got them it won't be easy to put them down again; and they have nothing to calm it down with, for they don't believe in their own strength. Do you know that sometimes, even recently, even now, as I take a close look at things, I've been struck by the idea of how strong the supreme power is in our country, and how it is supported by the people; and yet it is only a phantom—our people are both slaves, and 2) stupid. If there were a chance to hang half of them, I'd be glad to oblige, the rest will 3) act as raw material to form a new nation. Look (von Sohn, examples of morality, everything has come to the surface, everything has come to light). ~~Well~~ Who have they been working for, ultimately, but us? Why not fish in troubled waters? The Maksim Ivanovs will join us; the soldiers will join us. It is the boldness of our actions that will do it, the boldness of our propaganda. The rational, material law of morality. He who has a strong faith in himself is respected by everybody. One must stun the crowd by one's boldness. All Maksim Ivanovs will join us."

Uspensky: "Why, he's a scoundrel, a criminal."

"There are no scoundrels. There are those pressed by circumstances, all according to the laws of nature. In my opinion, Maksim Ivanov was fully in the right..."

Nechaev: "Remember, it is a dogma of our faith that there are no such things as scoundrels or criminals."

Uspensky: "Exactly as with the early Christians."

Nechaev: "Besides, all we need to do is destroy; anything will come handy for destruction, any material."

Explanation of why and in what sense he displays a complete ignorance of reality, whereas his theoretical part is good.

N.B. (Absolutely let the Chronicler comment on it.) On the part of the Chronicler, about Nechaev in connection with the question—is he a fool or isn't he? His theoretical side is strong, but he hasn't got the vaguest notion of reality.

N.B. At *Uspensky's*. His wife has taken a lover after all. Uspensky tells her: "Until now I have only loved you; but now I have begun to respect you." Yet he does cry a little. The lover actually moves in with them. The trio in the countryside nearby. Uspensky suddenly grabs him by the hair; later, he begs his wife on his knees not to let this fact become known. Later, they get used to each other. The lover suddenly decides to piss on everything and leaves town. Uspensky never does recover from this wound, but his wife keeps jabbering along, right by the book. Such is the condition of Uspensky's soul at the beginning of this story.

N.B. Shatov says (after having discussed the Slavophiles): "Now what is that, really? What kind of *narodnost* do we really have? We're still going to school."

143 N.B. After the Prince's death, the Chronicler should perform an analysis of his character (absolutely, a chapter entitled *Analysis*), in which he would say that he was a strong, predatory man, who got mixed up in his convictions and who, because of his immense pride, wanted and could arrive at only one conclusion, which *requires no explanation*, namely, he... etc.

"It is a curious fact that he had such a profound understanding of the essence of Russia, as when he explained it to ~~Nechaev~~ Shatov and aroused the latter's enthusiasm; but it is an even more curious and more incomprehensible fact that he did not himself believe in any of it after all."

N.B. Uspensky is a man seized by unrest, whereas Miliukov is a restless man.

Nechaev is terribly vain, but like a child (Livanov): "My name will live on for centuries, my proclamations are history, my brochure ~~will reach~~ will live as long as the world will."

N.B. After having already aroused Shatov's enthusiasm, and after their discussion about Orthodoxy, the Prince asks him: "By the way, do you believe in God?"

"And yourself?" "Absolutely not." On the next day Shatov asks: "Does this mean that you don't believe in what you told me about Russia either?" The Prince answers, maliciously: "Have you realized that only now?" "Have you been really deceiving me?" The Prince replies: "Oh, I was believing in it at the time; though, on second thought, perhaps I wasn't." "I'm feeling sorry for you." "Do feel sorry; *I'm so pitiable that I feel pity for you also.*"

More soberly. Simply, after three days of enthusiasm with Shatov, the Prince begins to turn cool toward him, and this to the point where he seriously and naïvely quits paying any attention to him. As regards his saying that he does not believe in God, he told that to someone else. Shatov happens to overhear it and asks: "Is it true that you do not believe?"

N.B. PUT DOWN A CLEAR NOTE EVERYWHERE: WHAT WAS IT THAT MADE SHATOV STATE HIS CONVICTIONS?—

The most important. N.B. The Prince was taking his discussions with Shatov so seriously that he would actually interpret the Book of Revelation for him. (He visited Shatov on 5 or 6 consecutive nights, then suddenly quit seeing him *in disgust.*)

N.B. Granovsky (is so petty) that, after having quarreled with his son, he actually rereads *What Is To Be Done?* for his lecture, trying to find some blunders in it. He was looking for them in a few other places also. The whole lecture was nothing but self-advertisement.

AUTHOR'S NARRATIVE

It must be done so that the Prince, *in spite of all the scandals which he has been involved in,* gains a great deal of authority after the murder of Shatov, and altogether after the conspiracy has been exposed. Up to that point the Prince has been taciturn, evasive, ironic (kind, with a tinge of lofty condescension), but here he suddenly seems to awaken from his apathy, and begins to talk. He gives an unusual display of energy (for a moment, he is suspected of the murder). A certain pudgy and poetic, grey-haired nobleman, an authority on literature and education, publicly denounces him for a predator, a wild beast,

Byron's Corsair, etc.: that to kill means nothing to him, that he had borne Shatov a secret grudge and killed him for revenge; so everybody begins to talk, and then everybody gets cold feet, and the pudgy (grumbler) beats an ignominious retreat. The Prince is the *only* man in town who does not lose his head and ~~everybody~~ it is he who straightens out the whole affair: he makes Miliukov and Uspensky confess; he captures Zaitsev; he delivers an inspired and formidable speech on the present unsettled condition of Russia and on how things really look in Russia today. "It isn't Russia's fault, or even ours." The response is a "hurray!" People actually want to elect him their Marshal of Nobility. The Princess is about to leave. Here, Granovsky dies. (By this time, the Prince has already abandoned the Ward, after having disturbed her greatly.) Here, *suddenly*, he leaves for Petersburg. Everybody is scared: "Is he going to inform the authorities, is he going to tell? Who knows, maybe he actually came here already having high connections, or even as an inspector, to check on us." (His speeches, in addition to their formidable tone, also sounded a good deal like a superior's contemptuous tongue-lashing. The Governor rushes to seek his advice, but the Prince remains condescending and aloof.) But while about to leave for Petersburg and though in a great hurry, he arranges a solemn public prayer to be held, inviting everybody to attend, and the whole town joins in, as a sort of penance–("We have been debasing our faith..."). He also organizes a subscription for the victims of the fire. But while about to leave for Petersburg and though in a great hurry, the Prince pays a visit to the Ward and offers her his hand–he looks as if he meant business, and as if he were in a hurry, full of plans; also, <he presents certain> conditions (the complete, passionate and somewhat somber, energetic confidence of a future leader). She accepts, fearfully yet enthusiastically. But instead of Petersburg, he writes her two weeks later from some small railway station, asking her if she would like to join him in becoming an expatriate; for he has already become a citizen of the canton of Uri, he is presently on his way there and is asking her to come to Uri all by herself–becoming an expatriate for good. Alarmed, she shows the letter to the Princess. "He is out of his mind completely!" exclaims the Princess ("Write to me in Uri," the Prince has given his address) and gets ready to travel to Uri with the Ward, i.e., at first to Petersburg. But that takes a while, what with travel arrangements and packing, five days to be exact, and suddenly, on the fifth day, they are told that the Prince has returned, quietly, to his suburban estate. The Princess and the Ward rush there, but he has already hanged himself. His suicide note is brief, disorganized, it explains nothing, but it is not mad; it is addressed to the Ward; not so much forgiveness as higher understanding. His papers show that he was really a citizen of Uri.

Only later, people in town begin to talk: Imagine him, knowing about Shatov's murder, being Nechaev's associate, admitting it all himself, yet preaching to us; it's as if he had cast a spell on us, the lunatic! The Chronicler says that he doesn't know what to think of it, i.e., whether or not the Prince was mad—that there are many people who act a hundred times more mysteriously, yet are considered clever, whereas here, in the Prince's case, I see, on the contrary, a very strong logical consistency (i.e., being uprooted from the soil, with no place to go, he thought that he might find rebirth in love, though not very much so, even ~~Nechaev~~ tried out Nechaev, and then shot himself).

As for ~~Golubov~~ Shatov, he was laughing at him, though perhaps through bloody tears, as he was firing up his enthusiasm for the pan-Slavic doctrine.

He was not laughing at Shatov, but was sincere. If not so, one has no understanding whatsoever...

But perhaps he was laughing, too, being a predator by nature. He suddenly tells the Ward: "I assure you that I agree with Nechaev in many respects."

June 8 <1870>

Shatov and the Prince, first meeting.

Shatov: "Society is moved by an aesthetic principle." "Paris."

"The aesthetic principle depends on Religion, Religion on itself only, on the revelation and direct intervention of God. The mystery of Christ."

"Only Russia can preach Christ. Only the Russian people are a God-bearing people."

In the Zemstvo's opinion: "why give it away, no control."

THE PRINCE—June 9

THE PRINCE HAS THE REPUTATION OF A GREAT DON JUAN.

Some more remarks on the Prince's character: The spoiled character of a young swell, yet a great mind, and great fits of passion. Much too passionate and too much in a hurry. He has succeeded in creating an ideal, yet feels at the same time that it is all only an invention of his (though it isn't actually his own either). Being the young swell that he is, he lacks patience; he also lacks breadth and depth, and eventually it all turns into a malicious joke. It is like certain sinners ~~even~~ (it is also said about demons) who may become believers, and who consequently clearly understand and see what they have come to believe in. Impatient as he is, he cannot forgive ~~either~~ Russia her deviations from the ideal; ~~nor~~ yet, due to his pride and narrow-mindedness, he does not see that he is himself guilty of an attitude toward reality which is incorrect, too exacting, and too impatient. However, it is most likely that his depraved nature has caused him to become more and more shallow, fit by fit, and eventually, toward the end, renders him completely insane.

AS A RESULT: A SPOILED YOUNG SWELL AND NOTHING ELSE. NOTHING BUT DISORDER.

N.B. Definitely insert a scene with the Ward at Skvoreshniki. The housekeeper has been bribed. The scene where the Prince insults her the Ward, and his terrible remorse. Shakespeare. They part as enemies. ("An ugly face.") First he rapes her, then begs her forgiveness. She also gets a letter from him about Uri—(a simple one, incidentally).

N.B. Definitely insert also the story about the government clerk and his wife.

?N.B. He has killed somebody. (Most doubtful.)

The Prince confesses his villainy involving the child (he raped her) to Shatov. He has written a confession, wants to have it printed, shows it to Shatov, asking him for advice. But after that, he begins to hate Shatov and is glad that he gets killed. He says that he would like people to spit in his face.

The Prince says: "It is stupid to blame people for one's own ugliness."

N.B. It is necessary that there be beforehand some instances of extraordinary unpleasantness between the Prince and his mother.

N.B. The Beauty has heard of him and is afraid of him. She makes fun of him. The Beauty hates him to some extent.

The Prince has been visiting with the Bishop. He has actually come to Russia in order to have his confession printed. But if he *can not make up his mind, then Uri.*

~~To the Bishop: "I don't believe in <God.>"~~

127 Marry the daughter of a minister of state.

The main thing. Prior to the Prince's arrival, rumors are heard in town about his connections with the highest circles in Petersburg, with ministers (Griboedov). (That's why he goes to the Governor, and that's why his mother allows him to go.) That he has *managed to worm himself* into a very high spot and that he may be about to get an absolutely special appointment. People in our town did not believe it at first, figuring that his rank was too low for that, even if he had the connections. But then there was another rumor that it wasn't rank at all that mattered here, but that he had personally managed to elicit the displeasure of a certain person in an incredibly high position, and that this was what the story was all about. That's when they started to believe it. However, there really wasn't too much talk, the whole thing being much too remote from us. ("A charming man, he really knows how to worm himself into your confidence.")

But when the Prince began to make speeches about town (on the other page), and to hold services, like a man in power, everybody started talking again, and when he announced that he was going straight to Petersburg, they were all frightened (the Governor).

A private person, friendly relations with a private secretary and an aide, and that one won't need to have any rank under these circumstances.

N.B. They got a scare: wasn't he in town acting in the capacity of a secret government inspector? Didn't he arrive exactly at the time when these proclamations started, and actually on the same day when the villain arrived? In fact, the notion of such a secret, entirely unofficial inspector, who wasn't even in the government service, seemed clever and enticing. "God knows, they've got everything going according to new regulations up there..."

The Prince comes to see Shatov (for the first time, after the slap in the face): "I haven't come to talk about that thing. I've noticed one of your ideas: an atheist cannot love Russia, or be a Russian. And I was struck by it."

Shatov (with a smile): "Why should I explain to you, why to an atheist..."

The Prince: "You don't have to. I know myself that an atheist cannot love Russia. That is my idea. I haven't ever run across it anywhere. And suddenly you are saying the same thing. I would like to know in what direction you are leaning."

Orthodoxy, Lutheranism. HERE.

N.B. The Holy Ghost is an immediate comprehension of beauty, a prophetic awareness of harmony, and so a steadfast striving for it.

N.B. Germany is our natural and perennial enemy.

N.B. Our whole strength lies in the fact that they do not know Russia.

N.B. An exclamation about Shakespeare.

N.B. Most important, couldn't it have been the Prince who committed that act of sacrilege in the church?

N.B. In his effort to become a Russian, the Prince has posed excessively high demands to himself, while actually not believing in them; and so, unable to stand such a state of doubt, he hangs himself.

N.B. Justify this.

The Chronicler, toward the end: He went much too far in his demands on himself. It remains unknown why he hanged himself.

The Prince: "I'm afraid ~~to hate~~ that I may hate Russia."

129 Without a steady basis for the development of small capital, and without a wealth of it, there won't be any credit. And small capital rests solely with the national character and, of course, depends also on how much free rein is given to this character.

They are corrupting people through *drunkenness.*

It rests with the national character and depends on it solely. Do you know that?

I am not praising the Germans, but rather, I am recognizing the fact that, with them, things have grown organically from their national character.

N.B. *The Prince and Shatov.*

The Prince: "Up there, they are worried about credit, and about revaluating the ruble. A terrible problem. And yet they won't understand that there can be only one remedy: ~~they are looking for it on the outside, nor will they understand when told that (the remedy) the disease isn't located on the outside, but deep inside the organism. There is only one remedy~~—the firm idea of a national principle. They'll laugh for sure if told that this is indeed so."

Shatov: "Why so? I haven't given any thought to this problem."

The Prince: "The remedy rests solely with the establishment of a firm national policy, and what is most important, with a steadfast, unwavering pursuit of that policy. It is important that this idea develop into a living organism and that everything be permeated by it. You are asking for proofs? I won't be pointing out any of the obvious, tangible facts which anybody can see for himself; but rather let's take, for instance, the fact that, once we have reform, and self-government, ~~the reform~~ they ought to be set up clearly, firmly, without vacillation, and with complete faith in the nation's strength. Any lack of stability is due solely to a lack of faith in Russia's strength, and because the German principle, viz. the administration, wants to suppress the ~~Russian~~ native Russian form., i.e., self-government. Neither will I bother to point out, for instance, that we have built 10,000 versts of railways, yet without having a single engineering plant in our whole country until very recently, as everything was being ordered from abroad, because we had no faith in ourselves, nor did we bother to start anything here at home. The same thing with armaments for our army. It is easy to find a hundred such facts, all showing how we vacillate while implementing an original national idea; which in turn has a most detrimental influence on the stability of the ruble, since you have brought up that topic. However, these are all only external considerations. The whole cause of it, I repeat, lies deep inside. The cause is a moral one. We Russians were derailed once and for all, and later kept under tutelage all the time. We have lost our moral self-assurance. (I am not speaking of the plain people.) We have lost our faith in everything, and are being blown about, like a leaf in a windstorm. What I want to say is that without that moral steadiness even the ruble won't become steady again. Why? Come on, look at our Russian capitalists and their capitals: it's as if they had all won it playing roulette. A father will make millions—and ~~is aiming~~ at he has made them not by accumulating capital, nor by labor, but rather by some ~~government contract~~ racket. Most of our fortunes have been made by racketeering. You can see that left and right. So no wonder that their heirs have all decided to become gentlemen, quit their business and joined the hussars, or simply squandered their fortunes. ~~That's not~~ ~~That is~~ Which means that it is all so much racketeering, and that these people have no idea how capital should really be accumulated. And actually there can't be any large capital if small capital is nonexistent, no legitimate natural proportion of the vast majority of small fortunes, to the large. Large capital exists only ~~where there are many small~~ because there is small capital. The whole credit system and your falling ruble depend solely on the stability of small capital. Without the latter there will be no economic recovery and no economic readjustment, nor will tricks do any good here. Does our society have even the faintest notion regarding how a capital is formed? A notion, perhaps, but nothing ingrained, nothing in the moral fiber of the people. But to accumulate a capital you also need a firm moral foundation, capital; capital is built only by labor and tenacious accumulation from generation to generation. The communist idea of the immorality of capital has had no success with us because all of our capitals were gained by racketeering, and not by stubborn work and labor. And even if not all of them were gained in this fashion, the notion of persistent labor and work has remained, over the centuries, unfamiliar to us, and we really do not believe in it either. I used to know a man in Germany who owned a house, ~~and meanwhile~~ a three-storey brick building which gave him an income, but meanwhile he continued to ply his shoemaker's trade, and kept working with his own hands, making shoes. ~~This man is thrifty and calculating~~, he makes it by being so persistent. He saves, knowing ahead how much he is going to save. ~~I don't know if this is good In Russia no <. . .>~~ He is calm and firm, he remains steady; even if he gets acquainted with ideas and acquires an education his shoemaker's mallet won't leave his hands. ~~Not that I am very much in favor of this.~~ You may approve of this or you may not, but there is one thing here that deserves credit, namely, that ~~all~~ this idea is firmly established, that it doesn't waver, that it has developed organically, that it believes in itself and in its own strength—and surely it must have taken centuries to build up such self-assurance in a nation, and certainly a firm foundation, and a firm, unwavering faith in its own strength—which is the very essence of nationality. ~~But we~~ We have nothing of the kind. We have no faith in ourselves and, truthfully, there really is nothing to believe in. A full two hundred years of unsteadiness. The entire reform begun by Peter has amounted to as much as taking ~~for instance, a solid~~ a rock which had been resting firmly on the ground and standing it up precariously on one end. And so we are standing there, trying to keep our balance. A wind will blow, and we'll be hurled down. And the further it goes, the worse it gets, because we have become so far removed from our national principle that we no longer feel a need to return to it, that we no longer understand what it means and why ~~to what purpose~~ one ought to be independent. Nor do we even understand ~~the highest question~~ : why should we love our soil? We understand nothing at all ~~we are vacillating all the time~~ , to the point where we've begun to like it that way."

129 "Everybody in Russia is now raising questions; we've buried everything under an avalanche of questions, haven't we? ~~But I swear And isn't it. But the most important~~ But isn't it most significant that, what we actually like so much about ~~posing~~ this mania ~~for new~~ for questions,

is the fact that they are ~~still~~ unsolved? Solve them, and you will cause grave chagrin to these questioners."

"Our habit of pretending to be Europeans carries with it as a first consequence, laziness and idleness; it relieves us of our responsibilities and cares; it deprives us of our initiative, as it makes us copy, unthinkingly and slavishly, ideas which are alien to us. It's easier to be a bookbinder than an author. That's why it is so tempting. They don't know themselves what they are bowing to."

Shatov: "You know what? You have been mentioning Germany as an example, and you are praising the Germans for their national spirit. Things have reached a stage where we have to learn even how to have our own national spirit from the Germans."

The Prince: "It is true that it has come to that, and if we have not entirely forgotten the idea of a national spirit, this is so because it does exist in the West. There is only one thing that strikes me, and that is how people in Russia haven't noticed as yet that the whole West, and its civilization, has developed and come into existence solely because, over there, everything rests upon a firm national foundation. Each nation believes in itself, to the point where it almost assumes that it is destined to conquer the whole world for its particular nationality. We are taking over a lot of things from them, yet we are afraid to take over this one, ~~because~~ 1) I repeat, because this idea would impose upon us labors and responsibilities, and we have become accustomed, ever since Peter the Great, to be doing nothing; 2) and you know what, the system of serf-ownership was really the veritable golden heritage of Peter's reform; it corresponded entirely to its spirit, and was its principal fruit. 3) They point to Kotoshikhin.[5] But read, for instance, the Book about the White and Black clergy, would you say that this is any better than Kotoshikhin? 4) You can see for yourself the progress we have made since Kotoshikhin. It is two hundred times worse, for two hundred years have passed since, if as much as one hundredth of it is true. 5) ~~And is this really the only thing~~ And don't forget, it is only too easy to write a book."

---

[5] Grigory Kotoshikhin, (born about 1630). He betrayed Russia by giving Sweden some documents, fled from Russia, and served Sweden. He wrote a book about Russia, describing its mores and conditions. In 1667 he was condemned to death for killing a man in a quarrel.

125 VALUABLE.

The Prince to Shatov, after their last conversation: "I don't believe in God."

Shatov: "I know it."

The Bishop advises him to wait. Self-improvement. Becomes free (St. Paul) (all of Golubov)—and then, after several years of hard work, act according to your own best judgment. But all this impatience and haste—that's that same untidiness once over again.

"I was always bored" (mention once).

"I am simply a scoundrel."

"You are a spoiled young swell," says the Bishop.

N.B. He only has a bite for dinner, then eats a big meal for his dessert.

Granovsky and Nechaev: "But I am your father." "Quite possible, though I wouldn't be positive about it. Judging by the character of my mother—a man is inclined to be blind." ~~Legally~~

Age and age, and Lev Kambek.

Nechaev to Granovsky: "It was you yourself who used to wake me up twice a night, and embrace me, and tell me the story of my mother."

~~Nechaev~~ (Granovsky: "Alas! I meant it in a higher sense...")

Nechaev to Granovsky: "You are talking about flunkies; why, you were a flunky more than anyone else."

Granovsky: "I? A flunky?"

Nechaev: "Worse than that, a hanger-on."

Nechaev to Granovsky: "Aren't you accepting money for marrying a girl who needs a husband?"

(He attacks him, mostly because of Varvara Petrovna.)*

Nechaev: "Because it is the most natural explanation. I was talking mostly about him. He has gambled away his estate, well, so he needs money. Incidentally, didn't you write yourself that you needed money,

---

* The sentence might also mean: "It is mostly Varvara Petrovna who attacks him."

that everything was mortgaged, and that you had decided to make a sacrifice? I am simply referring to your letter as I say this."

Varvara Petrovna: "What letter?"

Here it is revealed that Stepan Trofimovich had written a letter to his son, and Varvara Petrovna charges into Granovsky.

"I have shown all of your letters to Varvara Petrovna."

Nechaev to those present: "Allow me only 5 minutes, and you will all agree with me. As for the young lady, of course no one could have more respect for her than I. All that is required here is some courage to explain the whole thing."

Nechaev: "Well, good-bye, old man. Listen: don't feel hurt by what I am saying. In my opinion, which is of course the correct one, you are entirely in the right. You haven't got money, and you are being offered some for sacrificing yourself, and you're accepting it. Yet you're wrong in relation to the common cause. You're putting on a show and saying that you are a victim, yet you'd be very happy indeed to get married, wouldn't you? Well, and this is bad, if for no other reason then simply because marriage is based on a prejudice. So you are striking a pose, and shouting in a tragic voice, but isn't that stupid? And what's the most stupid part of it is that you are accusing me, ~~first of all~~ while from your very own viewpoint you've acted even more basely yourself. I'm going to speak from your point of view, not from mine. You're reproaching me for thinking ill of my mother, but who was it but you who suggested these thoughts to me, waking me up twice every night. That is baser still, to judge from your point of view. Don't worry about mine, I'm not passing judgment on you, for it is much better to spell out the truth, which you did. It isn't any of my fault that, with you, it came out so stupid; but could it be otherwise with the likes of you, what with your ideas of things? And tell me, please, what difference does it make if I am, or if I am not your son?"

"A mixture of Nozdriov and Byron. An opinion which, while both unfair and prompted by envy, is not entirely lacking in sense."

N.B. *Somewhere else, Nechaev says to Granovsky:* "Come on, why must you put on such an act? Tell me, what difference does it make if I am your son, or not your son, you my father, or not my father—nothing but trivialities, really. I'm telling you: what difference does it make if I am your son or not? Look at it from your own point of view: you put me away, with all kinds of aunts, ever since my childhood; you then saw me only twice in your life, which means that you can't have been overly concerned about me. So tell me, please, what are you whimpering about now?"

N.B. After all that has happened and been said, Nechaev suddenly shows up at Granovsky's as if nothing had happened: "Well, we had a talk; I'm curious to get to know all sorts of people, so why should I turn away from you?"

N.B. Everybody in town takes Nechaev's side. "Surely if you want to have good children, you must be a good father and bring them up yourself."

And other such moral admonitions on the part of the public.

~~A mixture of Nozdriov and <...>~~

The Prince and Shatov

The Prince: "They all (Renan,[6] Gué[7]) think that Christ was an ordinary man, and criticize his teaching as unsound for our time. Whereas there isn't any teaching, really, only incidental sayings, and what really matters is the figure of Christ, from which any teaching must emerge (for a contrast, look at the vanity and moral condition of these critics and tell me: are they qualified to criticize Christ?). From Christ there emerges the idea ~~for which~~ that the principal accomplishment and goal of humanity is equivalent to the result of having acquired a morality. Imagine that everybody would be like Christ—well, would the vacillations, the perplexities, the pauperism of our age still be possible? He who cannot understand that has no understanding of Christ, nor is he a Christian. If people would not have the slightest idea of the state or of any of the sciences, yet they would be all like Christ, would it be possible for paradise not to be realized on Earth immediately? On the other hand, look at civilization: the first question to be asked is that of a definition of happiness; not only has civilization failed to solve it, but it has actually confused it even more. And as for our own age, the less said about it the better. One would think that the foremost task of civilization ought to be to give firmness to the moral principles once

---

[6] Ernest Renan (1823–92), historian and man of letters; something of a positivist. His important and daring works are *The Life of Jesus* and *Origins of Christianity*.

[7] Nikolay N. Gué (1831–94) painted portraits of Hertsen, Tolstoy, Turgenev, and other men of letters.

acquired by mankind. But what do we see? The further ahead, the shakier these principles become, and Nechaev preaches that we really don't need any. Civilization has ultimately decided the question by using yardsticks, and by measuring the prosperity of the state by the number, size, and weight of the products manufactured by its people. An absurd definition, and a wretched and trivial one, whereas the only thing we really need are moral principles. And yardsticks, too, would come around, if there be need for any. The moral teaching of Christ can be expressed in a couple of words: it is the idea that an individual's happiness lies in his voluntary and self-desired renunciation of his individuality, if others would benefit from it. But the formula is not what really matters here. What matters is the fact that the individuality has been actually realized—try to refute the individuality of Christ, an ideal incarnate! You couldn't even think of it. That's where universal work (if everybody would be like Christ) would be realized, accompanied by joyous chanting, and not of Athenian nights."—Etc.*

N.B. Speaking of Russia, Shchapov[8] has altogether forgotten that she was in the process of creating a huge state, under impossible circumstances; he has also forgotten that all of Europe was actually even worse, ideally, because it measures things by yards and by weights (note that the more industrialized they are becoming, the more calamities, pauperism, heinous crimes, and moral vacillation they have to show for it). Russia is asked to do the impossible, in the past and now again, what is naturally impossible: industry, agriculture, the need for industrialization, research, colonization, are perhaps possible only when the population density has reached a certain level. A development, also, with a certain density of population. Add to this the fact that Russia's regular development was forcibly interrupted by Peter the Great. It is being forcibly interfered with to this day, and it has come to where our publicists consider every spontaneous activity both a disgrace and ludicrous wishful thinking. These people are mad. There is actually only one thing that we do need, and Russia had it even as early as the 16th century, the fact notwithstanding that these people are screaming about Russian Byzantinism. But they are simply dullards who cannot grasp the heart of the matter. To have such understanding, one needs to have

---

* . . . *no ne afinskikh vecherov,* "and not of Athenian nights," stands in no proper syntactic relationship to the preceding.

[8] Afanasy Shchapov (1830–76), a historian occupied with questions of church history, especially with the church schism. In 1864 he was sent to Siberia for liberal activities. He was somewhat influenced by Chernyshevsky and Pisarev.

a sharp intellect, and ~~much~~ a refined sensibility. What we need is more morality. It takes organization of the highest order to understand that.

The Prince: "The main principles of our 'Europeans' are, 1) not to be themselves, 2) to have no morality whatever—etc."

Shatov: "That's simply from laziness." *The Prince:* "Maybe." "But that's precisely what they haven't got in Europe; everybody is independent there, and that is their cornerstone. So it turns out that our Westerners actually stand for Byzantinism more than do Europeans."

Granovsky: "That is a new journal; that is real progress."

Shatov took a look, frowned, and shook his head:

"Eh! It will crawl along for a short while and then go bankrupt."

Granovsky: "Crawl along? What a strange expression to use for (the tendency) the activities of this journal!"

145 He turned away, toward the window: "I cannot marry someone else's sins; go, and you will see," with tired eyes.

Stepan Trofimovich during the sermon: "*Je ne suis pas pour les églises; vraiment, je suis pour le progrès.*[9] But if my Petrusha (Nechaev) were more clever, he would have thought up precisely this particular measure (consolidation of parishes) to deliver a fatal blow to Russia, and to cause her disintegration. But thank God, there is our wise administration which will correct Nechaev's error. It will nip the people in the bud, and Nechaev's cause will be on firm grounds. And what a fine and worthy goal: to increase the output of material goods, and hence moral and spiritual values, through self-interest."

L'enfer est pavé de bonnes intentions.
Grattez le Russe vous trouverez un tartare.[10]

Aliosha Teliatnikov.

Having come to see Shatov, the Prince, instead of explaining the reason for his visit, immediately begins to talk about the Antichrist.

---

[9] French: "I do not support the church; I support progress."

[10] French: "Hell is paved with good intentions. Scratch a Russian and you'll find a Tartar."

P.S. And from the letter which Shatov had sent him from America.

<Half a page of irrelevant arithmetic calculations.>

"If you've come to see me, the fool, you must have believed that I was wise."

"Come on, I can't challenge you to a duel, why should we ape the French?"

"~~But you should have~~ given him a good tongue-lashing but you got scared!"

"Meanwhile, a tongue-lashing—I understand."

"Yes, a coincidence."

"You keep insisting on your version, about that coincidence."

The Prince: "You said that duels were borrowed from the French."

"Isn't that a little too subtle for our local people?"

"You are judging things by the standards of our capitals: we have some most refined people here, Sir, we certainly do. People who'll grasp the subtlest things, Sir."

"The beating they'll give you won't be so subtle."

"Come on, Sir, I can't challenge him to a duel, can I?"

"You don't like duels, do you?"

"Not natural... and why should we be aping the French?"

Increase Kartuzov's role in the novel—and connect his part more with all the others.

Develop Liza.

The secret.

Schefel-Strasse No. 1.

I left being fully convinced that the man was mad. Perhaps he actually was.

June 13/1, 1870

Most Immediate Notes

Granovsky is a Slavophile. All this is a matter of schooling. "I assure you, my dear, we'll have to learn from the Germans even how to become nationalists."

About Belinsky:[11] "There was this incredibly young man who used to walk out to the railway tracks. But sometimes melancholy, too. I'll die—recalling they were playing cards. But how they loved Russia!"

~~On his own part~~ On his own part.

About the Slavophiles and about Russia he made bold to speak condescendingly, "school <boys> learn your nationality."

When the peasants,—nonsense—nonsense—axes, proclamations, nonsense, nonsense—

This "nonsense—nonsense" was heard more and more often. He moved to another flat—bedroom—and hysterics.

The explosion comes at the very end, but it actually coincides with the beginning of the chronicle.

Explanations about the other characters.

"As our malicious and very dear Shatov assures us."

"a gentleman's fancy."

"although, by the way, it is very funny."

"But listen to an old man,
study your nationality."

"He loved us all, and we loved him too."

He moved to a home where he felt more at ease. What was bad was that he kept losing. Before the emancipation of the peasants he was so frightened that all of us were amazed. As regards the revolution, he was a fine raconteur, ~~too bad~~ his glass of wine, a different flat. Too bad he played cards, but he was a matchless raconteur, in his later years he was bilious, yet he recalled his friends Belinsky, Granovsky, and Hertsen with gratitude. I don't know whether he was an atheist or whether he did believe in something. Naturally he never went to church to avoid compromising himself.

Even without their heads they wouldn't have understood a thing, though it is true that their heads were blocking their ability to understand things more than anything else.

All about Uspensky
a shitty little song

---

[11] These reminiscences about Belinsky spoken by Stepan Trofimovich found their way into Dostoevsky's *The Diary of a Writer* for 1873, in an article entitled "Old People."

an idea into the street
they copied it.
He used to make fun of Vera Pavlovna.[12]
the proclamations—"If you want fires, let's have some fires!"
nonsense—nonsense.

This "nonsense—nonsense" was heard more and more often, but the dream continued; ~~but~~ it was a long time to go until the explosion,—and suddenly everything broke loose.

Vera Pavlovna

a wretched little song

At Varvara Petrovna's.

~~Of course~~ The members of our circle held different views. Miliukov used to be in the opposition, but Stepan Trofimovich liked his caustic wit. All in all we loved him; there were many people who loved him. As for his convictions, excepting only a few so-to-speak sacred ~~beliefs~~ ones (rather in the department of saints), he used all the rest more or less to show off, or else kept changing his mind like a weathervane. I have already mentioned that he had acquired many bad habits, and actually to the point where Varvara Petrovna gave up on him, at least to some extent. All this, of course, from having grown fat and—to use a more delicate term—leading an idle life. Occasionally he would be in a mood to tell us God only knows what nonsense, as if he were laughing at us, and this would last for days and weeks. I've already mentioned his habit of speaking French.

pic-pic-pic-quedito <?>
Yes, he did have sensitivity!

Vera Pavlovna

He would often criticize an opponent from the point of view of reality, and occasionally even Russian reality, which was sometimes a little comical, for he had positively lost sight of Russia. However, this gave the old man a good deal of satisfaction, and we rarely contradicted him.

---

[12] The heroine of Chernyshevsky's *What Is To Be Done?*

About this terrible wedding... But before I do, I must explain some of the other characters, even though I'll do it briefly and indirectly, so as not to lose the thread of my narrative.

Uspensky. Incidentally, we loved him and even respected him—for his purity, and we are now sorry about the misfortunes that have befallen him. I want to make it plain that there was a lot more substance to that man than the comical nature of the dénouement might suggest.

19 Concerning nationalism.

In this respect he had firm ideas, settled once and for all.

"Why am I called an atheist? I believe in ~~the idea of a divine principle~~ God, as does any decent person, in God as the being which, in me, becomes conscious of itself."

Everyday life. The Ward to the Prince: "I am your slave." (the Bible) She received a letter from him and, on his very birthday, told the Princess that she was not going to marry Stepan Trofimovich. The Princess, very angry with Stepan Trofimovich, went to see him right away.

The Governor's wife to the Prince about the fact that she hasn't paid anyone a visit here so far.

About Teliatnikov: *"C'est un jeune homme charmant..."*[13]

The Governor and Granovsky.

The Governor (annoyed): "That is some kind of nonsense."

The Governor: "That is, how do you mean it?"

Granovsky: "That's what and that's how, your Excellency."

Nechaev ~~Nechaev~~ to the Prince, in our circle: "Look, of these people, only three are really active, the rest are just spying on each other. They can't be caught. Perhaps three, or six, will be caught—we'll escape abroad. One won't succeed, another will carry on for him. It smolders here and it smolders there, suddenly a wind, and—and—and you've got a general conflagration. Destruction, exactly what's needed."

20 1) Adding some administrative irritation to your private irritation—a mixture of private and administrative irritation.

---

[13] French: "He's a charming young man."

2) "How can you let me marry another woman?"
"You aren't a woman."*
"J'ai pris un mot pour un autre. Mais je suis...incapable."
"Oh, vous pouvez."[14]

3) "Wouldn't you like a glass of vodka?" (Granovsky to the police sergeant).

4) *The ear.* And though this happened in private, so-to-speak in the family, and therefore couldn't be too bad a stain upon the honor of this exalted government official, the General (*Gov.*) got so angry that he decided to take this extraordinary measure and executed it himself.

5) The whole Slavophile movement does nothing but sing its own praises, which means that it has reached its very climax and, consequently, won't go any further.

6) *The Prince's ideas.* A new idea. This isn't Anglo-Saxon law, nor is it Democracy or the formal equality of the French (Romance) world. This is natural brotherhood. The Tsar is at the head. Slave and yet free (St. Paul).[15] The Russian people will never rise against their Tsar (which some Tsars failed to realize, fearing an uprising). But they will come to realize it. The Tsar is for his people an incarnation of their soul, of their spirit. Uprisings could only occur as long as there existed a division of society into estates: the Moscow of December 14 (the people were always set against it). All this has come to an end with the emancipation of the peasants. Russia is not a republic, it is not Jacobinism, or communism. (Foreigners, as well as our Russian foreigners, will never understand this!) Russia is no more and no less than the embodiment of Orthodoxy (a slave, and yet free), and those Russians who have betrayed Christianity. In Russia, there live peasants. The Apocalypse. The millennium. The Roman Whore (for their Christ has accepted the earthly kingdom rejected in the desert). We have reached the last stage of our submission to Europe, to civilization, to the curse of Peter's reform. Intellectual irresponsibility—(socialism, communism, baseness)—but we shall eventually grasp this not only

---

* Russian *baba*, "woman," is pejorative. There is no exact equivalent in English.
14 French: "I took one word for another. But I am incapable..." "Oh, you can."
15 A free quotation from I Corinthians 7:22.

with our vigorous vitality (as we did finally grasp) <...> i.e., immediately and alive, but also with our intellect; we shall smash those European fetters which have been clinging to us for so long, and they will break like cobwebs; and we shall all realize, finally, that the world, the terrestrial globe, the Earth has never *seen such* a gigantic idea as the one which is now taking shape here, in the East, and moving to take up the place of the European masses <*sic*> ~~which~~ to regenerate the world. Europe will ~~either~~ flow into our waters as a living stream, ~~or~~ and the part of it which is dead and doomed to die will serve as ethnographic material for us. We are bringing the world the only thing we can give it, which is, however, the only thing it needs: Orthodoxy, the true and glorious, eternal creed of Christ and ~~regeneration~~ a full moral regeneration in his name. We are bringing the world the first paradise of the millennium.—And from amongst us, there will appear Elias (Enoch and Elias) and Enoch, who will give battle to the Antichrist, i.e., the spirit of the West which will become incarnate in the West. Hurray to the future.

This is the Prince's speech after Mass. Like a Samson with champagne. Leaves for Petersburg and hangs himself in Skvoreshniki.

This is important.

June 18/6, 1870.

N.B. *Prepare* the reader so that he can understand this speech. For instance, in his conversations with Shatov there is mention of what "a slave, and yet free" (St. Paul) is to mean.

A Russian will be ashamed if he is told, in Europe, that he is independent, and not entirely a European!

21 N.B. *The Prince and Shatov.* The Prince assures Shatov that all the mysteries regarding how to reach perfection and universal brotherhood have been given us by Orthodoxy and its discipline:

Self-perfection

Let no one be disheartened by the fact that this may be hard to achieve. And not all are needed, but only a few, so the idea will not die, and the world will be reborn.

Do you actually know how strong "one man" is? Raphael, Shakespeare, Plato ~~or~~ Columbus, or Galileo? He stays alive for 1000 years and regenerates the world—he does not die.

Some people are reborn too quickly and too obviously; with others it goes unnoticed.

N.B. PRECIOUS ~~REMINISCENCES~~ OBSERVATIONS.
"I cannot wait," says the Prince,
and *later:* "I don't want to wait."

N.B. *Shatov* conducts himself with extraordinary tact when he is with the Prince. He would very much like to ask: "Why is the Prince always with Nechaev, and what does he need that man for?" But, from a delicate feeling of tact, he doesn't ask this question.

The Prince notices this and says to him, with exquisite, deeply cordial familiarity: "You would like to ask me a question, but you can't. How tactful of you!" (And then he proceeds to tell him about Nechaev quite freely, i.e., why he has become involved with him.)

N.B. *Having bitten his ear.* One thing amazes me: "The Prince always showed respect for Stepan Trofimovich."

Chaque femme ne peut pas (ÊTRE COMME) *s'appeller Marie. Mais plusieurs maris sont comme diffemmes.*[16]

N.B. General Drozdov is writing denunciations.

N.B. ~~Young~~ Nechaev brought a letter for the Governor's wife.

N.B. The Governor sees that atheism is spreading, and is afraid of the atheist movement in town; that's why he started these discussions with Nechaev—that it is too early ("I perfectly agree, but it is too early!").

The Prince: N.B. "A Russian abroad (or a civilizer, Stasiulevich)[17] is just eagerly waiting for a chance to shine somebody's shoes. They, we are born flunkeys."

Shatov: "Those flunkey journalists and those flunkey journals are

---

[16] Dostoevsky is punning here on the sound similarity of Marie and *mari* ("husband"): "Every woman cannot be called Marie, but some husbands *(maris)* are like women."

[17] Mikhail M. Stasiulevich (1826–1911), a professor at St. Petersburg University, taught courses on the history of the Middle Ages. In 1861 he resigned with a group of other professors in protest against the conservative policies of the Ministry of Education.

out to prove at every point that there is no such thing as Russian independence from the West. Europe does not know us—we Russians have nobody but ourselves to blame for not having earned such distinction. Europe knows us because there is nothing in Russia that might be difficult to learn about.

N.B. Westernism is servility, intellectual servility.

(Article on Dickson,[18] *European Herald*, April, 1870.)

(The *European Herald* is mad at Pushkin for his ancient epigram.)

Convulsive hatred of Russia. If some fact comes up ~~positive~~ which speaks in favor of the Russian people, they are immediately peeved. Right away, they bring up some "but," and try to downgrade that fact, to reduce it to insignificance, and call to mind all of its flaws.

The Prince to Granovsky, at the Governor's: "*Maman* tells me that you were taken to the police station."

Granovsky: "No, not to the police station, for it wasn't a state case."*

Granovsky and Shatov: "Why, aren't you a Slavophile yourself, Shatov?"

Shatov: "Yes, a Slavophile, because I am not of the people—"

~~Shatov~~ *Granovsky:* "Well, if you aren't, who is?"

Shatov (interrupting him): "You want to say that I am the son of a house serf, and so of the people, but—"

Granovsky: *"Oh, mon Dieu, non."*

Shatov: "My dearest, no hard feelings—but though I may come from among the people, I am not now of the people."

Granovsky: "And so you have become a Slavophile because you found it impossible to become something better."

Shatov: "That's right, I've become a Slavophile because I've found it impossible to become anything better."

N.B. *An appellative:* PAPER PEOPLE.

Our whole liberalism is exclusively a sort of higher classicism, which is the reason why it has veered in false conservative directions. It

---

[18] Reference to an article which appeared in the May issue of *The Russian Messenger*. Dostoevsky made an error about the issue.

* There is an untranslatable pun in the original: *chast'*, "police station"—*chastny sluchai*, "a particular case."

watches with tender care that the German dominance be preserved. It keeps shouting that this is civilization and takes for granted that mankind can't possibly produce any other civilization but that which belongs to the Germano-Latin race. Exactly as if a German of the age of Arminius, instead of fighting the Romans, would keep shouting to his own people: "Let's submit! For there isn't and never is going to be anything but Roman civilization."

Our liberals are flunkeys more than anything else, eagerly looking for a chance to shine somebody's shoes.

A page: A SOIRÉE AT GRANOVSKY'S.

The Prince to Granovsky's son: "I saw your boots the other day." (Granovsky:) "Why doesn't he stay at my place?" Granovsky says to his son that he has become involved with some socialists. Nechaev: ~~"Eh, what's the difference!"~~ "Less trouble for you."

"I've been suffering for you here, and you tell me 'less trouble'!" *Nechaev:* ~~"I don't understand"~~ "What is there for you to suffer?"

Granovsky to the Princess: *"Il n'est pas grand, mais il est bon, ne parle pas trop."*[19]

(The Great Writer with Nechaev.)

~~I look~~ "Whenever I look at his face he reminds me of little Pisarev; why, we met many socialists in Petersburg."

The Governor's wife—"Socialism is a great idea," Shatov said quite suddenly and unexpectedly.

Everybody looked at him in consternation.

HERE "The idea is a great one, but its followers are not always giants, that's what you wanted to say, *et restons là mon cher.*[20] But as far as Pisarev is concerned, I find that he does look like him."

"Pisarev was a man of sense and of honor," Shatov suddenly cut in again unexpectedly, dropping his eyes.

Again, everybody looked in his direction ~~Granovsky frowned.~~

"Mais sans doute mon cher, sans doute et quelle mouche vous pique?[21] I used to have some special words of praise for him. He dropped in on me several times, though he had nothing to say most of the time. It seems that at one time he was detained at a lunatic

---

[19] French: "He is not big, but he is good; don't talk so much."
[20] French: "Let it go at that, my good man."
[21] French: "But assuredly, my good man, assuredly, but what's irritating you?

asylum...or was it somewhere else? He has left in my mind the impression of something small."

"Why small?" Nechaev asked, "he was ~~of average stature not at all~~ not of particularly small, but rather of average, stature."

"I am not talking about his stature, or about his talents. I—I don't know why, but he seemed so small to me, in a word, I was left with an impression of something small and *restons là*."

~~*Eh* I said that you were like him~~ "Don't take it personally," he said, turning to his son.

Nechaev: "Well, you're a giant yourself, aren't you?"

Granovsky was peeved. "The sound, *mon cher*, you could have YOU COULD HAVE EXPRESSED said ~~differently~~ this differently. But let's say it is a case of being frank on your part, and commendable, and I agree with you that it is indeed so."

Nechaev: "Well, if it is, what are you getting excited about?"

At the Governor's wife's, after the arrest.

Granovsky: "They are all like that! Remember, Varvara Petrovna, how he was sprawling on your divan in his dirty boots. Incidentally, I had to suffer for these boots in more senses than one. Do they still talk about Pushkin and the boots?"[22] he turned to his son.

Nechaev: "What Pushkin and what boots?"

Granovsky: "Soft-boiled, *mon ami*, as Pyotr our coachman likes to say. *Mais restons là* ~~You people keep mistaking rudeness for noble simplicity and sincerity, forgetting that it may be insulting~~. God spare me of giving you lessons."

Nechaev: "Didn't you give lessons at one time?" ~~So you've gotten into the habit—the way a schoolmaster treats his pupils, nothing else~~

Granovsky (after a pause): "If you want that he <...> You are mistaking your rudeness for <...> I am shocked and hurt by what you just said. ~~All of you are like that~~ I feel sorry for you. You are all—(from Renan)."

He is accepting alms.

"You have given away a lot, 80 copecks" (a beautiful, forceful tirade).

---

[22] A reference to Pisarev's excessively utilitarian view of art, expressed particularly in his essays "Pushkin and Belinsky" and "Realists."

("Try to remember honestly, when was the last time you gave alms to a beggar, and how much was it, truthfully?")

24 "You are smart, and you have caught me—it may be as much as 10 years ago when I last gave alms, I confess, *mais cela ne prouve rien,*[23] because <...>.

Nechaev: "On the contrary, that's exactly what proves it. ~~That is precisely the point~~ the proof."

"But the heart, the heart—" *Nechaev:* "I remember how you wouldn't let me sleep at night, you and your heart, waking me up at night."

"And you can bring back this memory in such a fashion?"

Nechaev: "It is all very well for you to say, you well-provided-for hanger-on."

Granovsky: "Hanger-on?"

Nechaev: "What else? Tell me, what are you doing? What are you drawing your salary for?"

Sound.

Granovsky: "But you have insulted me, and I won't suffer it."

Nechaev: ~~For God's sake~~ "I'm only repeating your own words. You wrote me ~~that this was so~~ yourself, here's your letter. You're writing me that you are being forced to marry a girl ~~and that you are forced to do it so as to cover up for someone else's sins~~ to cover up for someone else's sins."

(In the intervals the Great Writer talks to Pisarev.)

Granovsky: "I never wrote you anything of the kind."

Nechaev: "Here is your letter. To be sure, you haven't got anything here about sins, only that you are being forced to marry a girl, which is right here; and as for the sins, I found out about that from another source."

Sound. "Come to your senses! You don't realize what you are saying!"

Shatov and I after Granovsky's lecture,

I was teasing Shatov:

"...there are 100,000 of them (latent), yet they never get around to speaking their mind. But here, finally, there is one who decided to have his say, and spoke up. And how he did speak up!"

Shatov: "It would have been better if he hadn't."

---

[23] French: "But that doesn't prove anything."

I: "I'm not talking about the quality ~~of what~~ of what he said, I'm talking about the person who did." I regretted having teased him.

While visiting with the Governor's wife, Granovsky has an eloquent exchange of words with his son, etc. As if they had never quarreled.

XI
The Prince and the Consequences of Faith and Unfaith

These notes were written near the end of June, except for notebook pages 9 and 10 of notebook 3, which were written about July 23. This section comprises notes 27–40 and 9 and 10 of notebook 3.

As in the last section, but at greater length and in a more refined manner, the Prince rehearses the ideas that were to appear so often in Dostoevsky's *The Diary of a Writer*, and, mercifully, so fragmentarily in *The Possessed:* that Orthodoxy alone is truth, that the people are the unconscious carriers of pure Christianity, that science and reason cannot be guides to life, and that man left to his own resources will turn into a beast. In this long and unified dialogue-monologue, the Prince is more consciously a doubting expositor than in the previous section. It is not so much faith that he exposits, but the dilemma of faith and unfaith, and the logical consequence of each: Orthodoxy or Nechaev. The Prince says: "there are only two alternatives: either to have faith, or to burn everything. Nechaev has chosen the latter, and is strong and calm. I am just taking a good look at him, as I want to find out how much of his strength is derived from his convictions, and how much is simply due to his character." And he says: "And so, the whole question rests right here: can one believe in everything that our Orthodox religion tells us to believe? If the answer is no, it is much better, and more humane, to burn everything and join Nechaev." Nechaev is the alternative to the idea of Orthodoxy the Prince exposits so eloquently and believes in so little. Earlier in the notes the Prince was poised between Nechaev and Golubov; now he is poised between two sides of himself.

This section expresses powerfully the growing stature of the Prince as the ideological core of the novel. Dostoevsky comes back fragmentarily to the romantic intrigue of the novel, to the Prince's relationship to the Beauty and the Ward, but with little success, despite a note of satisfaction to himself. He is uncertain of what to do with Stepan Trofimovich: "Where shall we put Stepan Trofimovich?" In one note there is the suggestion that Dostoevsky is thinking of structural parallels to the Prince and to Nechaev: "<parallel> to these gentlemen we have the half-baked Shatov, that complacent Korsh, Stepan Trofimovich, who fails to realize that the whole thing was started by him, and his like." This may be the germ of that structural grouping in the final version of most of the characters about Peter and Stavrogin.

In the final version, of course, Stepan Trofimovich does realize "that the whole thing was started by him, and his like," and that realization leads him to self-awareness, remorse, and, so it seems, to some form of redemption. The notes do not support this view. There is no redemption of Stepan Trofimovich—here or elsewhere—but he does break with the "new ideas," which leads, however, only to "his old idealistic muddle": "Details aside, *the essence* of Stepan Trofimovich lies in the fact that, though ready at first to compromise with the new ideas, he breaks with them in the end, and indignantly so (preferring to go begging), and alone refuses to succumb to these new ideas, remaining true to his old idealistic muddle." There is even a sketch of his "redemptive" last pilgrimage, and what looks like remorse:

N.B. (Devote one chapter to him—after the lecture—where he says an eloquent farewell to everybody and talks brilliantly about God, Beauty, and Poetry.) N.B. ~~he act<ually>~~ God ~~therefore~~ and I am worse than you, I've made a mess of the world, but you are better than I, and I am happy. He takes his knapsack and actually leaves during the night. The elderly book-hawker woman, cholerine. A poetic chapter about how Stepan Trofimovich, on the one hand, weakly clings to the book-hawker woman, yet on the other, indulges in liberal platitudes at her expense, and how he is afraid of everything, while she considers him a babe. Recital of the Sermon of the Mount—he reads it himself and takes up selling. He is taken back to Skvoreshniki (or he comes running back himself).

For the Fantastic Page

The Prince and Shatov; the Prince: "These are only words—one must act."

Shatov: "What shall we do?"

The Prince: "Repent, keep building one's own character, keep building the kingdom of Christ. We are taking our religion from politics. Slavophiles and icons—Orthodox discipline and humility must prevail. No one is a slave, all are free. The lands of freedom, Christianity, the Pope-Antichrist comes forth blessing his flock. Our strength lies not in industry but in moral regeneration—*one needs full strength to ~~say the boldest word~~ express the idea in its entirety.*

We Russians are bringing to the world the regeneration of their lost ideal. The beast with one of his heads wounded,[1] the millennium. Imagine, will all Christians be poor? I used to know Hertsen—this is a vaudeville."

Shatov: "If this is so, mustn't you become a monk?"

The Prince: "Why? Proclaim Christ in the Russian lands, and proclaim it by your own deeds. Great feats are needed. Must one perform a great feat? It takes a great mind to go against common sense."

Shatov: "It is said that science gives power."

The Prince: "Science does not give one moral satisfaction, nor does it give an answer to the most important questions."

The Prince: "A moral feat is needed. Let Russian strength show that it can perform it. You will conquer the world through a moral feat."

Shatov became strangely pensive: "You know what, these are all mere fantasies," he said, "also taken from books or, or—religious madness. You go ahead and try to enlist everybody for your moral feat."

The Prince: "Why everybody? You won't believe how strong a single man can be. Let there be one, and everybody will follow him. What is needed is self-condemnation and moral feats; that's the idea which is needed; otherwise we won't find Orthodoxy, and nothing will come of it all."

The strength lies in the moral idea.

The moral idea lies in Christ.

In the West, Christ has become perverted and spent. The reign of the Antichrist. We have Orthodoxy.

---

[1] A free quotation from Revelation 13:3.

That means that we are the bearers of a clear understanding of Christ and of a new idea for the resurrection of the world.

"Do you believe in Christ's eternal stay on earth?"

So, in order to proclaim Orthodoxy, a moral feat is needed—

But factories and industry are needed also?

Why stop everything? Let things run their course. But when the world will have been regenerated by the moral feat, it will begin to see everything clearly, including the way it must proceed.

The most important: The main idea from which the Prince suffers and which keeps him preoccupied is this:

We have *Orthodoxy;* our nation is great and wonderful because it believes and because it has Orthodoxy. We Russians are strong, and stronger than everybody else, because ~~we have~~ we have immense masses of people who are believers in Orthodoxy. But if the faith in Orthodoxy were shaken among our people it would immediately begin to decay, as the nations of the West have already begun to decay (naturally, our own upper class is an import, actually borrowed from them, therefore it is just so much grass on fire, and so of no consequence), as their religion (Catholicism, Lutheranism, various heresies, a distortion of Christianity) has become lost and must remain lost. Now this question: who then can believe? Does anybody at all (among the Panslavists or even among the Slavophiles) believe? And finally, even this question:

28 Can one believe at all? And if not, why make so much fuss about how the Russian nation derives its strength from Orthodoxy? Which means that this is only a question of time. Over there, [decay] atheism appeared earlier, with us it has come somewhat later, but it will surely begin with the introduction of atheism. And if this is quite inevitable, one may actually hope ~~the sooner~~ the sooner the better.

(The Prince suddenly realizes that his position coincides with Nechaev's, that it is best to burn everything.)

The result is then:

1) That men of action, who consider these questions meaningless and are perfectly able to live without them are nothing but rabble and nonentities, so much grass on fire.

2) That it all boils down to one urgent question: can one believe while being civilized, i.e., a European? I.e., believe without a reservation in the divine nature of Jesus Christ, the Son of God? (For this is what faith amounts to.)

N.B. To this question, civilization gives a factual answer in the negative (Renan), also stating that society has failed to preserve a pure interpretation of Christ's teaching (Catholicism being the Antichrist, the Whore, and Lutheranism no better than the teaching of the *molokane*).[2]

3) If this is so, can society exist without faith (on the basis of science alone, for instance)? (Herzen.) The moral foundations of a society are given through revelation. Eliminate one thing from religion, and the moral foundation of Christianity will collapse entirely, for everything is mutually linked together.

So, then, is a different, scientific morality possible?

If it is not, this means that morality rests with the Russian people alone, since it possesses Orthodoxy.

But if it is impossible for an enlightened person to be Orthodox (and in a hundred years half of Russia will be enlightened), this is all nothing but hocus-pocus, and this whole Russian strength is a temporary phenomenon only. For in order to be eternal, a complete faith in everything is a must. But is it possible to believe?

So, then, the first thing is to settle this question, ~~and~~ to put one's mind at ease ~~regarding~~ this question: Is it possible to believe seriously and truly?

That's what it boils down to, that's the *whole* key to the life of the Russian nation and its mission, and to its existence in the future.

But if it is impossible, ~~doubtless~~ (even though nobody is asking for it now), it isn't quite so unforgivable at all if someone would demand that we rather burn everything. (Slow suffering and death, and quick suffering and death. The quick way, naturally, is even the more humane.)

So that's the quandary?

N.B. You might, of course, take exception to the logical correctness of this conclusion and of the entire preceding line of reasoning; you might also refuse to agree either with the learned right, which claims that Christianity is certainly not going to decline assuming the form of Lutheranism, i.e., when Christ is considered only an ordinary man, a beneficent philosopher (for this is the ultimate outcome of Lutheranism), or with the left, which denies altogether that mankind actually needs Christianity, or that Christianity is *a source of true life* (with the

---

[2] The *molokane* are a religious sect that arose in the eighteenth century. They rejected ritual, ceremony, and priestly hierarchy.

hotheads among them screaming that it actually does harm to it), and asserts that, for instance, science can give mankind the true life as well as the most perfect moral ideal. All these arguments are possible, the world is full of them, and will be for some time. But isn't it true, Shatov, that you and I know very well that this is all perfect nonsense,
30 that Christ as man is not the Savior and the source of our life, and that science alone will never realize the whole human ideal, and that peace of mind is a source of life for every man, and that the salvation of all men from despair, and the condition *sine qua non,* and the guarantee for the existence of the whole world, are all contained in these words: *And the word was made flesh, and faith in these words.* With which we can immediately agree. Sooner or later everybody will come to agree with this. And so, the whole question rests right here: can one believe in everything that our Orthodox religion tells us to believe? If the answer is no, it is much better, and more humane, to burn everything and join Nechaev.

29 "It seems to me that I believe," says Shatov.

"Which means that you don't," the Prince replies.

"That's because I have severed my ties with the people!" Shatov exclaims, rapping the table with his fist.

The Prince explains to him that Christianity (Orthodoxy) contains in itself the solution of all problems, moral and social (a slave and yet a free man).

"Do you believe?" asks Shatov.

"Why are you so curious?" replies the Prince, "haven't the two of us understood each other even without words?"

(N.B. They agree with the entire preceding logical construction, as well as with the conclusion drawn from it, even that *idea* belonging to Shatov. That's precisely what fascinates the Prince, that's why he has come to see him. If Orthodoxy is everything, then Russia, too, is *everything.* But if not so, it is better to burn everything.) "And so this is all a phantasmagoria," exclaims Shatov in despair, "and we must burn—"

"Burn we must," laughs the Prince. "However, we might also vegetate for some five or ten ~~years~~ centuries and turn into savages and—start a new civilization by burning<...>."

"Why are you laughing," Shatov screams, "you young swell!"

"That won't help to solve the question," laughs the Prince.

Or, finally, the assertions of those numerous people ~~for~~ who say that Christianity is compatible with science and civilization, that it is used by many to assure their after-dinner rest, and to facilitate digestion, who believe that one may very well fail to believe in the resurrection of Lazarus or *Immaculée Conception,* yet still remain a Christian.

"But Shatov, you and I know only too well that this is all nonsense, and that one follows from the other, and that one can't remain a Christian not believing in *Immaculée Conception.*"

Shatov is clinging to him, as if he were seeking his salvation through him.

Shatov is lost in thought.

The Prince: "I want to warn you that these questions are by far more important than may appear, even though it is a very ancient matter. What is new about it is that you and I have recognized the immense importance of these questions and realized that it is absolutely imperative that they be solved."

"Eh! Why decide things beforehand," Shatov exclaimed, "a thousand years ahead of time! (i.e., slow decay)—let us live ~~and how we live!~~ in the present, do only what is to be done from day to day, confident that God will help us eventually!"

"Go ahead and try to get used to such a life!" the Prince said with a ripple of laughter, and left.

"The reason why Nechaev is so very much at ease," says the Prince, "is that he believes that Christianity not only isn't necessary at all for the true life of mankind, but that it ~~even~~ actually does harm to it, so that if it could be eradicated, mankind would immediately come to life and begin to live a new, *real* life. That's where their terrible power lies. The West won't be able to cope with them, you'll see; everything will perish through them."

"So what is going to happen?"

"A dead machine, which is of course impracticable, but...perhaps it is practicable after all, because in a few centuries one can deaden ~~the people~~ the world to such an extent that, in desperation, it will actually want to be dead. Fall on us, ye mountains, and crush us.[3] And that's what is going to happen. (For instance, if science is unable to provide for people's subsistence, and there is a shortage of space, people are going to throw their babes into latrines, or eat them. I won't be surprised if they do both, especially if science suggests it to them.) (And

---

[3] A free quotation from Luke 23:30.

the voice of the bridegroom, and the voice of the bride shall cease to be heard.)[4]

"Would you mind developing this?" says Shatov.

"When food becomes scarce and science proves unable to provide for food and fuel, whereas the world population continues to rise, it will become necessary to stop the further growth of the population. Science says that it isn't your fault nature has arranged things that way, and the instinct of self-preservation being first and foremost, it follows that babes must be burned. That is the morality of science. Malthus[5] isn't so very wrong at all, for there hasn't been enough time to prove his theories. Wait and see if Europe is able to support so large a population without food or fuel. And will science come to the rescue in time, provided it is able to help at all? ~~Christian~~ The burning of babes will become habitual, for all moral principles in man are only relative, *if he must rely on nothing but his own strength.* The savages of North America scalp their enemies, while we, at least for the time being, consider this repulsive. (Although we are guilty of many abominations as bad as this, without being aware of it, and considering them rather to be virtues.) Now look: If you believe that Christianity is a necessity, and [a gift] to mankind by the grace of God, something which man could not have reached by himself; if you believe that man has been, from the cradle, in *immediate* communion with God, through revelation at first, and later through the miracle of Christ's appearance; if you believe, finally, that man, if left alone to rely on his own strength, would perish, and that it is therefore imperative that we believe God to be in immediate contact with man,—in that case, having surrendered yourself to Christianity, you will never become reconciled to the notion of burning babes. There you have, as you can see, an entirely different morality. Which means that Christianity alone contains in itself the water of life and that it alone can lead man to the living source of this water, ~~and that without it~~ saving him from decay. But without Christianity mankind will decay and perish."

"Christian religion teaches the contrary of this: i.e., it offers us its own morality, ordering us to believe that this morality is the normal, the only one, that there is no such thing as relative morality, and that

---

[4] A free quotation from Revelation 18:23 (or Jeremiah 7:34).

[5] Thomas Robert Malthus (1766–1834), English economist, who predicted that population would outrun the means of subsistence.

it was given to us by God, as an act of grace. Finally, that man does not have the strength to save himself, but that he has been saved by revelation, and later by Christ, i.e., by God's immediate intervention in human life—in other words: through a miracle both times."

"Consequently, one may believe one as well as the other. And so the question is: which is the surer way, and where are the living sources of the water of life? In my opinion, science by itself, as it reaches the point where it becomes insensitive to <the death of> babes, will deaden and brutalize mankind, and therefore ~~burn~~ it is better to burn everything than to die slowly. On the other hand, I firmly believe that Christianity ~~will save them~~ would save mankind."

Shatov: "How is that?"

The Prince: "(This includes all the conditions of salvation, a slave and yet a free man. If we imagine that everybody has become a Christ, how could there be such a thing as pauperism? With Christianity, even the shortage of food and fuel could be overcome—one can always choose to die oneself, for the sake of one's brother, rather than killing off babes.) This has been prophesied in Christian tradition; precisely the millennium, where there won't be either wives or husbands (in the millennium there will be no wives or husbands)."

Shatov: "If this is so, what's the problem?"

The Prince: "Always the same thing: can a civilized man believe?"

"It is sheer frivolity that prevents man from considering this question first and foremost. However, there are many who are concerned with it ~~We~~, who write and talk about it. Because of our frivolity and distractions we tend to be concerned only with our day-to-day existence, thinking that this is all that is needed. Then there are others who work out various philosophies for the benefit of their digestion, to the effect that Christianity is compatible even with an infinite progress of civilization, and not merely with the present. Yet you and I know perfectly well that all this is nonsense, and that there are only two alternatives: either to have faith, or to burn everything. Nechaev has chosen the latter, and is strong and calm. I am just taking a good look at him, as I want to find out how much of his strength is derived from his convictions, and how much is simply due to his character."

And the voice of the bridegroom, and the voice of the bride shall cease to be heard.

2)

"Are you interpreting the Apocalypse literally?"

"Listen, think for yourself: the wounded beast, the third part ~~of the~~

~~Earth~~ of all grass perished,[6] the whore (. . .), the woman who is with child[7]—Russia—Come, seriously, don't you really see any correspondence?"

"Are you serious?" Shatov asks.

The Prince: "I don't matter here at all, you look at my idea, not at me. Only recently you were shouting that I was a young swell, now you are saying that I'm a madman. There are lots of people who say that I am mad. Look at my idea, not at me. Is the idea a correct one? Isn't there a frightening correspondence?"

"Religious fanaticism!" said Shatov.

"Ready made phrases for the benefit of better digestion."

They said nothing for a while.

"I can't get away from you now, said Shatov, "you are mine from now on."

Shatov: "If man is to change, how then is he going to live a life of reason? The possession of reason is a property of the human organism only as we now know it."

The Prince: "How do you know if man will even need what reason he now possesses?"

Shatov: "What else? Something higher, I presume?"

The Prince: "Much higher, no doubt."

Shatov: "How can there be anything higher than reason?"

The Prince: "That's what science teaches us, but look at that bedbug over there. Science knows that it is an organism, that it lives some kind of a life, and that it has impressions <*sic*>, even its own way of reasoning, and God knows what else. But can science ever learn and convey to me the essence of the life, of the reasoning process, and of the sensations of a bedbug? Never. In order to learn about that, one must for
33 a moment become a bedbug oneself. If science can't do that, it follows that it is equally unable to convey to me the essence of another, higher organism or being. Which also goes for the condition of man upon having attained the millennium, even if reason were no longer around."

"You really make my head go round!" says Shatov, "however, I'm still going to hold on to you."

---

[6] Inexact quotation from Revelation 18:7: ". . . and the third part of trees was burnt up, and all green grass was burnt up."

[7] Revelation 12:2.

The Prince: "I don't know why you consider the possession of reason, i.e., of consciousness, the highest of all possible forms of being. In my opinion, this is no longer science, but faith, and if you don't mind, we are dealing here with a hocus-pocus of nature, to wit: it is necessary for the very preservation of mankind that ~~you~~ one (as a whole, i.e., man insofar as he is part of mankind) place a high value on oneself. Every creature must consider itself higher than anything else; the bedbug there surely considers itself higher than you, and even if it were possible it surely wouldn't want to become a man, but would rather remain a bedbug. The bedbug is a mystery, and there are mysteries everywhere. Why then are you denying the existence of other mysteries? Note further that unbelief may very well be congenial to man precisely because he puts reason above everything else and, inasmuch as reason is peculiar only to the human organism, fails to understand or even does not want life in any different form, such as life after death, refusing to believe that it could be higher. On the other hand, a certain feeling of despair and of damnation is peculiar to human nature, for it is inherent in the human mind to keep losing faith in itself every minute, to be never content with itself, so that man is inclined to consider his existence an unsatisfactory one. Hence then his tendency to believe in life beyond the grave. We are apparently transitional creatures, and our existence on Earth is apparently (A PROCESS) that of a chrysalis turning into a butterfly, made permanent. Remember the saying: an Angel never falls, a Devil has fallen so hard that he stays down for good, Man falls and gets up again. I believe that people become either devils or angels. You say that eternal punishment is an injustice, and that French philosophy which is so good for digestion has developed the notion that all will be forgiven. Yet ~~this~~ life on Earth is a process of regeneration. Whose fault is it that you may be regenerated to become a devil? Naturally, everything will be taken into account. But it still remains a fact, a result—exactly as everything on Earth comes of something else. Note also that devils have knowledge. Consequently, even ~~devilish~~ beings beyond the grave possess consciousness and memory, and not man alone; they may be, however, non-human. It is impossible to die. There is being, but no such thing as non-being."

Special and Important

N.B.

When Shatov comes to ask the Prince's forgiveness, the Prince does not resume that conversation at all, but asks directly:

"*Shatov,* I gather from your words on that particular occasion (at

Stephan Trofimovich's) that you have your own set of convictions, as well as some kind of faith. Why won't you tell me what you believe in?"

They get together. Shatov on Orthodoxy.

Shatov directly: "I believe in Orthodoxy, and that it is that very idea which Russia is bringing to the whole world in order to save it."

The Prince: "Alright, I'll come to see you."

Shatov: "There are innumerable conversations such as ours going on in Russia right now. Or are you really making fun of me?"

"What's wrong with that?" laughed the Prince.

Shatov: "I don't believe you. A man who has understood ~~such role~~ Orthodoxy ~~in essence~~ to be the essence of Russia, one who has understood it as you have, couldn't be joking."

The Prince: "Nor am I joking."

Shatov: "Aren't you really? I'm a bookish man. I wish I could change that. What am I to do about it?"

The Prince: "Believe."

Shatov: "In Orthodoxy and in Russia?"

The Prince: "Yes."

Shatov: "Yes, of course, this would bring salvation. It seems to me that I do believe. Why aren't you saying anything?"

The Prince: "This means, you don't believe."

Shatov: "What about you?"

The Prince: "Once again, what do I matter to you?"

Shatov: "Do we really understand each other with hardly a word said?"

The Prince: "Good-bye. ~~Incidentally~~ I shall never come to see you again. And let me tell you this beforehand, Shatov: you were just shouting 'I am going to hold on to you!' but I don't want you to follow me; on the contrary, I want you to leave me in peace, and perfectly so. I mean it. And I have my reasons for it. I'll never come back."—

June 23, 1870

34 1. A Fantastic Page

(for parts 2 and 3)

The Prince is seeking a great moral feat, some true accomplishment, something by which Russia would manifest her strength to the whole world. His idea is true, genuine, active Orthodoxy (for who, in our days, actually believes?). Moral power before economic power.

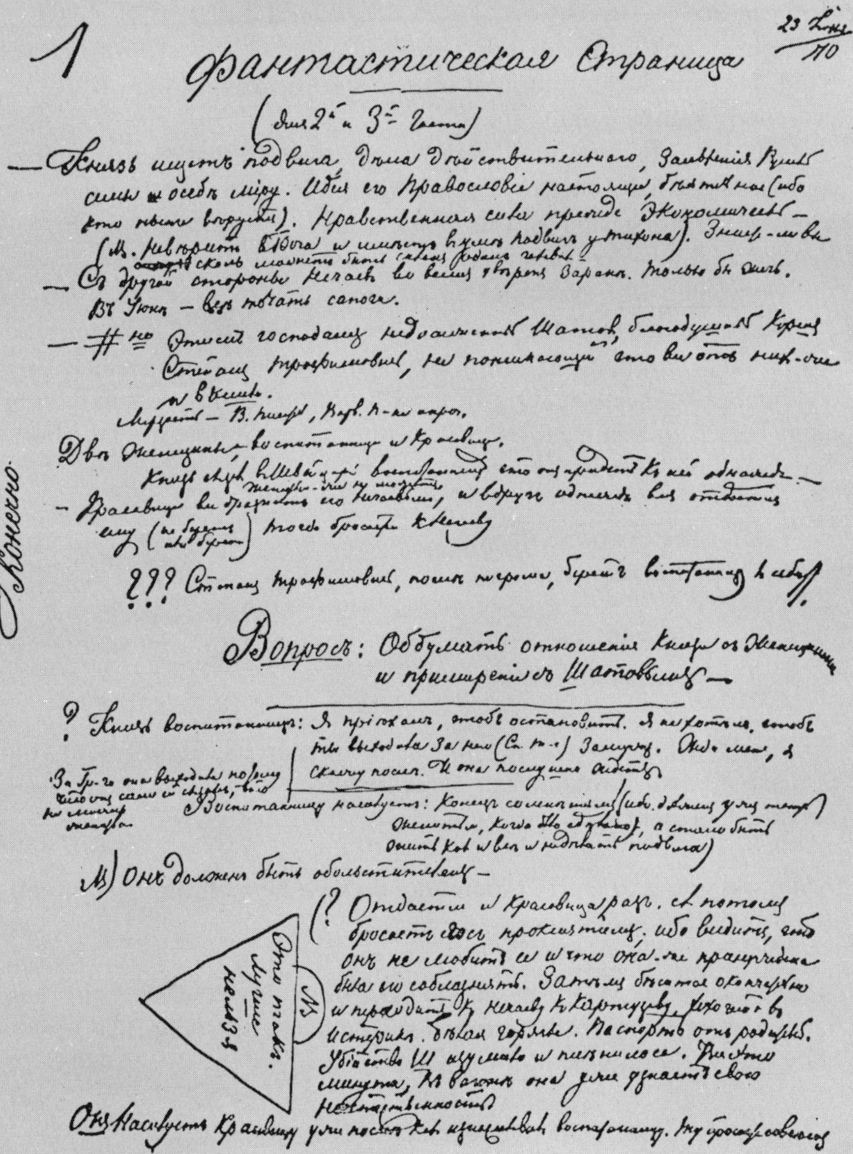

Notebook Page 34, Notebook 2

An excellent example of Dostoevsky's ordered disorderliness. The handwriting is varied in size, a marginal comment is neatly perpendicular, and one note is even enclosed in a triangle. The impression is one of contained restlessness.

(N.B. He does not believe in God, and what he has in mind is his moral feat at Tikhon's.) "Do you know ~~the strength~~ how strong a single man can be?"

Nechaev, on the other hand, is firmly convinced of everything beforehand. He cares for nothing but how to start burning things. By June, everybody will be making shoes.

<parallel> to these gentlemen, we have the half-baked Shatov, that complacent Korsh,[8] Stepan Trofimovich, who fails to realize that the whole thing was started by him, and his like.

Abomination—the Great Writer, Varvara Petrovna, etc.

Two women—the Ward and the Beauty.

The Prince has told the Ward, in Switzerland, that there would be a time when he'd come to her; however, he could never marry her.

The Beauty keeps teasing him with Nechaev, and then suddenly offers herself to him completely (he either takes, or does not take her). She then flings herself at Nechaev.

??? After the pogrom, Stepan Trofimovich takes the Ward into his house.

Question: Think about the Prince's relations with women, and his reconciliation to Shatov.

?The Prince, to the Ward: "I've come to stop it. I didn't want you to marry Stepan Trofimovich. Wait for me, I'll tell you later." And she waits obediently.

She was going to marry Granovsky because he had told her himself that he couldn't marry her.

He violates the Ward: an end to all doubts (for now, after this has happened, he must really marry her, and so go on living like every body else, without performing any feats).

N.B. He must be seductive.

(?The Beauty also submits to him once. But later she leaves the Prince, cursing him; for she sees that he does not love her, and that she

---

[8] Valentin F. Korsh (1828–93), journalist and literary historian.

actually had to entice him. Still later, she becomes decidedly furious, and goes through the hands of Nechaev and Kartuzov. Has a hysterical fit of laughter. Brain fever. A passport from her parents. The murder of Shatov shocks and fascinates her. All this takes only a minute. Only when already in the railway carriage does she finally recognize her own unnaturalness.

N.B. *This is so. Can't be any better.*

He violates the Beauty after he has already violated the Ward. He completely deserts her.

2)

Her mother sends her to Skvoreshniki. Stepan Trofimovich has come there to die.

A *tender,* terrible letter about Uri. The Ward immediately decides to sacrifice herself and joins him, leaving everything behind.

She loves him even more since she knows how unhappy he is; and she realizes that he is unhappy.

OR THIS WAY: Everything about Russia, about the Antichrist, and about the feat is said by Shatov (that is better, that is marvelous).

The Prince listens avidly, but remains silent. Although he says nothing it is clear that he is in command during the discussion. He listens and observes. He is somber and grave.

On one occasion he makes a speech: this is when Shatov has been killed. A wild speech.

Sometimes he is curious in a taciturn way, and caustic, like Mephistopheles. Asks questions like one who is in command, and appears everywhere like one who is in charge.

AUTHOR'S NOTA BENE:

AND SO, THINGS ARE SETTLED AS FAR AS THE WOMEN ARE CONCERNED, AND OUR DIFFICULTIES HAVE BEEN OVERCOME.

BUT HOW TO GET THE PRINCE TOGETHER WITH SHATOV?

? N.B. (I think, just as before, i.e., the Prince comes to see him. He conquers him, too, *with his charm.)*

And in general, keep in mind that the Prince is charming as a demon, and that terrible passions are struggling with . . . the feat. Moreover, unbelief and—torments—from faith. The feat breaks through, faith prevails, but the devils, too, believe and tremble. "Too late," says the Prince, and flees to Uri. Later he hangs himself.

36 3)

Occasionally, the Prince appears to be moved, so that the reader is shocked (he was sitting there with the children). The book-hawker, etc.

Among those present is *Liputin* (a liberal without a goal, like every Russian liberal).

Liputin says to Nechaev: "I used to be a plain Fourierist, but now I've come to think that it is actually better to burn down everything first."

Here. Liputin says this without actually believing what he says. He does not believe in what he is saying, and ~~yet~~ he is drawn into following Nechaev as into a machine. He is a type which is representative of that unaccountable restlessness, coupled with a dull feeling of superiority, which tends to be present in a Russian liberal. A restless and aggressive man, without brains and without a heart. However, he is witty at times.

N.B. Shouldn't one rather let Shatov come to see the Prince first, to beg his forgiveness?

The Prince initially gives him a cold reception. But three days later he comes to see Shatov:

"I appreciate your moral feat," he says. "It suggests that you are an extraordinary person." That is the whole conversation. The Prince comes two more times, then quits coming.

During the fire, the Prince is with the Beauty.

After the fire, "new ideas" score a signal triumph, and Nechaev is now definitely in fashion.

The Prince has cast his spell even on Nechaev.

N.B. Where shall we put Stepan Trofimovich? Varvara Petrovna for a moment veers into *new ideas*; but in the end she changes sides again, back to Stepan Trofimovich.

About Stepan Trofimovich, An Important Question?

37 4)

Details aside, *the essence* of Stepan Trofimovich lies in the fact that, though ready at first to compromise with the new ideas, he breaks with them in the end, and indignantly so (preferring to go begging), and ALONE refuses to succumb to these new ideas, remaining true to his old idealistic muddle (to Europe, *The European Herald,* Korsh).

Express through Stepan Petrovich that it is impossible to return to Belinsky, or to keep playing the European without going any further. "Accept the full consequences, for Europeanism, unnatural as it is for Russia, leads to that."—But this he fails to comprehend, and whimpers.

N.B. (Devote one chapter to him—after the lecture—where he says an eloquent farewell to everybody and talks brilliantly about God, Beauty, and Poetry.) N.B. ~~he act <ually>~~ God ~~therefore~~ and I am worse than you, I've made a mess of the world, but you are better than I, and I am happy. He takes his knapsack and actually leaves during the night. The elderly book-hawker woman, cholerine. A poetic chapter about how Stepan Trofimovich, on the one hand, weakly clings to the book-hawker woman, yet on the other, indulges in liberal platitudes at her expense, and how he is afraid of everything, while she considers him a babe. Recital of the Sermon of the Mount—he reads it himself—and takes up selling. He is taken back to Skvoreshniki (or comes running back himself).

N.B. Varvara Petrovna's reproaches at Skvoreshniki (nothing but Kapfig and Kapfig).[9] That is in the beginning, after she has chased him out on account of the Ward (N.B. when Shatov gave the slap in the face.) Then she wants to restore peace, and Stepan Trofimovich disgraces himself. Later, the public lecture and the farewell, a letter to Varvara Petrovna, a visit to the Ward, he leaves. He is returned to Skvoreshniki as a runaway (it is Varvara Petrovna herself who intercepts him) ~~in time~~ immediately after Shatov has been murdered, and a rumor about Nechaev is first heard. At this point, a last meeting with his son, whom he curses. Arrival of Varvara Petrovna, and his death.

A poetic promenade. An entirely new world which has a strange impact on the childlike Stepan Trofimovich.

Continuation of Fantastic Pages

The Prince has just arrived at Shatov's, and taken a seat, when he says:

"Well, what about Orthodoxy? How is it you believe?"

Shatov presents the above given logical deduction, while the Prince stops him now and then, adding some explanatory comments.

---

[9] Baptiste Honoré R. Capefigue (1802–72), French man of letters and historian, who wrote many works with a monarchist slant .

"This means that you also believe in this, doesn't it?" Shatov exclaims.

"Of course," replies the Prince.

Shatov: "But that is remarkable! I'm amazed! How could the two of us hit upon the very same idea?"

The Prince: ~~Don't bother to find out why~~ "I haven't run across such an idea before, and you think that you're the first to discover it. That's where you are wrong; this is a Slavophile idea and you naturally know that yourself."

Shatov: "Yes." (Then hotly:) "Yes, but it doesn't appear as strongly with them. They do not believe (Kireevsky,[10] the icon)."

The Prince: "Well, if this is so, how can you believe? Do you really believe?"

Shatov: "Of course I do."

The Prince (more coolly all the time): "Do you realize what the main point of the question is: Christianity saves the world, and it alone can save it—that's the conclusion we have come to and that's what we believe. That is one thing. Next: Christianity exists only in Russia, in the form of Orthodoxy. That's two."

Shatov (interrupting him): "And so Russia will save and regenerate the world through Orthodoxy."

The Prince (coolly): "If she will believe. But is it possible to believe? (The philosophy of digestion.) But you and I know that it is all nonsense. And so everything boils down to this: can one believe?"

The scheme of faith: Orthodoxy contains in itself the image of Jesus Christ.

Christ is the foundation of a great moral principle.

Develop further and carry it to wherever this principle might take you. (To the concept of happiness, to begin with; happiness anchored in law, so that others may be happy, too. This is not the gregarious organization *based on rights* which the Western socialists proclaim, for no rights whatever emerge as such from Christ's definition of happiness. My happiness lies not in the accumulation of material things, according to a ~~right~~ jealous right of the individual, but rather a *voluntary* surrender of all my rights. This is not slavery, for 1), the surrender is

---

[10] Ivan V. Kireevsky (1806–56), a philosopher, one of the founders of Slavophilism. His philosophy is best exposited in these articles: "On the Necessity and Possibility of New Principles in Philosophy" (1856) and "In Answer to A. S. Khomiakov" (1839).

voluntary, and consequently a higher manifestation of individuality, and secondly, the others, in turn, give me everything that is theirs.

We are seeking in vain, if this cannot be realized; if but every thousandth should be arrayed in white linen (The Apocalypse),[11] that would be quite enough.

From the awareness of what happiness really means there will follow, also, the organization of society.

But in order to keep Jesus, i.e., Orthodoxy intact, one must first of all keep oneself intact, and be oneself. ~~Then~~ Only then will the tree bear fruit when it has gathered and developed its strength. Therefore, what Russia needs is this: having become imbued with the idea, the precious treasure of which she is now the only remaining bearer, she must free herself from the German and Westernizing yoke, and become herself, in clear awareness of her goal.

Or thus: He comes to see Shatov: "What about Orthodoxy?"

Shatov begins to expound it.

The Prince nods his agreement ~~even (from the Apocalypse)~~.

The Apocalypse:

Try to realize that the beast means nothing but a world which has deserted its faith, reason reduced to its own resources, after it has rejected, on the basis of science, any chance of immediate communion with God, any possibility of revelation, as well as the miracle of God's appearance on Earth.

Shatov sees that their convictions are the same.

"How could this happen?" he says.

The Prince says: "Why, this is all ancient Slavophile stuff."

A Slavophile thinks that he can succeed through the virtues of the Russian people alone; but there is no succeeding without Orthodoxy, for all these virtues will be no help whatever, if the world loses faith.

Shatov explains the difference: "Slavophilism is a gentleman's fancy. The icon (Kireevsky). They could never believe spontaneously."

The Prince nods his agreement: "Yes, if they don't believe spontaneously, this is as if they didn't believe at all, and it's better to burn everything, as Nechaev suggests."

"How do you mean, burn?"

The Prince explains: (THE PHILOSOPHY OF DIGESTION) "A question of time, gradual dying out. You see: ~~if Christianity~~ that's precisely the

---

[11] Revelation 11:8.

difference between the Slavophiles and ourselves, that we consider this problem so important and that we posit it as a *sine qua non*. Orthodoxy and Russia. We believe that in Orthodoxy alone, and nowhere else, the image of Christ has been preserved intact, and that Russia is the bearer of Orthodoxy. On the other hand, I believe that Christianity contains in itself the solution of all the world's problems. The child, the millennium, the Apocalypse, the wounded beast."

The novelty of our conception lies entirely in the severity with which we have posited the problem.

Shatov is astonished: "Are you serious?"

"Effect a rapprochement."

"I won't lag behind you."

~~And so there is Orthodoxy~~ Shatov: "And so, everything rests upon Orthodoxy!"

"No, that's not the real point of the problem at all. The point is if one can believe in Orthodoxy."

The Prince: "The whole question is then: can or can't one believe?"

Shatov: ~~How's that~~ "So you don't believe after all?"

"You see: Either it is all a question of faith, or it isn't! We realize the importance of saving the world through Orthodoxy. And so the whole question is: can one believe in Orthodoxy, rejecting any philosophy of digestion. If so, everything is safe; if not, it's better to burn everything."

"Is it really true that you do not believe?"

"What do I matter to you—I am asking you; I have only come to ask you: do you believe? ~~do you really believe?~~ I was just curious."

"I... it seems to me that I do believe."

"That means that you don't."

Shatov: "It all comes from having lost touch with the people."

The Prince: "But this again is only a question of time. All the same, in a hundred years or so you'd lose your faith anyway, even if you haven't lost touch now."

"Tell me directly: is it really true, is it really true that you do not believe?"

The Prince: "I'll be civil and give you this reply: No, I do not believe. And listen, Shatov: let's try not to see each other again. You are saying 'I won't lag behind you.' But I do mean what I'm saying. I'm not talking about the slap in the face you gave me."

The Prince (incidentally): "Many people think that it is enough to believe in Christ's moral teaching, in order to be a Christian. It isn't

Christ's morality, or his teaching, that will save the world, but faith, and nothing else, faith in the fact that the word was made flesh. This faith is not only an intellectual acknowledgement of the superiority of his teaching, but rather an immediate striving for a goal. What one must believe in is precisely the notion that this is the ultimate ideal of man, the word all incarnate, God incarnate. Only if we have such faith do we attain the right worship, that ecstasy which, more than anything else, ties us to him immediately and which has the power to keep man from going astray. With anything short of such ecstasy, mankind would have perhaps inevitably gone astray, falling into heresy to begin with, and later into godlessness, then into amorality, and finally into atheism and troglodytism; and it would have vanished, and decayed.

Note that human nature absolutely demands worship. Morality and faith are one and the same thing, morality arises from faith, ~~worship is the inalienable~~ the need for worship is an inalienable property of human nature. This is a lofty quality, not a lowly one—a recognition of the infinite—a striving for an overflow into the infinity of the universe, a knowledge that one has arisen from it. But in order that there be worship, there must be God. Atheism, being precisely a corollary of the notion that worship is not a natural property of human nature, expects man to be regenerated solely from his own resources. It makes an effort to represent his moral aspect in the form it is going to take when man has become altogether free of religion. But they have actually represented nothing—a tree should be judged by its fruits—on the contrary, they have represented nothing but deformity and a philosophy of digestion. As for morality left to its own devices, or to those of science, it may easily degenerate and turn into the foulest abomination—such as the rehabilitation of the flesh, or even the burning of babes."

"How is that?"

"They have written that, if there should be a shortage of material goods, babes should be killed or burned, etc."

Shatov: "Can't this also happen under Christianity?"

The Prince: "Christianity is actually competent to save the whole world, and every question is contained in it. (If everybody were like Christ...)

Millennium.

The Apocalypse.

The Prince: "Oh no, the question does not rest there at all, but rather it is whether one can believe what is taught by Orthodoxy."

Shatov: "How is this? Didn't you just say..."

The Prince: "We merely concluded that one must believe; yet the question is whether one can believe in what one believes."

The Prince:* "You are a gentleman; you don't believe—"

"I've only come to satisfy my curiosity: do you believe?"

The world will become the beauty of Christ.

Man absolutely needs faith: if I am imperfect, vile, and wicked ~~and if at the same time~~, I still know that there exists another ideal of myself, which is beautiful, holy, and blissful. If there is just a spark of magnanimity and generosity in me, even this idea alone must give me joy.

From the image of the one whom I worship I also derive his spirit, and consequently my entire moral being.

.... And this is why it is absolutely necessary to worship.

I was curious to know—and that's why I came.

Shatov: "Are there very few believers besides me?"

The Prince: "Yes, but no believers at all at our stage of intellectual development. At least I haven't met one. As for the rest, even if they are believers now, you know yourself that it's only a question of time, as civilization advances. So what's the use talking about them?"

"Really, not a single one?"

The Prince: "Not one. The majority, as you know, is indifferent. But that is not the point, for it means nothing. Others, tormented by faith, gain their peace of mind from the philosophy of digestion. There are genuine believers even among the well educated, but it has appeared to me that they were fools ~~so that~~, whereas among clever people with well developed minds I haven't met any who were complete believers, not a single one."

Shatov: "But you yourself, you, you believe, don't you?..." etc.

"If I find one, this will be for me a fact.

Shatov and the Prince. Shatov: "Do you at least know why you did it?" (He has married the Lame Woman.)

The Prince: "Yours is a wise question. And you know what, I have a surprise for you: I know why I did it."

---

* Should be "Shatov."

Antonovich[12] and Zhukovsky[13]
June/July, "Dawn"

July 25 <1870>

LIPUTIN-ROZHDESTVENSKY[14]

N.B. *The fire* leaves a shocking impact upon the Beauty. It is after the fire that she apparently goes out of her mind and goes to Kartuzov.

This is Lermontov in a skirt.

Even before her flight and Shatov's death she complains to the Prince that Nechaev is stupid.

She wants to surrender herself to the Prince, but he scorns her.

She wants to go to Ivan Iakovlevich.

She comes running to Stepan Trofimovich for advice.

The Prince still remains a mystery to her: "What is he?" She also tries to find out what he stands for.

She suspects that it may be that of philistine happiness with the Ward.

(A showdown with the Ward.)

She goes on a wild spree.

She feels like rubbing herself with vitriol, or cutting off her finger.

She is shocked by the Prince's contempt, by how he has failed to understand her, and by how he has abandoned her. He gives her his own sincere view of women and says that the Ward is better than any *great* emancipated woman.

She equally despises vulgar women such as Mme. Virginsky.

She hates the Ward for the petite bourgeoise she is.

She is also right in asserting that she is misunderstood.

The Prince takes possession of her for nothing: "For nothing, for nothing!" After it has happened, they part cursing each other.

---

12 M. A. Antonovich (1835–1918), philosopher and critic. He was on the staff of *The Contemporary* and a co-worker of Chernyshevsky and Dobroliubov. A champion of the natural scientific outlook in humanistic matters, and a follower of Darwin, he engaged in polemics with the Dostoevsky brothers.

13 Iulii G. Zhukovsky (1822–1907), economist. He was on the staff of *The Contemporary*. He wrote an article, "Karl Marx and his Book on Capital," in 1877 in *The European Herald*. Zhukovsky was anti-Marx.

14 I. A. Rozhdestvensky, author of a pamphlet entitled "The Literary Decline of Antonovich and Zhukovsky" (1868) in which he defends Nekrasov against Antonovich and Zhukovsky.

A. Here.

The Beauty says: "Nechaev is stupid. You know, I've been expecting it to happen all along, because I've become convinced that it would take a stupid one to do it. The clever ones wander around aimlessly, whereas in order to be a man of action one must absolutely be, at least in some respect, a fool."

He who is very clever will never be a man of action.

10 The Prince and the Ward.

N.B. It is possible to create these characters in the flesh, not only as ideas. N.B. July 24 <, 1870>.

The Ward, fascinated by the words uttered by him on a certain occasion in Switzerland, fully surrendered herself to the Prince, totally submitting to him, without a will of her own. "*Because I love*, why do I love? That I do not know."

Here A. N.B. *She has lost the capability of judging him.* His actions do not frighten her. No matter what he will do, she knows she will follow him.

It isn't judgment over him, but boundless, unappeasable pity for him.

She tells him so herself.

Yet she is jealous of the Beauty.

The Prince tells her outright: "I consider you *the best* of all angels in the world, I know that *from here on* I shall always be coming to you, especially when I am unhappy, yet I cannot say that I love you."

However, he does take it upon himself to dispose of her fate. During his absence, knowing that she would never marry him, she was actually glad that, if she was to get married at all, it would be to Stepan Trofimovich.

But, immediately upon his arrival, he forbids her to go through with it.

When she conveys her refusal to Varvara Petrovna, *the latter*, who only the day before had been saying, "that's all nonsense, that talk about Daria," and who had been saying it all along, suddenly says to herself: "I have always expected this to happen!"

N.B. Develop and expand this.

XII
The Prince, Liza, and the Lame Woman

These notes were written in all probability between August 12 and August 22. They comprise notebook pages 14–15, 29–38, and 44–52 from notebook 1/10, and pages 14–15 and 56–58 from notebook 3. One might notice that the Princess is now called Varvara Petrovna, Liza mingles with "the Beauty" and "the Fiancée," and Lebiadkin with Kartuzov.

As we know from his letters, Dostoevsky had made important changes in his plans for *The Possessed* about this time, and was working feverishly on the novel. On August 17/29, 1870, he wrote to S. A. Ivanova the following: "Two weeks ago, having taken up the work again, I saw immediately what was going badly, where the error lay; and consequently, in a burst of inspiration, I conceived a new and harmonious plan. I had to change everything radically. After more than a little thought, I crossed out everything that I had written (about 250 pages) and took up the work from the very beginning."

Most of what we have here has to do once again with the romantic intrigue, something that has freighted his deliberations throughout so much of these notes. Once again the romantic intrigue has to do with the triangle of Liza, the Ward, and the Princess. The most frequent complication is the following: the Prince has seduced both the Beauty (Liza) and the Ward (Dasha). Liza hates-loves the Prince, and attempts to humiliate him and to entice him by pretending love for Shatov and at different times for Kartuzov (Lebiadkin). The Prince does not love Liza, but enjoys the power he holds over her. He is secretly married to the Lame Woman (Mary Lebiadkin), a fact he confesses to Liza in order to humiliate her. Liza's reaction is one of hate—she runs off to Shatov and Kartuzov and wants Shatov to kill the Prince; and it is one of love—she comes running to the Prince with love (as in the final version). The

Ward is for the most part compliantly patient, and in many variations she runs off with the Prince after the murder of the Lame Woman.

There are many variations of the central complication just sketched. Dostoevsky is unsure of most facts: for example, to whom the Prince will confess his marriage to the Lame Woman; what the Prince's feelings are for Liza, and hers for him. In one set of notes, a pregnant Liza runs to give birth at Shatov's; in another, Liza tries to bribe Shatov to love her and to marry her; in yet another, Dostoevsky is unsure whether the Prince should be married to the Ward, to the Lame Woman, or to a nihilist. He is sure that the Lame Woman will be murdered, but he does not know whether the Prince will be or will not be directly implicated. But he is sure that the Prince will hang himself, and that all the women will be fatally attracted to him.

In contrast to earlier variations of the romantic intrigue, Liza, her character, and her relationship to the Prince take on prime importance. Dostoevsky relates almost everything to the Prince and Liza's love. Varvara Petrovna's troubles and the frequent reference to a vinegar compress, for example, have to do with the projected match between Liza and the Prince, which is hurt by her son's attitude, and the machinations of the Governor's wife against the marriage. The feelings, motives, and actions of Liza are complicated. The Prince seems bored with her, or at best satanically interested in the pleasure he can derive from humiliating her. As before, she loves and hates him, turns to Shatov, and even to Kartuzov from motives of revenge and self-punishment. It is surprising to see how importantly Liza looms here. In the final version her role is largely vestigial, and one could cut it out entirely without great loss. Even her flight with Stavrogin at the time of the fete shows us only that Stavrogin has still some embers of desire left and demonstrates again his inability to love, something that has been amply shown in other ways.

The Prince's marriage to the Lame Woman—the prototype of Mary Lebiadkin—and the dramatic consequences of the secret marriage and its possible revelation are also significant additions to the romantic intrigue. Varvara Petrovna's plans for the marriage of the Prince to Liza are threatened by the rumors of his secret marriage as spread by anonymous letters and apparently by the vindictive whisperings of the Governor's wife. The Prince himself "confesses" the marriage to Liza, to Shatov, to the Ward, and apparently to Tikhon. The importance of the "confession" is beginning to emerge here, but all its moral, psychological, and metaphysical implications are not yet present. In only one note does the confession take on the metaphysical coloration of the final version: "The Prince is punishing himself and is testing his strength. He is wavering whether he ought to punish himself with the Lame Woman."

The political plot is present in bits and pieces, but there is still no coherent interrelationship between the romantic and political plots. We have Nechaev's plans for riot and revolution, and references to the printing press; Stepan Trofimovich is arrested; and Nechaev gains control over the spiritual heart of the town. Nechaev is brought into the romantic plot by his relationship to Liza. Liza is indifferent to Nechaev, and then interested. The Prince encourages the love affair of Liza and Nechaev, probably as a defense against her use of it to hurt him. All in all, though, the relationship is contrived.

The doctor, a family. Shatov is with the doctor; he has run away. The university, an affair at the university, he fled abroad.

He has returned from abroad, the doctor dies, work, half a year, and finally a position with Varvara Petrovna.

Varvara Petrovna and Stepan Trofimovich,

Liputin, Virginsky, and the Kartuzovs.

Shatov is hated by the family,

Varvara Petrovna's son.

Shatov's marriage. He hides his wife.

Stepan Trofimovich's relatives appear. Captain Kartuzov.

The Drozdovs. Liza and the Shatov woman are friends. They are expecting the Prince. Stepan Trofimovich is expecting his son. The proclamations.

The Governor. (Varvara Petrovna suspects Shatov.) The book of verse.[1] Emancipation. The poetaster[2] makes slanderous statements about Shatov. The Great Writer[3] is in town.

---

[1] In the novel itself, we have sundry poems composed by Captain Lebiadkin for Liza, and a poem, "A Noble Personality" *(Svetlaia lichnost')*, which Shatov was

A lecture in honor of the Polish priest.[4]

The Story of a Proletarian (Shatov)

Or: Shatov has brought back his wife, but the Prince makes her leave with him the first time he is back. She is now somewhere in Paris.

Shatov quits his job at Varvara Petrovna's (<and is now working> for one of the local merchants).

Meanwhile the poetaster is fawning on Varvara Petrovna (he would like to marry her Ward and 15,000).

—Varvara Petrovna wants her Ward to marry Stepan Trofimovich.

The latter confides his secrets to Shatov.

Anonymous letters. Liputin. Concerning how, for 8,000—

Proclamations.

Rhymes. Emancipation.

N.B. Shatov's wife willingly submitted to the Prince and left with him for Paris, where the Prince left her (for he never made any advances to her, nor did he ever promise her anything) and where Shatov, as her husband, kept supporting her.

Shatov's wife returns from Paris at the very beginning of the novel (they have been exchanging letters).

Shatov's wife suspects that he is in love with the Ward—(she tells him what, according to her conjectures, happened abroad between the Ward and the Prince).

The Prince. The Ward refuses to marry Stepan Trofimovich. Shatov slaps the Prince's face.

Stepan Trofimovich's son.

Shatov's wife has arrived from Paris as an aide in the conspiracy.

The Alfonsky's were abusing Shatov, even while being supported by him.

But if there's a book of rhymes, there should also be a carriage and gloves.

---

supposed to print on his press and distribute. It is a parody of a poem by Ogarev, dedicated first to S. Astrakan, and then, at the suggestion of Bakunin, to Nechaev. The poem appeared in *Kolokol (The Bell)*, where Dostoevsky became acquainted with it. It appeared in the legal Russian press in 1871 during the trial of the Nechaevists.

[2] A reference to Lebiadkin.

[3] A reference to Karmazinov, a caricatured figure of Turgenev.

[4] The priest, who appears a number of times in these notes, does not appear in the final version. Dostoevsky wrote to S. A. Ivanova on January 24/February 6, 1869: "Two or three characters have formed themselves terribly well in my imagination, among which a Catholic enthusiast priest, *à la* St. Francis Xavier."

August 12 (across the Vôsges)[5]

The Kartuzov family. They were dependent on Shatov.

Shatov returns.

Married or not?

Rhymes dedicated to Varvara Petrovna.

The poet has gained her favor and has everything in his claws.

N.B. (Through him, Shatov loses his job near to his wife. The poet is angry at Shatov's wife because he has courted her without success.)

They are expecting the Prince.

A subscription lecture in honor of the Polish priest.

The Great Writer is in town. (This worries the poet.)

Arrival of the Prince. Shatov's wife or fiancée.

Idea: Somebody has stolen Shatov's wife. He returns from a journey and does not find her at home. And later, rather toward the end of the novel, frightened by their rules and doctrines, she seeks refuge with Shatov.—(The day before he is murdered.)—

August 13. A pretty woman. Secretly, a happy marriage. Everybody considers him a monster. Two years of married life. She is wasting away. She is extremely frank with him.

The same setting. The family. The poetaster.

Varvara Petrovna, Stepan Trofimovich—

The dissipated Prince. Shatov is employed by Varvara Petrovna.

The Prince has sworn that he will steal her from the other man.

N.B. *An idea.* The effect of a desperate passion—it drives one to the point of delirium, of madness.

N.B. The setting all around. Change of governors. Stepan Trofimovich as a minor comic character. The arrival of Stepan Trofimovich's son. He kills Shatov.

Or: N.B. The arrival of Stepan Trofimovich's son (in the style of Khlestakov—some kind of nasty, petty, and ridiculous stories about town. ~~Finally~~ He is thought to be a nonentity. Finally he reveals his true self—in their eyes he is king). Yet, in the first part he is a worthless and idiotic creature.

N.B. Liza is the Prince's formal fiancée—

Or:

---

[5] A reference to the movement of Prussian forces at the beginning of the Franco-Prussian War.

The Beauty has been disgraced by the Prince. She wants to get even with him.

She realizes that Shatov is in love with her.

It gets to the point where she orders Shatov to kill the Prince. Yet ~~?~~ she knows that it is dangerous to play tricks on Shatov.

Shatov is married. He is trying to erase her from his life.

Varvara Petrovna. Stepan Trofimovich.

Kartuzov.

Or, the Prince has seduced his wife—

Shatov steals Liza from him (having promised her to kill him).

Kartuzov, etc.

(N.B. Stepan Trofimovich is married, and he <the Prince> also seduces his wife—)? Stepan Trofimovich in a comic situation.

N.B. (A clash of two strong characters: Shatov and the Prince.)

31 August 14 (Metz–Nancy)[6]

Final version

Shatov is not married, he is living by himself, at a merchant's. He shuns Varvara Petrovna. His sister is Varvara Petrovna's ward. It is she whom Varvara Petrovna seeks to marry off to Stepan Trofimovich.

N.B. The circumstances regarding the change of governors to remain the same. However, the Governor suspects Shatov, especially after the proclamations. He dislikes him even before. It is Teliatnikov who has denounced him. Shatov is a friend of Stepan Trofimovich's, and during the matchmaking Stepan Trofimovich confides in Shatov, asks his advice, etc.

Varvara Petrovna would be awfully glad if she could get Liza married to the Prince.

Liza is bored. ~~Meanwhile~~

N.B. Display Liza in a series of scenes.

Kartuzov as before.

Shatov has hardly talked to his sister.

Shatov writes Liza a letter in which he declares his passionate love for her.

Liza reads the letter thoughtfully, keeps it a secret, and after several days has a frank talk with him.

"They are *all* so very much lacking in originality that I actually

---

[6] French cities which figured in the Prussian advance into France.

might marry you," she says. And finally, she lets him know positively, in a letter, that she will marry him. She asks him for a rendezvous.

Rendezvous at Shatov's place. Shatov's definitive decision *not to marry* her after all; so he discourages her (she blurts out: "I couldn't possibly marry Kartuzov"). She wants to marry him and says: "I want to get married; *it couldn't be any worse*." She hints at 200,000. He says that 200,000 are no *obstacle*, "though I won't take them; I want *the whole* thing, that is, a wife." She tells him, reproachfully, that he has no passion. He says: "I've got more of it <than you>. You are not going to love me, are you?" "No, I am not." "Yours is a preposterous idea; you couldn't do any worse than get married on the spur of your eccentricity—you are doing it to spite somebody, or to distinguish yourself, I don't know which. Why, you wouldn't be talking to me that way if you considered me to be a human being." "Yes, but I'm still going to marry you." "Either those people who say that you're mad are right, or you have *the inordinately devious idea* to provoke his rage."

She: "I swear that I actually do not love him. He is much too ordinary a person, without any originality, entirely the same character as myself (he is very much like myself, this is why I hate him so)."

Later, *she* writes him: "Consider it *as not having happened.* I feel, *now I have begun to feel* that I can love you, and that this will really happen; and that's why I am not getting married *(not going to marry)* you."

2)

Meanwhile in town, Stepan Trofimovich's son makes a showing, rather in the style of Khlestakov. Wretched, banal, and vile. Nechaev's quarrel with Teliatnikov, in a tavern, or something of this sort.

He breaks up Stepan Trofimovich's marriage, spreads slanderous gossip; petty, comical little scandals (he is staying with Kartuzov); all as before, only his entrance is Khlestakovian.

The Beauty views him with contempt (though barely noticing him).

Meanwhile, his mysterious dealings with Shatov, with Kulishov, with the Prince, with the Governor's wife, with the Great Writer. N.B. The fire and Liza; for a certain reason she has become convinced that Nechaev and Liputin set the fire.

Liza takes notice of Nechaev.

He kills Shatov.

Liza is convinced that *he* has killed him. Rushes with him to Kartuzov.

(Meanwhile, the Prince and Tikhon, and prior to that, the Prince and Shatov, all as before.)

Liza flees with Nechaev. Stepan Trofimovich with the book-hawker.[7] He dies.

Liza has a fit of delirium tremens at the station. The Prince hangs himself.

All as before.

N.B. SOMETHING NEW:

A showdown between Liza and Shatov.

and Nechaev's Khlestakovian appearance on the scene,

and the dramatic form.

AND THE BEGINNING THROUGH VARIOUS SCENES, ALL OF WHICH ARE TIED TOGETHER INTO ONE KNOT.

N.B. One might begin with Liza, and even with a rumor that she has been taking treatments,

<or> with Kartuzov, Shatov,

and that she has a fiancé,

and that she took notice of Shatov all by herself, and invited him, having heard that he hates the Prince.

Shatov is working for her, doing a chronicle, but turns her down—he comes and turns down the job ("You know very well yourself that this is charity")—she tells him that he ought to be ashamed of himself—she won't let him go and starts to ask him various questions: does he hate the Prince?

Begin with Liza,

with Liza's character—her relationship with Shatov—(their conversations, Liza is quite frank with him, her proud character both fascinates and amuses Shatov).

There is no reason to kill the Prince.

I know, I'd accept charity, but I have brought a letter.

(Khlestakov, on the other hand, grows from a comic figure into *a personage.*)

THINK

Getting to the spot where Varvara Petrovna comes running to Stepan

---

[7] The prototype of Sofia Matveevna, the bookseller in whose company Stepan Trofimovich spends his last hours.

Trofimovich, the Ward sends for Shatov, and Stepan Trofimovich for Shatov. Then, Shatov to Kartuzov (Shatov also discusses Kartuzov with Stepan Trofimovich). Then the Governor, the proclamation, anonymous letters. ~~Meanwhile~~ Stepan Trofimovich's son arrives earlier; he is staying with Kartuzov.

Shatov's letter to the Beauty, inadvertently (as if before the shooting).

N.B. Nechaev, having had several *arguments* with Teliatnikov (his appearance on the scene), makes people take notice of himself with a stand against the proclamation. He appears at the lecture in honor of the Polish priest. Here, a scene with Stepan Trofimovich. Then, on the following day, he becomes involved in the affair.

2 *August 15*

Nechaev's appearance on the scene begins with a comical and paltry scandal, during which he is incognito, though he has a letter to the Governor's wife. "I wanted to see how this affair would be settled." Stepan Trofimovich is embarrassed at first, and doesn't know which way to turn, seeing what a wretched figure his son is cutting; but when the latter gains a position of importance, he greets him proudly and with pathetic tears—whereas his son keeps insulting him and destroys his marriage. (N.B. But it has not as yet become apparent who he is, so that Liputin, Virginsky, and the poetaster don't know.)

Shatov, a friend. She gives birth at Shatov's place.

But Shatov declares his love, and she goes to Kartuzov—because now she sees Shatov with different eyes and feels that she could love him.

But she hates the Prince.

Whereas he is despondent and wants to shoot himself.

Tikhon—

She has learned that the Prince is married and this is why she has begun to hate him.

(Who is he married to? *Could it be the Ward?*)

(N.B. No.)

Rather, in a Petersburg slum tenement. His wife is in town, somewhere.

(?He is married to the Kartuzov woman? or to a nihilist?)

Or: she is pregnant with the Prince's child.

Yet she has come to hate him,

and has fallen in love with Shatov.

But, struggling with the enormity of Shatov's passion, and after a psychological turnabout, she is seriously thinking of marrying Kartuzov.

(As for the Prince, she rejects his proposal immediately after his arrival, even though she is pregnant from him.)

Yet, at the last moment, realizing how monstrous a marriage to Kartuzov would be,

she comes running to Shatov, to bear her child (she used to be his enemy).

And so that he would accept her, not as his wife, but as a slave, for pity.

Or perhaps she is not pregnant?

But she hates the Ward and is spreading slanderous gossip about her.

33 Or: The Lame Woman, secretly, a relationship, the Lieutenant who begs for charity.

Thoughts about the murder,

and about the monastery. The rape.

N.B. In doubt about Nechaev?

August 16

The Prince is a somber, passionate, demoniac, and dissolute character who knows no moderation; facing the ultimate question he has reached "to be or not to be?" Should he go on living, or should he destroy himself? He cannot, in good conscience and judgment, go on living as before, yet he goes on doing the same things as before and commits the rape.

The Beauty, who had surrendered to him (abroad), now pretends that she hates him. All his sufferings and problems notwithstanding, the Prince, while not in love with her, still derives a secret and *extreme* pleasure from waiting until her patience will be worn out and she will come to him on her own accord, so that then, he may have the satisfaction of rejecting her.

He is amazed at her having fallen in love with Shatov, but he pretends that he is glad about it and encourages her in her love for Shatov.

She pretends that she is in love with Kartuzov, and for a while she actually finds it gratifying that everybody is wondering about her passion for Kartuzov. (For a while she quite seriously means to marry him. But then she throws <herself> at Shatov and begs him to kill the Prince.)

It is only then that the Prince quite frankly announces his <marital> status and tells her about the Lame Woman.

Relations with the Ward: To the Ward *alone* he has revealed, while they were abroad, the position he is in. This is to show to what an extent the Ward has impressed him. The Ward senses that herself, and from the fact that this somber and proud man has confided *such a* secret to her, she realizes how great an influence she has on him. *She* has fallen in love with him. But *he* thinks that *she* has no idea that he loves her. As for the slanderous talk about her relationship with him, she reacts to it with contempt, suspecting that it stems from the Beauty. *She* knows that the Beauty loves him and *lets him know* about it. But she knows that the Prince, having used her for his pleasure, now hates her. (For a while, she was actually jealous of him.) She lets him know about the Lame Woman, who has moved to their town (she has developed a liking for the Lame Woman). At first, out of desperation, she was willing to get married to Stepan Trofimovich, but later, after he suddenly arrived following Stepan Trofimovich's letter, she followed his command and rejected Stepan Trofimovich. He begged her *to wait* and revealed to her that he needed her. She was amazed by his words, but suddenly became afraid that he might kill the Lame Woman.

4 But when she gets jealous of the Beauty, she lets *him* know that she won't let him deceive the latter.

The Ward is Shatov's sister.
Retires to Shatov's flat, } ?
Breaks with Varvara Petrovna.

The Prince, realizing what a tremendous impression his confession will make, tells the Beauty about the Lame Woman. (He understands that this confession will humiliate ~~him~~ her.)

Then the Beauty has a fit of hysterical laughter and wants to marry Kartuzov, but at the last moment she rushes to Shatov: "Kill him, take me for your slave," etc. Hysterics. (Or, she tells Shatov that she does not want his love.) Or she stays with Shatov. But at the critical moment she flees with him to Switzerland; leaves him en route. He returns and hangs himself.

The estate is ostensibly *sold*, but actually given to the Lame Woman.

It is the condition under which she and her brother are willing to keep silence.

Her brother is an officer of irregular behavior; he gets the money, goes around bragging that he has got 4,000, and Kulishov is stalking him, planning to murder him for his money.

Brother and sister are killed one night.

The Beauty fears that he has done it, and so does the Ward.

Or: The Beauty has found out about his being married from the Lame Woman herself, who warned her.

The Beauty is to marry Kartuzov (hatred for the Prince).

Suddenly, the Lame Woman is murdered.

The Beauty, seeing that he wants to go to Switzerland with the Ward, informs the police.

Or: The Prince *orders* the Ward not to marry Stepan Trofimovich, asking her to wait. When the Lame Woman is murdered, he wants to take her to Switzerland, but she is in despair.

The Beauty wants to inform the police and flees to Switzerland with them (?); she abandons this plan and informs the police. He hangs himself.

Or: The Prince returns to marry the Beauty, but keeps putting it off and fails to make a forthright proposal.

~~But the Prince~~ The Lame Woman warns her—~~and~~

Suddenly the Lame Woman is murdered.

After the Lame Woman has been murdered, he suddenly abandons the Beauty, takes the Ward, and leaves for Switzerland.

35 *Or:*—He arrives, being in love with the Beauty, even though she already belongs to him. But she pretends that she hates him (perhaps it is actually true).

She gives thought to her feelings for Shatov.

With Kartuzov,

With him, however, an altercation, and in the end she runs away to Shatov.

Meanwhile the Lame Woman is murdered.

The Beauty abandons Shatov and flees with him.

But he takes the Ward and goes to Switzerland with her.

Or: He arrives with the ultimate idea of putting an end to everything, and to stop the Ward from marrying Stepan Trofimovich. He also wants to go to Switzerland with her.

To Tikhon. (But she is still marrying Stepan Trofimovich, i.e., she is willing to marry him.)

Meanwhile he is captivated by the Beauty's coquetry. They quarrel. He has gotten wind of her love for Shatov.

The Ward is jealous and fearful, for she knows that he can't marry the Beauty.

Suddenly the Lame Woman is murdered.

The Ward, like a madwoman, is ready to flee with him.

(While the Beauty clearly prefers Shatov.)

Yet, after the murder, she is ready to flee with him.

~~She~~

Theme: The Beauty's pride is wounded, for he has taken her virginity.

The Beauty, in the course of the novel, is at first attracted by Shatov; then, she abandons Shatov and, in a frenzy, offers herself to the Captain.

At this point, the Lame Woman is murdered (prior to which event he has broken up her marriage to Stepan Trofimovich).

He wants to leave with the Ward, but she leaves him (or else, she takes his word that *it wasn't he—and leaves*). He abandons the Beauty—the Beauty abandons Shatov and goes with him, etc. (?)

Or: The Beauty rejects him, as the novel proceeds, and goes to Shatov.

The latter despises her and loves the Ward (for which reason he spoils her plan to marry Stepan Trofimovich), yet he flirts with the Beauty.

But the Beauty, who is jealous of the Ward who has joined her brother's side, leaves Shatov and Kartuzov and comes running to him. From this the Beauty concludes that he will marry ~~her~~ the Ward; the Prince calmly explains to the Beauty, who is offering herself to him, that he is married (he does *not* take her virginity).

(Suddenly the Lame Woman is murdered.)

The Beauty is beside herself, and so is the Ward. And he hangs himself.

N.B. The Prince about the Beauty: "I don't like that creature; she is too full of life."

He thinks that she has fallen in love with Shatov purposely, in order to entice him (the Prince).

The Prince is punishing himself and is testing his strength. He is wavering whether he ought to punish himself with the Lame Woman.

N.B. Everything is contained in Stavrogin's character.

Stavrogin is EVERYTHING.

He has cast his spell upon Shatov, then drops him contemptuously and, among other things, makes him believe that the Beauty is enticing him simply because she is jealous of himself.

But he is wrong; the Beauty actually yields to Shatov's influence, though only to a certain point. But when she learns that he is married to another woman (the Lame Woman; she finds out from the Ward), she comes running and offers herself to him, simply and for nothing. She is convinced that he loves her and that he has been keeping away from her only because he is married to the Lame Woman, and suffers greatly from this, so that he actually wanted her to hate him. She gave it a magnanimous interpretation. Magnanimity!

? Stavrogin, who has had ~~her~~ the Beauty (he is in love with her) suddenly experiences a flare-up of passion. The murder of the Lame Woman and her brother (the killer is unknown).

The Beauty cannot stand this. She seeks the help of the chivalrous Kartuzov and, at his flat, while he is defending her against a general onslaught, she goes out of her mind.

Stavrogin suggests to the Ward that she leave Stepan Trofimovich and flee with him to Switzerland, to Uri.[8] This is even earlier. On this first occasion he offers to flee with her to Switzerland, *but* says nothing about his citizenship in the canton of *Uri.* N.B. At this point there occurs as misunderstanding with Stepan Trofimovich who shows his resentment at having been (so he alleges!) cuckolded, and the Ward goes over to the side of her brother, Shatov. At this very moment (the Beauty has shown her jealousy), suspecting that the Prince may not spare the Beauty, she warns her that Stavrogin is married to the Lame Woman. The Beauty, in desperation, for all her hopes have been shattered (she had thought that the Prince was in love with her, and she loves him madly, too), laughs at the Ward, goes running to the Prince, and offers herself to him. Immediately thereafter, the murder of the Lame Woman.

(He went to see Tikhon.)

The Prince buries the Lame Woman, while Kulishov confesses that he killed her all by himself. *A trick of fate,* as it were. It appears that the Beauty went out of her mind much too hastily.

---

[8] A Swiss canton, home of William Tell. Hertsen also lived there. This motif is retained in Stavrogin's letter to Dasha in the final version.

The Prince leaves. He sends the Ward a letter from the station. About the canton of Uri *(for the first time)*. Regarding the Beauty he writes that she went out of her mind much too hastily. He asks the Ward to join him. He hangs himself.

N.B. (What to do with Shatov in the end?)

Or: It is he who has killed the Lame Woman, through Kulishov, and a day later Kulishov is himself killed accidentally.

Nobody knows the secret of his marriage, except the Ward and the Beauty.

No pursuit and no suspicion.

About how Stavrogin makes fun of his brother-in-law and wife, ~~wanting~~ announcing to them that he will himself make the marriage public, and <give them> only 300 rubles.

He declares to the Ward: "There is something incredibly funny in connection with the Lame Woman," etc.

(Only Tikhon knows about the little girl.)

In the letter written to the Ward from the railway station: "You know all, can you share my life with me? I am in need of such a heart as yours. I more than love you (Christian love). Will you come, or won't you? However, as you wish."

If there will be a Nechaev, it will be he who incites Nechaev to murder Shatov.

N.B. Couldn't he incite Kulishov to kill <the Lame Woman>, not telling him directly, but merely mentioning casually that he has given 4,000.

Summary—*Stavrogin as a character:*

Every noble impulse in a monstrously extreme form (Tikhon), as well as every passion *(certainly when he is bored)*. He attacks both the Ward and the Beauty. He explains the secret to the Ward, but to the very last, critical moment, even in the letter written at the railway station, he does not tell her about the little girl. Yet the Ward thinks that she knows *all* about him. He egoistically demands that the Ward join him, with contempt and *without faith* in human compassion. He enjoys making the Beauty the butt of his mockery, also Stepan Trofimovich, the Lame Woman's brother, his mother, and even Tikhon.

As for the Beauty, he actually never loved her, but rather despised her when she submitted to him, but then, suddenly, he experiences a flare-up of passion (delusive and momentary, but immensely powerful), and commits a crime. Then, the disenchantment. He escapes punishment, but hangs himself. He has a talk with the Ward before leaving. The letter from the railway station. In the letter written at the railway station he does not ask the Ward to join him, but only tells her about Uri. N.B. (Makes fun of Stepan Trofimovich, etc.)

38 His pride is expressed in "I won't be afraid to tell everybody about the Lame Woman," *yet he is afraid.* He realizes that he is *not ready* for a moral feat, and that he'll never be ready.

He admits to Tikhon that he has fun mocking the Beauty.

Shatov has an extraordinary and real influence on the Beauty.

N.B. Perhaps Nechaev would be all right, but in a different form (incidentally, it is the Prince who brings him along, and it is he who encourages him)—

N.B. Nechaev's principal idea is—*to raze everything to the ground,* and that this is first and foremost.

He tells the Prince: "I admit, it isn't really any of my concern whether there will be general well-being or not; in any case, it will be better than it is now; and, what would have happened of itself centuries later, will be brought about much sooner by a blow of the axe. Everything will be aimed at eliminating differentiation and ignorance. Actually, everybody will be happy, because this is inherent in the system as such, whether they want it or not. They are going to have: a peaceful life—for everything will be aimed at establishing a beehive; 2) a common effort and a common goal; 3) the dissemination of common knowledge regarding certain facts through incessant research in the natural sciences; 4) general meetings, marriages in the evening, perhaps music and balls.

(N.B. He is asked a question.)

His answer:

"You are asking a lot of questions and want to know things beforehand. Let me tell you that this is precisely what has so far defeated men of action."

"But how is it possible not to know for sure what one is after, and am I not guilty of a crime when I cause a terrible upheaval without having previously made palpably clear to myself what the goal might be toward which I am driving?"

Nechaev: "Empty words ~~mere phrases, just so much idle talk and heckling~~. Aren't you satisfied to know that, first, all that is evil will be destroyed; and secondly, that from here on, social differentiation will be eliminated and mankind will be working together? This alone is enough reason to destroy everything, just to gain this advantage. ~~But what about the abolition of God, marriage, and family?~~ You see, I don't know what is going to happen later on, but I know this much: that God, marriage, family, and private property are the foundations of life as it exists now, and that such a foundation is the greatest poison. I don't know what is going to happen later on, but I know that, having all at once abolished God, marriage, family, and private property, i.e., society as a whole, I have got rid of the poison. Regardless of what may happen later, the poison has been eliminated at least for the time being —which is why I am abolishing society, for it is impossible to get rid of the poison in any different way."

"You know, I'm not the talkative type: my mission is of an entirely different nature. I know, once and for all, that others do talk a lot of nonsense, and that I've had enough of it."

"How do you know that?"

"Why, they can't help talking nonsense; even if they wanted to talk sense, they couldn't. This much I know. Resting upon erroneous premises, their argument must of course be false. Take a man who believes in God—it is quite natural for him to support all kinds of nonsense; or another, who may not himself believe, but who considers the eradication <of this belief> to be inevitable and imminent—again, he is talking nonsense; he has taken nonsense for his premise and is obliged to support it, etc. These people may have good minds, but they are using them in a way which creates falsehoods, and consequently nonsense. Incidentally, even their minds can't be all that good: bend a straight tree toward one side for a length of time, and it will wind up growing crooked. We intend to change all this, and it is all much simpler than is commonly believed."

4 Gradual rise of Nechaev's fortunes. He arranges for a reconciliation between the Governor's wife and Varvara Petrovna.

Nechaev has been almost flattering to Varvara Petrovna, and she wants to reconcile him with Stepan Trofimovich.

A soirée at Varvara Patrovna's, arranged to bring about a reconciliation between Stepan Trofimovich and Nechaev. Instead of a reconciliation, a complete break, and a scandal with the Ward. Stepan Trofimovich's marriage broken up. (Reckonings between Varvara Petrovna and Stepan Trofimovich at Skvoreshniki.) "I won't give up."

The Prince, a few words to the Ward. Liza is jealous; or vice versa.

Problem. DEVELOP THE LOVE AFFAIR BETWEEN THE PRINCE, LIZA, AND THE WARD, BUT THE SCANDAL AND EXPOSÉ THROUGH NECHAEV.

THE LAST, THINK.

Could it be that my difficulties stem from the style of the narrative?

Shouldn't the transition from "get ready for your birthday party" to the Drozdovs and Liza be *dramatic?*

What is needed is more coherence, it is a terrible mess.

Drozdov is angry about the proclamations.

Anonymous letters.

The Shatovs, the Kartuzovs, the secrets of the Lame Woman.

A new mystery every day, that's what makes it comical.

And the requirement that Stepan Trofimovich be destroyed.

Drozdov talks to Shatov.

Enter the cavalier.

The Polish Priest—Drozdov gave him.

Fedka—Kulishov.

Stepan Trofimovich fears that he may kill him.

Rumors about Kulishov roaming the area.

"This is a town full of intrigues" (Drozdov complains).

But he got to like the club; he was so well received there.

The Lame Woman falls on her knees before Varvara Petrovna when the latter is returning from Mass.

The Prince, after having paid a visit to the Lame Woman, goes to see Shatov, who has just slapped his face, and tells him that he is married, and what happened in Switzerland, also that the Ward is the only person to know about it, and that he intends to make the marriage public. Then he asks him about Liza.

About Liza,

and transition to ideas, the Apocalypse.

(Ideas in narrative form ~~and not in scenes~~, from the point of view of the author, and not in the form of scenes.)

Shatov says: "Why did you reveal your secret? You wanted me to see how guilty I am. This is noble, but it is also a terrible vengeance."

The Prince: "Oh no, actually I didn't want to dissuade you; I merely wanted to find out what you're thinking. I had a notion yesterday, during our conversation, that you believe in something. I am very fond of listening to Russians who believe in something."

Shatov: "And you really do not believe...in what you said?"

"N-no. Why, I don't believe in God."

The Prince, to Liza: "I am married."

"That's a joke, isn't it?"

The Prince pretends that it is a joke.

From part 3. Preparations for the Ward's wedding continue with the same urgency. Nechaev has driven Stepan Trofimovich to despair. Playing the atheist in a comical way. Stepan Trofimovich and Varvara Petrovna part tearfully.

On the eve of the wedding the Prince suddenly is passionate with the Ward: "I need you."

~~Liza~~ The Ward suddenly turns down Stepan Trofimovich—(scandal, and the Prince is compromised). The Ward, fearing for Liza, lets her know that he is married. Liza ~~to Shatov and to Kartuzov~~ submits to him, and then goes to Shatov, and to the chivalrous Kartuzov.

After the Ward has broken her engagement, Liza suddenly becomes quite furious (from jealousy, for she thinks that the Prince has encouraged her to break the engagement). Whereas she has not been in contact with the Ward up to this time (to the point of being contemptuous of her), she now comes running to her in a fit of rage, *strikes her* (?). She is informed by her that the Prince is married.

Liza is shocked, almost frightened (by the news that the Lame Woman <is Stavrogin's wife>). She is almost out of her mind and surrenders herself to the Prince in a fit of enthusiasm, with passionate naïveté and in a state of oblivion, also telling him, down to the most minute details, how she has loved him all the time. Naïveté (Princess Katia). The Prince's raging passion. He takes possession of her. (The Prince is also very charming.)

?She runs off to Kartuzov right after the murder of Shatov.

Meanwhile the Prince, who had talked to Kulishov earlier, proceeds to that part of town to look for him.

The Prince had been warning Shatov even before, while the latter had been trying to prove to him that he was just another spoiled young gentleman, that he had no roots, that he had more honor than the rest of them, that he couldn't stand it, and that he must become a naturalized citizen (of Switzerland). *He guesses it.*

Drozdov: "I am convinced that she's not simply another Lame Woman, and that something is being concealed here."

Later: *Rien de plus,*[9] about the Prince; and after the Prince, about Varvara Petrovna, management of the estate, worries, she's lost her acquaintances, Stepan Trofimovich—inert superiority, a handsome man, that's how it happened. Our Prince spent 4 years traveling~~—about Shatov~~ About Shatov, "it isn't your fault."

("Mr. Shatov, will you kindly leave."—"Why, I've actually come to take care of this.")

(On the same occasion they also talked about the Great Writer and about the Lame Woman.)

Liza inquires about the Lame Woman.

On a holiday. At the Drozdovs' ("settle down, have a bite!") (The proclamation, Stepan Trofimovich is at fault), Kartuzov. He is complaining about Kartuzov. "I insist that Shatov must not be around, or I'll leave the house. I also insist that Kartuzov is not to be around." They quarrel. Varvara Petrovna, very angry, comes flying to Stepan Trofimovich. "See to it that your relative gets calmed down." Kartuzov, and then right away about Liza.

About Liza and about Shatov.

The insult on the stairs.

Drozdov is in a rage over the insult and over the visit paid to Shatov. A certain cavalier comes to see him, puts in a word about Varvara Petrovna's patronage in Liza's presence (he also drops a hint about Liza), and also mentions that the Ward has sent a letter to the Prince. It almost comes to a quarrel about the Cavalier between Drozdov and Varvara Petrovna (reproaches regarding the anonymous letter). The situation at home has turned as sour as vinegar. (The news about the Ward's letter to the Prince and that the Cavalier is the buyer <of the Prince's estate>.)

~~Passed it on. Stepan Trofimovich and Liputin.~~ It was the Cavalier who passed on to Drozdov the news about the letter.

About the Great Writer.

News about the Great Writer.

---

[9] French: "nothing more."

Stepan Trofimovich about the subscription to the public lecture. "Eh, what do I care about your birthday."

They have a friendly heart-to-heart talk, that scene to be done more gracefully, "but where is your wife?"

There was a good deal of mystery about it all, ~~the Governor~~ about that relationship with the Drozdovs—she wanted the wedding, but the influence of the Governor's wife—the Drozdovs themselves—*Rejected*, but not entirely, and Liza's character—(she was in an agitated state of mind, so that for a long time Stepan Trofimovich had no hope).

Problem: Create the personality of the Lame Woman.

On distant terms with his sister.

The wedding of Stepan Trofimovich.

He was asked. He grinned.

"Why are you grinning? Your sister is being insulted. You're an idiot. A real idiot."

"Never mind."

Stepan Trofimovich tried to talk to him:

"I don't care."

However, it wasn't he who composed the anonymous letters, but someone else. However, Varvara Petrovna was much too irritated, especially by the fact that Shatov had done so well with the Drozdovs.

1st part:

6 Varvara Petrovna and Stepan Trofimovich. A lull. A handsome man. The Prince, matchmaking. Stepan Trofimovich's son. Assent to the marriage and a letter to the Prince. "Be ready for your birthday party." And straight on to the Drozdovs and Liza. But the match isn't meeting with the Drozdovs' approval. Varvara Petrovna goes excitedly straight to the Governor, a relative of the Drozdovs. The Governor's wife, in the meantime, has received an anonymous letter (about the wife). Relationships with the Drozdovs. She is being excluded. The proclamation and the intrigue against Stepan Trofimovich (the denunciation). The Governor as a relative of the Drozdovs. The Great Writer. But in spite of the fact that she has been *excluded* and that attempts obviously are made to annoy her (by all except the old woman: make this more typical and more anecdotal), she still hopes to overcome all this, and ~~combines~~ combine her upcoming labors and her struggle to succeed in the matter of this marriage with her planned humiliation of the Governor's wife. Putting her trust in Liza. Liza as a character. Traits. But

with Shatov and Kartuzov. About Kartuzov; later, Shatov's relationship and successes with Liza arouse an indescribable feeling of indignation in Varvara Petrovna. (N.B. It might be that Varvara Petrovna has developed a liking for the telltale Lame Woman. Moreover, her brother is a cavalier. The Lame Woman lives in the same house as Shatov.) Liza with Shatov, and the Cavalier insults Liza.

A digression, and begin to tell about Shatov, and about Liza. It wasn't he who wrote the anonymous letter. Relations with Liza. Liza went to see Shatov on her own. The old woman told Varvara Petrovna about it with tears, and complained that Kartuzov, too, had through them <...>.

~~Liza as a character~~ Sells a village. Vinegar: "Should we call the Prince?" Liza as a character. Liza and Shatov. Varvara Petrovna is more furious about Liza's relationship with Shatov than about anything else. Liza was a most extraordinary girl, twice married (with Kartuzov and with Shatov).* With Shatov (about his sister and the Prince, and everything), about Kartuzov. ~~Kartuzov told~~ The Drozdov woman also told Varvara Petrovna about Kartuzov. ~~Kartuzov told~~ The Drozdov woman told Varvara Petrovna that *she,* for her part, preferred the Prince. And it is at this point that the estate is sold. This is also where the Lame Woman enters the picture. (Regarding Liza's relations with Shatov) an air of mystery.

The birthday party, the situation is getting tense, Stepan Trofimovich gets angry. The Polish priest. The recital. Aliosha Teliatnikov, the arrest.

The Prince arrives. By means of description and dialogue (with his mother and with Liza). In these two conversations his character is revealed.

At the Governor's.

Kartuzov and the boots.

Evening. The son of Stepan Trofimovich, and a spontaneous marriage proposal. Rejected (perhaps not). ~~A quarrel~~ A scandal caused by Nechaev; Shatov strikes the Prince.

N.B. (The Ward is very sad that the Prince doesn't pay any attention to her; throughout the novel, he doesn't pay any attention to her, or to her marriage to Stepan Trofimovich.)

---

* "Married" is an obvious euphemism in this phrase, as proven by the preposition following: "with" instead of "to."

The Cavalier frequently visits Shatov.

N.B. Early in the 2d part, after the slap in the face, the Prince tells Liza straight out that he is married, but does not say to whom. She won't believe it (but keeps it to herself). But later, alone with the Ward and in a state of frenzy, she asks the latter: "Could it be true?"—

Or: Liza submitted to him in Switzerland. Later he told her that he was married. Liza returns to Russia and behaves foolishly. He owes her the money for her estate, yet in her excessive pride she refuses to charge it to him. Proudly, she releases him from all his obligations. He seems to be teasing her by remaining insensitive to her magnanimity and even politely derisive. "Why, you are one of those *new women,* aren't you, and isn't this what your convictions ought to be like?" Yet she won't believe that he is married. Even before his arrival, while in a state of frenzy, she went to see the Ward and asked her. The latter assured her that she wasn't his wife and that she seriously meant to marry Stepan Trofimovich; but that he probably was married, only she didn't know to whom.

A few lines in the same chapter, where <Varvara Petrovna says> "get ready," and then ~~directly~~, leaving Varvara Petrovna, turn directly to Liza.

The Cavalier: "A certain disorder in my affairs as a result of injustice, as a result of many... Amazones."

The Lame Woman, wearing a hat,* goes down on her knees before Varvara Petrovna in the Cathedral, and the Cavalier, rushing to the scene, explains that she kneels not from poverty, but from a different emotion. Varvara Petrovna takes her for a madwoman and, from here on, begins to visit her at Shatov's house. This is what the Ward had reported to the Prince in her letter.

7 2)

The Prince, having arrived on the following day, makes a clean breast about the Lame Woman before the Ward, and then suddenly asks her: "Are you getting married to Stepan Trofimovich? What's the reason?" And not a word more. The Ward, overcome with pride, says nothing either.

---

* Meaning "dressed like a lady."

The Lame Woman's brother. A visit to Drozdov

~~Put down~~

Conclude the 1st part with Varvara Petrovna's troubles with the Drozdovs, the Governor's wife, rumors about the sale of the estate, and "shouldn't I call him back?" Vinegar. Yet she has hopes.

N.B. *Put down.* 1st) ~~Vinegar the little spy shows up: "I'm not a spy, I'm doing it out of respect." He sends his poems: to tell of two things.~~

But she (Varvara Petrovna) puts her trust in Liza:

Switch directly to Liza—*a little chapter* on generalities (a few little anecdotes)—Shatov~~—she gave a horsewhipping~~ she gave a horsewhipping, entered into a relationship.

About Shatov in general, and all his relations with Liza (i.e., he returns the work). A final talk about his sister (i.e., his sister has told him to let Liza know that she is actually getting married, etc.) Liza is furious, but he has guessed her thoughts. She suddenly pays him a visit—Liza's fiery proposal, rejected by Shatov. The scene with the Lame Woman on the stairs. The Cavalier at Drozdov's—the insult. Kartuzov. A reproach to Varvara Petrovna: "You've made Kartuzov and the Lame Woman your protégés."

The Little Spy appears on the scene—The Ward has written to the Prince telling him that it was the Cavalier who bought the estate, and that Liza is with Shatov.

"That Lame Woman who was here on her knees," a visit by Varvara Petrovna, a good deed, the Lame Woman kisses her hands. And suddenly Varvara Petrovna learns that it is they who have bought the estate.

The Ward is sent for: "Yes, I did write; no, I can't say, but there is nothing to it ~~?~~."

Secrets. Vinegar.

~~The Ward comes upstairs and tears up the rough copy.~~

She calls the Ward: "Yes, I did write." Then about Stepan Trofimovich. Then about the strained emotional state. "I have put my trust in you."

The Ward returns to her room. She gets out the rough copy of her letter and gets to thinking about Switzerland (everything that happened in Switzerland), and reads the letter.

The Polish priest. 2d part.

Begin the 2d part with Liza (a few traits of her character; why not bring in Kartuzov and the Officer), Shatov, the Lame Woman, Kartuzov, etc. The Cavalier at Drozdov's, Drozdov is angry and complains to Varvara Petrovna, even about Kartuzov. About Kartuzov. Through letting him meet the Ward at Shatov's—who is the Ward's brother—(or at Varvara Petrovna's). Meanwhile the incident with the Polish priest. The lecture and the scandal. The arrest. The Prince arrives. Scenes with his mother and with Liza (invitation to the club for dinner). At the Governor's. Kartuzov—the boots. ~~The nameday party, evening~~

3d part. ~~The nameday party~~ The nameday party, evening. ~~Liza~~ The Ward refuses. Scandal. Nechaev. Shatov slaps <the Prince's> face. On the next day the Prince reveals to Liza that he is married. (Majestically, proudly, and derisively.) He speaks with Liza about Nechaev. He offers the ~~Lame Woman~~ Ward an explanation regarding the Lame Woman. Thanks her for having written him about the Lame Woman, (speaks of Liza in a bored and condescending tone and appears to be strangely interested in Kartuzov); it appears to the Ward as if he were talking of something that was of minor importance, and in passing. She sits there facing him with trepidation. Continue about the Ward and about their relationship in Switzerland. He declares to the Ward that he is about to make public his marriage to the Lame Woman. "À propos, are you going to marry Stepan Trofimovich?" Here, a funny idea. He goes to the club to have dinner. Insult, challenge; he goes to see the Lame Woman. To Liputin's house. The Officer acts as second to his opponent, also Kartuzov. How subsequently opinion about the Prince is firmly established.

After having seen Kartuzov, the Prince spends some time with Nechaev. Then he pays a visit to the Lame Woman and drops in to see Shatov also. Conversation with Shatov and the Cavalier. On the following day, the duel—and after that, the 3d part, and directly on to Nechaev.

Then, the 3d part. Nechaev and Liza. In her ~~despair~~ disappointment she acts foolishly ~~for she has been told that he is married~~. The rise of Nechaev, the fall of Stepan Trofimovich. The Prince trying to match up Liza with Nechaev, etc. Relations with Liza. The Ward lets Liza know that he is married.

The wedding of the Ward and Stepan Trofimovich is called off that day.

The little spy.

The Poetaster.

N.B. No rendezvous with the Ward is necessary, for he didn't tell Liza in Switzerland that he was married.

(For Liza is convinced that the Ward has broken her engagement because of the Prince.)

48 August 19 (leave it).

The Drozdovs are related to the wife of the new Governor. The Great Writer and their social set are *à part.* Varvara Petrovna *feels* that she is different in this particular society, and that she is being purposely excluded from it. However, Liza is friendly to her, though even she keeps somewhat aloof.

Varvara Petrovna is a stern woman, set in her ways; she isn't easily shaken, but she has a native talent for intrigue. Incidentally, she has convinced herself that she must absolutely be an enemy of the Governor's wife. The latter has not paid her a visit as yet. The Great Writer.

She has the feeling that the whole business of a match between the Prince and Liza is about to fall through. She is convinced that the Governor's wife has played a major role in this intrigue, and that it was she who put forward the Officer. (The Officer is a good man, of a good family and with a fortune—he is more closely related to the Governor's wife than to General Drozdov himself.) Yet Varvara Petrovna does not want to give up her hopes for a match. She would like to call the Prince home—but hesitates to do it until Stepan Trofimovich has sent his own plea to him. Regarding the Ward, she has acted too hastily.

New motives, which change the earlier form:

1) The Drozdovs are related to the Governor's wife. The Governor's wife is actually pulling strings for a marriage between the Officer and Liza. This is why the enmity between her and Varvara Petrovna becomes more pronounced.

?2) Shatov as a person. Shatov's love for Liza. Sometimes, Liza also imagines that she loves Shatov. In the further course of the novel, she confesses her love to him and wants to visit him at his flat: N.B. For a while she is interested in Nechaev; but soon enough she is critical of him when he says: "You'll be given satisfaction." The Prince has succeeded in convincing Nechaev that Liza loves him. Proclamations, boots, under interrogation.

3) *Liza is bored.* She keeps saying that she is bored. Hence her crazy

ideas. (Shatov's wife. What do I care for my wife! Liza is interested in her and is asking questions about her.)

4) The Lame Woman; a mysterious air; already in the first part, a mystery. The Lame Woman's brother insults Liza during a visit at the Shatov woman's, and suddenly pays a visit to ~~the Captain~~ Drozdov.

5) The Ward is Shatov's sister. Introduce Shatov along these lines, as early as in the 1st part. The Ward alone knows the secret and fears for Liza. Already in the 1st part, Liza speaks with Shatov about his sister.

6) When Nechaev makes his appearance, neither Miliukov nor Shatov know anything about him. (He later reveals his identity.) Nechaev knows the Prince, and the latter knows him. Liza is an acquaintance from abroad. And what is more important, he had at one time been a protégé of the Great Writer's.

7) *The most important thing.* The Prince, after his arrival, not a single word with the Ward. From Stepan Trofimovich's letter he had guessed *(without telling anybody)* that she had fallen in love, and upon his arrival he refuses purposely, in a Pechorinian[10] manner, to start a conversation with her. He even fails to advise her against her proposed marriage to Stepan Trofimovich. She is hurt by this. In the further course of the novel she finally asks him to come and talk things over with her. Having received her letter, he says: "Aha, she couldn't resist after all." But when they meet, she immediately brings up her fears regarding Liza, and he can see right away that her fears are serious.

The Ward is not a serf girl, but from the Poetaster's family.

The Poetaster had warmly supported the idea of her marrying Stepan Trofimovich. The Poetaster is in love with Lizaveta Nikolaevna.

If the Ward is from the Poetaster's family, then what should be the reason for the beginning of a relationship between Liza and Shatov?

The slap in the face.

Varvara Petrovna, the family of the Doctor with the growing poet. The late Doctor had insulted Varvara Petrovna and Stepan Trofimovich; Varvara Petrovna had been helping out on occasion. Then, Shatov appeared (she had been supporting him at the university, too). Shatov started to help them. (?) A poet: an image of the bosom of a family; the Poetaster slanders Shatov with Stepan Trofimovich; he

---

10 The hero of Lermontov's *A Hero of Our Time.*

would like very much to gain favor with Varvara Petrovna; he reads his verses to Shatov. Captain 2d grade Kurmyzhnikov,[11] Liputin, Virginsky. The story of Varvara Petrovna and Stepan Trofimovich. The Prince is still abroad, appearance of the Amazon. (Varvara Petrovna suspects that Shatov may love the Ward.) Stepan Trofimovich's wedding, and meanwhile, suddenly, some of the Poetaster's poems have appeared in *The Contemporary*. The wedding doesn't come off, because something goes wrong at the Drozdovs'—Shatov and Liza, Kartuzov, Stepan Trofimovich sends a letter to the Prince—the Lame Woman and the Captain 2d grade are also among those present. Anonymous letters (the Poetaster and Liputin).

Start from the first moment, then, in the course of the narrative, relate what has happened in the past.

The Prince arrives on Stepan Trofimovich's nameday. Stepan Trofimovich, all of a sudden, spontaneously proposes, receives a categoric "no!" from ~~Liza~~ the Ward. Shatov slaps the Prince's face.

(Change of governors, and the lecture in honor of the Polish priest, and everything, only without Nechaev.)

~~65 45 33~~

(Give the Prince a bigger role, make him more important; the Drozdovs are related to the wife of the new Governor) which is why they have returned; also, the Great poet—

The Governor and the Drozdovs are afraid that Liza may marry Shatov, and also of Kartuzov's unseemly escapades.

Still, they would like it very much to see her marry the Prince. That's why they are expecting him. That is also why they supported the match between the Ward and Stepan Trofimovich. The Poetaster, too, is fidgeting around, seemingly pleased with the way things are going. The mysterious appearance of the Prince. The Prince tells the Ward outright: "An awful lot of things are funny around here."

The Prince is received at the Poetaster's house, as they hope that kinship ties with him may be in store for them as a result of his relationship with the Ward.

If Nechaev arrives (that is together with the Prince) and the Prince assures him of Liza's love for him, and provokes the cold jealousy of Nechaev's vanity against Shatov.

The Beauty teases Shatov with Kartuzov, i.e., Kartuzov's love.

---

[11] He does not appear in the final version.

She shows him an anonymous letter.

~~The Kartuzovs~~

Everything is clear about Nechaev, to the point of being comical and repulsive.

As for the Prince, everything about him is a question mark.

August 18 <1870>. *Attempt at a program.*

Change of governors, and the proclamations. An altercation with Varvara Petrovna, and the denunciation against Stepan Trofimovich. Stepan Trofimovich at the time when he was getting married, and his relations with the Drozdovs. In a word, gossip and moral decay in town. The Drozdovs had not been socializing with anybody.

It is necessary to tell about Varvara Petrovna. Then, about Varvara Petrovna and Stepan Trofimovich before the lull. This, then, is the Stepan Trofimovich who was very nearly accused of spreading proclamations; but meanwhile there came the reform, Anton Petrov, faith in God, etc. (N.B. Shatov, Liputin much too casually)—there's one thing he firmly believes in, namely the effect he has as a handsome man, and there, suddenly, this marriage. This must be told in more detail.

Initially, about the Prince. Abroad. The Drozdovs. They went abroad. They returned after a genuine quarrel. N.B. The Drozdov woman has a discussion of some length with Varvara Petrovna (among other things, about Stepan Trofimovich's son). Finally, also about the Ward.

Varvara Petrovna wants the Ward married. Goes to see Stepan Trofimovich. He agrees, nor can he help agreeing. Varvara Petrovna has got things pretty well under control on her side, but over at the Drozdovs they are certainly heading toward a violent break. About the Beauty, mostly Shatov and her relationship with Shatov before the break, and about the visit she paid him. Asks him about his sister: "Is it true that she is getting married?" And this is a victory and a triumph for Kartuzov.

N.B. Yet ostensibly it is still the Shatov girl and Stepan Trofimovich, even in front of Varvara Petrovna. Shatov has a talk with his sister.

Varvara Petrovna seeks to steer clear of trouble by arranging this marriage. Later, she is angry at 1) the anonymous letter (to a lesser degree), 2) at the Great Writer, 3) at the letter sent to the Prince, and at Kartuzov. THE NEW GOVERNOR, for whose appointment *she* is being blamed. Varvara Petrovna's hatred for Shatov.

Nevertheless, the match with Stepan Trofimovich wasn't coming off. Necktie, Shatov, etc.

N.B. In a word, there has been so much distressingly wrong with everything, and everybody has become so angry with everybody else that even Stepan Trofimovich loses his patience.

This is what Kartuzov has to say, in passing: "There's this bit of news that the Prince has sold a village."

A public lecture in honor of the Polish priest. Varvara Petrovna advises against it. "Couldn't it lead to trouble?" "You know what, there's this bit of news that the Prince has sold a village (to the Lame Woman)." She had a vinegar compress tied around her head. Stepan Trofimovich about the Polish priest and about the birthday party.—

"Oh, you and your birthday party!"

This birthday party is due tomorrow.

~~Shatov goes and returns his work to the Beauty, refusing to continue it. She comes to see him herself.~~

There is a commotion at the Drozdovs' house. "Did the Beauty go and see Shatov? Find out about Shatov."

N.B. (Tell how Shatov met the Beauty, and beforehand, tell about Shatov. Some things remain unsaid between the Beauty and Shatov. Yet *two* things are hinted at: 1) that Shatov is already infected with either a serious love or a serious hatred for the Beauty, and that she has noticed it; ~~Shatov~~ she says to Shatov: "You are in love with me." Shatov replies: "I certainly won't take you; what I need is a wife." *Shatov:* "Please leave me alone!" (getting his hand on the lintel). And, 2) that the Beauty entered this relationship with Shatov with a purpose, and Shatov quite bluntly tells her what purpose—("Because I am the Prince's enemy, and you hate him for some reason.")

BRING OUT THE LOVE.

N.B. In a word, this is *the last word* between the Beauty and Shatov, a word which has left much unsaid, which was spoken hastily, which was misunderstood and said in anger. It happened at Shatov's flat. She drove in together with the Officer (à propos the Lame Woman).

(N.B. During this very encounter, Shatov inadvertently reveals a thing or two about the anonymous letters, also about Liputin and Stepan Trofimovich's son.)

She lets out some secrets.

Thereupon, a public lecture with the Polish priest, a scandal—arrested and taken away under escort. The Prince arrives. The tryst. At the Governor's. Boots and Kartuzov. The soirée.

At Stepan Trofimovich's. The Great Writer. Nechaev. The Beauty shows Nechaev her favor, but she is only making fun of him. It turns out that she is involved in the proclamations without herself knowing it. Nechaev speaks disparagingly of Stepan Trofimovich's marriage. Shatov slaps the Prince's face.

2d part. The Prince and ~~Shatov, Nechaev~~. Nechaev is constantly cutting a ridiculous figure (yet he is successful everywhere, having been well recommended). And suddenly, Nechaev begins to grow.

N.B. *The most important.* The writer himself says that, here, Nechaev has made a kind of mysterious self-discovery, but that the author is not aware of it.

N.B. The most important about Nechaev.

Nechaev reconciliates Varvara Petrovna with the Governor's wife. He manages to gain control over Varvara Petrovna, since the Great Writer, and everybody, is for *Nechaev.* The sudden downfall of Stepan Trofimovich. There is a persistent rumor about Nechaev that he was originally among those guilty and was also active in Switzerland, but that now he has not only been forgiven, but is actually in the employ of certain personages (because everybody seeks his company, and everybody is for him). Varvara Petrovna even becomes an atheist. (Everybody goes to see Tikhon and Ivan Iakovlevich.) Sacrilege. The fire. Liputin. The Polish priest. (All this, in a *fragmentary,* mysterious manner.)

Even Shatov with the printing press. And the Beauty herself is involved in the conspiracy and has been distributing proclamations. Kartuzov and his projects, etc. A temporary trance.

Nechaev has been inadvertently teasing Stepan Trofimovich about the latter's naïveté, suggesting to him that he has been cuckolded.

Stepan Trofimovich's flight—a showdown, and death.

The murder of the Lame Woman.

The murder of Shatov.

Kulishov's death and Nechaev's flight.

The Prince's departure and words—(the authority <claims> that he is with the Count).

Letter from the railway station about the canton of Uri—

He hangs himself.

After the Beauty has gone out of her mind, Kartuzov's death.

The Lame Woman's brother has also been distributing proclamations. The Poetaster and the Correspondent (instead of Virginsky), to whom Shatov had done a good turn in the beginning.

Shatov, in his last conversation with the Prince, concerning his intention to inform the police, says this about all of them: "*Buffoons!*"

? What is most important, *Nechaev* arrives *mainly* with the plan to stir up riots in the area, and to prepare it for a June uprising.[12]

About Nechaev: Nechaev is acting two roles, the 2d of which I, the Chronicler, don't know at all, so that I'm not trying to present it (I do not know, for instance, what was going on between him and Liputin, and Shatov, so I'm not presenting it; but I know about the meeting, and this I do present).

August 21

14 I am doing each thing in its proper turn.

1st part. Up to *Rien de plus* (with alterations).

After *rien de plus,* about the Prince. (In the Prince's presence, about the rule of Varvara Petrovna, about her being stingy, and a good manager. Her son has come to mean everything to her, and in many respects *she is disappointed* with him. Also, about Liputin.)

Our Prince has been traveling for 4 years. A lull. A letter from the Drozdov woman. Varvara Petrovna went abroad, returned, and is now eagerly expecting the return of the Drozdovs, getting the house touched up.

Her hopes were fulfilled. ~~She has become a competent manager~~. The new Governor (she was afraid of the influence of the Governor's wife) about the Drozdovs. (The General on atheism.)

The Drozdovs have arrived. Liza is offended. About the Ward and about how she <missing verb> Shatov—she gets to talk with the Ward.

She rushes to see Stepan Trofimovich (here, about bad habits and about how he is a handsome man).

Rushes in, and a proposal.

He couldn't but accept, Nechaev. He accepts.

---

[12] Dostoevsky was more or less historically correct here: Nechaev arrived in Russia in August, 1869, in order to cause an uprising on February 19, 1870.

And nevertheless the wedding was slow in coming off (Varvara Petrovna is worried). Stepan Trofimovich can't stand it and goes to pay a visit. A scene because of the letter: "Still you aren't so very guilty yet."

Notre (…) Chatoff, discussion about the marriage agreement. Yet the letters were written by a different party.

Still, the marriage wasn't coming off, and here then, about the proclamations AT THE DROZDOV PLACE. ~~He expressed himself~~ Stepan Trofimovich has been very critical. "I am surprised." "It isn't us, not us," and still, Drozdov did write it. Varvara Petrovna handed it over to him. He hid the manuscripts. "I am surprised: *a birthday*. You and your birthday!" But he had gotten in her way at an inopportune moment: Varvara Petrovna had just received word that the anonymous letter was in the hands of the Governor's wife, so that the Great Writer could be laughing with her about it right now. The Great Writer arrives—a letter to Stepan Trofimovich about the Great Writer. At the end of the last letter about Shatov, Shatov didn't let sleep; she found out about his sister, about Shatov. (She has gotten the idea that the Governor's wife, Shatov, and others.) Success with Liza. She decides to investigate the matter.

She went to see the Drozdovs (she loved Liza). "I don't want Shatov, or Kartuzov." The Lame Woman. This is a proud type (the nervous and wry General). Sells the estate.

~~Gets it for Kartuzov~~ About Virginsky. ~~Sells the estate.~~

As for Kartuzov—he sells the estate <…>.

Home. Stepan Trofimovich gets it. Vinegar. Virginsky—Kartuzov.

Here, the insult on the stairs takes place.

Liza (Varvara Petrovna used to love her) and Shatov—she refuses until that insult on the stairs.

Lebiadkin and Drozdov, the Ward's letter to the Prince. The news that Lebiadkin is about to buy.

This Lebiadkin is a socialist, yet he goes begging from Stepan Trofimovich. Virginsky.

Lebiadkin and the Lame Woman.

Where to insert about Captain Lebiadkin?

Compare with the first program.

Note (in the 2d part). 1) The Prince asks the Ward: "So you are getting married? How did you get this idea? Congratulations." (She turns pale, returns, and falls on her bed.)

2) After the boots, about the Ward, who is getting ready to leave, and about the Prince in Switzerland; the Lame Woman.

3) Also in the 2d part, before the duel the Prince goes to see Shatov: "A secret—your sister let me know."

Note 2. ~~In the chapter "Bad Habits"~~ Varvara Petrovna says to Stepan Trofimovich: "You are getting old frightfully early."

15 A man before going out of his mind.

The Great Writer. The new Governor.

Kartuzov.

The proclamation.

Reproaches for the letter written to the Prince.

Ce Chatoff.[13]

Advance notice on Shatov.

I've quit going there, but he invited me in and started giving me all the ins and outs about the Governor. The Great Writer, Kartuzov.

Meanwhile strange rumors are heard about town.

The new Governor, a family feud, the proclamations.

A quarrel with the Drozdovs (she has created her own image of Liza, as Stepan Trofimovich emphatically observes. "The affair with Liza will come to an end, and I'll be relieved.")

~~Anonymous.~~

The Great Writer, Kartuzov—(Stepan Trofimovich calls for me: "Find out what Kartuzov has come up with.")

Varvara Petrovna comes rushing and reproaches him for Kartuzov. A quarrel. The letter.

She comes and reproaches <Stepan Trofimovich> for having written that letter to the Prince. The mystery of the anonymous letters.

It is Shatov.

Warn the Drozdovs about Shatov.

1) Varvara Petrovna resents the Drozdov woman's letter and decides to have a formal showdown. She lets Stepan Trofimovich know, and he hides the books. He asks: "What about the birthday party?" "You

---

[13] French: "This Shatov."

and your birthday party. There will be nothing. This is all nonsense." He has come at a bad time: anonymous letters all over (?). Visiting with the Governor's wife. The Great Writer. The Kartuzov woman has paid a visit and has begged to save her from Captain Kartuzov. And, while *she* is glad about it, Drozdov himself is annoyed. "I've arranged everything; A Teniers[14] for you.

Society.

2) Varvara Petrovna notices that Shatov is among those present. "Why yes, Shatov." "So he is an acquaintance of yours?" "Liza's"

Society, anonymous letters. The Great Writer, about Shatov. "In the postscript, imagine, about Shatov!"

~~At this time, suddenly, Mme. Drozdov's visit, the lecture of the Polish priest.~~

This mysterious note about Shatov related to the fact that the Drozdov woman was, on that particular day, out of humor, and greatly so, and about Shatov.

~~And as luck would have it, Captain Kartuzov had been on another binge at about the same time, which annoyed her so much that everything almost collapsed~~. Thereupon she decided to clear the air drastically.

4. This Captain Kartuzov.

After mass, at the Drozdovs', the proclamation, Lebiadkin, the Lame Woman, secrets, Shatov.

Firstly, Captain Kartuzov had been on another binge, and everything came down on Stepan Trofimovich.

Society.

Anonymous letters and the Great Writer.

The proclamation.

The letter, getting ready for the trip, but just then, Kartuzov.

"Liza, who has fascinated Kartuzov, has not, I think, fascinated Shatov."

---

[14] The Teniers were a family of Flemish artists who flourished in the seventeenth century. The most famous of them was David Teniers the Younger (1610–90). His favorite subjects were scenes of peasant life and historical scenes. Barbara Stavrogin sends Stepan Trofimovich her Teniers to hang under the portrait of Goethe. Part I, chapter 3:3.

56 August 22

1st Part—(I'm telling one thing after another.)
—Till *rien de plus* (with an alteration),
after *rien de plus, about the Prince.* In the chapter about the Prince, about the reign of Varvara Petrovna, about her boredom, stingy, a good manager, how Stepan Trofimovich was beginning *to lose ground* (?), actually moving to a different house; but then there is Varvara Petrovna's need to love and to give herself up to something or to somebody (at one time it was the Ward, then Shatov, if only he hadn't responded with black ingratitude, but more of that later); and so she threw herself at her son. Stepan Trofimovich, too, had advised her to go abroad.

A conversation is more characteristic:

"He has got knowledge, culture; he'll mellow." "Let him have a good time abroad, and in the meantime I'll save some money for him," thinks Varvara Petrovna.

Our Prince spent 4 years traveling (about his travels). Varvara Petrovna at first avidly received his letters, but later she didn't even ask him to write. Description of his travels. Many things worried Varvara Petrovna. "It isn't any of my business," she thought. "We'll see each other in 4 years, and in the meantime I'll save some money for him." Everything is quiet over here, Stepan Trofimovich definitely is being pushed into the background. He was actually glad to be left alone—which she promptly took to heart; everything about her was now focused on her son. Meanwhile we had a circle of sorts, consisting of Liputin, Shatov, and Virginsky. We used to discuss this and that. He possessed a strange, inert calmness; he believed in God. I made a point of observing him. ~~Still earlier, at the time of the reform~~ I can recall that 19th of February, a year after her return from abroad, but before the Prince was back. He was getting into the habit of forgetting what he would be talking about. *Bad habits*, "Without sputtering!" Of late, Varvara Petrovna had been casting strange glances. *Elle a changé ses idées voila tout.*[15] A handsome man. And suddenly he disappoints her.[*]

A letter from the Drozdov woman. She has made a trip, and returned

---

15 French: "She has changed her ideas, that's all."

* The editor has changed the original text to read: "And suddenly he has become disappointed," which seems unwarranted (*razocharoval* emended to read *razocharovalsia*).

from it, energy, "get the house finished." To Stepan Trofimovich about certain secrets, and about Liza. "She is such a child." Varvara Petrovna: "Why a child, on the contrary, she's got character, and I approve of that." She couldn't get along with them: "Drozdov is a worthless character." He remembered about Liza and the Ward. Incidentally: children used to love him. Varvara Petrovna's dreams were becoming real. Yet we are having a revolution. The Governor and his wife. The secret amounted to this—the Governor's wife. Conversation between Varvara Petrovna and Stepan Trofimovich about the Governor and his wife: "She was sitting there in my drawing room, with that fly on her forehead." Stepan Trofimovich observed that women tend to sense the attitudes of others beforehand; for instance, she would say "she is my enemy," and then everything would eventually bear out that notion. He wanted to make her a compliment, but got entangled in his words, and Varvara Petrovna tore into him: "You are sputtering when you talk."

N.B. *That's when*: "You are aging awfully early!" And to the mirror.

"Elle a changé ses idées."[16]

qui boivent en zapoy[17]

A handsome man. But how this opinion was destined to crumble!

The Drozdovs have arrived. Liza acts hurt. About the Ward, a superficial description of the Ward. ~~Conversation and marriage proposal~~ (Some sort of vain jealousy on the part of Liza.) Three days have passed. "Liza is right, and Drozdov is a worthless character. She has not been getting along with them, and swears to me that it is *Nikolas'* <*sic*> fault." She is convinced that she has been turned down by the Drozdovs, although not quite. The General on atheism. The officer. "It's all the Governor's wife's doing!" Inspiration: a conversation and a marriage proposal. She comes running to Stepan Trofimovich. The proposal, which he accepts.

He couldn't help accepting. Nechaev, 8,000. Yet the wedding won't come off. ~~Varvara Petrovna is annoyed (society has turned its back on Varvara Petrovna), but what is most important, <she is worried> about her son: "Can it be true?" She won't dare to ask him in a letter and decided to expect him home for Christmas~~. Stepan Trofimovich could not contain himself and paid her a visit. A scene on account of the letter. "You aren't as guilty." Busy days. The proclamation, and she

---

16 French: "She has changed her ideas."

17 French: "who drinks hard" (*zapoi* is Russian for "hard drinking").

falls in love with Liza. *Chatoff*. His sister. Yet the wedding wasn't coming off. A falling-out with Drozdov about the proclamations, which almost leads to a complete break. He has written about Stepan Trofimovich.

Kartuzov.

57 She has returned from abroad, energy, the Drozdov house. She summons Stepan Trofimovich (he has been living a distance away). He was flattered by the fire of her avowals: with Liza, the child! But here the Governor's wife enters the picture and the intrigue is under way, "the fly!" ~~I did force her to~~ "You must imagine, Mme. Drozdov was most surprised by my arrival, yet I did force her to state her position." "Oh you Bismarck!" "Though no Bismarck, I still realized that an intrigue was brewing there; Drozdov, then there's that officer—they're complaining about Liza's being self-willed, yet there is no way to get along with that man, he is simply an old woman. I remember him, there's her <. . .> afraid of atheism; and so, around the day-after-tomorrow." But most important, these intrigues, the Governor, "the fly."

Stepan Trofimovich: "The Governor has arrived; she is expected any moment now, as you know; and imagine, she is coming with the Great Writer."

At this point, about "the fly."

Stepan Trofimovich: "How typical of you. I can virtually see that fly—but aren't you exaggerating? A woman will always be a woman," he laughed, spluttering. "You are aging awfully." The mirror. "Gone to seed."

Mme. Drozdov: "Lizaveta Fiodorovna's favorite phrase is 'either you or I must leave the house.' "

Varvara Petrovna arrives. Her carriage almost runs into that of the Governor's wife. The Tragic Mother, Liza, makes her angry; doesn't seem to mind Kartuzov's verses. Steps straight up to Varvara Petrovna: "You are bearing a grudge." To Shatov: "How do you believe?"

But the trait that is characteristic of Varvara Petrovna is *the assurance with which she carries on an intrigue.**

Shatov, an odious character. He is the one responsible for the proclamations.

---

* Unclear; might also mean: "her firm conviction that an intrigue is going on."

"What do you think of the proclamations?" (a question which she incidentally addresses to Stepan Trofimovich).

"Lebiadkin the purchaser?" Varvara Petrovna laughs out loud.

Lebiadkin plies Kondraty, Varvara Petrovna's valet, with drinks and assures him that he is the purchaser. Varvara Petrovna is laughing aloud; which means that this is all nonsense and the first report <. . .>: "We aren't concerned about either Kondraty or Lebiadkin (I don't want to hear any servants' gossip), but about Shatov. De-fi-nitely, and would you imagine, I'm being told that he actually shares a stairway with that Lebiadkin!"

Kartuzov's verses.

Split up Kartuzov into two parts:

1st part, before the visit and before the officer, that's what Drozdov had been complaining about to Varvara Petrovna. Shocked by all these mysterious goings-on, Varvara Petrovna comes rushing to Stepan Trofimovich: "Why won't you stop that relative of yours?" For the first time, *Stepan Trofimovich* is rude to her: "I'm having a headache (please allow me to have a word with the Ward)," etc.

Varvara Petrovna returns and says: "If that's the kind you are." And she ties a vinegar compress round his head.

Stepan Trofimovich derives some comfort from the fact that he has actually been rude to her, and naïvely summons Kartuzov. Kartuzov then ends up writing the letter which causes the cup to overflow.

"It must be Shatov, it must be Shatov," said Varvara Petrovna.

N.B. (Couldn't the Great Writer be brought in here?)

Liza and Shatov.

After the Ward's letter to the Prince: Varvara Petrovna interrogating the Ward ~~She wants to~~. "But would you marry Stepan Trofimovich?" The Ward replies: "Yes, I will; but allow me to ask you: what is this all about?" "It's too early for you to know, that's what." "If it is to be Stepan Trofimovich, believe me, Varvara Petrovna, if I tell you that I doubt whether he has any desire to marry me. He has written me a strange letter. (A rapturous and tender letter.) It is as if he wanted to forgive me something. No matter how great my humility, it still affects me; I have the greatest respect for this, and I understand that it is his character that causes him to act that way."

"His character? Eh, why, you're even smarter than I thought you were, if you've understood that it's his character. So why don't you take him into your hands, you'll be better off for it. He absolutely wants—a Polinka Saks."

"Oh, what a funny man. I've been struggling with him all my life, haven't I!"

Letter to him: "*Get ready for your nameday party* (BIRTHDAY PARTY), invite your friends."

"(How is it between you and Liza?)"
"We never meet and never see each other."

"How was it between you and her in Switzerland?"
"Very much at a distance. I was having a sad time there.." etc.

"Kempen, I'm a Russian, I'm more than a Russian."

"I'm surprised how Slavophilism is, in his case, compatible with Nihilism of the extreme, active, émigré variety. He is actually serving as an adjutant, and considers it an honor. And now, after we have told each other so many nice things, shouldn't we two make up, Shatov? Why are you grabbing your hat? ~~Sit down~~ Sit around for a while with an old man."

Lebiadkin—Kempen.

58 ## Rough Draft of Program

1) As I begin my chronicle of ~~our~~ some extraordinary recent events in our town, I affirm, firstly, that this is a particular case. However, nonetheless ~~it is incomprehensible~~ it would be incomprehensible if this weren't so. I'm warning you beforehand that we shall be striving for clarity, accuracy, and if so, that I must make use, I must make use of a good deal of space to explain the details of the friendship between Varvara Petrovna and Stepan Trofimovich. Up to *Rien de plus.*

About the Prince and a few *special* words about Varvara Petrovna (N.B. 101).

Our principle—I'll save some—quiet, our circle, a lazy calm, a red nose, bad habits, Liputin, Shatov, Virginsky. His wife walked around wearing glasses and was serving the cause of her modern convictions. Capt. Kartuzov (a few words will have to be said, unfortunately, about that most trivial personage).

We used to discuss (still before the Prince's return) the reform, and to tease Shatov.

"If he had to be Mme Högg's adjutant, he would do it, whereas you are only a windbag, and nothing else."

"All we want, you and I, is to have a nice chat, that's all."

I'm amazed at how well Slavophilism is doing.

The Drozdovs have arrived from Paris after almost 4 years of absence. They have returned with a lot of energy left in them. A conversation with Stepan Trofimovich, who feels flattered, the Governor's wife, "you are spluttering when you talk, you've aged," he looks into the mirror, "you have really gone to seed." Her conviction, that he was a handsome man, was destined to meet with disappointment!

The Drozdovs have arrived. Liza seems offended (the officer ~~Drozdov himself~~). For the Ward, the portrait, "that's all nonsense" Marriage.

She comes rushing to Stepan Trofimovich; he agrees, he couldn't help agreeing.

Nechaev, 8,000 rubles—he agrees, no marriage. Stepan Trofimovich's excitement. He tells me: "She's all excited about the Governor's wife; society has turned away from her." Paid her a visit. A scene on account of the letter. "You aren't quite as guilty as some others. (I'm surrounded by intrigues.)"

It was not Shatov who was spreading that anonymous letter about; nor was it Shatov who had written it, and it is to Stepan Trofimovich's credit that he did not think "*Ce Chatoff*..." etc. before his involvement with Shatov's sister. ("It does not surprise me at all that his wife has deserted him...")

Yet the wedding wasn't coming off; there is a near break with the Drozdovs. Drozdov, the General, is being caustic. Varvara Petrovna was maneuvering, but it was quite impossible to come to terms with the General. She went to see him, listened to his reproaches. But what was most important, a number of accusations were being leveled at her. It all started with Kartuzov. You couldn't imagine a more ridiculous or trifling affair, yet I'll have to say a word or two about that Kartuzov, even at the risk of dragging out my narrative, for he does play a certain role in our chronicle. *Kartuzov* ("I have served my Sovereign, such people, Stepan Trofimovich.." etc.) The accusation.

But at least one could not have any argument on account of Kartuzov, but one could on account of the proclamations. "The proclamation, it's not of our doing." Drozdov: "It's you, a letter to Petersburg." Varvara Petrovna let Stepan Trofimovich know about it, being herself offended. He mentions his birthday party. "What do I care about your birthday party, there won't be any." But he ~~was in a terrible~~ got across her way while she was terribly out of sorts. It happened to be precisely at the time she learned about that anonymous letter to the Governor's wife. And the Great Writer has just sent her a note concerning Shatov. "Imagine, I've learned that he has designs on Liza—he is her favorite right now."*

This bit of news about Shatov caused the cup to flow over. If there was anybody at all she had counted on, it had to be Liza (and there, Shatov). She was anxious to find out all about it and if necessary force a showdown. "Daria, maybe nothing will come of it all."—

At the Drozdovs—a showdown about the proclamations and Stepan Trofimovich. "He has told me that there is no God, and gives me a story about the Club. Shatov shouldn't be around." ~~And why is he selling the estate~~ She's not just another lame girl; enter Shatov; a discussion; he refused to leave. "Why are you refusing?" "Why are you selling the estate?" (This is a city of many secrets.)

She returns and ties a vinegar compress round his head. "If he would only come home now!" "He is selling the estate to the Captain. Shall I write him or not? Who am I afraid of, not Daria?"

Liza and Shatov. A visit to him, the insult on the steps, the horsewhip. Everything is in a turmoil. Lebiadkin pays a visit to Drozdov; the Ward has written to the Prince. "I am the one who is buying the estate."

Drozdov to Varvara Petrovna. In a towering rage, she interrogates the Ward regarding the letter. ("But she is going to marry Stepan Trofimovich anyway. *I am ready.* He is ready. The day after tomorrow is your nameday, get yourself ready!")

And so Stepan Trofimovich's fate had been decided once and for all. The Ward blushed. "I'll marry him. But... suppose Stepan Trofimovich? And I don't know how one does these things. What does one write? What are people saying?"

No matter how superfluous and inane, and verbose this might appear, its essence is closely linked to the very heart of the matter. So it always happens in real life. An item you would never suspect, a mere trifle, suddenly becomes the thing that really matters, with all the rest revolving around it as mere secondary or subordinate items.

Nicolas treated him with justifiable contempt.

---

* The feminine ending of the predicate suggests that these words belong to Varvara Petrovna.

But Stepan Trofimovich's fate could not be decided so soon—it was destined to go through several more phases. It all started from some trifles, Kartuzov.

These anonymous letters were being spread around. Little does she care. She noticed very quickly that over at the Drozdovs' they were simply trying to provoke her (an intrigue). The General is being caustic, his wife is saying whatever she pleases. It was necessary to act more energetically, to call Nicolas, get a showdown, but definitely, with the Drozdovs.

About Kartuzov.

Later, they were talking about this event all over town, and it did a good deal of harm to that extravagant Lizaveta Fiodorovna. But Drozdov wanted to leave.

"I will be given a hard time at the Club."

Liza also wanted to leave, she almost had to take to her bed. I'll pass over all of these scenes, mentioning only that which is relevant to the main events of my narrative: Lebiadkin paid a visit to Drozdov, about the Ward, etc.

XIII
The Prince and Nechaev, a Secret Connection

These notes were mainly written in the fall of 1870. The outermost dates go from September 12, 1870, to February 3, 1871. Most were written in November and December, 1870. They comprise notebook pages 1 and 59–89 of notebook 3.

It is November, 1870 (a little more than a month before the beginning of the publication of the novel), and Dostoevsky asks himself the following:

"Where (characters, and the main, direct idea aside) is the intrigue of the novel?

It consists of this:

1) Liza is passionately, extraordinarily in love with *Nicolas,* with all the manifestations and peculiarities of her eccentric nature."

The romantic core remains, even though its form resembles more and more the vestigial remnant we have in the final version.

The Drozdovs had suggested a union between the Prince and Liza, and it is a union that Varvara Petrovna energetically pursues. But rumors and anonymous letters hint at the fact that the Prince is already married to the Lame Woman. It is because of this and because of the Prince's eccentric actions that the Drozdovs wish to back out of the marriage. In the meantime the Prince's mother hurries to marry off Dasha (here called so for the first time) to Stepan Trofimovich in order to remove the obstacle of the Prince's possible love for Dasha. The Prince is—for varied motives—indifferent to Liza, though not above exploiting her love for him. Liza does everything to punish and attract him, including provoking his jealousy by encouraging Lebiadkin (called consistently so now) and Nechaev. When she finds out that he is married, she gives herself to him without reservation, on the reasoning that the Prince's indifference had proceeded from his consciousness of his marriage and not from distaste for her. Dostoevsky says: "Liza has used every means to enthrall him, lacerate him, insult him, excite his jealousy (through Shatov, Nechaev), anything to attract him. Sometimes he is disgusted by it; but on one occasion he let himself be carried away."

The Prince (Nicolas) is possessed by two impulses: the impulse to reach for some moral feat, and the impulse rapaciously to possess Liza; that is, he is possessed by the impulses of moral regeneration, and moral fall through exploitation of Liza:

And really, Nicolas was in a terrible and mysterious frame of mind when he married: there were two ideas struggling within him: 1) Liza—take possession of her—a cruel and rapacious idea, 2) the moral feat, a surge against evil, the magnanimous idea to overcome. Therefore he seeks the company, first of Shatov, then of Tikhon. He also wants to confess before everybody and to punish himself through the shame of the Lame Woman.

At the same time he amuses himself by bringing together Liza and Nechaev.

In section XI, written in late June, the Prince was torn between faith in Orthodoxy and Russia, and Nechaev and destruction. The antithetical principles are now dramatic and part of the romantic intrigue. Stavrogin of the final version will not, of course, be torn by desires for moral feats or for passionate despoilation of Liza, nor will he be torn by faith in Orthodoxy and temptation to the destructive principles of Nechaev. The fires of love, temptation, destruction, and faith will have died in him, and his relationship to Peter Verkhovensky will be ideological and metaphysical: he will be, as Peter himself ecstatically shows, Peter's spiritual father, and represent the principle of unfaith and moral indifference from which destructive actions spring. One wonders if Dostoevsky has begun to see something of this special relationship in the following quotation:

Most Important

The Prince and Nechaev are tied to each other by mutual secrets which they accidentally share.

Yet Nechaev is concealing a good many things from him (though he is tempted to initiate him, seeing his colossal stature. He is studying him).

The Prince reveals his thoughts to no one, and is a mystery to everybody. There aren't many love scenes between him and Liza.

One should note finally that Kirilov makes his first appearance in these notes, under the name of "The Engineer." As in the final version, he is to take the blame for Shatov's death, although here for it is for "the common cause" and not because of his indifference. He is actively involved in the conspiracy here, running errands, carrying messages, and apparently believing in the cause. There is no hint of his colossal metaphysical significance, and he comes into being apparently because someone other than the Prince is needed to take the blame for Shatov's death.

---

59 *September 12* <1870> Great Ideas

Shatov enthralled by the Prince to the point of idolatry.

Shatov *receives guests* at Mme. Virginsky's (or at his wife's).

The Beauty is indignant that Shatov is so enthralled and suddenly reveals her whole passionate love (he is in a frenzy of passion and *suddenly the Prince takes all* (?)).

(Or, she won't submit to the Prince until the end, *la haine dans l'amour,*[1] but when she learns that he is married, she does submit? Reasoning thus: "He spared me because of his being married, for he did know that I would submit to him."

The Prince, seeing her tenderness, and her readiness to submit to him, *takes her*; and the murder of the Lame Woman and the Captain on the following day. Shatov keeps aloof, while the Beauty is down with brain fever.

---

[1] French: "Hate in love."

Then, Shatov's wife returns to him ~~and the murder of the Lame Woman~~ to give birth to her child ~~the murder of Shatov~~; Nechaev and Kulishov. The murder of Kulishov, the murder of Shatov.

A passionate and swift love scene between the Prince and the Beauty; the Prince is full of new life, he is tender and passionate. He isn't the man he was before—he also mentions the Lame Woman—she runs off to Kartuzov, virtually in a frenzy, barricades, *Nechaev*: "you shall receive satisfaction," and serves as a mediator with Drozdov, proclaiming the rights of the Beauty.

In the meantime, her frenzied condition leads to an inflammation of the brain. She dies.

N.B. Nechaev, Kartuzov, and the Prince were all convinced that she loved them, even Shatov.

They burned down the town just to show off their *bravado*. Liputin and Virginsky were too trustful. The sacrilege—and meanwhile Stepan Trofimovich with the book-hawker.

The visit to Tikhon, and the insult to him.

The visit to Ivan Iakovlevich.

(The social teaching of the *complete* dependence of man upon his circumstances.)

A children's party!

The Engineer[2] smuggled the proclamations across the border, spread them in the South and, together with Fedka, at the factory, etc. The *Enforcer* is with Nechaev, reasoning in this fashion: "If they find out, they'll grab me alone. But I will sign a written confession and then shoot myself, for it is all the same to me."

An important note: The factory hands with Shatov. The possibility of Tveretinov. Some are freethinkers and reject everything, *after their own fashion*; these are with Nechaev (though not all of them). Others are more cautious; at Shatov's flat, they listen to objections, and are willing to be enlightened. Nechaev quarrels with the Raskolnik. These popular characters and types are sort of like those in the House of the Dead.

---

[2] This is the first reference to Kirilov.

N.B. Important: The Engineer has paved the way for Nechaev; he was the first to establish contacts with the factory hands.

2d Important Note: The personality of the Governor's wife. The Governor's wife represents the bad type of the party of the *European Messenger*.[3] A conservative, the principle of large land ownership. One of those conservatives who do not mind getting together with the nihilists, just to stir up a lot of trouble.

(N.B. Find out about the actions of the Kholm town council. She is trying to influence her husband so he'd be disposed to take a similar course of action. Don't mention it in detail, but accurately, and make the point clear by means of an example. Find an example for what the Kholm Zemstvo was doing.

"Governor von-Lembke, the fool, is stupid as a mule."

Nechaev accommodates himself to the Governor's wife and her ideas. She is glad that he is saying "yes" to her and consciously forgives him his nihilism. Besides, there are some points about his nihilism which she believes in anyway.

Some people, Liputin for instance, think that Nechaev is simply playing politics as he simulates full agreement with the Governor's wife. But much to the surprise of Liputin and everybody else (the Prince had guessed, and actually observed it before), Nechaev quite sincerely sympathizes with the conservatives—to be more precise, with their principle of displaying a cynical nihilism regarding everything heretofore considered good and honorable, i.e., their contempt for the public interest, their people, their country, anything that won't directly affect their own aristocratic interests.

63 N.B. The Governor, having inspected the Captain's project, says to his aide: "God knows what he was talking about! However, the project does have some sense."

(He hears arguments against this view.)

"I'm not saying that, but you must agree that it isn't any worse than the other."

"You may be right there."

"No worse and no better. One may even keep it in mind, i.e., that one leading idea. As regards the project itself, it is of course complete nonsense."

---

[3] A liberal journal edited by Stasiulevich.

N.B. Shatov says: "Germany is Russia's natural enemy; he who does not want to see that, sees nothing at all. What have they to boast about? What have they done for us? They are inferior to us in everything. They have a coalition working for them in Russia, one is promoting the other. A conspiracy that has existed for 150 years. Due to special circumstances they have been always on top. All of their mediocrities have been holding high-ranking posts, and treated Russians with stupid contempt. They've been sapping Russia's strength all along. They have had a veritable coalition," etc.

The most important thing. N.B. naïvely and directly.

The Ward and the Prince, tête-à-tête during evenings in the village:

The Prince: "And you were thinking seriously that I was in love with the Beauty?"

The Ward: "Yes."

The Prince: "How boring that was. I am bored."

The Ward: "What is this boredom like? I've heard about it, but I can't understand it."

The Prince explains it to her, sincerely, as best he can.

"And you, after all I have told you, after my *attentat* on you, you still love me?" "Ahem. I'll think about you." (She hadn't the strength to tell him that she would never become his wife, but her mind was set on that score. She began to feel sorry for him.)

The Prince: "You know what, perhaps I actually love you" (proudly and condescendingly).

The Princess assures her that he is a madman. (She is sorry for him.)

(The Ward.) She tells the Prince directly: "I feel sorry for you, terribly sorry."

Shatov says: "You'll see, the moment we'll become concerned with our truly urgent needs, science and the arts will appear in Russia. Had we only stayed what we were, we would have become ourselves. We are paralyzed ever since Peter's reform. Yes, all we've gotten out of it is a copper penny. That's true, a copper penny. A copper penny is a lot, you can't make one from nothing. A copper penny is incomparably more than nothing, but the trouble is that for this most useful penny we had to pay 5 rubles of our own. Genuine, silver rubles of the kind you won't find today, and besides, it was the last thing we owned; we gave away everything we had."

N.B. *Most important.* During his last meeting with Nechaev, at the village, Granovsky suddenly exclaims, in despair:

"Oh God! If you have really decreed that the whole world should perish, if you are really so determined, and if it pleases you to overthrow and to destroy everything, isn't there really a single tear, isn't there a drop of pity and compassion left in you for all the things you are about to destroy? Why are you so calm, why are you so heartless, and so inhuman? Why won't you shed a tear? ~~A stone~~ Are you a stone, or are you a man, or is it that I no longer understand anything at all?"

"We are a special breed of people; we are the new people; so don't shout, please! All this is nothing but old, sick nerves, old wives' tears, and besides, not without danger for you."

"If this is so, I curse you in my own name!"

"Now look what nonsense you've come up to! E-eh! ~~When Good-bye, old man!~~ How stupid you are, in my mind. By the way, au revoir—I haven't got time, and even so I have, because of you<. . .>"

~~and then about~~

64 1) THE NOVEL

November 1, 1870

(CONSEQUENTLY, STEPAN TROFIMOVICH IS OF THE ESSENCE.)

It was necessary that the Prince knew for sure that Fedka would commit murder, *but did not say a word*, even though he did not personally participate in the killing.

He had the intention to hire a killer, but he merely let him see that he was taking 1,000 rubles there.

Upon his arrival, the Prince actually didn't know whether he would announce his marriage or not.

Where (characters, and the main, direct idea aside) is the intrigue of the novel?

It consists of this:

1) Liza is passionately, extraordinarily in love with *Nicolas*, with all the manifestations and peculiarities of her eccentric nature.

2) *Nicolas* is, in a certain sense (with regard to the idea which fascinates him and which has taken possession of him), a lost man; yet at times his nature (its live, immediate side) is fascinated by Liza. This happened in Switzerland when he suddenly came to his senses and fled. It also happened later, in our town.

3) Liza has used every means to enthrall him, lacerate him, insult him, excite his jealousy (through Shatov, Nechaev), anything to attract

him. Sometimes he is disgusted by it; but on one occasion he let himself be carried away.

4) Liputin has told him about Liza and Shatov. He has seen Nechaev himself.

5) And really, *Nicolas* was in a terrible and mysterious frame of mind when he arrived: there were two ideas struggling within him: 1) Liza—take possession of her—a cruel and rapacious idea, 2) the moral feat, a surge against evil, the magnanimous idea to overcome. Therefore he seeks the company, first of Shatov, and then of Tikhon. He also wants to confess before everybody and to punish himself through the shame of the Lame Woman.

At the same time he amuses himself by bringing together Liza and Nechaev.

At the same time he also picks out Fedka.

Regeneration and resurrection—they are closed to him solely for the reason that he has lost his roots in the soil, and therefore does not believe in, nor recognize the morality of the Russian people. For instance, he considers feats of faith to be a fraud. Yet the abstract concept of a universal human conscience is empirically unsound. Point that out. He suddenly breaks down, though he has, for instance, already made arrangements regarding Uri. But he does not tell anybody about it, except Dasha, toward the very end.

6) He knows that Dasha loves him, but for a time he finds it merely repulsive, nor does he want to help her; on the contrary, he maliciously brings her all the closer together with Stepan Trofimovich.

7) Here. The plans for Dasha's wedding continue through the entire course of the novel, but it is Nechaev who more than anyone else distorts her image and has a strong influence on him <Stepan Trofimovich>. He tells his father outright that he is a fool. He frankly assures him that he is about to marry someone else's sins, which (as could be expected) disturbs him. Varvara Petrovna says that the marriage will be pro forma only. Even so, Stepan Trofimovich feels offended and complains that everybody has deserted him and that his erudition and his talents are held in contempt; he gets excited and writes to Daria, has a heart-to-heart talk with her, and hurts her with his questions. Nechaev proves to him and to Varvara Petrovna that his father (Stepan Trofimovich), selfish and vain as he is (and hoping to be rewarded for his feat), is trying to move Dasha to tears, repentance, and admission <of her guilt>, but that he simply *does not know how to go about it,* "because you certainly are not a new man, and because you'd like to play the role

of Saks, and be rewarded for it, but you simply don't know how to go about it." Nechaev cruelly makes fun of him. Yet Stepan Trofimovich ultimately insists on her admitting <her guilt>. Nechaev, on his own part, is absolutely convinced that Dasha has had an illicit relationship with the Prince. ~~Here suddenly~~ Stepan Trofimovich has a frank talk with the Prince also.

8) But the Prince suddenly takes recourse to a new maneuver. He proves that nothing has happened between him and Daria, makes a whole story of it, accusing Liza, Praskovia, and questioning Nechaev. Nechaev shows that he has been merely quoting the words and the letters of his father and quite clearly proves to his father that he has acted like a cad. Here now, at Skvoreshniki, Varvara Petrovna reveals everything, and promises Stepan Trofimovich a pension. Stepan Trofimovich flees after the lecture. The Prince talks to Daria, a scene, asks her if she would accept him if he came to her all smeared with dirt and blood—*in a word, a few mysterious words.*

9) But Dasha has observed that the Prince is inflamed with a bestial fire for Liza. (Though her rival,) she runs to Liza and warns her that he is *married,* and that this is why he is avoiding her. Then Liza forgives him everything and, seeing only his unhappiness, passionately surrenders to him. Death through a Jesuitical scheme involving Fedka, and Dasha tells him so directly. (Nechaev feels that this is how it is to be done.) At first, Liza wants to flee with him, but later she goes out of her mind. Shatov's wife gives birth to a child (with the Virginsky woman helping her). The Prince makes an apparent gesture to warn Shatov, but then leaves with a sneer. The murder of Shatov. The death of Stepan Trofimovich. The Prince, in a frenzied state, makes certain statements. Mocking and haughty words addressed to the public. Reveals everything that he has secretly observed about everybody. Wants to hand over ~~to the Polish priest~~ to the Pastor <. . .>. Lembke is trembling. Leaves—at the railway station—Death.

65 November 1, 1870

A Most Important Note

. . .I must, however, once and for all make this reservation:

Let the reader, from the very beginning, accept this apology, and excuse me:

I am not describing a town, a local setting, a daily routine, people, offices; nor the relationships—or the curious vacillations of these relationships—which exist in the essentially private, provincial life of our town, as a result of both an ancient, perennial order of day-to-day life under which the town has grown to become what it is, as well as of recent perturbations of this order ~~by new forms~~ caused by the reforms of these past years. Nor have I the time to draw a picture of our little town. I consider myself the chronicler of a certain curious event of private character which took place in our town suddenly, unexpectedly, quite recently, and much to the surprise of all of us. Inasmuch as this event took place, not in the sky but, after all, in our town, it goes without saying that I shall have to touch upon the day-to-day aspect of our provincial life in a purely descriptive way, yet I would like to warn my reader that I will be doing this only if and when it will be of the utmost and unavoidable necessity. I shall not be going into the particulars of the descriptive aspect of contemporary daily life in our town.

Is this necessary or isn't it <. . .>

6 A NEW PERSONAGE: the brother of Virginsky's wife,

ZAITSEV.

With a dull sort of indignation. Zaitsev.

~~With indignation~~ He has arrived together with Nechaev. He follows the debates at Stepan Trofimovich's with indignation. He represents the opposition against Nechaev.

With Virginsky's wife against Virginsky.

With Shatov (with indignation).

Brings about a reconciliation between Shatov and Nechaev.

Indignantly about the fact that the Engineer has shot himself. Against Tikhon.

In the end Shatov winds him around his little finger.

He protests against the murder of Shatov.

He leaves—

Thinks a lot of himself, and is stupid.

As they were killing Shatov, he had already left the scene of the murder because of some principle of his.

N.B. Or: "No, you haven't got the right to exploit the Engineer's life."

Always in the opposition—including when it comes to murdering Shatov.

~~1~~ "You are a fool."

"Me, a fool? As a matter of principle you did not have the right to say that to me."

The Engineer

volunteers to shoot himself for the common cause—AND, WHAT IS OF THE UTMOST ESSENCE:

The Engineer's role is a factual one.

Nechaev knew about Shatov's *betrayal* while still in Switzerland, through Mme. Virginsky's sickly little brother (Zaitsev).

N.B. That sickly little Zaitsev showed up in our town (might as well be together with the Polish priest, a month and a half before Nechaev's arrival). He immediately got into some arguments with Shatov and had started an intrigue against him, but the moment ~~with Shatov~~ Nechaev arrived, he was found standing with Shatov, against Nechaev. Mme. Virginsky knows all about Shatov and his crimes, but this is being concealed from Virginsky. Liputin, all the more, knows nothing at all at this stage; he merely knows that Nechaev is expected to arrive and has an inkling, which he keeps to himself, that he will become involved in the conspiracy.

That means that *Nechaev* has detached the Engineer (leaving aside the spreading of proclamations, and the hope that he might be of some
67 use if he would shoot himself), 1) to find out, through him, what the score is; 2) to look into the disagreement between Zaitsev and Shatov and, since Shatov is apparently the guilty party, prepare to shoot him; also, inasmuch as the Engineer will also shoot himself, in order to take on himself.

This is why the Engineer must, upon his arrival, pretend to have quarreled with Shatov and show himself hostile to him.

The reason why the Engineer stops at Lebiadkin's is, first, that he is one of them (recommended by the Virginsky woman and Zaitsev), having already been spreading proclamations in the area and being ready to continue this work (which is what the Engineer has been asked to verify, i.e., "is Lebiadkin reliable, and is he on our side?")—and, second, that the Engineer used to know Lebiadkin well in the past. Knowing him for a frivolous and disorganized person, the Engineer has given Nechaev misgivings regarding Mme. Virginsky's and Zaitsev's wisdom in trusting Lebiadkin with such an important matter. And what is most important, the Engineer knows Lebiadkin since he had been an usher at the Prince's wedding to M-lle Lebiadkin, and thus a witness of this event of the *obscure* past of the Prince's Petersburg period. The Prince has confided this secret to Dasha, because she is worthy of such trust (the Prince is most sensitive and susceptible to beautiful characters such as Dasha). He has trusted her with handing the money over to Lebiadkin, because he would confide in no one else, and besides, Dasha just happened to be around. ~~N.B. Here, a *qui pro quo* develops: the Engineer~~ He also asked the Engineer to quiet down Lebiadkin and put some sense into his head. While the Prince was abroad, Lebiadkin had been writing him rather too insistent letters demanding money, and threatening to expose him. The Engineer was to tell Lebiadkin that the Prince would soon come home and take care of the matter, that he had already sent *three hundred* rubles, and that if he would be sensible, he would get another 1,000; also the Prince would then turn over the estate to him. The Prince entrusts the Engineer with this mission precisely because he had been an usher at his wedding. Incidentally, the Prince is unaware of that other message, delivered to Lebiadkin by the Engineer on behalf of Nechaev.

N.B. The Prince is ~~a great~~ *a friend* of Nechaev's. Nechaev, incidentally, does not trust him with all his secrets, even though he is very frank with him, respects him greatly, and knows that the Prince would not report on him. He is almost ready (and actually would like) to reveal all his secrets to him, but stops short of it every time (and so to the end) because there is always something that holds him back, something which tells him in a most convincing manner that the Prince is *not the right man.* The Prince, though, actually guesses almost all of Nechaev's secrets and schemes anyway, and Nechaev knows that he does, and even seeks his advice in a number of instances.

N.B. The Prince never is completely frank *with anybody,* not even Tikhon. With Dasha more than with anyone else. He tells her almost everything (in his suicide note).

But when the Engineer (who is very glad he can deliver the Prince's message to Lebiadkin, for that gives him a pretext *to approach* Lebiadkin) brings up the matter of money, he mistakenly tells Lebiadkin that Dasha was to hand him 1,000 rubles. Lebiadkin thinks that Dasha has stolen the money and starts bombarding her with letters.

(N.B. One letter was intercepted by Varvara Petrovna. It was also sent to Stepan Trofimovich. *This also comes up during Stepan Trofimovich's nameday party, at which occasion the Prince's secret is bared.*)

And so, Dasha, the Engineer, Nechaev, and Lebiadkin know the secret of the Prince's marriage. They all keep silent about it. But Liputin, who has been plying Lebiadkin with drinks, strongly *suspects* something, and he would very much like to know more. That's why he seeks the Engineer's company and introduces him to Stepan Trofimovich. Liputin would also like to learn *a lot* about Nechaev from the Engineer.

N.B. While with Stepan Trofimovich, the Engineer cleverly simulates hostility toward Shatov, thus preparing himself for the role of his murderer.

N.B. The Engineer has been detached to watch Shatov, but not as an emissary and, besides, he himself does not know about the printing press. Zaitsev does not know anything either; Nechaev has concealed this information even from them.

71 Virginsky is a serious socialist.

He says: "I would die for it."

He moves away from Nechaev and the Engineer: *"That is not it."*

Nechaev, who has great erudition about socialism, never enters a debate with anybody, always agrees with everything—what matters to him is *the conspiracy.*

The Prince has more serious opinions regarding socialism than all the others.

~~Virginsky, a new generation of people.~~

Virginsky conveys his "*this is not it*" to the Prince, who immediately comes to see him. They get to talk about the new generation of people (much as in France, however without the classicism of the Germano-Romance race). He talks to him for a while, and *leaves for good.*

Virginsky, even as he is doing the killing, at the scene of the murder in the grove, keeps saying to himself: *"This is not it, not it."*

72 2D HALF OF PART 2, November 29 <1870>

Preface.

About how we are sitting here.

Liputin's visit; he becomes acquainted with the Engineer. About Lebiadkin. An obvious hint directed at Dasha. Stepan Trofimovich's despair.

In the morning, my meeting with the Great Writer. A note. Stepan Trofimovich full of remorse. A letter sent to Varvara Petrovna. ~~Three letters to Varvara Petrovna~~. His intention to send three letters. He orally tells the content of his letter to the Prince, and reads his letter to Dasha. "Oh, how I am ashamed of you!" He is very nervous, I quiet him down. He leaves.

Meanwhile, Varvara Petrovna's adventure in church. The Lebiadkin woman pays her a visit alone.* ~~They meet~~ Varvara Petrovna is

---

* Might also mean: "Varvara Petrovna, alone, pays a visit to the Lebiadkin woman."

quite beside herself when she returns home. Stepan Trofimovich is already waiting. "So you are here," she says indifferently, "what about that Lebiadkin woman?" "There is a certain Engineer here," Stepan Trofimovich tells her. "Am I to marry her?" "If you'll be found worthy of her ~~but that is not the point, or is it? I have received terrible news. *Nicolas* is selling the estate, and who is he selling it to?~~" Lebiadkin's visit. He is nervous, declares: "~~I am buying the estate.~~" 15 rubles. Leaves. Varvara Petrovna is beside herself. Arrival of the Governor's wife. "This is Stepan Trofimovich." A spilled cup of coffee. The Governor's wife about ~~Varvara Petrovna~~ the Great Writer. "*Nicolas* is selling the estate, I've heard it from the Drozdovs—to a certain Lebiadkin." Varvara Petrovna is desperate. "I'll let you know, stay at home."

I was waiting for Stepan Trofimovich at his house. He came. He quickly muttered: "I've just met an angel" (about Liza). Liza has left —"What about Lebiadkin?"

Liputin reaches this conclusion while at Stepan Trofimovich's: "What do I care? ~~Why~~ I can make enough noise for the whole town to hear, if necessary. However, in the meantime Lebiadkin is already raising his voice in every tavern in town. He certainly isn't fussy. He is telling Shatov to his face: 'what's so wrong with my passing it on to you?' "

The Engineer: "Sorry, I'm in a hurry."

"For heaven's sake, I'll come with you."

"I…I…I can't—there's some nonsense here."

With indescribable naïveté.

"How do you mean, nonsense? Haven't you told Lebiadkin yourself, in the name of Nikolai Vsevolodovich, that a whole ~~1,000~~ one thousand rubles were sent to him? Why, Lebiadkin has told me himself that Daria Pavlovna has kept 700 ~~0~~ rubles of his money. It seems that Nikolai Vsevolodovich asked her—and no one else to deliver 1,000 rubles to Captain Lebiadkin, and it seems that she handed him only 300 and kept 700."

"Liputin, I am warning you!"

~~That's the engineer~~ "The Engineer has made a turnabout, and you <…>."

~~After Liza's visit:~~

~~"Oh, I believe, she is divine <…>."~~

Words and Essentials

~~I'm waiting~~ Stepan Trofimovich in the 1st part:

"I am waiting for Petrusha! Will he come, my boy, my good, my dear boy? Oh, how I have wronged him, and... and—how I am suffering for it..." etc.

"Forgive me, I... haven't seen Petrusha in a long time. I have heard almost nothing about him..."

Lebiadkin is shouting about *Dashka:* "I am a gentleman, while she is a servant girl; *she* is a peasant slave; I'll teach her a lesson"... Stepan Trofimovich hears about it, takes offense, and demands an explanation.

A cup of coffee.

She did not become angry.

And later: "You know what, she was actually very kind to me."

"Yes, maybe precisely because you poured coffee all over her."

"You know what, I think so myself, I was only afraid to say so..."

"Ah, why are you doing it? Why this *wedding?..* Why is it that I know nothing?.. Now, as I am happy once more, how do I wish that nothing of this had ever happened..."

And suddenly: "But I do love her!.. What this woman has meant to me! Why, I would have rotted without her," etc.

He enters: "I'm dead, I'm dead, dead forever! But I've come across an angel..." (about Liza, and only after he is through with Liza, an account of his wanderings).

"I have ordered myself a dress coat."

"I need *a poem,* look (...).

"Here you are, singing a hymn, and he won't open the door.

Shatov, Shatov, how good it is to be alive!"

"Don't you understand, you ass, I'm in love!"

"And I am dispatching to her, and to her ailing mother, a tear of mine."

Earlier, they almost had a fight:

"I've come to you with greetings
To tell you that the Sun has risen,
That its warm rays

Are trembling upon the leaves."*
Shatov is listening, bewildered.
"To tell you that the forest has awakened,
All awakened... in"
"To tell you that my song is ripening,
Song is ripening..." "how's that?
I don't know and ~~I'm afraid~~ what I'm going to sing,
Better let the devil take it;
well, never mind. But... still, I've come to you with greetings!"
"You are drunk, get out."
"And yet there are things higher than petty quarrels."
~~"But for such a fool"~~ Silence.
~~"I'm in love."~~
~~Silence.~~
"S-s-son of a bitch." (He leaves.)
A piece of paper.
A grenade.

"Shatov, Shatov! I'm in love."

"Shatov, Shatov, open up before I put you to shame."

"Shatov, I love an amazon, an aristocratic, divine gal. To hell with proclamations!"

"You are a fool, you drunken scoundrel." (1)

(2) "I was nothing, but now, as I have gotten some money for my sister from that villain <...>."

"You have taken money for your sister and spend it on drink."

"And your sister, and yourself, you are a peasant slave. You ought to be ashamed of your sister. Your sister (IS PREGNANT) is a slave girl (...). She has stolen my 700 rubles. But my sister, do you know who she is? You don't know, do you?"

"Who?" asked Shatov.

Lebiadkin said nothing. "You scoundrel!"

"Do you think I'm afraid to tell you?"

"Precisely."

"So I'm afraid?"

---

* A poem by A. A. Fet-Shenshin, incorrectly quoted by Lebiadkin. Trochaic tetrameter, rhymed abab.

"You sure are."

"Don't say I'm afraid; I'll tell you!"

"You scoundrel! Go ahead, spell it out!"

74 WORDS AND BONS-MOTS

"Lebiadkin, my dear, aren't you, too, a Lebiadkin?"

"They'll disgrace the Ward, his mother will (I'm not talking about *Nicolas*)."

The Lame Woman to Shatov: "Why don't you ever ask me what it is he keeps beating me for?"

"Well, what is it?"

"I'm not going to tell you, no I won't—you can cut my throat, and I still won't. Let me suffer whatever may come, and I still won't tell." They began to laugh. "Offer me tables of gold—of velvet, and I still won't tell. But if you asked me, I just might tell you. ~~Oh~~ And how I would like to tell ~~to tell~~! Even if (...) I could tell this man here. I've had a dream: he comes to me, my Prince. Or it may have been for real, too. For real it was—no, it was not. ~~What I mean~~ At least to somebody (what I mean is to find a friend)."

"Is it true that your wife has run away? Etc."

Shatov to Lebiadkin: "If things are going to continue in this way, I'll pull your nose off."

Lebiadkin: "I'll go, I'll go."

Lebiadkin: "I came to you with the greeting,
To tell you that the sun has come up."

"I am cunning!"

"Do you know the song (...)"

The Engineer to Liputin: "If you want to know why I visited Lebiadkin, well, that doesn't concern you."

The Engineer about the madness, about civilization, the sooner the better.

I do not stand whatsoever for universal destruction. I try with all my might not to have an opinion.

The Engineer was laughing and Stepan Trofimovich was amusing him. But as soon as they go.

Oh, how all that.

After some vacillating.
That is not a treatise at all.
I wrote it myself.
And you, Liputin, invent a great deal.

We were standing on the threshold.
Varvara Petrovna was being amusing.
How she did make us laugh.
He even trembled. He felt that Liputin had come precisely for this, and that the important thing was about to begin.

Liza: "I came to invite you personally, proud man."
"I know, I know; you are unhappy, unhappy, right?"
"I am happy."
"Take off your hat, take it off"; she kissed him.
"I'll come to you forthwith."
Stepan Trofimovich returned, threw himself on the divan and broke into tears.
Liza about her aunt, making fun of her.
"It's my aunt's fault."
"To give him some books for a present, and some tea."

I won't be describing her beauty, I'll only say that she was a blonde —a very tall blonde, and besides, that she may not have been such a raving beauty after all. There was an air of inconsistency and anxiety about her, and affectation, too, a good deal of affectation, but also a certain childlike quality. She was meandering along like the water of a brook, seeking its own level.

Liza to me: "I thank you for your visit, and most of all, for Shatov. ~~Yesterday~~ Let's be friends. Yesterday, the impression you gave me of yourself was a comical one."
"If you are a confidant…"
"But if you are speaking ill of him…"
"All right, I am stupid, let's be friends."
"But I'll leave you here, so you can talk to Shatov. You are very clever."

Liza to Stepan Trofimovich, about the officer: "This is my friend, a wonderful person, you must get to love him." You can actually read something to him, and he will listen to you. You can cry on his shoulder, or even embrace him."

75 "Having sacrificed my health, my very life to a study of my poor Russia, I have all the facts about her at my fingertips, and I can tell you."

But then again she got angry with him because he had asked this question quite seriously, and because he had declared that he would oblige, and actually had expressed his consent by getting all dressed up for the occasion.

The tryst?

"I swear, if I hadn't agreed she would have been terribly angry, but still not quite as angry as she is now, after I have given my consent."

—2d chapter: One morning I came to see him; I had met with a small adventure on my way (the Great Writer), and *I used to tell him everything* <...>.

In the 1st chapter, only about ideas.

SHORTER. SHORTER.

He told me many things about her, and altogether, I got the impression that he was sentimentally involved with her. "She (...) has taken to new ideas." Stepan Trofimovich's main supposition, and indeed a very shrewd one, was that she had been quite serious about arranging that match for him.

On one occasion he broke into a positively lyrical tirade.

"She has taken to new ideas."

"She is having her ideas, and I must suffer for it and—that she is not in love with him. My time has passed."

Liza in a mood of hysterical gaiety.

"I'd be willing to marry your brother—I'll marry nobody, ever!"

Lebiadkin's letter to her: "About Sevastopol, the armless."

She is going to marry her fiancé (the officer). She beckons to him and comes out. "There's an excellent, rare, wonderful person."

"Call Daria." Varvara Petrovna cross-examines her, and defends her.

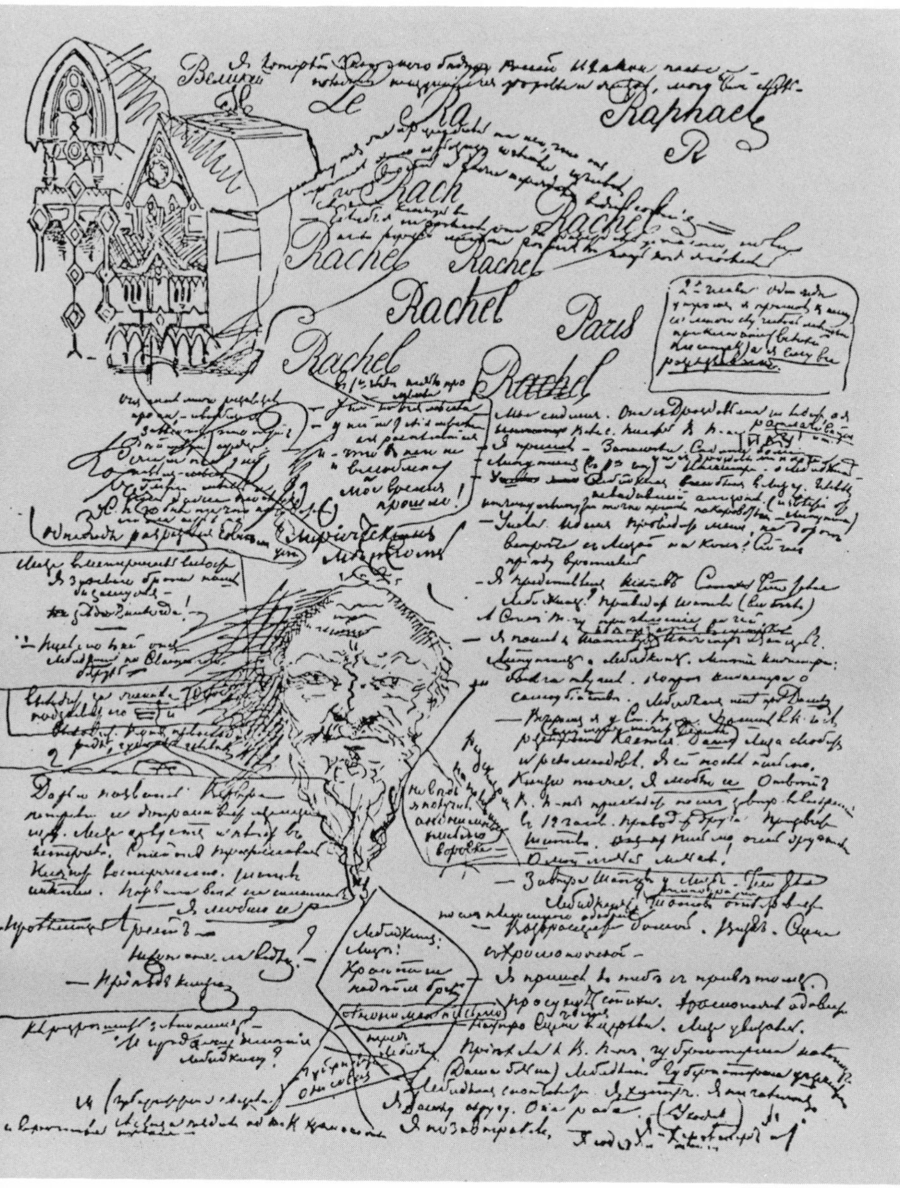

Notebook Page 75, Notebook 3

A restless and varied notebook page of drawings (characteristically of men's faces and gothic windows), calligraphy, and, across the page, the barely discernible technical reminder "koroche," *that is, "more concisely." The impression is at first one of messiness, and then, upon closer examination, of neatness and control.*

Liza kisses her, and cries hysterically. Stepan Trofimovich vows rapturously. Shatov laughs. She invites everybody to the nameday party. "I love her."

The proclamations. The arrest.
"Would you like some vodka?"
The Prince arrives.

How to solve this: an anonymous writer?
And the sale of the estate to Lebiadkin?
N.B. (The Governor's wife said so.)
And Liza, alone, went to see the Lame Woman and returned very nervous.

Lebiadkin to Liza: "Beauty, do not hope for marriage as you are facing Lebiadkin."

The anonymous letter.

The Governor's wife: "They are quite <...>.

"We are sitting around here. She can't get along with the Drozdovs, and I am to suffer for it," etc.

~~The Engineer~~ The Great Writer. Varvara Petrovna: "*I am coming!*"

"I've come." Little notes. "Stay home." "She's having trouble with the Drozdovs."

Liputin (just before 11 o'clock) and the Engineer. About Lebiadkin.

~~They are gone I~~ Lebiadkin is in love with Liza. A man who has never seen an amazon (news from Liputin). The Engineer and Liputin apparently had come for the sole purpose of exchanging nasty remarks.

They are gone. "Let's go. Why won't you come with me?" Along the way, meeting with Liza who is on horseback. "I'll be with you in a moment." They've returned.

I am being introduced. Shatov. ~~Verses~~ What about Lebiadkin? "Get me Shatov!" (everything in passing). Stepan Trofimovich gets invited to tea.

I went to see Shatov, but I found him at home only when it was already getting dark. The Engineer and Zaitsev. Liputin and Lebiadkin. The Engineer's opinion: "He has received some money." The Engineer's question about suicide. Lebiadkin tells me about "Dashka."

Later that night, I am with Stepan Trofimovich. He comes

home at 10 o'clock. He is downcast, remorseful. (Embarrassed about "Dashka"). Liza loves Dasha and speaks well of her. I've sent her a letter. Also one to the Prince. *I love her.* Varvara Petrovna's reply: "Come the day after tomorrow, Sunday, at 12 o'clock. Bring your friend along. Invite Shatov." ~~He~~ A very friendly letter. "Oh, my dear boy!"

Half-and-half with the narrative.

But I have received an anonymous letter—that thief!"*

The next day, Shatov at Liza's. What about Lebiadkin? The printing press. Shatov turns down her offer, after having enthusiastically approved <her project>.

He returns home. The visit. The scene with the Lame Woman.

"I've come to you with greetings." He forces his verses on him. The Lame Woman gets dressed and leaves. In the morning, the scene in church. Liza insists on accompanying her. They arrive at Varvara Petrovna's. The Governor's wife, finally. (Dasha is ill.) Lebiadkin. The Governor's wife leaves. Lebiadkin stumbles. "I'm shrewd. I'm a nihilist. I'll take care of Dashka. She is a slave girl." (Exit.)

"I've had breakfast—"**

"I'll keep the secret."

"I have character."

No. 1.

2d chapter: "If she has been concealing such trifles as those little notes, she has probably concealed more important things, too."

The answer is simply: "Stay at home."

"I'm coming, I'm coming—you won't leave me—otherwise I'll have to go in and see Varvara Petrovna." (I was acquainted with her to some extent. I can go in.)

"I bet you think I am a scoundrel—"

At Varvara Petrovna's: Lebiadkin! (The officer: "He shouldn't be received.")

Another variant: Lebiadkin is not drunk at all, and behaves with dignity, white gloves, a dress coat, a carriage, and all.

---

* The Russian noun is in the feminine gender, so the thief is a woman (apparently Daria Pavlovna).

** The ending suggests that the subject is a woman.

N.B. Stepan Trofimovich, *rapturously,* when Dasha emerges: "Why these questions, why this examination?"

Last night, I insulted *her,* I love her, I'm thankless," etc.

"You haven't insulted her at all."

"I love her." "Whom?" "Her, her."

"Oh, how unhappy I am! Oh my dear boy! Come soon!"

N.B. Varvara Petrovna had never heard of the Lebiadkin woman before until she met her in church. Here now, everything became clear to her in one day. Due to her forceful character, she wished to finish the whole business all at once, and therefore admitted Lebiadkin into her presence so that she could then and there find out about his secret, expose the calumny, and utterly wipe out all libelous talk. Yet the facts about the Lebiadkin woman (i.e., that she was a victim of *Nicolas*) were inexorably coming to light. And to top it all, that anonymous lettter. *And this is why she was so depressed* and made the sign of the cross over Liza when the latter, in front of everybody, said "*Yes!*" to Drozdov. (Liza, incidentally, is laughing at Lebiadkin's verses.) Also, right then and there, she exonerates Dasha and *insists* on her marriage to Stepan Trofimovich (i.e., to show everybody that she never meant to marry Dasha to Stepan Trofimovich because of Nicolas to begin with).

Stepan Trofimovich was delighted, yet back home again, he showed even more despair than earlier, and less faith in Dasha: "And now these Liputins, Lebiadkins! Nobody will believe it!" And—he seemed *repulsive* to me.

77 Bons-mots. (N.B. He has listened to too many nihilisticisms.)

The Prince visits Lebiadkin for the first time. The latter addresses him swaggeringly:

The Prince: "First of all, I warned you not to get drunk."

Lebiadkin, with dignity: *"What strange demands."*

Important

Stepan Trofimovich has written his son that he is marrying *someone else's sins,* which were committed in Switzerland.

Nechaev: ~~Why do you have to~~ "When are you going to Switzerland?"

Stepan Trofimovich: "To Switzerland? Why?"

"Well, to marry someone else's sins. Do you actually want to get married, or is the word *marriage* only an allegory here?"

After they've got it straight: Nechaev: "Well, I wasn't aware of that.

This misunderstanding is your own fault. And it seems that there has been an important misunderstanding. Why write long poems, instead of a simple letter?"

Important

Stepan Trofimovich, after returning from his visit to Liza in the evening, first of all, kept assuring us:

"Oh, I believe in *her* (Dasha). You are quite wrong if you think that I don't."

And finally, I to him: "To cut a long story short, you want me to find out about those 1,000 rubles?"

Stepan Trofimovich blushed:

"Oh, no!"

"Oh, yes!" I exclaimed, indignantly. "All right, I'll make inquiries as best I can, but you—you aren't worthy of that girl."

"I'll prove to you that I am."

N.B. As a result of which I started to make inquiries, got to see a few things, made up a few more, etc.

1) "She doesn't say much—and it seems that she is none too clever, but I can use her (in the household)," he whispered, "in my declining years, in the evening of my tempestuous life, and we'll get along together. Her angelic and calm gentleness will help me to face the impending afflictions of old age with equanimity."

2) "I can see that you seek to justify yourself by claiming that you are pursuing a useful economic goal, but you still want to find out about those 1,000 rubles."

8 The Last Word on Part One

(most important)

With Liza hysterical, Stepan Trofimovich full of matrimonial enthusiasm, and Varvara Petrovna ~~dropping~~ *dropping a last hint* to Liza, suggesting to her that her son ought to be forgiven his affair with the Lebiadkin woman, it being very much a thing of the past, Praskovia Drozdov, most irritated and full of spite against Varvara Petrovna, as she has been all along, suddenly says:

"But what if she is the wife ~~daughter~~ of your son?"

Liza turns pale, and Varvara Petrovna starts, but responds with calm contempt—though later she *falls ill* (N.B. N.B. N.B.—)

Praskovia: "Never mind what I said. I just mentioned it *à propos.*" Varvara Petrovna turned pale, and Liza said: "But *maman,* you can't say such things *à propos!*"

"Well, forgive me if I said something stupid."

Liza: "Dasha, do you see that man? He is the best of them all, our Pavel—come here, let us shake hands."

"Ah, Liza," exclaimed Praskovia.

Liza: "*Maman,* if you please, if you please."

Pavel: "Lizaveta, calm down."

Liza: "I am giving him everything, and he says 'calm down,' you have fallen in love with a foolish woman, a senseless, foolish woman."

Varvara Petrovna: gets up without saying a word, makes the sign of the cross over Liza, and kisses her.

"So make me like you, you must make me like you."

Liza: "Isn't it so, auntie, isn't it really?"

Varvara Petrovna: "If you want it that way. Each according to his own nature. There are people who can forgive and forget the past. Suit yourself."

(She had to force herself to say that.)

Praskovia Petrovna: "Varvara Petrovna ~~,my dear,~~ never mind that, but don't you see that we could take offence at that?"

Varvara Petrovna: "What has there been for you to take offence at (even if there has been something, certainly nothing has come to light so far)?"

N.B. *Praskovia:* "Well, how could a married man seek a girl's hand?"

Varvara Petrovna: "A married man? Who is a married man?"

Praskovia Petrovna: "Suppose M-lle Lebiadkin <is his wife>?"

79 The half-witted* Lebiadkin woman to Shatov:

"I am sitting in the monastery. The song about Eudocia."

N.B. She is unable to distinguish her *phantasies* from *reality;* other than that she is in no way demented. She loves rapturously: "He would come to me, begging me, saying, 'come, my little kitten.' It's his calling me his little kitten that made me happier than anything else. 'He loves me,' I thought, 'he still loves me.' "

---

* The adjective *iurodivy, iurodivaia,* is often, though not necessarily, used with special reference to foolishness-in-Christ.

HERE: "Take this golden ringlet," he says, and always look at it at sunset, before you go to your little bed. If you will, I shall come to see you in your dreams."

"Where is your ringlet?"

"That villain, my footman has sold it for drink. He also beats me, being the footman he is."

"I had a child with him."

"Where is the child?"

"I threw it into the pond."

"Mother of Eustigneus."

"Is it true that your wife has left you, Shatushka?"

"It is true, Maria Timofeevna, she's left me."

N.B. Stepan Trofimovich says: "They all have such narrow, such *very short* ideas."

N.B. Praskovia Petrovna: "What professor?" Artificial minds. The little dog—etc.

Mme. Drozdov: "What Prince Harry?"

N.B. Stepan Trofimovich: "People with very short ideas, as I call them."

The Engineer develops a strange relationship with the Lebiadkin woman and defends her from the Prince, *claiming his right of best man,* ~~and also~~ (compassion) (only one minute, incidentally).

Liza *to Dasha,* during the last scene at Varvara Petrovna's:

"Never get married to anybody."

To Stepan Trofimovich: "Why would you get married? Aren't you satisfied with enjoying the fruits of your learned pursuits?"

To the officer: ~~Here's~~ "I just might marry somebody: ask me—perhaps I even might. Hey, ask me now, hey, don't waste any time!"

Mme. Drozdov: "And I'd give you my blessings."

Liza: "Well, that's where you lost your chance—now I'm not going to get married." ~~It wasn't you I~~

Mme. Drozdov: "Why then?"

"I wasn't asking you to hurry up, but him."

Stepan Trofimovich after his visit to the Drozdovs.

The Drozdov woman got her first notion of *Nikolas'* <*sic*> being out of his mind only after his escapades (the one where he pulled somebody's nose) became known here. "Well," she said, "he was acting strange even in Switzerland." Stepan Trofimovich about Prince Harry. Mme. Drozdov: "No, he is mad, and everybody in town says so." N.B. And yet she was the one who suggested the match and wrote a letter to Varvara Petrovna from Paris. Now she is trying to back out of it as best she can. The Drozdov woman has made a hint to Varvara Petrovna about her son's madness. An argument. Stepan Trofimovich was questioned regarding the incidents of the nose <pulling> and the <bitten> ear. The Governor's wife got involved also. Liza acts very independently. "I doubt if she loves *Nicolas*," thought Stepan Trofimovich. "What do they need Shatov for?" They were asking about Lebiadkin. Stepan Trofimovich assumes that he was invited for the purpose of being questioned.

81 Lebiadkin is buying the estate.

"Do you really believe that Liza was so overjoyed only because she could call on you? What a sceptic you are." "Oh, no! I, about Liza... no, she is an angel, while I have fallen low indeed." About Daria Pavlovna. Liza has hardly seen her *at all.* Liza stands up for her indignantly. "She asked me all about my would-be marriage. I told them a great deal. Liza was listening with great curiosity. And do you really believe that I have no faith in Daria Petrovna's <*sic*> honor? You are sitting there thinking just that." "Oh, no! (or rather, yes indeed.)" ~~You want me to investigate~~ "(Here's a letter from Varvara Petrovna; she has set the date for the day after tomorrow.) Perhaps I am guilty in that I have written to *Nicolas,* Daria, and...and..." ~~"You want me to <...>"~~ "She'll come in handy." "(Economically?) Do you want me to find out exactly about those 1000 rubles? I'll do what I can." N.B. "As I see it, we are simply facing an intrigue. He actually did dishonor her, and is paying now."

Stepan Trofimovich: "This much money?"

"~~Oh, my poor boy!"~~

Fundamentals

Nechaev is active in a certain educational institution.

"Wouldn't it be something to start some activity among secondary school teachers!"

When the Drozdov woman said: "Perhaps he is married."

"Are you going out of your mind? What are you raving about?"
Liza has a fit of hysterics.

N.B. "He used to be Falstaff with Prince Harry," said Shatov, having read the verses.

Liza, while at Lebiadkin's place, doesn't know yet that she is at Lebiadkin's, and when she does find out, cries: "So that's Lebiadkin!"

32 Stepan Trofimovich: "When God created woman he knew only too well the chance he was taking.

"So enjoying the fruits of your learning is not enough for you,"—that's during Stepan Trofimovich's first visit to Liza.

Last Adjustment of Program

December 25

Without the Arrival of Nikolas <*sic*>

II. At the Engineer's, a discussion about suicide, a meeting with Lebiadkin. At Stepan Trofimovich's—"I love her"—drunk. "You aren't worthy!"

III. At Liza's. Shatov has left. Liza to me, energetically: "I want to see that Lebiadkin woman. Today, immediately." I took off.

I talked her into waiting until the next day, and went to see Shatov. He wasn't in. At night—the lop-eared man and the Engineer.

About Liza, about America. "Let's go and see the Lebiadkin woman."

(To explain why Liza wants to see the Lebiadkin woman. "Once you have seen the Lebiadkin woman you may guess why.")

She actually did guess it. Yet she didn't say a word.

Noise. He's home. Verses.

~~Went to see Stepan Trofimovich. Confiscation of his papers. Cleared up. In the morning. Varvara Petrovna makes the sign of the cross over him and sends him off to the Governor. She is off to the Cathedral herself. Kneeling before her <. . .>.~~

In the morning, at the Cathedral. She has brought with her the Lebiadkin woman and Liza. Turmoil. The Drozdov woman with anonymous letters. Lebiadkin, not drunk. His sister is giving orders:

"Lebiadkin, let me have something to drink." Lebiadkin recants, and is almost chased from the house. Perusal of the anonymous letter. Dasha questioned. "Perhaps she is his lawful wife." Calls her a fool. Blesses Liza. "Well, and meanwhile we must finish this matter," and suddenly a question to Stepan Trofimovich: "Is it agreeable to you?" He is delighted, supports Dasha. (Dasha about the letter.) Varvara Petrovna, suddenly: "Nonsense, never mind, he isn't worth it."

2) 2d part. The nameday–arrest. And later, arrival of the Prince and Nechaev.

"Except that I've already refused Stepan Trofimovich."
"On what grounds?"
"Well, he wrote a letter to Nikolai Vsevolodovich."

83 ~~*Lebiadkin:* "One must instil respect in a woman."~~

~~*Nikolas* <*sic*> respectfully offered his arm to the Lebiadkin woman: "Don't be afraid, he (your brother) won't touch you now."~~

~~*The madwoman:* "Why, I'm not afraid of him at all; he is my footman. Lebiadkin, get me my burnous, and let the coachman drive the carriage up to the door."~~—

~~PART ONE ENDS WITH THE ARREST OF STEPAN TROFIMOVICH~~
~~December 25~~
~~In part two~~

~~The entire morning scene:~~
~~The arrest.~~
~~The half-witted woman in church~~.
~~At home~~.
~~Arrival of the Prince (he has been intimate with Liza).~~*
~~Lebiadkin and the half-witted woman.~~
~~*Mme. Drozdov:* "His lawful wife."~~
~~Appearance of Nicolas and Pyotr Verkhovensky.~~
~~*Nicolas* offers an explanation ("the half-witted woman is in love").~~ ~~Lebiadkin nods his approval.~~
~~The young Verkhovensky about somebody else's sins in Switzerland.~~
~~Scandal. Dasha can't marry Stepan Trofimovich. Dasha says: "Why not, I'll marry him."~~

---

* Literally, "He has seen the soles of her feet" (obscene).

Shatov slaps the Prince's face.

Stepan Trofimovich *moves out* (rather than flees) from Varvara Petrovna's house. Negotiations with Varvara Petrovna. With the son. A public lecture on Sheakespeare. For money.

The meaning of the finale of the last part lies in the fact that Varvara Petrovna is totally convinced of *Nicolas'* guilt, and is thunderstruck by Mme. Drozdov's assertion that he is a married man.

The Prince to Lebiadkin: "I shall have yet to ask this gentleman to render an account of the money."

Lebiadkin obsequiously agrees with him: "You must absolutely ask him."

4 Nechaev arranges a reconciliation between Varvara Petrovna and Stepan Trofimovich, inviting her to the old man's nameday party. The latter acts as if he were out of his mind.

"Let them expound their convictions, and I shall expound mine." He is looking for a quarrel. He is left with no one but Dasha.

Nechaev finally manages to embroil him even with Dasha, having told him about a meeting between Dasha and the Prince.

THE ARRIVAL OF NIKOLAI VSEVOLODOVICH.

Varvara Petrovna suddenly says: "My son Nikolai Vsevolodovich is here. He will presently give us an explanation (regarding Mme. Drozdov's statement about "*his lawful wife*")."

THIS MAKES A STRONG IMPRESSION UPON EVERYBODY.

HERE THEN, FOR THE FIRST TIME, LIZA LEARNS OF NICOLAS' ARRIVAL.

N.B. LIZA AND HER MOTHER HAVE ARRIVED (IN THE MORNING) INADVERTENTLY, BY LIZA'S WISH.

Nicolas, in the meantime, made several visits.

Varvara Petrovna herself, very shrewdly, had kept her son's arrival a secret, so that she might then refute all slanderous allegations and completely crush Mme. Drozdov's suspicions.

In the meantime, Stepan Trofimovich, who has withdrawn and is sulking on account of Varvara Petrovna, with terrible ardor prepares to challenge the nihilists to battle. Also, there is his romance with Dasha, broken by *Nechaev*.

~~N.B. But the nihilists do not accept his challenge, but rather, rout him part by part, yet savagely. Stepan Trofimovich turns into a ludicrous figure. Varvara Petrovna joins the camp of the Governor's wife and the young generation. Meanwhile the nihilists set fire to the city, spread proclamations, commit acts of sacrilege, kill Shatov and Lebiadkin.~~

~~Stepan Trofimovich finds out about all this and flees in despair~~.

~~In the beginning of the 2d part:~~
~~Here's the whole dénouement:~~
~~Stepan Trofimovich's fate is decided~~.
~~Varvara Petrovna's doubts are dispelled~~.
~~Mme. Drozdov makes herself clear.~~
~~The Prince shows his true nature.~~
~~Nechaev takes the stage.~~
~~A face is slapped.~~
~~Later, the Lame Woman's romantic love for the Prince is explained~~.
~~Lebiadkin confirms this~~.
~~WHAT IS MOST IMPORTANT: Varvara Petrovna gets even with the Drozdov woman in a big way. She forces her to make herself clear ("his lawful wife"). "I have been suspecting that myself. I've been getting anonymous letters myself. Here is my son Nikolai Vsevolodovich," he enters: "Are you married, or aren't you?"~~

85 Stepan Trofimovich to his son: "You people are the last, and that's precisely why you consider yourselves to be the first."

"In your complacency, there rests your judgment."

"Such people ~~in love~~ cannot develop further."

1st part. Finale. *December 27*. Scene with the Lebiadkin woman at Varvara Petrovna's who is thunderstruck, *as everything suddenly becomes clear to her* (Mme. Drozdov: "his lawful wife"). Varvara Petrovna says:

"Let there be a wedding anyway, they aren't worth it." She makes the sign of the cross over Liza. A vinegar compress round his head for four days. Stepan Trofimovich announced the night before* that he was officially engaged to be married. Dasha begs him not to visit her, nor does she receive him. Lebiadkin has suddenly quieted down and

---

* *vechera*—probably a misspelling of *vchera*.

Кн. Сыну — Вы последние и именно потому что считаете себя первыми.

Въ самодовольствiи вашемъ осужденiе ваше

— такимъ вашимъ путемъ развитiя. /

1-я Часть финалъ 27 Декабря Сценой Лебядкиной у драпированной Варвары Петровны, передъ которой все открывается (Хромоножка: Законная жена). В. П-на говоритъ: — А все таки свадьба, не отпопятъ он из того. Креститъ? Миз. || На четыре дня голова въ укусъ. Ст. Т-ч вечера открылъ — формальный женихъ. Даша проситъ его не ходить и не принимаетъ его. Лебядкинъ вдругъ притихъ и заперся. Рискнулъ было письмо Лизавете Николаевне, въ которомъ, чортъ знаетъ что. Лизавета Николаевна больна. —

Черезъ четыре дня начинается днемъ именинъ и ареста Степана Трофимовича

Затемъ прiездъ Nicolas, сына и на вечеръ скандалъ пощечина. —

??? ... — НЕ ЛУЧШЕ ЛИ ТАКЪ?

Ст. Т-ч объявляетъ свою любовь к В. П-не уже после того как он наставилъ ее вовсю официально Прасковьи поутру после обеда.

27 Декабря. Не кончить ли после стиховъ арестомъ? 1-я Глава

Н.Б. Держаться Зоны, не уничтожить ли совсемъ арестъ?

Notebook Page 85, Notebook 3

A clean sheet, one gothic motive, characteristically evenly lined. Dostoevsky's linear divisions between passages—expressed in these notes by spacings—can be easily seen, as well as his frequent habit of capitalizing for emphasis, as seen toward the end of the page in the phrase "Ne luchshe li tak?" *("Isn't it better that way?").*

doesn't leave his house. He nearly takes a stab at writing a letter to Lizaveta Nikolaevna, a letter in which he'd have written God knows what. Lizaveta Nikolaevna is sick.

Four days later: It starts with the nameday and the arrest of Stepan Trofimovich. Later in the day, arrival of *Nicolas* and Stepan Trofimovich's son, and finally at the soirée, the scandal and the slap in the face.

???—ISN'T IT BETTER THAT WAY?

Stepan Trofimovich declares his love for Varvara Petrovna only after he has insisted on getting officially engaged to be married earlier in the day, after mass.

December 27. Shouldn't the first part end in his arrest, after the poetry recital?

N.B. HOLD IT HERE. Shouldn't we do away with his arrest altogether?

86 BONS-MOTS

Varvara Petrovna to Mme. Drozdov: "Why did you have to blurt it out?"

"I don't know myself why."

Mme. Drozdov: "My dear, why won't you take the pressure off us a little?"

Varvara Petrovna: "All right, forget about it." And she makes the sign of the cross over Liza.

Such was Liputin's character.

Liza: "You will forgive mother; when her feet swell up, she gets very capricious."

Nechaev: "Is this you, old man? ~~I see, I see~~ Please, no nonsense, no nonsense, and no gestures!"

"Please, would you mind acting a little more soberly, I beg you—control yourself if you can! I knew that you were going to cry. How can one be such a child at your age? And here is Nikolai Vsevolodovich."

"Nikolai Vsevolodovich, ~~tell me, without approaching me~~, is it true that this unfortunate woman is your lawfully wedded wife? Stay where you are and tell me this without approaching me."

He did stop for a moment, smiled, but then walked up to her.

Most important. "Say something to us, do say something," Liputin, Shigalyov, et al. are constantly entreating Nechaev, who keeps spouting words, yet never to their satisfaction, even though he gets them more and more deeply involved in the conspiracy.

Here *the Great Writer:* "There was actually a war going on there and ~~of course~~ miasmata, and ~~temporarily~~ of course I have come to Russia, on which occasion I shall also sell my estate and have done with it all."

8 Nechaev and the Prince, without any comments, rather through their actions, while the narrative about Stepan Trofimovich should *always* be accompanied by comments—

Most Important:

The Prince and Nechaev are tied to each other by mutual secrets which they accidentally share.

Yet Nechaev is concealing a good many things from him (though he is tempted to initiate him, seeing his colossal stature. He is studying him).

The Prince reveals his thoughts to no one, and is a mystery to everybody. There aren't many love scenes between him and Liza.

Nechaev is actually trying to get Mavriky Nikolaevich married to Liza. He studies the Prince through Liza, thus clearing the way for the murder.

The Prince with Nechaev. Nechaev clarifies things for the Prince (he is one of two witnesses), as Lebiadkin shamefacedly voices his agreement and clears out. Nechaev exposes his father—"those sins of another man in Switzerland." ~~Varvara Petrovna disdainfully turns down Stepan Trofimovich,~~ Dasha faints—Nechaev apologizes and volunteers to clear up the whole affair. Shatov spits.

This is how these two new characters appear on the scene.

Then, a description of how Nechaev cleared up the whole affair.

But the Prince wants to fight—then, putting both characters on stage. A new intrigue. Nechaev makes Varvara Petrovna come to terms with the Governor's wife. He reconciles her to his father. He seeks the Prince's advice in everything. The latter seems to be nodding his approval, and finally goes to see Shatov.

Then, a new intrigue begins.

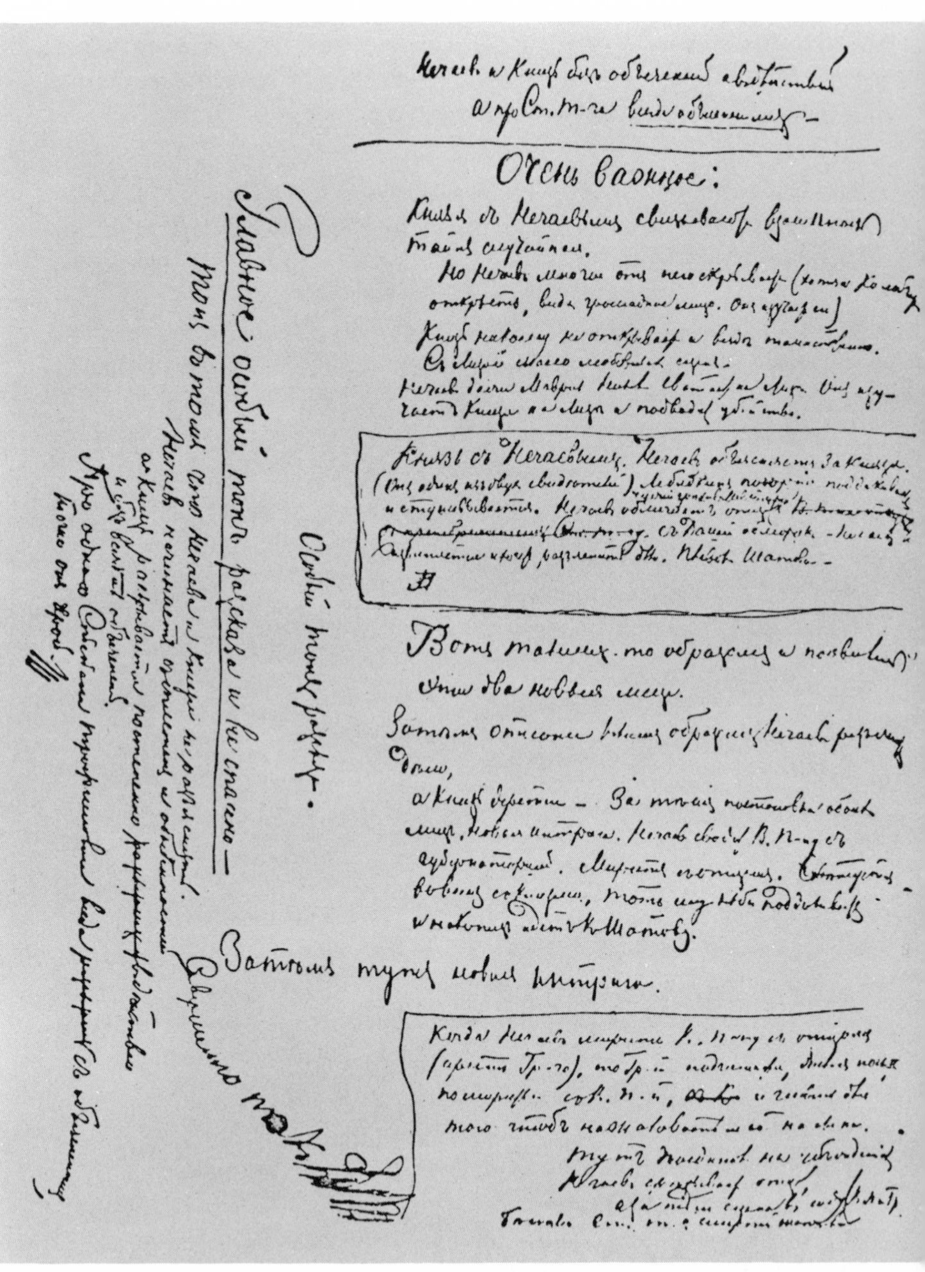

Notebook Page 88, Notebook 3

Of special interest in this page is the long sideways marginal comment. The comment is a reminder about tone, and is expressed in this edition in the last spaced section.

When Nechaev is seeking to reconcile Varvara Petrovna to his father (Granovsky's arrest), Granovsky obeys, as he wants to come to terms with Varvara Petrovna as soon as possible ~~with V.~~ , mostly because he would like to complain to her about his son.

Here, a duel of convictions. Nechaev cuts down his father, and then the scene in the garden (Varvara Petrovna and Granovsky).

The flight of Stepan Trofimovich and Shatov's death.

Special tone of the narrative.

Most important, the special tone of the narrative will save everything.

The tone consists in not explaining Nechaev or the Prince.

Nechaev starts out with gossip and trivialities, and the Prince reveals himself gradually ~~through the narrative~~ through the action, and without any comments.

Only about Stepan Trofimovich, always ~~through the narrative~~ with comments, as if he were the hero.

9 Exactly so. December 28 <1870>

December 28, 2:00 A.M. <1870>

DEFINITIVE PLAN.

The entire first part ends with the Lebiadkin woman getting dressed up, riding to the Cathedral, and getting down on her knees before Varvara Petrovna.

PART 2. The Lebiadkin woman was taken to Varvara Petrovna's house. ~~Lebiadkin himself is following her.~~ The Drozdov woman had *blurted out* even before Lebiadkin's arrival on the scene. ~~Lebiadkin explains~~ She seeks to justify herself by the anonymous letter, calls in Dasha: "Did you write a letter?" "I did." "Did you hand over the money?" "I did." At this point Lebiadkin shows up. He makes a brief, yet ambiguous statement. He is stupid, plays *the role of a flunky,* doesn't answer some of the questions? Liza laughs loudly, then cries over the Lebiadkin woman. Enter Mavriky Nikolaevich; *Nicolas* has arrived.

More briefly.

The unexpectedness of his arrival. Varvara Petrovna's joy. He escorts the Lebiadkin woman out most chivalrously. ~~He refuses to give a full explanation.~~ He says that a certain impression may have been produced; Lebiadkin then offers an explanation in his stead, agreeing

28 Декабря 2 часа ночи. 89.

Планъ окончательный.

— Конецъ всей первой части въ томъ, что Лебядкина нарядная поѣхала въ Соборъ и стала на колѣни предъ В. П-й.

Notebook Page 89, Notebook 3

Dostoevsky again places his stylistic and technical reminder athwart the whole page: "Make the narrative shorter—a special tone and a special manner. A brief, narrative, special tone, without comments." The page is neat and orderly and corresponds to a unified subject matter.

to everything he has said; finally, he turns him out with ignominy, and Lebiadkin leaves meekly.

Varvara Petrovna, immediately: "Stepan Trofimovich wouldn't be worth it, but ~~Liza~~ Dasha, would you like to?" "I would." Nicolas offers his congratulations. (Dasha suddenly faints. Never happened before.) Mme. Drozdov excuses herself, Liza is secretly delighted, yet she lets everybody know that Mavriky Nikolaevich is number one. Suddenly, Shatov spits in his face. ~~The latter~~

Liza and Mme. Drozdov leave. Varvara Petrovna hugs him: "Don't I know that you lived with Shatov's wife. But what's more important, that Drozdov woman has suffered a defeat, and God knows what's best, and we haven't any use for them anyway, so it's all to the good."

Then a quick confession of mother to son. "What has been going on here?" He listens respectfully, but says nothing most of the time. Varvara Petrovna is still mad at Shatov.

However, this scene was not without consequences, as it was the cause of a particular turn of events. He hadn't paid anybody a visit yet, and on the following day, there came this challenge. ~~A fight, broken up. A son of the landowner Istom <the rest of the name is illegible>.~~

After having been home, he went to see Shatov, then Lebiadkin—(the Engineer acted as his second, Mavriky Nikolaevich was second to the other party). There was going to be a fight the next day, and there was. The whole town talked about the results of the fight. With respect, too, for it is such a romantic story.

Make the narrative shorter—a special tone and a special manner. A brief, narrative, special tone, without comments.

Information on Stepan Trofimovich.
Prince Harry and matchmaking.

He kissed her before everyone's eyes, took her in his arms, and carried her off.

Pyotr Stepanovich yells after him: "Shall I give the fifteen hundred to Lebiadkin?"

"Are you making fun of me?"

"No, I am not making fun of you." He cast a glance at her not looking her in the eyes. "What else? It is simply the truth."

From abroad. About the Drozdovs, about the Governor—Arrival of the Drozdovs.

She has made the match.

"That's where I was needed."

Nearly going out of his mind.

(Explain the story of the arrest and Alyosha on the part of the narrator, in a brief narrative, and just let the scene stand out.)

Beginning of the 2d part.

Now it is time to explain how all this has come about, i.e., the wedding.

The Governor's wife, ~~the Great Writer~~

Anonymous letters.

He went there and complained: "That's Shatov."

Vinaigre de toilette.[4]

Shatov is summoned. About Shatov; his sister is about to get married.

Stepan Trofimovich is annoyed.

The Great Writer. "She simply isn't received at the Drozdovs."

Quarrel because of Kartuzov.

Stepan Trofimovich has been rude—("Ungrateful! I'm glad!")

Letter about the Prince.

"You aren't all as guilty as that: It's Shatov and Liza. He is working for Liza."

They rushed to warn them of Shatov. He carries out the proclamations (also, about Lebiadkin, prospective buyer of the village). Shatov is shown the proclamations.

The books were being dragged from one place to the other, while she was getting some vinegar ready.

Liza at Shatov's. Lebiadkin has given a beating.

Lebiadkin has informed the authorities.

The wedding (feverishly). The public lecture, because he is now a bridegroom, must express himself.

The Drozdovs knew about Lebiadkin even before they returned from abroad, but they did not actually believe the story.

Kondraty[5] is not there.

That's why the Drozdov woman exhibits a mocking expression on her face, and interrupts Varvara Petrovna when the latter approaches

---

[4] Toilet-Vinegar.

[5] A valet in the employ of Barbara Stavrogin.

the subject of the wedding. She won't listen to her and interrupts her with a mocking remark.

At Liputin's. The lecture about Słończewski.

Stepan Trofimovich had to be talked into agreeing to give a lecture.

P.S. Concerning Section IV, January 3, 1871.

A PRECIOUS OBSERVATION

N.B. *About the proclamations.*

Varvara Petrovna: "... ~~since~~ I am an ignorant woman compared with you, yet I have become convinced," etc.

Stepan Trofimovich: "Convinced of what?"

Varvara Petrovna: "That we ~~you and I~~ aren't the only clever people in the world, Stepan Trofimovich, at least not you and I, but that there are some who are more clever than we are."

Stepan Trofimovich: "What you've just said was witty, and elegantly phrased, but..."

"...why won't you talk to Liputin..."

Later, Varvara Petrovna is interested in hearing her son's views on that subject, as she sees that he is on close terms with Nechaev. What bothers her most is this: is it really all that simple (as it says in the proclamation, N.B. write it out)? It just couldn't be that stupid. It must be that something else is implied.

Her son answers drily that nothing is implied and that it is all that simple.

Varvara Petrovna: "I asked Stepan Trofimovich, and this is how he explained it."

Her son: "Does he, too, explain it *that way*? I'd have never thought. Most interesting."

Her son: "That's one of the reasons why these affairs progress as well as they do, everybody thinking that it can't be all as plain and simple as that, and that there must be a deeper meaning somewhere."

Varvara Petrovna: "And you think that this isn't clever?"

The Prince: "Terribly stupid!"

October 22.

I've come to grief, usually,

(...) a cruel fate,

at three o'clock, everything most definitely
Olga Nikolaevna (. . .)

Unnecessary cruelties, he has driven the girl to desperation. She knows that he is persecuting her without a good reason. An unsuccessful declaration of love. He dies in jealousy and contempt.

Laziness and limpness, apathy.
I was a universal man, and I have ended up becoming a misanthrope.[6]
I loathe my land.

87 N.B. Liza's engagement to Mavriky Nikolaevich.

(*Nota-bene, February 3*—that's definitely how it should be. *Nicolas* abducts her on her way to the altar.

That's how it happens:

First of all, *after the finale of the first part*, Liza is engaged to be married to Mavriky Nikolaevich. *Nicolas* greatly supports this match. (He also spurs on Nechaev).

Liza, meanwhile, has become convinced (early in the 2d part) that the Lebiadkin woman is just mad, and not Nikolai Vsevolodovich's wife. And though she does insist on marrying Mavriky Nikolaevich, she does it only out of frustration.

Practically on the eve of the wedding she has a heart-to-heart talk with the Prince. Everything is up in flames again. And suddenly Liza learns by accident that the Prince is really *married*, and that this is why he had withdrawn from her. (She learns it either from Lebiadkin or from Dasha.)

She elopes with him, in order to show him that she loves him boundlessly, and willingly submits to him, even though ~~he can't marry~~ he is married.

Here, immediately, the murder of the Lebiadkins.

Liza in a fever.

Etc.

---

[6] Russian *obshchechelovek*, which is literally "general" or "universal man," but probably best rendered as "abstract man." As used by Dostoevsky—it is a favorite expression of his—it is always pejorative.

XIV
Nechaev's Principles

Except for pages 114 and 115, which were written in March, 1871, the bulk of these notes were written in late spring or early summer of 1871. The notes, comprising pages 90–103 and pages 114 and 115 of notebook 3, are a connected exposition of Nechaev's ideas, and would seem —from unity of subject matter—to have been written about the same time. Some of the content would seem to indicate that Dostoevsky used information from the trial of Nechaev's co-conspirators; but if this were true, the notes could not have been written before July, 1871.

The notes of this section comprise the most extensive exposition of Nechaev's ideas that we have, and the reader may want to supplement them by the undated and miscellaneous section XV on Nechaev. Most of what Nechaev says here is close to what Peter Verkhovensky tells Stavrogin so ecstatically in Chapter VIII, Part II of the final version. Nechaev's program is designed to turn man by monstrous vice into a happy, contented, and gregarious animal. All aristocrats, special talents, and manifestations of special ability are to be ruthlessly exterminated in the interest of a deadening equality. One wonders how Dostoevsky planned to reconcile Nechaev's insistence upon collective will and the extermination of individuality with his insistence on the importance of self-interest: "Satisfying one's own interests is higher than the state, higher than morality, higher than religion, higher than society. If you satisfy your own interests, you have by so doing satisfied those of society and the state as well. Society is higher than the state. Society has been formed only in order to give <each individual> more strength, only to satisfy the interests of each single member." Perhaps he felt that what seems to be a blatant contradiction could not be reconciled, because Peter repeats in almost the same words the destruction of Ciceros and Shakespeares, but he does not repeat Nechaev's views of the importance of self-interest. Yet a form of this contradiction is to be found in Chernyshevsky's works, from which it was probably taken. Chernyshevsky believed in rational self-interest as the highest goal of man, and in the collective will as the highest goal of society; and he believed that the two could be reconciled, because the truly rational man would see that his highest self-interest lay in the service to the collective.

The Engineer, now called Kirilov for the first time, appears in these notes, and brief mention is made of his idea that the belief in God must be changed if society is to be changed, and of his belief that man will actually undergo a physical change if he stops believing in God. These ideas are our first hint of the immense metaphysical stature that Kirilov is to assume in the final version of the novel.

Finally, Dostoevsky seems to see more and more clearly that the most essential relationship in the novel must be between Nechaev and the Prince. Earlier in the notes for *The Possessed* Dostoevsky had discovered that everything was to be centered in the Prince, and now he tells us: "N.B. And so, *everything is concentrated in the person of Nechaev.*" And on the same notebook page: "Therefore, the most important thing about the novel is: The relationship between Nechaev and the Prince."

---

114 SHARP WORDS.

1) *Bons-mots. Nechaev*: "There are things which not only can't be discussed in any clever way, but which it isn't very clever to discuss in the first place."

Von Lembke: "That was a well-turned phrase (clever and not very clever)."

The Lebiadkin woman, during her meeting with the Prince:
"Allow me to go down on my knees before you."
"Aren't you ever going to kiss me?"
"Say 'my little kitten' to me!"

Flattery.
Nechaev has put Varvara Petrovna under his spell through flattery:
Nechaev: "I'm an awkward person. I don't see how ~~everybody~~ one can be agreeable to everybody, how one can please everybody—I just don't know."

Varvara Petrovna: "Never speak about yourself to anybody, but quite the contrary, listen to everybody when they are speaking about themselves—and they'll find you adorable. Do ask them to talk about themselves—and they will all be on your side."

Nechaev: "What a subtle observation."

"And yet you've never done me justice before."

Shatov: "We have a long way to go, learning to be ourselves."

Nechaev actually hadn't meant to flatter her at all, but here the thought suddenly struck him: "Well, it might not be such a bad idea to flatter her a little. I ought to do that more often."

N.B.—…"Well, I'll tell him the whole truth directly, that is, of course, not the whole truth."

N.B. Stepan Trofimovich inadvertently says this to his son: "But, my dear boy, you don't seem to be so very clever at all, tell me, how do you manage so well?"

Nechaev to the Prince: "I am not putting on an act for them; I'm just using my wits in dealing with them" (that is, with Lembke).

He imagines that he is using his wits.

5 REGARDING THE 2D PART.

The whole setting and the whole plot involving Nechaev amounts to the circumstance that, in the beginning, the reader sees nothing at all about him, except some character traits suggesting buffoonery and a certain oddness.

Don't do as other novelists do, i.e., blow your horn at the very beginning, announcing that "here is an extraordinary personage." On the contrary, conceal it, and reveal his true character only gradually, by means of strong artistic strokes of the brush (for instance, the contrast between his cleverness and cunning on the one hand, and his absolute ignorance of reality on the other).

MARCH 1 <1871>

Nechaev talks with the Prince about the Engineer: His idea is that all attempts to reorganize society are doomed to failure until the cornerstone has been removed from the structure upon which society rests. He believes that God and man's faith in him are such a cornerstone.

"I don't know if he is right, ~~but~~ I think that the mistake lies precisely in making God alone <the cornerstone of society>. Too bad I haven't the time to think about it, though it is a rather forceful idea. There is of course some reason to assume that, inasmuch as every society in the world so far has believed in God, all the societies that will quit believing will undergo some changes. He says that man will actually undergo a physical change. There's an idea in that, eh?"

The Prince: "Really a great one. Reverse his arguments a bit and here's what you get: if man ~~changes~~ will undergo even physical change once he has lost God, couldn't one also put it this way: without a physical change ~~the faith in God among mankind~~ he won't lose his faith in God either."

"Come on, that's only a play of words," said Nechaev, "and today it's no longer words that count, as it used to be before."

Having heard that literacy is about to spread among the people as a result of soldiers being taught how to read and write, *Nechaev* observes right away:

"That's an idea... That's a good idea. This literacy of theirs can be taken advantage of. There's nothing better than such rudimentary education. It creates a most receptive type of people. Literacy will make them excitable, irritable. What fun it will be to get to work on them! Some material!"

47 May 13, 1871

After the fire, Tikhon sends a note to the Prince: "Was it you, or wasn't it, who caused the fire? Are you the murderer of the Lebiadkins and of Shatov? Don't worry about my messenger, he is reliable."

Tikhon: "I am terrified."

"Don't you see that nobody will ever forgive you?"

The Prince: "Why?"

"You lack a sense of the beautiful (your feat is great, but the beautiful is lacking in it). This lack of beauty is going to kill you; you won't be able to stand it."

"There are many who don't believe in God, but do believe in devils."

"(Unto the angel of the church in Sardis write—")[1]

"(More than one crucifixion took place on that cross.)"

"Who am I to pass judgment; as you wish, you have my blessings."

---

[1] Revelation 3:1.

"Yet I am afraid."

"There is nothing beyond these torments. There can't be anything higher than this moral feat of yours."

Tikhon: "There are many who love, but very few who believe. What is one who loves? One who wishes and would like to believe."

"Yet only perfect love coincides with perfect faith. Only the indifferent do not believe at all. The most complete atheism is perhaps closest to faith."

—The Most Important

At Tikhon's

The Prince confesses to him his violently passionate love for a certain woman.

I have received word that she will come to see me. I won't be able to resist, the very thought plunges me into the madness of passion.

That he is violently passionate.

Bons-mots

The Great Writer: "Eh, for goodness's sake, Moscow could be destroyed in a fire, and with it my article. We can't allow this to happen—for it has happened, you know."

Varvara Petrovna about Stepan Trofimovich: "You can't yield your position with dignity."

Stepan Trofimovich at Lembke's: "The study of Russian history obscures human common sense nearly for centuries."

The Prince after the speech at the meeting.

This is irony.

This is vanity.

The Prince: "Leave me in peace, I was laughing."

While Nechaev says to himself: "No, there's something else here. There's still some hope here."

Tikhon, taking leave: "I am afraid—"

The Prince: "Leave that to me."

Tikhon: "I am afraid because right now you are terribly close to committing a crime—"

The Prince (theme): "I've come to you <asking you to> prove God to me."

"Why do you need Him so suddenly? Aren't you an educated man?"

The Prince: "Yes, I do know, more or less, all the *pro* and *contra*; also that there is no proof, and rather many more facts suggesting His superfluity. But that is not the point. I have been told that you are one of those who really do believe. Well, you must have something to tell me why you believe, if you actually do believe. I have never met a man who actually believed. Tell me anything. Forgive my rude, feverish impatience."

The Prince: "All this would be very naïve if I'd come to you without a serious reason.—But there ... there is one thing—"

91 1)

ABOUT

WHAT NECHAEV WANTED

On the part *of the Writer*

Everything in connection with Liputin.

How it all appeared to Liputin as he was trying to read Nechaev.

The author describes all of these products of Liputin's *imagination* as he addresses his public.

N.B. N.B. N.B.:

Liputin had imagined that an extensive conspiracy existed. Imagination is corroborated by facts. Also, Nechaev seconds his opinion (i.e., does not contradict him) that Fourierism will be established immediately.

And yet all this is founded on the *naïveté* of these people and on their *ignorance* of Russia.

What's most important is this: that through the entire novel nobody actually establishes quite clearly why Nechaev came to this town in the first place.

On the other hand, it is made emphatically clear that at the bottom of all this *breathless* bustle, all this fussing around, and all these crimes, there was really:

90 2)

a false conception, worked out somewhere in Switzerland, about the actual condition of Russia (her being ready for mutiny and insurrection, etc.).

As a result of which a shrewd and self-assured man (Nechaev) is sent out to give it a try. Uprooted fool that he is, he goes with high hopes of actually achieving his goal, and with ridiculous ease:

And therefore:

He decides to base his activities upon the following:

1) Organizing local cells. These cells would derive their strength from their members being compromised, for good, by some drastic action which they had been drawn into and which he would keep threatening them with.

N.B. To this end, Nechaev carefully looks over, examines, and sorts out people. Some of his activities are presented in the novel.

His tactics with the Prince: he drops a hint, much too naïvely. The Prince to him: "Are you trying to scare me, too?" Nechaev: "Why, even without my doing anything you are..."

"Scared?" asks the Prince.

"Oh, no; I want to say that you are with us without my doing anything about it."

"Don't you know that I am not bound by anything?"

"Yes, but in your thoughts, in your thoughts..."

N.B. (Nechaev, aside: "No, you're wrong there, and you're afraid to admit it; you have tied yourself up, and I've tied you up, too."

Nechaev to the Engineer: "There is one captain here in town, a company commander, who is a malcontent. I got to know him, and seeing right away that he has a fancy for such things, I began to prove to him that there was no God. Would you imagine, he got to think about it, and here's what he said: 'If there's no God, what kind of a Captain am I then?' "

The Engineer, incidentally, asks Nechaev to, please, not bother him with politics.

2) Through these cells, he spreads proclamations and actually prints some in Russia, for Switzerland is none too active. (Nechaev talks to Shatov about that, and that's why there is a clash between them.)

3) Distributing proclamations and acting upon factory workers and soldiers—Nechaev has come to get it started and show how it is done; and later, let the cell carry on by itself.

4) Get all this organized in two-three provinces. Acting upon the Raskolniki, and upon the nihilists in the capitals. (An investigation to determine what the latter are capable of. Nechaev's criticism.) ~~Upon the peasants~~

5) Act upon the peasants, not with "Golden Bills" anymore, but by causing riots, disturbances, fires, *by troubling their minds,* and by making them expect something.

92 3)

6) Teachers, secondary school and divinity school teachers.

7) By organizing an imminent uprising: when everything is ready and in a troubled state, let the factory or the country side stage an uprising (any reason will do, just think up anything, and get them ready: fires, acts of sacrilege, etc.) It would be a good idea to arouse *the Jews.*

8) They'll send soldiers to quell the uprising. The soldiers must be prepared, and their commanding officers as well. If just one officer were prepared, that would do. If it might be impossible to get them prepared properly—kill ~~the soldiers and~~ the officers. Let the soldiers fraternize with the peasants, or at least part of the soldiers. Just for the sake of *making an example,* for this has never happened before, and the whole province is on fire. (This is Liputin's project who, in part, proposes it ~~to Shatov~~ to Nechaev. His idea is to precipitate a civil war. Nechaev takes cognizance of everything, but remains silent.) Nechaev reports to the Prince that this is Liputin's idea.

9) Toward the beginning of the affair, a colossal local exposé (of the Governor). Issue a bulletin about every civil servant in the province, revealing their past, bribes taken by them, and all kinds of slander. Spread it among the people. This leads to the following:

The absolute need of our own printing press. *The clash with Shatov.*

A bulletin about private individuals. That's where Liputin will be a valuable man, and it ought to go well. Nechaev's report.

10) Increasing the incidence of villainies, crimes, and suicides, so as to shake the morale of the people, to undermine faith in the stability of the existing order, and to get the criminal element among the people stirred up.* Increase sin and debauchery, liquor. Distribute money.

About the conversation with Kotzebue.

11) Inciting the capitals to rebellion.

12) A cattle plague, for instance. Rumors that they are *mixing in* <poison> and *setting fires.* The murder of a governor, somewhere, etc.

A cut-throat and a poisoner.

Generally, a few apt turns of speech about "those who are mixing in <poison>, and those who are setting fires."

~~A year of such Finally, the beginning~~

A year or less of such conditions, and you've got the elements of a

---

* *Stenka-Razinovskaia chast' narodonaseleniia,* literally, "the Stenka-Razinite part of the populace," after the notorious seventeenth-century bandit and insurgent.

huge Russian insurrection. Three provinces will go up in fire simultaneously. Everybody will start killing off each other, *traditions will not remain intact.* Capitals and private fortunes

4)

will be ruined, and then, with the people crazed after a year of insurrection, establish at once a social republic, communism and socialism. Liputin insists on Fourierism. If the people won't accept it—kill some more of them, and *so much the better.*

Nechaev's principle, *his new word,* lies in aiming everything at an insurrection, "but let it be a live one," and "the more rioting, disorders, bloodshed and ~~general~~ collapse, fire, and destruction of traditions, the better." "I don't care what will be later: what's most important is that the existing order be shaken, ~~shattered~~ shattered, and exploded."

13) ~~In~~ Finally, if this is actually possible, let's have Karakozov—~~(Sometimes.~~ He counts on the Engineer. "I admit that I had set my hopes on Kirilov." Inasmuch as the Engineer refuses to accept responsibility for *the fire* and *Shatov* <'s murder> (the fire and the acts of sacrilege took care of themselves; the Engineer was held responsible for Shatov).

"Russia won't stand up under this onslaught, there's nothing that could stand up," says Nechaev.

The Prince: "The people are strong."

Nechaev: "Make them drunk, we must make them drunk, we can make them drunk."

Of course, it all turned out to be a mere soap bubble. But such were Nechaev's plans.

Nechaev is not a socialist, but a rebel. His ideals are insurrection and destruction, after which *"let happen what will"* on the basis of the social principle according to which whatever might come would still be better than the present, and that the time has come to act, rather than to preach.

5

From All This There Follows the Most Important, Nota Bene:

That Nechaev, as such, is still a *fortuitous and isolated* individual. He only thinks that everybody who resembles him is like him—*which is where he is wrong,* to the point of vile naïveté ("let me talk to them from my window for a quarter of an hour").

But as such, this entire group, detached as it is from society, is weak and insignificant—it is half dead, and badly lagging behind times, for it is unable to register not only what is going on in Russia, but even the day-to-day, superficial mental attitudes within its own, uprooted party.

This is to be stated by the author.

And don't forget, in this connection, the project, contemplated by Nechaev, concerning an alliance between the nihilists and the large landowners.

N.B. And so, *everything is concentrated in the person of Nechaev.*

Nechaev as a person:

As already stated above, an abstract shrewdness, and an absolute ignorance of reality.

But whenever he does understand reality, he either takes advantage of it shrewdly, almost brilliantly,

or,

or, as a result of his one-sided understanding of the facts, an interpretation which directs him toward the most foolish objectives. He is the last Russian conspirator.

Nechaev says to the Prince: "I am the last Russian conspirator."

95 6)

Therefore, the most important thing about the novel is:

The relationship between Nechaev and the Prince.

It all started with Nechaev's blunder, for he let himself be guided, to some extent, by his heart—if such a tarantula has a heart.

Nechaev, from the very beginning, even while still in Switzerland, is fascinated by the Prince and actually falls in love with his intellect and his character. ("I am telling you, you would really be the man *our cause needs.*") The Prince enthralls everybody, and Nechaev is greatly impressed by it.

He is fascinated by his ideas, and by his capacity for crime.

For a while he actually suspects that he may be acting as the head of his *own* conspiracy.

"How can you let such a man stay inactive, let him sit around twiddling his thumbs?"

And therefore:

He is around the Prince all the time, he analyzes and *studies* him, even little-by-little reveals things to him.

Finally—oh joy!—he has maneuvered the Prince into a situation where he is compromised by the murder of the Lebiadkin woman (which, incidentally, has been done so well that there isn't a trace leading to him; nor has the Prince admitted his guilt to Nechaev, which the latter doesn't like a bit).

Here. Nechaev reveals to him *his entire plan, which he has been pursuing up to this point* ~~and about~~. The Prince listens with utmost attention, but does not reveal any of his own secrets and says nothing at all when Nechaev announces that he is making him his successor, but quite the contrary, proceeds to let Shatov know. Then Nechaev is suddenly stricken by doubts, and he decides to kill the Prince—but he runs out of time and flees, leaving Liputin, or more correctly, *no one* to act in his stead.

2d part. The Prince is at Lebiadkin's. They bring in his wife. He looks, looks again.

The Prince: "Get out!" (to Lebiadkin) "Out into the yard?" "All right, into the yard." He is left alone with his wife.

The Lebiadkin woman to the Prince: "Can I go down on my knees?" "Yes, you can."

6 *Nechaev* 1

Nechaev's Views on the Development of Internal Policies

1) "An attempt to introduce retrograde policies, an attempt to strengthen the power of the governors, for instance, all this means as much as *playing into our hands* (disturbances). All the reforms of the present reign have produced precisely the thing we need—disturbances."

N.B.$_1$ But the point is that Nechaev assumes that the government has acted by design—that it has been creating disturbances and lawlessness on purpose (following the example of Napoleon <III> in France), in order to seize power.

N.B.$_2$ Shatov's idea about the Russian Tsar and about how the Russian Tsar has nothing to fear.

(Read the *Moscow News* on the happenings in Perm,[2] and about the proposed strengthening of gubernatorial powers. Nechaev expounds this at a meeting, or to the Prince. He tells him: "I wonder who that

[2] A reference to strengthening of police powers there. Articles appeared in the *Moscow News* in January, 1871, on this subject.

clever man may be (in the government); I'd like to go and embrace him for it!")

Look Here. (No. of the *Moscow News.* Saturday, January 16 (or Friday, the 15th) Feuilleton signed "Voice of A Transient," Saturday the 16th, or Sunday the 17th of January.)

Von Lembke, in a conversation with Nechaev, when the latter tells him about certain recent events (in Perm province) is at first naïvely shocked by the untidiness of it all, but later comes around and is greatly impressed by the *higher reasons,* presented to him by Nechaev, regarding this being conducive to a strengthening of gubernatorial powers and a *paralyzing effect* upon every reform of the Tsar—(feuilleton signed by "A Transient"). He is deeply moved (he also expresses his opinion on the subject of birch rods, namely that they are indispensable) and declares to Nechaev that he has already *sent the Minister a memorandum regarding two sentries to be posted at the gate of the Governor's mansion*—~~for~~ which he considered most essential to a strengthening of gubernatorial power.

97 2)

Nechaev replies: "Essential not only to strengthen gubernatorial power, but simply so people would know that you are the Governor."

Nechaev gets von Lembke confused right off the bat by telling him that in 200 years there won't be any fuel left in Europe. Because of this it will be inevitable to reorganize society on a new economic basis, namely in workers' communes, in connection with which the family will also ~~suffer~~ disintegrate. And if so, the sooner the better. The fuel reserves will last so much longer.

Lembke is very much impressed. "But maybe they will invent some new fuel?"

"But allow me," he suddenly strikes his forehead, "haven't we got our vast forests and a vast amount of land? Shouldn't we be able to retain the family longer than everyone else?"

"Hungry Europe is going to take it all away from us, seeing we've got so much of it."

"And how soon will that be?" asked von Lembke most worriedly.

Nechaev: "Well, not in your lifetime anyway. However, one must get ready for it."

Lembke was relieved.

Nechaev (answering the Governor's questions about the Engineer) ~~says~~ *apparently* defends him, yet also insinuates that he is a mysterious character and that, quite likely, he may be linked with those proclamations. He speaks about the Engineer's madness, and about his atheism, about *America,* etc. He even gives the Governor a scare; *though he did reassure him temporarily.*

N.B. "I've been at the Engineer's: his *Essay on Suicides.* We talked a lot."

Nechaev, while discussing Shatov and Slavophilism with the Prince:
"Is he a Slavophile? Isn't he a Slavophile, pure and unadulterated?" (Nechaev actually does not know what exactly a Slavophile is.)
"I wouldn't say that he is a pure Slavophile," the Prince replies casually, "rather, he is one of those who are seeking to regenerate Russia through her own resources."
"You know what," says Nechaev, "I've heard that they've been very much on the increase lately. It might be a good idea to let the government know about them, perhaps through certain generals. What do you think, oughtn't we do it?"
"Look there now," says the Prince, "there you are, being indignant about Shatov's informing, and you yourself want to inform on him."
"Come on now, that's not the same thing! We are doing it for the common cause, and that is honorable. ~~Decided~~. I'll talk to Lembke about Shatov. We must point him out to Lembke as a troublemaker, just in case."

8 May 13, 1871 At Virginsky's

Nechaev's principles. Every man's goal is to strive for maximum protection of his own interests. This is the whole goal of man AS A WHOLE. There is no such thing as national, (or moral), or social purposes, for the principle just mentioned covers everything. Satisfying one's own interests is higher than the state, higher than morality, higher than religion, higher than society. If you satisfy your own interests, you have by so doing satisfied those of society and the state as well. Society is higher than the state. Society has been formed only in order to give <each individual> more strength, only to satisfy the interests of each single member. Each member of society has immediate control over it. An association may act by means of violence, falsehood, fraud, murder, slander, and larceny, as long as it hasn't conquered its opponents, but is still struggling. By the way, it may act in this fashion even thereafter.

Each member of society jealously watches every other member, and thus each controls the other. ~~Each member must~~ All ~~each~~ for each and each for all—there's your best guarantee. If all are asking services from each, without reciprocating in kind, we get despotism. If each single individual, while receiving services from all, which have no other purpose but his well-being, does not wholly surrender himself to all, he is an aristocrat, a despot, and an enemy of society. Social control every hour and every minute. Everyone must spy on everyone else, and inform on him. That isn't spying, for it serves a higher goal. In the last resort, slander and murder are the best way: everything is permissible, for it serves a higher goal.

99 But what is especially important is to take great pains to ensure absolute equality. To this end, one must first of all lower the level of education, of the sciences, and of talent in every field. Nothing has served despotism more than science and talent. A high level, in the sciences and in intellectual accomplishment, is accessible only to the highly gifted. The highly gifted have always seized power and become despots. And this is why we have no use for the highly gifted—a highly gifted person is incapable of love. It might be argued that a high level of achievement is open to everybody. Let it be so, yet the majority has only mediocre natural gifts (...) and never has achieved (OR COULD ACHIEVE) that which has been achieved by the highly gifted. And this is why education ought to be well within the range of all, and there should be no attempt made to look for anything higher. Any time a person shows any special or higher gifts, or knowledge, he must be ~~executed~~ expelled from society, or executed, if there is no place to drive him out to. Cicero is to have his tongue cut out, Copernicus is to have his eyes put out, Shakespeares are to be stoned. In my opinion, there shouldn't even be allowed men or women with very handsome faces, nor individuals who are too strong physically, or anyone who excels too much in any way. The same with those who are too stupid, for they might give the others occasion to feel superior, i.e., a temptation to despotism.

Level the mountains—etc.

But, one might argue that this is harmful (IT MAY BRING HARM TO SOCIETY ITSELF, THEY SAY,) even from the viewpoint of your very own economic and social principles. A talented individual may make discoveries which may be of some use to society.—Nonsense. According to today's principles, YES, but not according to those of the future. The mean is the highest of all goals. Also, there have been enough inventions, enough science. "We've learned a trade and we want to be honest people: what good is any more science to us? That's what,"

At Virginsky's

answered the English workingmen.

"That's not what you find in the novel *What Is To Be Done?* That's not the picture you get from it. They've got halls built of aluminum, and concerts which would put Beethoven to shame."

Nechaev: "I haven't read that novel. Its author hasn't gotten to the main point yet. If he'd live and see for himself, he'd wind up realizing that there can't be any concerts. Luther rejected the authority ~~of the Church~~ and founded a free Church. ~~Alas~~ But of course he failed to realize that his religion would, in the process of its organic development, arrive at a negation of itself, i.e., at a negation of all religion. That's exactly what will happen here. Even if certain accommodations for general use could be built of aluminum, one ought to reject them as a matter of principle, so that there wouldn't be any aluminum, and no colonnades, no art, no music, for all these things only corrupt people. Only the absolutely essential is of the essence. That's the motto of this world, and the absolutely essential is always attainable. And if, ultimately, there would be a shortage of even the most essential, nature will take care of that."

"Yet 'the absolutely essential' is also a relative concept."

"Society, at any given moment, decides for itself what the level of the 'absolutely essential' should be. It will go down, of course, but nature draws its own protective limit."

At Virginsky's

"With the abolition of the family, there will be fewer children also, down to a level of absolute necessity."

"They will be wolves."

"They will be honest people. Each will know his trade, and his obligation to watch one another."

"But they will devour each other."

"All the better! That's the highest goal of all. For they'll be devouring each other, once again, only up to a certain point—for as a consequence of it all, they'll change altogether, human nature will change, and man, as a result of long practice, will become organically assimilated ~~in~~ by society, and they will become so that *each is for all, and all for each.* What's most important here is to induce a physical change in human nature. It is absolutely necessary here that individuality be changed into herd instinct, quite spontaneously, though man may have long since forgotten the original formula."

"But in this case you see man's whole interest in securing food and drink for himself?"

"Yes, and equal rights, and organic regeneration of equality."

"It's going to be very dull."

"That is an aristocratic idea. And why should it be dull? People who have unsatisfied strivings and desires are bored. But man will be satisfied, and in our new society there won't be any desires. Desire is something aristocratic..."

"Enough, enough." ~~Shatov~~

N.B. *The most important. Nechaev concludes:* "Generally speaking, you are going too much into details. I for myself have mastered only the idea. It isn't any of my business either. There are others who write books and who willy-nilly do some occasional daydreaming, and who talk nonsense. Experience will show, the future that is. One thing is sure: a radical reorganization of society and its very nature. And therefore, destruction. And that is my specialty."

102 *Nechaev* to the Prince and Miliukov: "I know very little, guide me."

"But how can you, not knowing reality, want to make a revolution?"

"Oh, knowledge—that's so trivial. Always one and the same thing. The same everywhere. I'd only like to find out about those who have been bribed."

N.B. That *niveau* which it won't be possible to transcend in the society of the future. Give a man just a little bit of education and understanding—and already you have to deal with aristocratic desires, to the detriment of the commune. Give him just a little bit of a family, or of love—and already you face the desire to own private property. And, excessive desires will, in a dissatisfied individual, lead (in the absence of guidance and education) directly to crimes on the part of those who desire. He will kill. But even this is better than education. (WE SHALL KILL DESIRE, WE SHALL LET <...>) Drunkenness is quite useful also, and pederasty, masturbation, as in Rousseau. All this tends to bring things down to a median level. ~~But~~ Best of all, destroy literacy and all books. We shall extinguish every genius even in his ~~soc. adolescence~~ infancy. Everything down to a common denominator, complete equality—but there must be a leader. There must be despotism—there has never been such thing as equality without despotism.

"Then everybody is going to enjoy most complete equality, i.e., despotism; ~~but such~~"

"But such equality is despotism."

"Oh, no! Such despotism is equality. There is nothing else. Fools who are dreaming of aluminum colonnades are lagging behind times."

"Call on the Jesuits and Catholicism, and let them guide us."

"An excellent idea! ~~Neither is it~~ yours. The Jesuits have known for a long time that they are going to be called on. But at this stage, certain words are still presenting an obstacle—republic, equality, Christianity. Some ideas, too, are still in our way: for instance, the Jesuits make everybody a slave, and equal, so they could themselves rule and live in luxury. They will never become the equals of everybody else."

"Yes, but things will get to that, too."

"No doubt this lofty idea will be realized one day! Despotism is of the essence, as are privileges to the few, so that all the rest could live in equality. To achieve this, one might even resurrect the papacy and turn the world over to it. I've been thinking that this is what Catholicism has been after all along. And all the rest of the people will be their slaves, yet equal among themselves, and free, and each spying on the other, and each informing on the other."

Nechaev: "We'll let the West daydream about aluminum, but we Russians have a much higher goal. Unlike the West, we aren't tied down by anything. The West finds it too hard to part with its heritage, though it be an evil one, because it is *their own*, developed by themselves. Whereas we are a vacant nation. Peter the Great relieved us of participation in our affairs, and so we can proceed directly to our bright idea of destroying everything."

"We are a consequence of Peter the Great."

03 *Nikolas <sic>*

Nikolas to Shatov: "Oh, no; I'm healthy, I'm not an epileptic, nor does a legion of demons dwell in me.+Our kind looks after our health; even in debauchery, we are careful. I lack the ability to go to any excesses, no matter what I'm doing."

"Did you say that you lack the ability to go to any excesses?" says Shatov (almost immediately after the Prince has admitted his marriage to the Lame Woman).

Nikolas to Nechaev, in Fedka's presence: "Lebiadkin has just received 2,000 rubles."

Nechaev takes the cue: "They don't even keep their doors locked."

(Nechaev shows Fedka a revolver and promises to give him one. Fedka shows his knife.)

Fedka has left. Nechaev tells the Prince (with deliberate naïveté): "Come to think of it, he was standing there and listening as we were talking about how they've got 2,000 rubles, with their doors unlocked: I'm afraid something might happen to them."

"It's all in God's hands," the Prince answers with a sneer, and both fall silent. (Nechaev knows perfectly well that the Prince deliberately said these things in Fedka's presence, and actually helped him to seal it, by mentioning that the door wasn't locked.)

Fedka later says to the Prince: "I ought to get a thousand or two from you for my services. I didn't find the 1,000 rubles at Lebiadkin's; in fact, I knew that I wasn't going to find them."

(The Prince kills him under a fence; nobody finds out about it.)

I.e., Fedka means to say: "You'll have to give me the money, *or I'll inform the police*" (even though he does not say that he will).

The Prince makes him believe that the money is hidden at such-and-such spot, under a fence.

N.B. Shatov says to Nechaev: "I know that you've caused the fire."

Nechaev, as he is about to leave Shatov, says: "I know that you know too much" (i.e., "you must be killed").

Shatov's formula: Salvation lies in Christ, and only we have Christ. If this is so, salvation must come from us.

All social doctrines are, at this stage, mere self-delusion. Nothing but bright patches. We must become completely regenerated, and therefore destruction—destruction for the sake of destruction! etc.

N.B. Shigalyov has developed his own system. Virginsky is rather more interested in aluminum. Shigalyov reaches a certain point and—stops. He quotes examples—the commune. Nechaev corrects him—*destruction for the sake of destruction, and then let happen what will.*

The Prince later asks Nechaev: "Are you making fun of them?"

Nechaev: "No, I am serious. Did you think that I was joking?"

The Prince: "No, I actually thought that you were serious: for this thing is as ridiculous as it is serious."

Here, Shatov: "Who then, can show us the way out? Christ!"

He gets up and leaves.

XV
Nechaev—Uncertain Chronology

Although these notes appear on successive notebook pages, they were written at different times and on substantially different subjects. Names such as Uspensky and Miliukov indicate early entries, and Virginsky and Liputin, later entries. Uspensky is, by and large, the early name for Virginsky, and Miliukov, for Liputin. No exact identifications are possible. These notes comprise pages 50–53 from notebook 3.

The content of these notes has a miscellaneous and fragmentary character, but the picture of Nechaev is not different from his portrayal throughout the notes.

---

0 ABOUT NECHAEV

After the first meeting. THE CONSPIRATOR Uspensky is not quite satisfied with Nechaev. He had been waiting for Nechaev as one waits for Heaven; ~~he~~ he won't *dare* to stand up openly against him, and for that matter, is afraid to admit his dissatisfaction to himself. Nevertheless, he wants to advertise himself, as well as to satisfy his own self-esteem, and so he is expounding his dreams of a Golden Age become real both to the Society (at the meeting) and to Nechaev himself, whom he manages to corner in private. A moral concept of happiness; happiness lies entirely in sacrificing everything to your neighbor; my own happiness rests with my neighbor's happiness; and so everybody will be happy in the society of the future (Fliorovsky, the Golden Age, *Dawn*, January).[1]

Miliukov who has been sniggering at these ideas even before, says that happiness lies in a rehabilitation of the flesh, that the rich should all be forced to work, that everybody should be rewarded according to his talents, and talent according to its proficiency, and that Uspensky's happiness is Christian religion all over again.

Nechaev, having listened initially to Uspensky only, says that all this

---

[1] See note 92.

is of course very good and may be realized later, but that for the time being this is not their principal object, which is to destroy everything. They immediately start to *battre la campagne,*[2] i.e., a torrent of verbiage to this effect. Altogether, they all speak very little, but rather each of them, after only a few words, mounts his own hobby-horse and stays there.

But when Nechaev hears Miliukov say that this is nothing but Christian religion (Uspensky's theory), he retorts: "If this is indeed Christian religion, let's pay no attention to it at all, because Christian religion must be totally eradicated, so that one could start a new life, and this one without any kind of God."

Miliukov and Uspensky get into an argument regarding the concept of happiness. Miliukov makes fun of the clergy, while Uspensky asserts that the formula *à chacun selon sa capacité*[3] is wrong, as is the rehabilitation of the flesh, but the important point is to sacrifice and sacrifice; then everybody will be mutually happy, for one need only assume that everybody will become like Christ (Shatov).

Shatov on the need to develop Orthodoxy. Miliukov points out Shatov to Uspensky and says: "There is your theory, everybody should become a monk and be humble." But Uspensky says: "No, enough of being humble."

Nechaev listens to them dully—he asks the most trivial details to be explained, and "what really matters is destruction." He hasn't come to argue, but to get things done, and, most important, to destroy. He's got an arsenal in our town and he is organizing.

Nechaev is in part Petrashevsky.[4]

51 (Here) 1.

Nechaev has only a few ideas which he uses to the hilt. He does not take into consideration locale, time, nationality, diversity. Whoever disagrees with him "has been bribed." Uspensky and Miliukov actually think sometimes that he is simply a nonentity, and stupid. He doesn't

---

[2] French: "scour the country."

[3] French: "everyone according to his capacity."

[4] Mikhail V. Petrashevsky (1821–66), leader of the mildly subversive circle, "The Petrashevsky Circle," which met in St. Petersburg between 1845 and 1849, which Dostoevsky attended from 1847 to 1849, and for which he, Petrashevsky, and others were arrested in 1849. Petrashevsky was condemned to life imprisonment. He remained an uncompromising enemy of the government to the end of his days.

care much for debating, is rarely interested, and usually indifferent. He has only one idea: *organize destruction.* Miliukov actually goes so far as to make fun of him, but sees to his surprise that the other man is so dense that he doesn't even understand it, and in fact doesn't seem to have time to try to understand it. But invariably, Miliukov and Uspensky end up viewing him once more with respect. ~~Every time~~ More and more, they become convinced that he is a man of action, who has no reason to become involved in debates like them, that he actually has no time for this. What then, is he doing? This always remains a mystery to them. However, the proclamations are being scattered all over. Kulikov gets killed. He has powerful friends everywhere; he goes to all kinds of places and is really setting himself up all around; and they begin to revere him. The notion that they have been sitting around, arguing and getting nothing done, while he is not ~~doing anything~~ arguing at all, but just doing everything, inspires them with awe. Little by little they begin to feel that they, too, have been sucked in, as if by a machine. He cleverly gets them involved in the murder of Shatov, so that they didn't have a chance to refuse.

As a type, he is pretty close to Petrashevsky.

Virginsky says: "How many mistakes, but then, how much fire!.."

Stepan Trofimovich: "And how many Yids?"

"There have always been Yids."

N.B. The difference between Nechaev and the rest of them. None of them would have used his *tone* in telling the story about those 80 copecks for the poor, or the story of how Fedka was sent away to be a soldier; but he does, and in the end everybody is convinced that this is how one must talk; in fact, everybody feels ashamed not having talked like that before.

(This is how Miliukov explains to Uspensky the difference between them and Nechaev.)

Shatov says to Uspensky: "The kingdom of heaven is at hand."[5]

Nechaev joins in: "Yes, in June."

The most important thing: Nechaev's denseness is simply outrageous, the denseness of a practical man.

---

[5] Apparently Matthew 3:2.

52 Here, 2

Somebody has brought Ivan Iakovlevich some tea. Nechaev says that one should not encourage <such things>, for the price of this pound of tea could be used for the common cause... (The lop-eared man and the girls.)

Liputin: "Why, hasn't it been used for the common cause?"

From among those present, several wits raise their voices asking: "What is the common cause?" "Aren't these the same good-for-nothings?" One of whom is indignantly ejected; whereupon a protest note, signed by everybody, is submitted.—

N.B. "So you think that the common cause is nothing but a bunch of good-for-nothings?"

"I think that they are, the way things are shaping up."

The Great Writer says to Nechaev: "I have made everybody here believe that you are an extraordinarily clever man, and they are quite crazy about you (the Governor's wife)." (N.B. While Varvara Petrovna, acting against the Governor's wife, started having her own soirées *to lure* Nechaev away. The rivalry contributes to Nechaev's fame, and *explains* his success. Nechaev then reconciles the two, in his own interest.)

Nechaev failed to grasp the caustic wit in the words of the Great Writer, who is thinking to himself: "Not only did he not understand my witticism, he actually couldn't care less if he did."

N.B. And so the Great Writer helps to spread Nechaev's fame, becoming the cornerstone of his fame.

The *Chronicler* describes this as simply as possible, *precisely the way it is written down here.*

Then the Chronicler adds, as a comment of his own: "It is amazing how ideas can spread: the Governor's wife and Varvara Petrovna were the first to be converted; then a lady comes home with the news of the reconciliation between Varvara Petrovna and the Governor's wife—and cuffs off her children ('Eh, you ought to be sent to reform school!'). Another one stops going to church (invent appropriate anecdotes for that), the third quarrels with her husband about the idea of free love. Finally, everybody joins in a pleasure ride to Ivan Iakovlevich's. (During the outing, The Prince and the Beauty, and the fire.)

The Governor talks to Nechaev and tells him that he is in perfect agreement with him. Alyosha Teliatnikov.

Some were sober.

Sacrilege in the Cathedral, an insult to the Bishop, and finally, leading to the two little merchants shedding tears for the Lord, to Captain Kartuzov, the lady who keeps discussing Finland, and the elderly couple.

1) Ivan Iakovlevich:

"Good-for-nothing stuff. He's got some good-for-nothing stuff and makes no bones about it, while you've got the same good-for-nothing stuff but think that it is the greatest wisdom."

Nechaev thinks that Ivan Iakovlevich has been bribed. Miliukov assures him that he is simply an imbecile.

2) Nechaev has this idea:

"Too bad! In his place, with the influence he's got, a lot could be done." (And he makes plans to convert him to his own beliefs.)

Baretails.

Blockheads.

Dearviews! Dearviews!
Newthoughts, newthoughts.
Highbreasts, highbreasts.

3 *The Great Writer* to Nechaev: "I've been always struck by the *absence of genuine knowledge* in our writers."

Nechaev has this to say about novelists: "Tell me, what good are they?"

The Great Writer: "Aren't you insulting me, saying this?" And later: "You are right, though, of course they are good for nothing."

Nechaev: "It is up to you to improve your activities, so that they would be of some use."

Nechaev tells Shatov, in part 1 (after the blow of the fist, in the street): "If they are clever, they can be talked to, and they will be ours in a quarter of an hour. If they are stupid, or if they have been bribed, they'll serve as kindling wood."

N.B. In these first brief words to Shatov, Nechaev appears sharp, self-assured, triumphant, expecting to meet no obstacles.

It has a sickening effect on Shatov, who feels a wave of cold and hatred surging inside himself. What he has been expecting for a long time, with fear and with anger, has come true.

Shatov: "I'll turn (the printing press) over to you."

Nechaev: "That's one of the reasons I've come here—where have you got it?"

"I've got everything buried.

"Underground?" "That's right." "That's good."

"Also, to talk to some people and to take certain measures."

"Try to talk."

N.B. Initially, Nechaev has the notion that Shatov, though a Slavophile, is an embittered man and could therefore be of some use, and work with them. He actually tries to persuade him in this sense, displaying an unwavering moral superiority.

"This is incompatible," says Shatov.

"If this is so, you've been bribed," Nechaev decides, and informs Liputin accordingly. The latter seeks to convince Nechaev that one can have different convictions without having been bribed, but Nechaev would not accept that.

Nechaev is stupid as the *elder Princess,* Bezukhov's relation.[6] But his whole strength lies in the fact that he is a man of action.

---

[6] A reference to *War and Peace;* a relative of Pierre's natural father, one of the Mamontov sisters.

XVI
The Prince and Tikhon—Miscellaneous Entries

These notes comprise pages 25, 26, 41, 46, 104–07, and 110 from notebook 3. The pages have been grouped by subject matter from those notebook pages whose chronology is uncertain. Some of the entries are more or less, by name and subject matter, chronologically determinable, but there is not enough data to make a fairly probable determination, and it was consequently thought better to present them in this way.

1 *A page on* THE BISHOP AND THE PRINCE.

The Prince is about to leave (after the question "Do you believe in God?") when the Bishop calls him back:

"Tell me, I adjure you, were you telling me the truth, or did you make it all up?"

The Prince, looking at him: "Did I make it all up?"

The Bishop looks at him, thinks for a moment, and blesses him: "Go in peace."

Whereupon, on the following day, a note from the Prince: "I made it all up myself, and rest assured that ~~as I say this~~ I am not lying now. If for no other reason, though I am not afraid of it becoming public ~~this now~~, as I am writing this, for you are not going to tell it to anybody, then ~~only~~ because of desire my ~~desire~~ to mitigate somewhat my unworthy conduct toward you. I was not quite myself; it is an affliction of mine; forgive me then, and pray for me,

your son Stavrogin.

The Bishop responded on the very same day:

"And I beseech you to postpone your great moral feat for the time being, as I advised you, for I can see that you won't be able to cope with it. Fortify yourself first, ~~find the strength in yourself~~ gain mastery over yourself, acquire the power of persistence, get prepared, and then, if you ~~have the strength~~ can, do it. For the feat it too great ~~strong~~.

N.B. *Later,* the Prince must absolutely, once more in the novel, drop a hint (he actually says it in his note about Uri written at the railway station) which would make it quite clear to the reader that he actually did commit the sin, and that he did not lie to Tikhon. "Let Tikhon pray for me," he writes.

N.B. Shatov reads an article entitled "The Russian Liberal" at the public lecture.

N.B. The Prince tells Shatov about the happiness of being in contact with nature (a surge prior to an epileptic seizure), *Götter Griechenlands,** and that God speaks to man.

The Prince tells Shatov about the Apocalypse, about the mark of the name of the beast, whose head was wounded.[1] The whole difference between the Prince's and Shatov's convictions lies in the fact that Shatov is still standing before a locked door, while the Prince has already accepted all the consequences as well as *the main idea,* namely that *Orthodoxy* is the main foundation of a new civilization out of the East. The Bishop then deals the Prince the final blow by imposing on him the obligation of self-regeneration, self-improvement, i.e., the necessity of the practical duties of Orthodoxy as one conceives of Orthodoxy.

26 2)

It then develops that the Prince fascinates Shatov with his idea of Orthodoxy, i.e., with the catechism of a new religion which must be accepted, at any cost, by every new man.

The Bishop says that a catechism of the *new religion* is fine, but that faith is dead without deeds, and demands not a superior feat (superior classicism), but something even more difficult—Orthodox *work,* i.e., *"well, you fine gentleman you, do you think you can do it?"* And the Prince must admit that he is still a gentleman, assures the Bishop that he has been lying, and disavows his own words; as a result: *Uri.*

The meaning: The Bishop proves to him that one must not make a leap, but that one must rather regenerate the image of man in oneself (through long-lasting work, and only then vault ahead).

"So one can't do it all at once?"

---

* German: "The Gods of Greece," a poem by Schiller (1788).

[1] Revelation 13:3, 16.

"No, one can't. It would only turn the work of angels into a work of the devil."

The Prince: "Alas, I knew that myself."

THE PRINCE AND THE BISHOP.

In the Prince's note on the rape there is this spot:

..."I did all this as a gentleman would, as an idle man, uprooted from the soil. Even though I can see that most of the fault lay with my own evil will, and not with the environment alone, ~~but you~~. Of course, ~~few~~ nobody commits crimes such as mine; yet all of them (those uprooted from the soil) are doing the same, though on a smaller scale, and not quite as strong. Many of them don't even notice their own dirty game and consider themselves to be honest men"... etc.

My future judges.

The Bishop says that it might be better to omit this section. The Prince seems offended.

"I am no man of letters," he says.

THE PRINCE'S CENTRAL IDEA, WHICH FASCINATED HIM AND WHICH HE HAD FULLY AND PASSIONATELY ADOPTED, WAS THE FOLLOWING:

WHAT REALLY MATTERS IS NOT INDUSTRY, BUT MORALITY, not the ~~industrial~~ economic, but the moral rebirth of Russia.

"You go ahead and tell them, and you'll see what they'll tell you!" says Shatov.

"If they won't understand me now, they're bound to understand me eventually."

"Of course, everything will come about in due course, but we will fall far back in our development if we won't be aware of our goal. Whereas if the contrary were true and we would achieve moral self-awareness, we would not only increase our economic power tenfold, but would also allow its development to assume an independent character."

(—"Words, nothing but words.")

"Yes, but I wish this idea would spread at least in words."

Nechaev guffaws at Granovsky's having gotten so high a price for his estate.

1 The Polish priest later complained that Stepan Trofimovich had

kept some of the money that was due him, and Nechaev picked up that matter.

At this point we do not need socialism yet, and it is with us merely a result of excessive sentimentality, one might say, and... and... also a kind of gentleman's fancy.

Socialism. (Stepan Trofimovich:) "I suppose it may actually come from sentimentality (yet how many houses, Yids feathering their own nests, etc.)."

N.B. This is said during his argument with his son, as they are exchanging caustic remarks.

THE STOCK-EXCHANGE ASPECT OF SOCIALISM.

1) *Tikhon.*

Tikhon: "I am a *daydreamer.*"

"I imagine it to be like this: a soul, while wandering about, will suddenly see its whole sinfulness, but not the way it does now, but the *whole* of it, and at the same time see that God is opening his arms to receive it in his embrace—then, having realized the whole truth, it will become most exasperated and will itself ask to be punished, and will seek punishment; but it will get love in return—and thus it will find its hell. To be conscious of an unfulfilled love must be the most terrible thing of all, and so that's what hell really is.

"What did I give you?—Eternal happiness. And what did you make of it?—Eternal unhappiness."

"This is quite clear to me, quite clear!"

The soul will learn that ~~there is~~ each and every one is responsible for everything.

"It was as close as possible to you; it was in your hands; man will realize with the utmost clarity that everything, absolutely *everything* in the world, during his earthly existence, depends on Him alone! Everything that did happen, and even things he wasn't even aware of ~~I thought to bear~~ could have followed the example of Christ, could have been full of His love, and His love alone."

The notion to surrender ~~I~~ *one's own I* has been confirmed to the point where there exists an urge to surrender it.

There is a higher being and, in return for it, happiness.

There is a spider creeping there.

A small one.

There is so little time in the world that one is surprised that we are still devout people; that we still remember God; somehow or other; that we haven't forgotten Him despite all our business. Frivolity devours us.

The Prince: "I do not believe in God, while you do believe. How can you say that God will forgive?"

"Oh, I really don't understand it myself. Sin is infinite ~~yet~~ yet God in His wisdom is infinite also."

The end in sight.

1)

THE PRINCE AND TIKHON

1) "How can we have such high understanding?" says Tikhon.

"Say 'how can I?', please do!" says the Prince.

"Why do you want me to say that?"

"When one says *we*, it is as if one were hiding behind everybody else, so say it simply for yourself: 'How can I?' "

"How can I have such understanding?" Tikhon repeated.

"That's it. *I love you very much*," said the Prince. "You must be a great prelate," he adds with a mocking smile.

Tikhon looked around: "*Fever*."

The Prince: "Tell me, what good are all these moral feats, if there is no God."

2) Tikhon: "Why do you absolutely need God? Doesn't your conscience speak to you through your suffering? Later you will also come to believe in God."

The Prince: "Yes, of course, my question is an inane one."

Tikhon: "Perhaps not quite so."

The Prince: "The Woman question—that is my sore spot. Women and the Woman question. A lack of originality. They are foolish enough to think that they have solved all the problems by establishing a new order. How can you accomplish anything but trivialities if you lack individuality, if you lack originality. You'll be unfaithful to your husband in a trivial way, you'll go to work in the same trivial bookbinder's shop, and you won't ever come up with anything better. Look at your needlewomen: they're all doing the same kerchief or embroidery, and that's why it is so hard to sell the stuff and make a living. You become midwives in droves, one after the other. There just aren't enough babies born. You simply can't do things without having your own initiative and your own individuality. And that's what you haven't got, an individuality. And how could you get one, never having had one! An individuality must be developed, it must grow according to laws. An individuality must be *earned through long service*... and where are you going to serve? You have no originality, no individuality, *no manhood*—how vile!"

"I get down on my knees barefoot and pray, but the next morning my faith is gone again."

"Because everything I say comes naturally, while you are only putting on a show."

"They are telling you that there is no God, and you believe them, not knowing yourself why, because you've let a seminarian talk you into it."

The Prince and Tikhon. "Mine is an idle mind, and I am bored. I know that one can (and must) be happy on Earth and that there really is something that makes for happiness, but which I am not aware of, ~~and therefore~~ and that's why I am so sad, because I don't know what that thing might be."

"No, I am not one of those disenchanted people. I think that I am one of those depraved and idle ~~minds~~."

Tikhon gives him the advice to conquer himself, and says exactly what *Nicolas* has been telling Shatov only recently. *Nicolas* listens in wonder and says to Tikhon: "Go on, go on, tell me more, continue." And later:

"I said myself exactly the same things only recently, and while you were speaking I was wondering all the time how our minds could have met so exactly."

Tikhon says: "So then, there's the solution, and you believe in it."

"No, I don't."

"No, you do, but you lack the strength."

The Prince to him: "I want to try my strength." And he tells him about the little girl.

Tikhon advises against it and suggests that <he should reform> gradually.

As a result, he goes to Dasha and suggests Switzerland to her—to repent. She agrees—and suddenly—the murder.

Tikhon says: "One must be happy on earth."

4 The Prince says: "Do you know that there is such thing as a passion for the pangs of conscience?"

That's what Tikhon says.

The Prince realizes that he could be saved by enthusiasm (for instance, monkhood, or self-sacrifice through a confession). But to have enthusiasm, he lacks *moral* feeling (partly from lack of faith). *And unto the angel of the church in Sardis write.*[2] In part, from vehement bodily instincts. *He got married out of proud irony at his own lack of control over himself.* From his passion for torture, he violated a child. *A passion for the pangs of conscience.* Sensuality—Liza, HERE after having taken possession of her, he kills the Lame Woman. After the murder of Shatov, a fit of madness (words of supplication), and he hangs himself. Melancholy. But the most important thing is still—his lack of faith. Horror at himself: for instance, at his realization that he derives pleasure from inflicting suffering.

The Prince says to Shatov: "It was then that I got the idea of killing myself; but that wasn't enough for me. Why not ruin other peoples' lives? I had a desire to play some awful joke on myself and on I-don't-know-what."

"A passion for the pangs of conscience. What a case of overstrained nerves!" says Shatov.

The Prince tells Tikhon outright that he sometimes deeply suffers from the pangs of conscience, but that sometimes these very same pangs of conscience turn into a pleasure for him. (Pins under the fingernails of a child.)

Moral feeling has nothing to lean upon.

Tikhon tells him directly: "You have no soil <to take roots in>. A foreign education. Learn to love the people, their sacred faith. Learn to love to the point of exaltation."

The Prince to him: "I also love the foreign, I love science, art."

Tikhon: "Like a visitor, and not like a master in his own house. You love science—why haven't you become a man of science? You love all mankind—but do you believe in it? Do you believe in God and in Christ?"

5 *Tikhon:* "Strong sensations, never guided by anything. Millions get

---

[2] See note 186.

away with that. Some have their fun with various toys (being decorated, having their calling cards, carriages, accumulating money)—but *strong characters* are not so easily pleased with themselves, and they are looking for a solid rock upon which to rest. You haven't found that rock. For there is only one, and you don't believe in Him.

"You know of nothing sacred!"

"Try to hold something sacred, no matter what it be."

"What for?"

~~"If you say 'what for?' this means that you are utterly unprepared."~~ "This isn't done '*for something*,' it is done '*just so*.' ~~It carries its own reward~~. It has irresistible attraction—for it is harmony. If you do not feel a need, and if you love nothing, you're obviously incapable of it. But woe to him who is the cause of temptation."

Nikolai Vsevolodovich: explains how there can be beauty even in the scalded little hand of a child.

(Because he hasn't got any soil.)

The Slap in the Face

A Moment:

The Prince: "Why won't you tell me what you wanted to say? Maybe you wanted to say something?"

Shatov: "I've said everything." (And he leaves.)

The Prince does not love Liza: he acts from boredom.

N.B. Perhaps he does love her, but only sensuously, for a moment, and even that from boredom. Before Shatov, for instance, and before Dasha, he denies that he loves Liza only a few days before he takes possession of her.

106 The Prince hands Nikon a handwritten note after their first conversation.

Then, the handwritten note.

Then, the second conversation, and finally, "at Tikhon's" (ONE CHAPTER).

Stepan Trofimovich's wandering—also one chapter.

The Prince's relations with Liza and Dasha:

Having taken possession of Liza—and having put the Lame Woman out of his way—the Prince tells Liza that he apparently never did love her at all, but that it was simply one of those things.

(N.B. Better make it so that Liza, after having submitted, falls ill and keeps repeating to him: "Don't or didn't I know that you were incapable of love"—she falls into a delirium, and dies.)

As for Dasha, not a word about her throughout the entire novel. The Prince is treating her as if she were a stranger. It was she herself who wanted to get married to Stepan Trofimovich, right until his running away.

And here, suddenly, the Prince proposes to her (before Uri).

The Prince fully believes both in the Antichrist and in salvation through Orthodoxy. But inasmuch as he, in his own conscience, has *insufficient* faith, he proposes this formula:

"If I believe insufficiently, I believe in nothing at all."

Incidentally, *Tikhon* has this to say on this score:

"Yes, this is true in the cases of some ~~strong~~ people who take a strong stand, WHO INSIST, and who are asking for much. But there are others who are content with a small faith, and who get accustomed to living on trembling soil, as long as the tremors aren't too strong."

0 *Tikhon*: "I am making my suggestions according to your own wishes. I don't mind if 10 years hence it will turn out to have been all nonsense, i.e., you didn't become a believer after all. But then at least you've done all you could, for your conscience."

Tikhon's main idea:

"The only freedom is to conquer oneself."

"A slave and yet a free man."

XVII
Miscellaneous Entries

No attempt has been made to place these notes in any order—either chronological or by subject matter. In both, they are varied. Many of the notebook pages have entries from different times; some have entries of an ambiguous nature, such as reference to one of the commonplaces of the romantic intrigue; and some, though partially identifiable, are sufficiently vague to be placed here. They are presented in numerical order. The notes comprise these pages from notebook 3: 2–6, 13, 16–17, 28, 30, 32, 42, 44, 45, 116.

---

2 After a day had passed he began to look for the reason why they were trying to get him married. The locomotive was puffing and pattering along the tracks as if it were repeating over and over again: *Vek i vek i Lev Kambek*[1] <"Age and age, and Lev Kambek.">.

33 minutes past 11, page 1

20 minutes past 12

Half past 2

<A page of arithmetic calculations and book-keeping entries.>

~~He~~ A moment later, it seemed, he had already forgotten what had happened and was viewing the events that had taken place as if from a distance. Having looked all around, and having realized what had happened, he smiled in a way that seemed both malicious and gay. Another moment later he was pale and shaking all over. There was a most frightful noise—nobody was understanding a thing, yet no one dared to take action. ~~Finally, right then and there, Nikolai Vsevolodovich was unanimously expelled from the Society.~~ He began to laugh and left.

---

[1] This ditty appears in the final version as the refrain Stepan Trofimovich murmurs to the noise of the train as he and Barbara Stavrogin return from their disastrous trip to St. Petersburg liberal circles in the mid-fifties. *Vek* was a weekly liberal newspaper which appeared in St. Petersburg in 1861–62. Lev Kambek was the publisher of *The Family Hearth* (1859–60) and *The St. Petersburg Messenger* (1861–62). The rhyme parodies journalistic nonsense.

Pale and trembling. Having cast a glance at them, he left, seemingly downcast.

"You aren't angry, of course, are you?"

"The ear—why shouldn't I be pulling it?" he burst out laughing. "Liputin, my coat."[2]

Varvara Petrovna: "Don't be afraid, he won't dare in front of the Great Writer."

On Shakespeare:

This is non-tendentious, and eternal, and it has survived.

This is not a simple reproduction of everyday life, ~~in~~ which, as many scholars assert, exhausts the whole of reality.

The whole of reality is not exhausted by everyday life, for a ~~great~~ huge part of it is present in it in the form of a still latent, unexpressed, future Word. From time to time there appear prophets who divine and express this integral word. Shakespeare is a prophet, sent by God, so as to reveal to us secrets about man, about the human soul.

"A prophet and anointed, you can't say that, Sir."

"Do you know what the word 'anointed' means?"

Thou shalt not be saved unless thou hast sinned.

3 We have two kinds of gentlemen. There is something half-baked about the first kind, while the other is almost absurdly ~~firm and defined~~ sharply outlined. Then there is naturally also the golden mean, those who are just having a good time of it.

Granovsky: "And we are the half-baked ones, while the well-defined ones are all those seminarians of ours. And here they are. There is something frightfully precocious about them."

Cheap self-satisfaction.

That's where he was simply showing off. Any influential person has a tendency to show off in the circle of his friends, if he is their acknowledged leader and if these friends ~~to him~~ are beginning to bore him

---

[2] The reference to the ear and to Liputin and the coat probably are sketchy references to Stavrogin's scandalous deeds of the first part of the novel: biting the Governor's ear and kissing Mme. Liputin.

somewhat. ~~However, he said~~ He was doing it all to make Shatov furious. He dearly liked it to drive Shatov mad on occasion.

~~But Shatov~~ "Before you start talking to him you must always tie him up first," Stepan Trofimovich concluded. He was laughing very hard.

While it was possible, indeed, to get Liputin involved in a frenzied debate, nobody could ever tease him with impunity, for he had his own malicious way of killing an argument with a joke. Yet Liputin—a gossip and a scandalmonger, and ~~perhaps~~ an unscrupulous man—was not a young man. He enjoyed Stepan Trofimovich's hospitality because of an old acquaintanceship. He was the oldest of us all and, moreover, a proven liberal. Shatov and Virginsky, on the contrary, were still young men and, on occasion, the hapless victims of Stepan Trofimovich's wit.

Shatov, even though Shatov later <. . .> "One must tie Shatov's hands." Yet he used to make fun of Shatov, while Liputin <. . .>

As for Virginsky, he was not very different from some seminarians whom I have <. . .>

"We are all half-baked, there aren't any well-defined characters among us."

"And who am I?" asked Liputin.

"Why, you are the golden mean, he who has a good time of it."

He liked to tease Shatov.

To make them furious, Virginsky, Shatov

"I was talking about Liputin."

(. . .) so

you must talk with Shatov only after having tied his hands first.

Believed in God.

Later. It may really turn out later that this is even more than necessary. "In any case, you shouldn't believe me," which is true of all of us,* and as Herzen said of them.

He would insist, much too strongly, on never giving in to Stepan

---

* Or, ". . . which, *entre nous,* is true of everybody. . ."

Trofimovich, and would actually go into a frenzy during his debates with him. "One must tie Shatov's hands," etc.

Return to me, Paul,
I'd straighten you out myself.*

4 <Calendar entries for 1870>

The idea of panslavism. The help of the committees must be extended not only to the Slavs, but even to Russians, in order to prepare them for the idea of panslavism and to confirm it in their minds.

And to this end:

Set up courses in the history of Russia and of panslavism aimed at demonstrating the organic ties linking all Slavs.

Classical education is mandatory, in order that the new Panslav might completely understand the West and consciously realize what he is about to give ~~in~~ to the world, something that is so different from what the West has given it, and why he has a right to hope that the Slavic idea will regenerate the world.

It is impossible to get to know the West without a classical education.

And so, help the Slavs, while preparing the material in Russia <...>

Pascal

"I'm sure you didn't say that: that must be somebody else's."

......

"Occasionally, I succeeded even in Russian, not often, but occasionally, yes."

"Aren't you a Slavophile?"

"*Oh que non!*[3] I leave that to Shatov."

"What about him?"

"He has fallen into Pietism—keeps preaching."

The day after tomorrow.

"What about Liputin?"

"A member of your family? This was a most unexpected surprise for me."

Did he really consider him capable of such a trick ~~in his~~ while in full possession of his faculties?"

---

* Trochaic tetrameter, with rhyme.

[3] French: "Ah, but no!"

In Moscow, across the post office. School of Painting. Vasily Grigorievich Perov.[4]

5 <Arithmetic calculations and calendar and book-keeping entries.>

6 *Shatov,* the day before his death, tells his wife (about Uspensky). While on earth, love everybody more than oneself, do good deeds, pass on regretted, receive even from others the good that comes with the torments of happiness, ~~a happiness which~~ for them, etc. A rapturous tirade.

Shatov to the Prince (rapturously): "We are the new Russia, independent Russia, we are looking for and we are pointing toward her independence. We are a hard rock in a weathered stratum."

Shatov says: "Russian freethinking (ATHEISM) never went much beyond a pun."

Stepan Trofimovich: "The destruction of our forests, that's an idea. Already after rods. This idea is more serious than you think."

Shatov speaks with his wife about the ideals of the holy elders and the impotence of nihilism and all new ideas, about their petit-bourgeois lack of talent, about envious equality, about the leveling effect of mediocrity.

13 PRINCIPAL IDEAS

"That can't be us, not us," says Stepan Trofimovich, looking at his son.

"It is you!" Shatov says to him, "only you aren't recognizing yourself; you were godless while wallowing in your humanitarian sentiments; you considered it a crime to be like your people; nor did you understand that a man cannot live without God, but will ask for a new morality; that he can't lose his independence without surrendering to spiritual sloth; that he can't despise his native country."

The Ward, seeing Stepan Trofimovich's humiliation, tells him about her love (she makes a confession).

---

[4] Vasily G. Perov (1833–82), a painter. One of the famous portraits of Dostoevsky was done by him.

She fears for Liza, comes running to her: "Take care, he is married, he is capable of anything.

The Prince does not believe in God and yet fears: "What will happen to me in the other world? (There absolutely must be something there.)"

3d part. Had Nechaev wanted to attain his objective (TO BEGIN) through cunning, and through knowledge of human nature (to reconcile the Governor's wife), he could not have invented anything more suitable. "A smart man," people say, yet he acted quite naïvely.

6 BON-MOTS IN GENERAL

He spluttered.

Pascal.

The half-baked and the overcooked.

"I'm telling you, it will turn out that this is a most unusual Lame Woman."

We pray to God that he may save ~~beloved~~ our beloved Russia from any trials. But if she is destined to experience such in this most difficult age of ours, we pray to God that he may save her Monarch, the Emancipator, and that his ministers might be such as you are.

Shatov pawns his revolver when his wife comes home to give birth to her child.

THE PRINCE SAYS TO NECHAEV: "YOU AREN'T AN AGENT OF THE HIGHER SECRET POLICE, ARE YOU, SENT HERE TO EXTRACT FROM US THE FINAL REMNANTS OF THIS ABOMINATION?"

At the literary matinee (~~after~~ Stepan Trofimovich, in a frenzy, lectures on the Madonna and develops his idea on the abolition of history; the fires at the Tuileries). Nechaev says to his father: "You did, however, didn't you, lose Fedka in a game of cards? How do you mean, it isn't the environment? But for you, he would not have become a murderer and a convict."

All: "Yes! yes!" etc.

Stepan Trofimovich, after having met *the book-hawker*: "I didn't know that *here* (among the people) things are so solid. *C'est presque beau c'est beau tout à fait,*[5] if I hadn't been afraid of being a retrograde."

---

[5] French: "It's almost beautiful, it's completely beautiful."

"A kingdom of lumber as opposed to a kingdom of stone; plenty of birch trees, and therefore a Spanish grandee has developed one notion of honor, and we another, precisely because we had so many birch trees. The abolition of corporal punishment will coincide with the annihilation of our forests."

(This, at the time of his arrest.)

plus de moines que de raison.[6]

"Why, it's his nameday."

"Mais il a tant d'esprit."

"Madame je ne suis pas si bête que j'en ai l'air en votre présence."[7]

A particular case.

It was uttered in so loud a voice that I had no choice but not to hear it. Naturally I didn't hear a thing.

So that I didn't hear it, of course.

17 "Yes, I do feel that I am going somewhere."

Stepan Trofimovich, after his arrest and after having returned from his visit to the Governor: "Somehow, I have just budged from a place I had occupied for twenty years, and I have gone... or flown somewhere. I don't know where to, but I have taken off."

Tikhon: "He who will come at the twelfth hour." Song of the angels.

The word is infinitely generous.

"And I shall bury him, like a neighbor."

"He says that a cockroach <...>"

"My dear."

There is no greater freedom than that of conquering oneself.

Stepan Trofimovich: "The recipient of a good deed invariably experiences, aside from the natural feeling of gratitude toward his benefactor, also a certain feeling of hatred—I don't know why, but it is always that way."

---

[6] French: "more monks than reason."

[7] French: "But he has so much spirit." "Madame, I'm not as foolish as I may seem to be in your presence."

Nechaev: "There must be a constant rumor abroad, about some sort of a conspiracy against the people."

"A rumor that the land will be taken away from the peasants is most useful."

"Every cattle plague, every fire, they must all be exploited by us. But most of all, disorder."

The idea of man's irresponsibility.

Support the enthusiasm generated by shattered nerves, along with the crookedness of a Stellovsky—and the resulting clash will create desperation.

Question: "Who is it they'll rebel against? Now it is good."

Answer: "Even if it were good, that would mean things are very bad. The more delay in the further course of progress. The better the worse, and the worse the better. It's only a pity that we don't have any proletarians."

"We've got some."

"If so, then only as an exception. There will be some in the future, no doubt, but still it's a long time to wait for them. Might be a good idea to make some, like say, by spreading literacy."

Karmazinov: "I can't understand why you people are so much against me."

Kartuzov: "As for God, I don't recognize him at all."

Nechaev and Karmazinov: "There is no great guiding idea. There's *au jour le jour,*[8] it has always been that way. We conservatives are the greatest (EVEN GREATER) nihilists, I've always felt so. You people at least have enthusiasm. So he has killed a coachman—*Enthusiasm of shattered nerves.* It has always been that way. I've taken a close look at our conservatives in general, and here's the result: they only pretend that they believe in something and that they stand for something in Russia, whereas in reality we conservatives are even greater nihilists. The boy and Château d'Yquem, Smolny monastery, the Crusades. A good cook, an estate. I'm hastening to sell my estate and get out of here. When is it going to happen (i.e., the revolution)?"

---

[8] French: "from day to day."

Who: Speransky[9] or Karamzin? The question ought to be put that way—who is progressive: Speransky or Karamzin? Yet he takes exactly the same view, and only asks that one be a trifle more respectful toward Karamzin. Why, that's worse than nihilism. Exactly the same thing with religion.

The lectures are marvel<the rest of the word is illegible> of the sun, the moon.

116 CURRENT INCIDENTALS FOR PART 2.

After the slap in the face. I must shorten my narrative. This slap, a difficulty, in a week <her> marriage to Mavriky.

A beneficient genius had arranged everything—Nechaev. A description of him, his row with his father, etc., his role in the incident with the slap in the face ~~etc.~~, at the Governor's, at Liza's, etc.—

The Prince says to Nechaev: "I do, however, owe you a debt of gratitude for the service you have done me in clearing up ~~the matter involving~~ the Lame Woman. N.B. He is saying this with a sneer, seeing that Nechaev is seeking to ingratiate himself with him, trying to make himself useful: however, he does take advantage of his services.

Toward the very end of the novel, when the footman announces that the Prince has suddenly arrived at Skvoreshniki, the Prince orders a *rabbit,*[10] inspects the gallery in the ballroom, "the old musicians, they've lost their mouthpiece."

"All because I don't know which is better, pins under the fingernails, or Christ" (in his letter).

121 IDEAS FOR NEW NOVELS

Nastasia is a tall house serf, actually with a pock-marked face, quiet. The master arrives, lives with her, gets her with child, Grigory and Fedosia, he marries, she dies in childbirth.

---

[9] Mikhail M. Speransky (1772–1839), a government official who came to have great influence on Alexander I, especially in regard to domestic affairs. He drew up many reforms and envisaged a constitutional monarchy. He is satirized in *War and Peace.*

[10] Compare with the conversation between Stavrogin and Shatov in the final version (Part II, Chapter 1:7) concerning catching one's hare before cooking it, symbolically believing in God before having a doctrine based on his existence.

The Prince and the Beauty

The Beauty is in love with the Prince. She is afraid of him, and angry at herself for being afraid. She conceals her feelings from the Prince, because of her pride. ~~Very glad~~ She won't admit to herself that she loves the Prince and is very glad that she can become involved with Nechaev. She happily lets herself be carried away by the moment. She is shocked by the murder, but is still struggling with herself. Finally, loathing overcomes <her love for> him; she leaves Nechaev, but it is already too late.

What is needed here is an ambiguous (AND BEAUTIFUL) scene where she, for once, reveals her feelings to the Prince, wanting to entice him, where she gives herself to him, where she *calls him*. But he won't follow her. "My life is not destined for happiness!" Then she leaves him with *bloody revenge* in her heart, and surrenders herself to Nechaev.

The Prince tells her outright: *"I never loved you, I can't love you."*

His mother to the Prince, playing with his hair: "You are melancholy and bored, it becomes you well."

The door closed: the Beauty blushed and began to stamp her feet. She is in love with him.

Though the door was closed, the Prince saw everything, knew it as if by heart, that's what is strange.

Bons-Mots

Our liberals are flunkeys by their very nature; all they are looking for is a chance to shine some German's shoes.

All this is long gone and forgotten.

It really takes a great man to resist common sense, if necessary.

It may also take a fool, or a scoundrel.

Kartuzov: "Your Excellency, Russia is *a freak of nature* (and enough)."

The Governor: ~~That is how~~ "A freak of nature?"

Kartuzov: "Russia is a misunderstanding, a tremendous misunderstanding, and therefore a caprice of nature, and not of the intellect."

The Governor: "So you are a philosopher?"

Kartuzov: "Of the Cynic sect, your Excellency."

Granovsky: "The whole of Russia is a tremendous misunderstanding, and one is inclined to believe the Captain when he says that Russia is a freak of nature."

Lizaveta asks: "If I were to break my leg, Captain, would you lose your affection for me?"

"Even if you broke both legs."

"Can you love a woman who is on crutches?"

He takes out a poem: "Only to you,

"In the event *she* might break her leg."

"Allow me, do allow me to read it, Captain."

Reading. She blushes, gives it back to him, and nods.

A puny little captain, from a little sheet of paper—*

She leaves. Nechaev says that if he weren't so stupid he could very well be a socialist and—what's the use of being clever? When everything is cut down to the same size? (Granovsky on the attack) (This, in reply to Lizaveta's question: "Do you know him? He reared you.")

The Great Writer's bons-mots.

Granovsky: "Every time I look at his face he reminds me of little Pisarev."

"Why little?"

"And you, you are so great, aren't you?"

Granovsky: "Ivan Turgenev, Bazarov, puppies in the sun."

"Leave me the initiative of the good."

"He has given the poor 80 copecks."

"Himself marrying a dowry of 8,000."

32 Current Page

"*Je suis un* man with his back to the wall."

42 In a word, he raised so much fuss that they preferred not to put him on trial.

Current Notes for Chapter 5.

Varvara Petrovna's education

He was in America for three months—in the East.

She expected her son back for Christmas (rumors about him in Petersburg, with the Minister), and that's why she was in a hurry to get the Ward married before he was back.

---

* This rhymes in Russian: *Kapitashka iz bumazhki* (which sounds like a ditty).

Varvara Petrovna, in a brief note to Stepan Trofimovich. He has changed in many respects, but is full of joy as ever, and still suffering from his old boredom, though he is not complaining.

Our former governor, the kindly Ivan Osipovich, was relieved because of important instances of dereliction of duty. It was rumored that, to some extent, it happened on account of Varvara Petrovna, that is, because of her running the province. The Chief of Police displayed his patent disrespect for her by arresting her personal valet for creating a disturbance in the street.

"Well, he's really got himself in a pickle! One thinks of a man, while he..." "Why, isn't that, too, ~~isn't it~~ a translation from the French; what do you think?" exclaimed the Prince, pointing at the book.

"No, Sir, not from the French. This, Sir, is a translation from the universally-human, from the language, Sir, of the universally-human republic, that's what it is, Sir."

"Fie, the devil take it, why, there isn't such nation!" remarked Stavrogin.

He was walking along and thinking to himself, how propaganda, ~~in~~ a government official, in a far away town, of the judiciary, taking bribes, living by intrigue, keeping his wife locked up, counting short, keeping her in the fear of God. Nobody within a hundred versts has even heard of Fourier, and yet there he is, a Fourierist, and thinking. Propaganda. That's how it works. He will take you for a walk, then wipe his feet clean, and who could figure out how all this was brought on, or how it is going to be taken out again.*

The Princess to Granovsky: "I am convinced that it was Shatov who wrote (the anonymous letters)."

Granovsky: "Exactly, I think so too, but I don't want to get mixed up in this, and I suggest that even you, my dear Varvara Petrovna, hint to no one. Besides, I like the boy. He is in love *sans que cela paraîtra, sans que cela paraîtra*."[11]

("It may well be that you are actually glad about that letter," thinks the Princess.)

---

* The meaning is not quite clear in the original. There is also an untranslatable pun in this sentence: *provesti* means "to accompany, to take for a walk," but also "to cheat, to fool."

[11] French: "without seeming to be, without seeming to be."

The Princess: "You insisted on presenting a scene from *Polinka Saks.*"

Granovsky: "But for goodness's sake, there isn't any similarity at all."

The Princess: "Forget about your erudition for the time being. You've understood me, and that's that."

Liputin had arranged the lecture at a local landowner's house. But somehow a *police officer* got in. He was incessantly mentioning the name of a certain Podvysotsky,[12] perhaps a former patron of his, or simply a person who had somehow captured his imagination, and whom he kept assiduously advertising all the time.

C'est un chenapan,[13] but there's a principle involved here.

Stepan Trofimovich, though *a bit fearful,* was finding the notion of being accused a most intriguing one. Perhaps, Varvara Petrovna, too, will show up with the daughter. Shatov gave him a ruble, expecting to meet Varvara Petrovna. As for Liputin, he actually had some relatives on the police force. Stepan Trofimovich always used to call him "a provident man."

44 The Prince and the Beauty. He left (their house, on the first day), kissing her hand.

There follows an analysis: The Prince knew what was going on here, he could guess it. He saw clearly that she was in love with him, whereas her love for *the other man* was just a fancy. She wanted to cut him to the quick by the kiss of the hand. He rather ~~liked it~~ liked it. "That cat has scratched me up, but is suffering herself, as if this meant goodbye forever! *What use is that to me?*"

He entered the Governor's mansion, lost in thought. He caught up with the coachman, and drove up to the entrance.

Chatoff

While his wife is resting, Shatov keeps walking up and down the tiny room, saying to himself: "How good it is to live quietly, to love, to have children," etc.

When it became known that Shatov has been killed, Varvara Petrovna is the first to scream out loud and to burst into tears.

---

12 He does not appear in the final version.

13 French: He's a scoundrel."

Shatov pawned his revolver when his wife returned to him to give birth to her child.

They used a trick to lure him to the place where the printing press had been buried. For Shatov thought that they had already removed everything.

Nechaev does not recognize any differences between nationalities and asserts that everything happens according to one and the same law. He sees nothing about Russia that might be different from Europe. He displays an utter lack of attention to the individual traits of the Russian national character, and hardly bothers to answer. As for the opinion that, before anything else, one must become an individual, he hardly listens to it at all, apparently finding it unnecessary to even consider it, and directly moves on to other matters.

Stepan Trofimovich. He says about God: "Give me God! If nothing else, knowing that there is a being superior to myself reconciles me to life and won't let me fall into despair (and, a small-minded person, into depravity and savagery)."

When told that this isn't the way he used to talk about God (but rather, like Hertsen, Belinsky, et al.) he admits that he had only been making jokes—for what wouldn't a man do for a *bon-mot* or for a well-turned French phrase.

STEPAN TROFIMOVICH ANNOUNCES THAT SHAKESPEARE AND RAPHAEL ARE HIGHER THAN THE RUSSIAN MUZHIK, HIGHER THAN NARODNOST',[14] HIGHER THAN SOCIALISM, HIGHER THAN THE PEOPLE, HIGHER THAN THE NEED TO SATISFY ITS NEEDS, HIGHER THAN MOST ANYTHING HUMAN —FOR IT IS THE FRUIT OF ALL HUMAN LIFE, ALL THAT WE MUST LIVE FOR, "AND WITHOUT WHICH I DON'T WANT TO LIVE."

"Mankind can survive without the Russian, without the Englishman; but without Shakespeare mankind should not exist at all, nor could it, it seems to me."

"Without America, without railroads, mankind can stay alive, even without bread."

---

[14] An abstract noun derived from *narod* ("people"). It is probably best translated as "national identity," with the qualification that it is the "spiritual" or inner identity that is in question, and not simply the legal and historically empirical identity.

"Beauty is more important than bread, beauty is more useful than bread!"

"Not only that it can't, it must not live, ~~because~~ it must reject life, for that leaves it with nothing to do. Railroads corrupt man. They couldn't fill your life with that; beauty alone is the goal of man's life; and the young generation will perish though it be wrong only as regards the forms of beauty."

XVIII
Notes for Part III of the Novel

These notes (notebook 1/6) have to do exclusively with the last part of *The Possessed.* The first two parts were serialized in *The Russian Messenger* in 1871, and the last part was published a year later in the November and December, 1872, issues of the journal. There are four dates in the text, but only one—September 10—gives the year 1872. The Russian editor conjectures that the notes of this section were all written in 1872. There seems little doubt that they are Dostoevsky's last notes on the novel: all the names are those of the final version—even Nechaev has at last become Peter; and the exclusive concern with the last part supports this conclusion. And yet, I am not sure: the portrait of Stavrogin is sufficiently different here from what was appearing in published form in 1871 to support the conjecture that at least some of these notes may have been written in the second half of 1871. To a lesser extent the same is true of Kirilov.

Most of the material of this final section is close to what we have in the third part of the novel. Kirilov is prominent at this late hour, whereas, before this, he appears only fragmentarily, and except for one reference, under the name of "Engineer." His conversation with Peter Stepanovich about the necessity of suicide because God does not exist is close to what we find in Part III, chapter 6:2 of the final version. But it is sketchy, suggesting that the immense conception of Kirilov, which developed so late, continued to develop even after these notes.

Dostoevsky continues to emphasize Peter's remoteness from reality and his ignorance of reality. But in the final version Peter's ignorance does not come through. Peter is incomprehensible; his motives are impenetrable; he enjoys some reasonless, goal-less love of manipulation and destruction, some Iago-like love of evil for evil's sake. But he is not ignorant. Unconcerned, uninterested, untouched—but not ignorant. Ignorance implies a fact unknown, and an aim misjudged. When Dostoevsky says the following: "Author's note: All his clever cynicism notwithstanding, Verkhovensky was terribly stupid in believing that it would be possible to make everything collapse. With regard to this point, he was as much of a theoretician as Liputin.)," Dostoevsky was —probably for personal reasons—misunderstanding Peter.

When Dostoevsky calls Peter a theoretician, he means that he has an abstract illusion about reality. But nothing in the final version supports this. Peter called Shigalyov an aesthete, because Shigalyov believed in a system, and all systems, for Peter, are dreams; all beliefs are unreal. Peter had no systems and no beliefs, and he knew that Stavrogin had none. They understood each other. Nechaev, Peter's life counterpart, was like him, for he confounded the *émigré* liberal establishment with what appeared to be ignorance and bravado, but was neither.

Stavrogin here is close to his final portrait, but he explains himself too much. He protests that he cannot believe and why he cannot believe. The tone is all wrong: garrulous, superior, self justifying. Here is an example from the notes for his final letter:

Unlike all of our young generation, I cannot welcome the reign of mediocrity, envious equality, stupidity coupled with a lack of individuality, the rejection of any kind of duty, or honor; of any obligations. I can't welcome the rejection of my country, just as I can't welcome those whose only goal is destruction, and who cynically reject any principle that might reunite them after their goal of total destruction has been realized, when the ~~rout~~ profanation and plunder of everything will have brought about the moment when it will no longer be possible to continue life even with the small supply of products and things left intact in the general destruction of the old order. They say that they want to work—they won't. They say that they want to create a new society. They haven't got the bonds ~~to create one~~ for a new society, but they give no thought to these things. They do not think! But their doctrines have all become so complex as to divert them from thinking altogether. The golden mean. No. I am not a democrat.

Somewhere between this and the final version, Dostoevsky knew it was all wrong.

Please note that substantial skipping of original notebook page numbers in this section comes from blank pages, which were nevertheless enumerated by Dostoevsky's wife. The intervals are particularly great beginning with page 49.

March 7 No. 85168

1 <Irrelevant arithmetic calculations.>

<...> and a vague, though most serious, urge of the heart.

An old, leaky boat, ready to be scrapped.
"Really? I'll strangle him."

But let us retrace our steps a little. Even before the conference at Erkel's, Shatov had to lie down with a bad headache.

The dead Christ.

"Could anybody stand this thought, where the world seems to be mocking itself? I don't want to live."
"Just because of that?"
"~~Scoundrel~~ You worthless creature, you don't understand (YOU CAN'T UNDERSTAND) that this can be enough to kill a man!"

Kirilov about Stavrogin:
"Stavrogin doesn't believe that he believes when he believes, and doesn't believe that he doesn't believe when he doesn't."

Stepan Trofimovich, dying: "Long live Russia, for she is the bearer of an idea."
"They, I mean the nihilists, are the bearers of an idea."
"We, too, were the bearers of an idea."
"Their ideas are in a concealed state."

"That perennial Russian urge to be the bearer of an idea, that's what is so wonderful. *Je ne parle pas* that everything that they've got is opportune and proper: poor flock of God!"

"Et puis toujours des idées et rien dans les faits."[1]

"However, it suits us well enough."—

2 Liputin and Nechaev

After having had his face slapped by Fedka, Pyotr Stepanovich drops a hint to Liputin: "Tomorrow he is going to have his throat cut." Had he not dropped that hint, perhaps Liputin wouldn't even have participated in the murder of Shatov. But Fedka's death, which became known on the next morning, suggested to him that Nechaev had in fact great power. But in the meantime he was *walking along with him*, arguing that there won't be any uprising in the summer...

~~Liputin~~

Fedka and Pyotr Stepanovich.

Fedka: "If you weren't my lawful master, I'd do you in right here."

"Do you know that the holy man has taken off his chasuble?"

About Kirilov: "He is a philosopher."

"I only stole the ~~stones~~ pearls, but you put a mouse in there, and that's why I'm going to dishonor you!" (he slaps his face).

"For you, two (...) drink no milk."

"You've dared to stand up against me!"

Upon his return, Liputin says to Nechaev:

"Well, it seems they aren't expecting our 'student' so very impatiently, 'all the way from Smolensk to Tashkent.' "

Pyotr Stepanovich: "You don't like this poem?"

Nechaev: "I submit to instructions from above."

Liputin: "I wish I knew what these instructions are like."

"If he weren't such a buffoon, and just a mite smarter, I'd..."

Psychology

Pyotr Stepanovich and Kirilov. ~~If~~ On the eve, when ~~initiated~~ informed, Kirilov gets mad and chases him out.

But the next day, during his last minutes, he is spontaneously expansive.

Whereas Pyotr Stepanovich has lost everything, i.e., he has lost sight

---

[1] French: "And always ideas, and never facts."

of Stavrogin. As he comes after the murder of Shatov he is in a nasty mood. He feels like venting his anger on somebody.

And that's where Kirilov refuses to sign the paper. This makes him twice as mad. ~~He signs that I and~~

"I don't want to leave. What's the difference if you do it in my presence. I'll watch."

"Look out, I might chase you out of here."

Pyotr Stepanovich: "If you really mean to do it, what difference does it make to you?"

Kirilov: "I really mean to do it. Only I'd like to do it ~~differently~~ not in this way."

Something, a fantastic question.

(About self-will. But what if there is God? What if there is?)

"Chicken, won't you care to eat?"

"No."

Contempt.

Kirilov: "The world is wicked. Let me sign it. What's the difference. The fouler, the better."

He signs.

"Tell me when."

"In a quarter of an hour."

(Takes a look into the hall, he's still walking up and down.) "Right away, leave!"

4 o'clock. "You're disturbing me." He takes another look. He's hidden himself. He bites his finger.

Liberté, égalité, fraternité.

3 Lembke: "It's all arson, that's what nihilism is. If there's anything on fire, it's nihilism. Believe me, believe me!"

"The unfortunate will be consoled, the guilty will be put on trial before the whole people."

Here ~~?~~, even the regretted <…>

~~Tears~~ "Your Excellency, would you deign to remove yourself from this place?"

"They will dry these tears, but burn down the city. This is the plot of a single villain. Arrest the villain! He invades the honor of our families. The family is inviolable. ~~Orthodoxy, autocracy Autocracy~~

~~and *narodnost'*~~ But ~~still~~ it is too early, too early for us! In Russia, ~~tories, but~~ it is still ~~too~~ early for whigs. ~~The Governors~~ We shall gobble up the whigs. Gubernatorial power feeds on whigs, and proclamations mean nothing, though there is a lot of fire. Put out the fire, put it out. Where are the water barrels? There aren't enough barrels, and they're getting as fat as barrels themselves. ~~In At the next fire use all of your fat merchants instead of barrels, also the Arch-Priest, and the members of the Club.~~ Get him down, get him down, he is lost, the poor wretch! What is he doing there? Put him out, put him out—why, why has he climbed up there?"

"To put out the fire, Your Excellency."

"Rubbish, don't put out the fire! The fire is deeper, ~~the fire is in the hearts it is time~~ the fire is in the minds, and there aren't enough barrels. Barrels, barrels! ~~A whole Or you'll have a whole barrel full of tears.~~ Where are the governesses? Forward, use governesses to set fire to these houses! Oh! ~~Isn't that~~ That old woman, that old woman, drag out that old woman."

"To put out fires, gubernatorial powers must absolutely be increased."

Both whigs and tories.

Kirilov and Pyotr Stepanovich. "If there is no God, a new era."

"But more likely, people will devour one another."

"In that case, God is indispensable."

"And since He doesn't exist, He is indispensable to deceive people."

"In that case I don't want to be alive."

("I don't want happiness with deceit; better blow up everything.")

Pyotr Stepanovich: "Go ahead, blow up everybody... It can be done. I'll teach you how."

Kirilov: "No, better just myself, only me."

4 June 26 <1871 or 1872>.

Pyotr Stepanovich at Stavrogin's in Skvoreshniki, on the morning of the fire:

~~But not~~ "They were killed, but not burned. But don't worry, I have taken the necessary steps: Kirilov will take the whole blame. If anyone is dangerous, it is Shatov and Shatov alone. ~~He will~~ If he hasn't already told the police, he certainly will now. I really shouldn't have told you that ahead of time. But I want you to know everything."

N.B. *In its own place.*

In the morning fog. Stepan Trofimovich and Liza. "How did you arrive at this decision?" "I've been analyzing things for some time: amazing how clear a man's head becomes ~~without~~ when he is awaiting his execution. I wouldn't have expected it. I want you to know that my undertaking is not a symbolic gesture, but rather like an algebraic formula according to Taine.[2] I'm full of fear, but my mind is set. I was actually afraid of the darkness of night, and when dawn came I was frightened and trembling. The light of day is returning me my courage. I've been told that story about the major who, a believer at night, turns atheist at dawn, as the light of the day revives his courage and he no longer needs God. In 1793, Rohan[3] was full of fear, but there, the blood of sacred royalty, of Charlotte,[4] of his friends the marquises —and he *went* to the guillotine. And had he been told: 'Ask forgiveness, recant, and you'll live!'—he wouldn't have recanted, though he was trembling. Neither shall I recant. I, too, am trembling like he, but like he, I shall not recant."

"I have a presentiment of what has happened to you, my dear, I can guess it, don't tell me about it. This town is accursed—I'm shaking its dust off my feet. Accept my blessings—a midge's blessings."

Kirilov and Pyotr Stepanovich, before Kirilov's death: "Why kill <oneself>?" "You won't understand." "Yes, of course, I'm busy with other things, but I'll be listening to you with pleasure, especially since it appears that you have a strong urge to talk." *Kirilov:* "If there is no God, I have a right to put an end to my life, and I want to prove that I have that right." "But who will know, tell me?" "That doesn't matter. Everything will be revealed one day." "All right, and what if there is a God?" "In that case one can't be master of one's own fate." "All right, what if there is?" "~~No~~ I wish there were one." "Really?" "Certainly!" "So you'll be punished?" "I hope not." "But still, you can't be quite sure?" "The point is that there really is no God. That's why I'm

---

[2] Hippolyte Taine (1828–93), historian and critic. He devised a theory of literature based on the triple influences of race, milieu, and times. His important works were *Histoire de la littérature anglaise* and *Origines de la France contemporaine.*

[3] Louis Constantin Rohan, (1730–94), an enemy of the republic established by the revolution; he was arrested in 1794 and guillotined July 24, 1794. Dostoevsky is wrong about the year.

[4] Marie-Anne-Charlotte Corday d'Armont (1768–93) murdered Marat on July 13, 1793.

going to shoot myself. If there is no God, I don't care to stay in this world. Christ died on the cross, thinking of God, a victim of this world of ours." "Well, go ahead now, I'll be watching."

N.B. (He was watching, but for the sole purpose of being able to tell himself: "What a man I am, looking on, as this other man is shooting himself.") Vanity, thinking about himself.

"So what? All right, what if he doesn't shoot himself? That would be worst of all."

1) "If there is no God—I am God."

"But if there is God?"

"There isn't."

"Come on, what do you care, why are you so much interested in this?"

"Because I am not you and because I can't stand the idea that I am God without making it manifest."

"~~God~~ You mean, your divinity?"

"That's right, my divinity. If I am God, then the highest self-will. I must, I can't help manifesting my self-will, if I feel that I am God. I owe it to humanity, to the world. While God existed, I wouldn't dare dispose of my own life."

2) "If he does not exist, I am obliged, by my conscience, before myself and everybody (even if I am all alone), to make it manifest that my will is the very highest phenomenon that exists."

"Why not kill someone else?"

"That is the very lowest form in which my will can manifest itself. That's the whole difference between you and me."

"A crawling creature can reason in this fashion, but not supreme man. There exists no higher idea for me than that there is no God."

This is so high it will regenerate mankind. I cannot remain indifferent. I must state my atheism in full before all mankind."

"But nobody will know about it."

"Everybody will. It was he who said, 'for there is nothing hid…' "[5] (pointing at the icon).

5 Pyotr Stepanovich argues with Liza at Stavrogin's that she can still marry Mavriky Nikolaevich.

---

[5] Mark 4:22.

Pyotr Stepanovich with a revolver. Stavrogin: "You might as well kill. No, later."

"Of course you will kill me."

"Won't it be degrading for you to get killed by me?"

~~Stavrogin:~~ "No."

Pyotr Stepanovich: "What suffering a man won't bring upon himself! So, to the devil with all of it, and the sooner the better! Let's shake up Russia, but good! What if out of spite, yes, out of spite? What do you care now, if you've gotten to where you're asking me to put a bullet through your head?"

Silence.

Pyotr Stepanovich: "Once more, I shall wait for a while. Stavrogin, listen. Three more days, a week, and then I'll come for the last time, to get your answer. But in the meantime I'll butter up and smooth over everything."

"Well, as for that ~~?~~, how would you like me to handle it? She ought to be married off as fast as possible, right? I'll see to that. Kirilov will write a note on the fire, and everything will be all right as far as the Lebiadkins are concerned."

"We'll manage to do it all today."

Stepan Trofimovich. He lies to the book-hawker woman, making up a whole romance between himself and Varvara Petrovna.

A teacher who makes an attempt to stop the distribution of gospel texts. A taciturn one. Stepan Trofimovich confounds him.

Liputin catches Pyotr Stepanovich at the railway station as he is about to leave on the 5 o'clock special.

"Liamshin is going to tell the police."

Verkhovensky: "No, he'll be sick in bed. He is badly scared, but what can he tell the police? Even if they'd reduce his sentence by two degrees for his confession, he'll still be sentenced to hard labor plus deportation."

Liputin: "I understand, and also that your remark was addressed to me really."

Verkhovensky: "Do you intend to tell the police?"

Liputin: "Tell me, are we the only quintet, or are there thousands?"

Verkhovensky: "What if there is only one?"

"Socialism was invented for fools. Where, then, is the truth, and what cause should one serve?" ~~In order to~~

Verkhovensky: "So that everything would collapse, and we could take their place."

Liputin: "That's not what I've been thinking about. What, then, are you leaving us to find comfort in?"

"I'll come back in the summer; there'll be an uprising for sure. Stick to Stavrogin, who'll be in Petersburg. Stavrogin is working on our behalf in Petersburg."

Virginsky protested, but did not tell the police.

"I have received a prearranged cable message from Stavrogin, from Petersburg."

6 Liputin and Nechaev. Liputin criticizes the "Noble Soul," which offends Nechaev.

Liputin is angry and contradicts him on every step.

Nechaev looks to him like a punk.

The distortion of a man, and of reality.

"You are a fantastic person." Upon which the other man only laughs.

Nechaev—absolutely make him go to a restaurant and eat a beefsteak.

Liputin is contradicting him biliously all the time, and says this to Nechaev at the meeting: "All right, granted that in Europe the collapse of everything is a desirable contingency, but why should we in Russia ape what they're doing? ~~their wishes~~ For no special reason? *For love of the game?* Just raising dust."

He contradicts Verkhovensky with bitterness, and yet goes ahead and helps him to kill Shatov.

Shatov: "Yes, since we have become so corrupted that we can't be Russians anymore, I have become a Slavophile."

"For want of anything better?"

Liputin and Nechaev. About the sedition (about how everything has collapsed);* even without us, they ~~will~~ are working at it. ~~?~~

Liputin: "Who?"

Nechaev: "Everybody, absolutely everybody."

Liputin: "Come on, not really everybody?"

---

* The gender of the verb form suggests that it is not the sedition that has collapsed.

Nechaev: "Everybody to the last man." (He is absent-minded and taciturn.)

Liputin: "Well, if everybody is working at it, even without us, why should we bother?"

Necheav: "To gain control over the movement, that's why. (That's why we must get organized.) Get organized—work. You won't get a thing without working for it. Gone are the times of idle talk."

Liputin: "What shall we do then?"

Nechaev: "Get organized, ~~and~~ support ~~sedition~~ the general sedition movement, while waiting for the key move."

"What key move?"

Nechaev: "You are asking more questions than I can answer."*

Liputin: *"We're just raising dust!"*

7 N.B. Those characteristic little sayings were also showing up here and there.

For instance, in answer to the question of one man who had just come in: "Well, brother? ARE YOU WORKING HARD? Are you getting ready?"

"Well, in a way: *just raising dust, Sir.*"

Up to: "We can't afford to lose the printing press, can we?"

The murder of Shatov.

"He has shown us where he buried it; well, that's enough, time to do away with him."

(Author's note: All his clever cynicism notwithstanding, Verkhovensky was terribly stupid in believing that it would be possible to make everything collapse. With regard to this point, he was as much of a theoretician as Liputin.)

Liputin and Verkhovensky, at the last moment before Verkhovensky's departure.

Liputin asks: "What shall we do? Tell me, what can be more serious than that?" Verkhovensky replies, now seriously, though with some

---

* The Russian version is a proverbial saying, literally, "he who asks too many questions ages early."

bitterness, that it all boils down to making sure everything will collapse.

Liputin is astonished and says that it is of course necessary that there be no private property, no God, no family, etc. Having achieved this, socialism would achieve everything else as well.

To this:

Verkhovensky looks at him as if he were some nitwit, and says, in a light and condescending vein, that this has been made up for fools only, though it might be a good idea to use it as bait, among other things, but that it is really even more stupid than the present order of things. "This Fourier, for instance, is some kind of Christianity without Christ."

"But what then is our goal? We must have some goal if we're doing what we're doing."

Verkhovensky views him with derisive astonishment: "*Chacun pour soi,*[6] and catch your fish."

Liputin: "You never speak in that tone."

Verkhovensky: "A clever man must wear a mask."

("What good are those quintets then?"

"The earlier one gets organized, the more surely one will seize power later.")

8 *Shatov and his wife.*

"We are living together and, suddenly, a third person. A mystery." Almost pleadingly: ("It's a mystery, isn't it?")

"It isn't yours, it's Stavrogin's."

She: "There is no mystery: simply an organism and its development."

The midwife: without reverence, or joy, she handles the child with distaste.

Shatov runs to the midwife: at first, curses, but later "I'll be there."

Shatov, with Kirilov: "We used to lie <on that floor> together." ~~"You have~~ Kirilov: "You've got a wife, that's good." "You'll leave, and I'll be thinking of you."

Shatov: "Ah, Kirilov, forget about your terrible ideas, and then, then what a man you'd be!"

---

[6] French: "Everyone for himself."

Kirilov: "Come *again* if you need some tea. Money: a ruble."

Shatov to Liamshin: ~~No~~ Liamshin: "No, I simply can't; no, better leave me alone; no, I simply can't; and do you realize that it is the middle of the night..."

Shatov: "You took 25."

Liamshin: "I can give you 15, but only the day after tomorrow."

Shatov: "No, right now."

Liamshin: "5 rubles now, and 10 the day after tomorrow."

Shatov: "No, 10 rubles now, and 5 the day after tomorrow."

He thought it over for a moment, then gave him 7 rubles. "Take it or leave it, I can't give you more."

Shatov's wife, handsome, brunette; she has put on some weight; she has been ailing and is ~~capricious~~ nervously excited. She is capricious and condescendingly disgusted with everything; 85 copecks of money. She makes an imperious entry. A tiny room.

"I haven't the slightest intention of taking up living with you, so please don't think that you are doing me a favor."

"What has been happening in these parts?"

He tells her about the death of Stavrogin's wife (seeking to find excuses), and about Liza.

"Aren't you doing famously!"

They get to talking about Stavrogin: "I beg you, not a word, not a single word."

Shatov immediately proceeds to prove the existence of God.

They keep interrupting each other.

And the next day, after she has given birth to her child, with her eyes flashing: "Stavrogin is a scoundrel."

Shatov, to his wife, as he leaves to hand over the printing press: "Perhaps I am acting basely."

N.B. Kirilov didn't know that they were going to kill Shatov.

9 *Marie* has come back hoping to find work as a bookbinder.

"Eh, *Marie!* People here even don't have books, (PEOPLE HERE DON'T READ BOOKS) much less books to be bound."

"People here won't ever think of having their books bound."

A witty remark: "Having a book bound means as much as having respect for books. Mind you, this stands for an entire *period* of development."

Marie: "You are just showing off your wit. I know your manner of being witty" (while, at the same time, her hand is stroking his hair), "what bristly hair you've got, though."*

Kirilov: "I don't know how to bear a child. I mean, not to bear a child, but make somebody bear one... Or ~~the devil~~ or, the devil take it, I don't know how to say it."

"You can't help, ~~that's all~~."

"Yes, yes, help, personally, but... if necessary..."

"No, no, I'll get a samovar by morning, and... and a woman, some sort of a woman, to take care, an experienced one, by morning, while I—I'll run along to get a midwife."

Shatov and his wife. "And suddenly, a new *I*. Say what you want, that's a terribly important fact."

"Simply the fact of a further development of an organism."

"And you could! Ivan, Ivan!"

The midwife: "Come on, you'll need a funeral, and all you've got is eighty kopeks. It's cheaper to have a baby. First thing tomorrow, I'll take the baby down to the village and find someone to nurse it ~~and that's all there is to it~~. That's all as far as he is concerned. Later, when you get well, you'll pay him for all the expenses in a few months."

10 An Idea

A government clerk: "I'm so bored, oughtn't I set a fire?"
Somebody slapped his face. He set a fire (in his imagination).
He killed. Terrible impressions. He got busy.
Daydreams about an island in the Baltic.
(The Pruzhansky woman.)

The emptiness in the soul of today's suicide.

The murder of Shatov.
Liamshin doesn't show up.
The Lop-eared one leaves before it happens.

---

* Literally, "what a hedgehog you are, though."

Virginsky protests after the murder (also, prior to the murder, he demands that Shatov be heard and tried).

Erkel, Tolkochenko <*sic*>, and Pyotr Verkhovensky do the actual work. Liputin.

In the morning, Virginsky comes running to tell the others that Shatov isn't going to tell the police—knowing the human heart—that a child was born to him, and that his wife was back. But he finds no one at home. He is the first to arrive at the scene of the murder. He states his reasons.

Pyotr Verkhovensky: "If you suddenly became happy, ~~and~~ would you delay, not your giving information to the police, but some risky feat of civic virtue which you had planned even before you became happy and which you are considering a duty and an obligation?

"No... I wouldn't delay it, I most certainly wouldn't..."

"Would you rather become unhappy once more, than a scoundrel?"

"Yes. In fact, quite the contrary, I would very much like to be a scoundrel... that is, not at all a scoundrel, but on the contrary, unhappy rather than a scoundrel."

"All right then, are you aware of the fact that Shatov considers reporting us to the police his feat of civic virtue? Such convictions are the most dangerous of all. Another day, and he'll regain his senses and go to the police. ~~He Certainly~~ Note that he is himself taking a risk, in fact more so ~~than anyone else~~. That's precisely what makes him think of his action as of a feat of courage. He is the type who'll never lay off, he'll go ahead and do what he feels is his duty. If he were but an ordinary sentimental lump, no good..."

Liputin: "But has there actually been a report to the police?"

"I haven't the right to reveal all of my channels. There has been such a report."

"I've come... if this is so, I've come to put a question to Shatov... a trial, and then, if it turns out <that he is guilty>, make him give his word (if otherwise, I protest, I protest, I protest!)..."

Pyotr Verkhovensky: "That can be done, we shall see."

11 *Kirilov's suicide.** Pyotr Stepanovich checks his pistol, which he had loaded already in the morning, and suddenly he is struck by this thought: "I've got to watch out that he doesn't shoot me." So he imme-

* The text actually reads "Kirilov's murder," obviously a *lapsus calami.*

diately takes out his revolver and lets the other man see that it is fully loaded.

Kirilov: "You just thought that maybe I'll get the idea to shoot you instead of myself, and so you want to warn me that you've got something to defend yourself with."

AND, AT THIS POINT:

Kirilov: "What made you think that I won't shoot myself?"

Pyotr Stepanovich: "That is so natural."

Kirilov: "For a scoundrel such as yourself."

Pyotr Stepanovich: "Precisely, precisely—but I never knew the reasons" (and here then, their conversation).

Nechaev and Liputin. "I don't see any so-called differences between Russia and the other nations. But even if there were any, it still wouldn't mean a thing, and only an idle person who can't see or know what he's got to do, will actually bother to discuss it in his idle mind. All this Russian history, all these Slavophiles and Liberals, or whatever they are called, that's all nothing but tightrope walking, a pastime for frivolous people. That a man can become passionately devoted to the most ridiculous kind of tightrope walking, is proven by such people as Kirilov who, incidentally, was simply a fool."

"Do you really mean all this seriously?"

"Get everybody saddled, and let's ride along!"

"Well, what are you taking people for?" ~~after all this~~

12 "For a bunch of crooks, of course."

"And yourself?"

"That is, in what sense? He who was the most clever of them all was always thought to be holy. However, let's quit all this nonsense."

"You are saying then, that all of us who have let you get to the top are stupid, and you are openly admitting that you want to 'saddle us'?"

"On the contrary, I'm suggesting that you participate in beginning to saddle others, since I've found you to be more capable and more clever than the others."

About Fourier: "That is, I actually don't want to argue against this; however, the principal task we're facing right now lies not here, but in making everything collapse."

Liputin: "Well, there are some sincere socialists around, too."

"That is, bribed?"

"How do you mean, bribed?"

"What a fool you are. What the devil, let's talk of something else."

The murder of Shatov.

Shigalyov protests and leaves, because this murder is only *a loss of time,* which could be used to immeasurably greater advantage in listening to his system.

N.B. ("This murder is at odds with my system.")

"I am not talking of those causes which are anchored in religion."

Pyotr Verkhovensky yells at him: "Do you know at all, Mr. Fourier, that you may have to pay for this?"

Shigalyov answers: "So what, you'll kill me, but you'll still end up using my system."

~~And besides, I~~ "Allow me to remark that I am not Fourier. I beg you not to get me mixed up with that sugary and abstract milksop."

Pytor Stepanovich: "That is not the point."

Shigalyov: "I understand, Sir; ~~that~~ are you threatening to kill me? Is that so? ~~All right, you will kill me.~~ All right, and still you will sooner or later adopt my system."

5 Liputin: "The kingdom of Heaven is at hand."

Nechaev: "Yes, about June, or so."

Liputin: "And you think that everybody will follow you?"

"Whoever is wise enough will join us within a quarter of an hour. Those who are stupid, or who have been bribed, will have to burn."

N.B. (Nechaev's mediocrity and narrow-mindedness leave a painful impression on Liputin. He sees quite clearly that, all his self-assurance notwithstanding, he is inferior to them as an ideologist and visionary.)

Before the murder, Nechaev on Shatov: "I knew that he was a Slavophile, that is, one of the most stupid people there are. But I also knew that he was embittered and, insofar as he did, after all, whether he wanted or not, belong to our organization, I kept alive my hope that he could still be employed in the common cause, being, as I said, an embittered man; moreover, having already once changed his convictions, he might well have another change of heart, and rejoin our ranks. But now this has become impossible. He is about to inform the police, believing this to be his sacred duty. As far as your personal relations with him are concerned, I don't care if you kiss him, but you don't have the right to betray the common cause. And that's why he must be destroyed. I believe I've just told you the same thing for the thirtieth time."

Liputin: "Isn't socialism taking the place of Christianity? Isn't it the new Christianity ~~only without God~~ which will lead the way to a regeneration of the whole world? It is precisely that same Christianity, only without God."

Nechaev: "Well, if it is indeed Christianity, why even talk about such nonsense ~~for Christianity must be destroyed and an end put to it~~."

"But Christianity without God, doesn't that make a whole lot of difference?"

"As far as I am concerned, God isn't even quite so bad. God could actually be retained, if necessary."

16 About Liputin.

(N.B. What about him? As he was leaving, he was still talking about socialism!)

Virginsky's exclamation after the murder:

"That isn't it, that isn't it!"

(N.B. See the enclosure to T. Filipov's letter.)

N.B. ~~In~~ A Russian ~~is something~~ gets worn out very fast. He must be used while he is still good for raising some dust.

N.B. ~~After chapter~~ October 24. General plan.

After Kirilov's suicide. Pyotr Stepanovich enters the railway carriage. Forget about Liputin. Erkel is the only one he sees.

A Chapter on *Stepan Trofimovich*

Chapter. Meanwhile strange things had happened in town:

In a rapid narrative, the instructions left by Pyotr Stepanovich.

His sharp mind and his failure to understand reality.

However, he did make his escape. Instructions left—pass on to Liputin. He firmly believed in the cell.

Yet the crowd of people, forsaken by him...

How everything came to light suddenly. Kirilov's letter. Suspicions on the part of the authorities. Shatov's wife comes running. Liputin's flight. Carousing in Petersburg.

Meanwhile, suspicions.

Virginsky is overwhelmed by the sight of Mrs. Shatov. He confesses.

Shigalyov will be acquitted. Erkel arrested.

Tol<ka>chenko flees. Liamshin arrested, squealing.

7 News from Petersburg. A cable with orders to arrest Pyotr Stepanovich. The local authorities in trepidation.

A senator is due to arrive. Stavrogin's mysterious appearance. Public prayers.

The return of Varvara Petrovna. The citizen of the canton of Uri.

Erkel and Pyotr Stepanovich, the railway carriage.

"I'm positive they're not going to tell the police!" (annoyed; he knows himself that they're going to).

8 "You're the last to be with me. I wouldn't like to leave you with something between us."

"Be assured that I never had anything against you personally."

"You are a scoundrel, but I am no better myself."

"God is necessary, and that's why he must be."

"Yet I know that there is no God and that there can't be one. That's enough reason to shoot oneself."

"Don't you understand that a pure man cannot go on living with this double-faced idea."

He was eyeing the other man timidly, afraid he might accidentally drop a wrong word: "Did I hear you say something about God?" ~~I'm sad~~

"I'm sad <because> you are lying—"

A maniac and a child, but—

Stavrogin is also ailing with that very same idea.

"Did he admit this to you?"

"No, I guessed it. Stavrogin (a phrase)."

"Stavrogin's got some other things, more clever than this one."

Stavrogin (a phrase).

"Well, enough, what the devil, don't talk about him."

If he <. . .>

"An extraordinarily clever man, but with a certain frivolity, continuous blundering even where he could have known better. A certain touchiness and lack of self-control."

"If he had literary talent, he would be second to none among our great critics-and-leaders of the early 1860's. Of course he would have been writing something different, but it would have had much the same effect. It goes without saying that I'm leaving morality out of the picture entirely. I'm not appealing to morality at all, nor am I, at this point, passing judgment on anybody. I am talking only about his intellect and his talents."

"He is active abroad even today, and is a fascinating speaker."

He understands, for instance, that Kirilov is having a terribly hard time shooting himself, and that he is perhaps more of a believer "than many a priest."

He very cleverly outlines his plan to Stavrogin, and takes an intelligent view of Russia. Still, it is all very strange: he actually does believe, quite seriously, that "it will start in May, and be all over by October."

How then should one call this? An abstract intelligence? An intelligence which is groundless and rootless—without nationality and without a truly necessary cause? Let my readers decide for themselves.

20 Preface

Kirilov embodies an idea which belongs to the people: to sacrifice oneself, without a moment's hesitation, for the truth. Even the wretched, blind suicide of April 4 did, at the time in question, believe in his truth (it is said that he later repented, thank God!), nor did he hide himself, like Orsini,[7] but was ready to take what was coming to him.

To sacrifice oneself, to sacrifice everything for truth—that is the national trait of this generation. May God bless it, and may He give it a true understanding of truth. For the whole problem amounts to no more than the question as to what ought to be considered "truth." That is what this novel is all about.

"I've been looking at ~~our~~ negators, our own and those in Europe. Oh, if I only could be with them, at least."

"I used to be so full of spite I actually got involved with ours, and wanted to join them."

---

[7] Feliche Orsini (1819–38), Italian revolutionary who was guillotined on March 13, 1858, for an attempt on the life of Napoleon III. He was particularly brave at the trial and at the time of punishment. Dostoevsky's remark about his fear is not accurate.

"Yes, I am capable of wishing to do a good deed. But besides, I also like what is evil, terrible, cruel."

"But this is a small love, and nothing will come of it. One can cross a river on a plank, but not on a sliver."

"I've tried debauchery. I ~~rather~~ spent my strength on it. But I got nowhere. I've tried love."

"Most importantly, I didn't want debauchery, nor did I like it, too much for me."

"I am looking for some sort of peace."

"The consolations of religion are for me impossible, because I can't believe." ~~I've lost God a long time ago.~~

"I hate my neighbor—(I DON'T LOVE HIM) (. . .) ~~Probably~~ I shall probably get to hate you, too, if you'll be around me all the time."

"I've tried out my powers. A few trial demonstrations have proven them to be boundless."

"I was able to bear having my face slapped by Shatov, I—"

"But where should I apply these powers? I haven't found my main goal."

22 "I am not out to deny anything, yet I am also indifferent to everything."

"I am a walking mummy."

"I have been always aware of my baseness."

"There's nothing that makes me belong to Russia."

Stavrogin's Letter

Unlike all of our young generation, I cannot welcome the reign of mediocrity, envious equality, stupidity coupled with a lack of individuality, the rejection of any kind of duty, or honor, of any obligations. I can't welcome the rejection of my country, just as I can't welcome those whose only goal is destruction, and who cynically reject any principle that might reunite them after their goal of total destruction has been realized, when the ~~rout~~ profanation and plunder of everything will have brought about the moment when it will no longer be possible to continue life even with the small supply of products and things left intact in the general destruction of the old order. They say that they want to work—they won't. They say that they want to create a new society. They haven't got the bonds ~~to create one~~ for a new society, but they give no thought to these things. They do not think! But their doctrines have all become so complex as to divert them from thinking altogether. The golden mean. No, I am not a democrat.

But the senseless and ancient idea, developed by a society of landowners, of an imitative socialism, sentimental, yet with a new strain (. . .) of hatred and greed ~~has, with them, changed into some higher form of generosity, some higher sort of liberalism~~. I felt nauseated. I am an honest man, I can't come to such a stupid end. Yet (I fear nothing, not even ridicule, ~~but~~ I fear only myself). Strange creature, he ~~?~~ is actually himself seeking to persuade me that I should destroy him. The magnanimous Kirilov could not bear the idea; I could bear it, I can bear anything. 2) What has come from me is nothing but fearless negation without any sublimity.

... Despite my vanity and posing, I was at all times aware of my baseness.

I know that I ought to kill myself, wipe myself off the face of the earth, like a loathsome insect, yet I ~~basely~~ fear suicide ~~not believing in~~, for I'm afraid to make a display of magnanimity. ~~My cynicism stops me from doing it~~ Besides, there is nothing in the world that I respect enough to make me consider myself a loathsome insect. In my mind, there could never be room for indignation. The tedium of these past years.

Better if you don't come. And yet I am expecting you, and calling you. What could be more shameful?

Here I am, writing: "What could be more shameful?" But do you know that I am not ashamed, because I never knew any shame in anything?

Don't look for love; I am not going to love you, I am a stranger everywhere. Now I am getting verbose. At times I am rather ill; ill with a terrible disease. I would like to lock myself in, all by myself. Underground, if this were only possible. I have a frightful hatred of everything in Russia.

26 *Little ideas*

—Fools
—Dialogues

A pity that I can't turn to Molière, but have to turn to Ostrovsky.

27 The officer who shoots himself is an average man.

That is to say, society as such, statistically. That is an important fact.

Prospectus

"Lick the floor."

"What about China. The marriage of the Chinese Emperor. Look, if I were living in China, I'd know what to say. But here in Russia; what a boring life. Not quite; habit, gotten used to. But certainly an ant-heap."

"How much superior to *fraternité, égalité*... etc."

"The Chinaman sees it differently. You'll get there, you'll get there. (Haven't you got many principles, while you go on living?)"

"In China I'd know what to say. Ask for a phrase and I give it. But here, it is difficult. People don't understand you. Hertsen. But I'm not afraid of them."

"Boredom! What is boredom?" "A sensation of unfreedom, unnaturalness."

On suicides, a sore spot. How they die. By his own hand, or an executioner's. Tropman, the officer. Château-d'Yquem (from trifles, no struggle whatever). No mystic terror. ~~It is said~~ From education? Hardly. How much of an education did he have anyway? Mysteries. Nothing but mysteries.

Boredom and chinoiserie, the lady and Meshchersky,[8] the perfect image of Tatiana.[9] "Not boring at all." "Certainly, ~~she~~ Tatiana is bored." "It is gratifying that this will never happen."

The General who sings Alexis, Man of God. Pushkin. The ideal of womanhood is found among the people. King Athenio—*

"For me, this is higher than everything, everything!" "Do you believe that this, too, was created by the people?" "Not what is trashy about it, but its ideals." Incidentally, they misunderstand each other frequently.

---

[8] Vladimir Petrovich Meshchersky (1839–1914), editor of *The Citizen* for which Dostoevsky wrote in 1873–74 and in 1876–77. His column in 1876–77 appeared as a separate supplement. These articles have been collected under the title *The Diary of a Writer*.

[9] Heroine of Pushkin's *Evgenii Onegin*.

* Afinion.

Hertsen commended them both to him as clever men.

A and B.

Anecdote about Hertsen. He used to have fits of melancholy.

Belinsky wouldn't have been melancholy. Anecdote about Christ.

"Nobody ever gets to be thoughtful any more, and perhaps nobody even gets to think at all, except about money. I have nothing against money, I'm only against disorder. Practically speaking, we aren't in the least different from China, except that there isn't any kind of order in our country. I'm so fascinated by China, because I've read an article on the marriage of the Chinese Emperor."

"That is marvelous."

Each suspects the other of ~~mutual~~ stupidity, without giving the matter any real thought, or asking the inverse question, i.e., if he's perhaps stupid himself. A terribly comical phenomenon.

N.B. Jurors.

The runaway boy.

"You can't demand of a hireling <. . .>

Yet, an established *modus*. Abroad.

We, the nobles, are really flunkies. We shall never become marquesses.

Be what you wish to be, but stick to the ceremonial. As for ceremonies, they are essentially the result of a thousand years of past historical life, the result of realism and experience. Be what you wish to be, it is your business; be a murderer, scoundrel, beggar, fanatic, but stick to the ceremonial. Ceremonies are the bond which keeps the ant-heap from falling apart. What good are those freedoms to you? Oh, of course, *liberté* and *fraternité* are still alive.

28 FOR THE DIARY OF A LITTÉRATEUR.

THEMES:

One lady wrote:

About Tatiana (from a lady's letter to Meshchersky).

About suicides (life is boring, and why).

Belinsky and Christ (half true).

Conversations with a fool. Hertsen and Belinsky (conversation between Mr. A and Mr. B).[10]

---

[10] See Note 9 or Section V.

I heard this anecdote from Hertsen, in Naples (description, the daughter, high-class people).

Simply *la Mort*[11] is even higher, but surely a Chinaman sees these things differently.

In China, I'd be a good writer.

The lady in a railway carriage and the man who is about to take his vows.

The scene with the fool who is en route to his wedding:

10 rubles lost.

Socialism in Europe and socialism in our country.

The type of a pure nihilist. (*Nihil.* Chernyshevsky.) Here's my orchard, come. Takes an axe and hacks it all to pieces. Without feeling any pangs of conscience. Later, he will shoot himself. Château d'Yquem, grapes.

The runaway high school boy (treat his thirteen years with respect).

Heard of a boy who was said to have been expelled from a certain institution.

Children. Develop a certain attitude toward them. A foundling. A government clerk who used to adopt foundlings.

There is no such thing as crime. The coldbloodedness of the shooting. The idea about the jurors. Have they a right to acquit? One or two examples of *circonstances attenuantes*.[12] The coachmen-killers.

Chinoiserie, ant-heap. Lick the floor and eat rice.

Alexis, Man of God, the General, a woman superior to Tatiana.

29 What is a lie? Every bite of communion bread has been counted.

How do, at certain times, liberal views come into existence?

A Voltairian view. In St. Theodosius.

A nihilist who had had commerce with the devil.

Confrontation of photographs, Katkov, Krasovsky.[13]

THEMES FOR A PAINTER.

Belinsky, after a rapturous <harangue?>, so boring <. . .>

But how can you make merry, if there's Château d'Yquem awaiting you?

---

[11] French: "Death."

[12] French: "attentuating circumstances."

[13] Apollinary K. Krasovsky, a student in the engineering school which Dostoevsky attended and author of a book entitled *Public Architecture*.

(On how death must not be boring.)

But (. . .) even in a rapture. She is not bored, but how must Tatiana feel?

Confrontation.

For orphanages or for scholarships.

I don't understand a thing about Shakespeare, and suddenly you become a great man.

32 Notes.

Every bite of communion bread has been counted } review.
Tolstoi's ABC-Book }

41 Reminiscing is for me equal to suffering ~~and actually, the happier the memory, the more so;~~ happy for a moment, while yesterday was an unhappy day.

48 *Bons-Mots*

He who is not aware of his calling most often lacks a sense of dignity.

Happiness is to my disadvantage: I can't bear happiness and immediately forgive my enemies.

He who lacks the ability to appreciate a joke ~~is~~ will never be truly happy.

He has stuffed his pockets with twenty thousand or so.

I have looked through (GLANCED THROUGH) ~~your entire~~ this marvelous album of yours, and I became envious ~~of it; as~~; I got to regret not having started one myself ~~early in my life~~ some thirty years ago. How many friends and associates of yours have entered ~~their thoughts on these beautiful pages, at least upon~~ their thoughts in this splendid memorial volume, or how many fine ~~moments~~, or rather, living moments of our past life do these ~~sheets names~~ sheets recall. I have ~~possess~~ left with me several photographs of people whom I loved most in my lifetime and who are no longer with us. I am very glad to have ~~these photographs~~ their likenesses, yet I hardly ever look at them: ~~I fear~~ the more touching, the more beautiful these memories, the more ~~from it~~ suffering they cause. And ~~simultaneously~~ at the same time, all these losses notwithstanding, I ~~myself~~ love life dearly. I love life for life's own sake, and I am always *getting ready to start my life*. I'll be fifty soon, and I still don't know if I am completing my life, or just starting it. This is the principal trait of my character; perhaps of my life's work.

F. D.

69 *Addresses.*

Pleshcheev, 2 Vladimirskaia Street, Apt. 17.

Vasily Grigorievich Perov,[14] Moscow, across from the post office, School of Painting.

70 1872

DIARY

September 10. A letter from Vladislavlev,[15] and an invitation to a christening. Strakhov[16] had dinner with us. Yesterday my brothers Andrei and Kolia had dinner with us. The children are healthy and sweet. Anna Grigorievna looks tired. The weather is damp, rainy, on the windy side, but warm.

Yesterday, my brother Andrei told me that Askochensky (!) had been looking up my address at the address bureau. I told Strakhov about my idea for an almanach.

20 Putsykovich[17]—10 years of reforms.[18]

Meshchersky—Aleksei Slobodin.[19]

Myself—The Monasteries.[20]

ABC-Book.

P.—don't know what.

26 FITS—

September 3, in the morning, while asleep, of the more serious type.

October 10, while asleep, in Moscow, of the more serious type.

---

[14] See note 4 of this section.

[15] Mikhail I. Vladislavlev (born 1840), a conservative philosopher and fellow worker in Dostoevsky's journals, *Time* and *Epoch*.

[16] See note 17 of section I.

[17] Vladimir F. Putsykovich, a journalist; from 1874 to 1879 the editor of *The Citizen*.

[18] *Ten Years of Reform,* 1861–1871, a book by Aleksey A. Golovachev (1819–1903), published in 1872. Golovachev wrote for *The Russian Messenger, The Russian Thought,* and other journals. He also published *The History of Railroads in Russia* in 1881.

[19] Aleksei Slobodin, a novel by A. I. Palm published in *The European Herald* (1872).

[20] "I and the Monasteries" is a review by Dostoevsky of a group of articles entitled "Our Monasteries," which appeared in *Conversation* in 1872.

130 <Irrelevant book-keeping entries and arithmetic calculations.>

131 Feodosy[21]—And that was all, that was how long his anger lasted, all of that and no more—

About Feodosy in an earlier passage.

About how there is no time to think.

He returned, his face pale.

A fitful, shocking diatribe about how one ought to blow up—

"I hate everything."

"They are plotting to blow up things. What they've got going is stupid, but if I get involved in it, it won't be stupid anymore. All they've got going along these lines can be turned into something not so stupid."

Tikhon: "If I'd dare to do it; it ought to be regulated, and order established."

Find God.

Stavrogin: "A toy, that is? The crucified and the malefactor. A sordid lot."

He leaves (immediately after his fit of temper, as if he were ashamed).

"And I thought you might stay for a while. Wouldn't you like to have a cup of coffee? Why won't you? I'd be very happy." ~~He is trying to make him talk: "Didn't you say you liked my coffee?" He admits it.~~

Tikhon: "What a fine person you are—you are a superior man, the superior ones cannot <. . .>"

He is trying to make him talk: "You are saying that you intend to make your marriage public" (about Stavrogin's mother).

"Don't do it."

"Either you will take revenge for it later, or you will commit a terrible crime before."

"And here, the more terrible the more to your advantage, for the thing is so ludicrous. So, to divert people's attention from the ludicrous, on to the terrible."

"~~Yes~~ Fie, how many different passions you suspect in me! Why, in such case it might be better indeed not to make it public."

---

[21] Variant name for Tikhon.

"That would be best, yet you are going to make it public. Because you are ashamed of people thinking that you might be afraid."

"You want me to end up by becoming a member of the Club."

"Regulating your life."

Feodosy—find God.

The crucified: you know what, Kirilov was once struck by this thought.

About Feodosy.

"What a healer, what a Christian you are, as you are pulling me away and rescuing me from my demon, saving me from going mad."

"Enough, enough, I've done nothing!"

He is undoubtedly an ideal for socialists and even for nihilists, except the most stupid ones among them.

And, yet, this ideal, who had believed in his resurrection and in his divinity, as one believes that twice two makes four, quite naturally dies, and of course without any resurrection.

This is strongest of all, and the last word art has contributed to this idea, is really Don Quixote.

"Come on, don't I know instead, that even if I should become a believer 15 years hence, it would still be a lie, for there is no God. ~~Better~~ For I do know that there isn't. ~~Better~~ No, better let me remain unhappy, but with the truth, rather than happy with a lie."

32 "But if there is no God, how will your world, and you in it, stand up, even for a single minute? Why do good deeds, if this is so? Why sacrifice oneself?"

"Come on now: you have thought up some sort of humanitarian ideal, ~~as if it weren't~~ exactly the same kind of a contrived toy, ~~so that~~ guided by the instinct of self-preservation."

"Yet it is more natural for anyone who is strong to think that he is sustained by his own strength, rather than by some contrived toy, and he'll suppress any turmoil <. . .>"

"That's what every strong man has been doing so far, since times immemorial."

"Oh, if only they had something more clever going for them!"

"More clever what?"

"Oh, nothing. A pretender."

"Wha-at?"

"A pretender—ha, ha, ha. Are you satisfied? By the way, this isn't stupid at all. But nevertheless, to hell with it, good-bye."

"Don't make your marriage public."

"You are going to commit a crime."

"The urge for self-inflicted punishment, yet at the same time you can't stand even being with me."

"I assert that an improvement in the condition of our agriculture will lead to the disappearance of atheism in Russia."

"This is a confession. It tells of an injury to a child (I don't have to read it)."

Tikhon: "I know, it is just too shameful."

N.B. "Conquer the whole world, conquer oneself, conquer disorder."

"I don't want order, I want disorder."

"Better use your own strength—coffee, please?"

"I never have coffee at this hour, but I'll have some with you, for you are a most venerable man."

"Regulate yourself, get to know yourself, there's hardly time to think. I'd give my whole life for equality. I heard about equality only a few days ago, whereas a man's personal dignity stands above equality. Get to know yourself, and if you are lower than very many others, position yourself in the highest row, and you'll be equal to anybody, and higher than many. A slave is free, and truly free, and truly, by this very fact, he abolishes slavery."—To the Hermit—Diatribe on the Club—St. Theodosius.

"Be, I see strength in you."

"Give me a hare," he came out laughing out loud. Then he got pale, and spread out the sheets for distribution.

"And this is your whole story."

"No, all there is here is an injury to a child."

Self-inflicted punishment.

2) A spiteful fit of temper, blow up—"I shall most definitely make it public." "And will you also announce your marriage? You are going to commit a crime."

Final

"Won't you read it? Will you start reading it or not?"

"No, under no circumstances, for if I read it, your pride will not stand it, and you would commit a crime."

"I do not love evil, but right now I want it with all my might, purposely, every day, every hour."

"Your common sense will save you from crime, but not from despair."

Name and Topic Index

Dostoevsky did not want to write *The Possessed*. He wanted to write "The Life of the Great Sinner," the great novel that was to be the culmination of his artistic life. He interrupted his work on "The Life of the Great Sinner" to write a small political pamphlet, which he intended to finish in one season. "The Life of the Great Sinner" was never finished, and the political pamphlet grew into *The Possessed*, one of the world's greatest novels.

The development of *The Possessed* was as tortured as the life Dostoevsky lived while he wrote it. As Mr. Wasiolek writes in his introduction, "This is the longest of the notebooks, and the distance between the first note and the final version is also the greatest," The Notebooks are a record of false starts, errors, mistakes, repetitions, and obscure gropings. Dostoevsky does not know what he wants to say, and when he discovers what he wants to say, he resists saying it. What emerges is *The Possessed*, according to Wasiolek